Professional Ethics for Accountants

Professional Ethics for Accountants

Leonard J. Brooks

Professor of Business Ethics & Accounting
Faculty of Management
University of Toronto

WEST PUBLISHING COMPANY
Minneapolis/St. Paul   New York   San Francisco   Los Angeles

PRODUCTION CREDITS

Composition: Parkwood Composition Service

Copyediting: Jan Krygier

Interior Design: Roslyn Stendahl, Dapper Design

Cover Design: Sean McKenna

Cover Image: Photonica

WEST'S COMMITMENT TO THE ENVIRONMENT

In 1906, West Publishing Company began recycling materials left over from the production of books. This began a tradition of efficient and responsible use of resources. Today, up to 95 percent of our legal books and 70 percent of our college and school texts are printed on recycled, acid-free stock. West also recycles nearly 22 million pounds of scrap paper annually—the equivalent of 181,717 trees. Since the 1960s, West has devised ways to capture and recycle waste inks, solvents, oils, and vapors created in the printing process. We also recycle plastics of all kinds, wood, glass, corrugated cardboard, and batteries, and have eliminated the use of Styrofoam book packaging. We at West are proud of the longevity and the scope of our commitment to the environment.

Production, Prepress, Printing and Binding by West Publishing Company.

British Library Cataloguing-in-Publication Data. A catalogue record for this book is available from the British Library.

COPYRIGHT © 1995   By WEST PUBLISHING COMPANY
610 Opperman Drive
P. O. Box 64526
St. Paul, MN 55164-0526

All rights reserved

Printed in the United States of America

02 01 00 99 98 97 96 95   8 7 6 5 4 3 2 1 0

Library of Congress Cataloguing-in-Publication Data

Brooks, Leonard J.
    Professional ethics for accountants / Leonard J. Brooks.
      p.   cm.
    Includes bibliographical references and index.
     ISBN 0–314–04603–8
     1. Accountants—Professional ethics. 2. Accounting—Moral and ethical aspects. I. Title
HF5657.B74   1995
174'.9657––dc20

95-1648
CIP

To Jean, for her love and support.
To our children, Catherine, Len, Heather, and John for their
patience.
To my parents, Dorathy and Leon, for the values I live by.

Contents

PART **2**   **Ethical Decision Making**   115

CHAPTER **3**   *Codes of Conduct   116*

PART **3**   **Important Ethical Issues and Opportunities   239**

CHAPTER **5**   *Important Ethical Issues and Opportunities   240*

Preface

Professional ethics are a prime differential between professionals and people who are just experts in their chosen field of endeavor. Professional ethics are the reason why professionals are held in high repute, and why their services are in demand. Professional ethics are at the heart of the public's expectations for the level of trust, of integrity and credibility that they have for those who serve them as professionals. The public respect professions with high ethical standards, and look with disfavor when their trust is betrayed.

During the 1980s there have been many challenges to the ethics of the business-oriented professions. Examples such as the crash of the savings and loans, the BCCI scandal, and bankruptcy of two banks in Alberta, Canada, leave no doubt that ethical risks are growing rather than subsiding. Hard economic times are compounding the problem by adding stress to ethical dilemmas, and by pressing professionals to judge their activities in terms of their bottom line rather than on the basis of service to clients.

There is little doubt that business professionals striving to maintain good ethical practices are increasingly "in harm's way." But, it is only relatively recently that accountants, for instance, have begun to revise their codes of conduct to make them effective, and to consider where and how ethical matters ought to be integrated into the curriculum for accountants. Indeed, only a short while ago the battle raged as to whether ethics could and should be taught, or whether it should continue to be left to osmosis.

The simple fact is that a revised code of conduct is only the foundation level of the ethical framework needed by today's professional accountants. Modern accountants must be sufficiently aware of potential ethical problems to be ready to deal with them, and if their code doesn't cover the problem specifically, they must be able to apply ethical reasoning and values to ensure an ethical solution—that, at least, is what the public expects.

PURPOSE OF THE BOOK

To facilitate the development of sound ethical decision making by members of the accounting profession, this book provides an understanding of appropriate values, an awareness of ethical pitfalls, and an understanding of the applicable codes of conduct, and of the application of sound ethical reasoning where codes do not apply. By providing this material in an orderly framework, this book complements many texts that offer no treatment of ethical reasoning, little in-depth treatment of major issues, and scant development of the historical and sociological perspectives that are essential to the understanding of the proper role of a professional accountant. The framework used is comprehensive; each topic begins with text to put the major issues into perspective, then follows with readings selected to enrich the discussion, cases to deepen the understanding of issues, and pedagogical notes and research findings to provide contextual background.

APPLICABILITY

Professional Ethics for Accountants is a comprehensive treatment of the topic, and as such is intended to be used as a sourcebook for both students and graduate accountants. By virtue of its coverage of issues and of approaches to ethical reasoning, this work may be used as a stand-alone text for an ethics course or independent study, or as an adjunct to traditional accounting texts to provide access to interesting, real-life dilemmas at all levels of accounting study.

The coverage provided is North American in orientation. Examples, readings, and cases are drawn with that perspective in mind so that the book will be most useful in the United States and Canada. The basic ethical problems and principles are the same in these two countries, because they are driven by the same concerns, markets, and similar institutional structures and legal strictures. Where points of difference are noteworthy, they are dealt with specifically. In the future, arrangements like the North American Free Trade Agreement (NAFTA), will ensure that the ethics required of professional accountants will become ever closer in the U.S. and Canada.

The perspective adopted is that the fundamental principles of professional ethics apply equally to accountants engaged in auditing and to management accountants employed by corporations. Specific differences in ethical responsibility are also addressed. As a consequence, *Professional Ethics for Accountants* will be useful to all accounting students and to members of the following professional organizations: American Institute of Certified Public Accountants, Institute of Management Accountants, Canadian Institute of Chartered Accountants, Society of Management Accountants of Canada, and Certified General Accountants Association of Canada. The relationships and mandates of each of these organizations is discussed in Chapter 3. Together they, with other regulators, form the ethical environment for accountants in North America.

AUTHOR'S APPROACH

To the greatest extent possible, *Professional Ethics for Accountants* focuses on the development of a practical understanding of ethical issues, and of the practical skills required to deal with them effectively. Of necessity, this means providing a learning experience embedded with real-life cases and examples. At the same time, these real-life problems will be interpreted through exposure to classical positions and articles that have had a lasting impact on business ethics in general, and the accounting ethics in particular. That the author is a professional accountant with substantial practical and teaching experience, as well as experience in the teaching of business and accounting ethics, will contribute to the development of the issues and discussions offered.

ORGANIZATION OF THE BOOK

This book is divided into three parts: (1) developing an awareness of issues, (2) ethical decision making, and (3) an in-depth treatment of important issues encountered in practice.

Part 1 consists of two chapters. The first provides a historical understanding of the ethical challenges that have faced business in general, the responses business has generated, and how thinking about business ethics has changed as a result. Because the profession of accounting is practiced within this environment, background information of this type is essential to a full understanding of the role of a professional accountant, which is the subject of the second chapter in this book.

Why devote an entire chapter to the role of a professional accountant? Because a proper understanding of that role is essential to making proper ethical decisions. A professional must understand what standards and behavior the public expects, and what these expectations imply for the services offered. Judgment and underlying values need to reflect these expectations, and their importance and development need to be explored. The chapter concludes by introducing the other sources of ethical guidance: codes of conduct, laws and jurisprudence, and independent decision making.

Part 2 concentrates on developing practical approaches to ethical decision making. Beginning with a discussion of professional codes of conduct, it moves on to examine how these are or are not integrated into corporate/employer codes and the potential conflicts these may generate. Although it is apparent to anyone who has been a practicing accountant that many of the most difficult ethical issues are not covered in formal codes, the importance of the need to resolve issues beyond codes is made clear for students.

How to develop practical and defensible approaches for such ethical decision making is developed in Chapter 4. Here, the role of values is confirmed, and a discussion of the concepts and techniques of stakeholder impact analysis is provided, including how nonquantifiable factors might be taken into account. Three approaches to comprehensive decision-making analysis are then examined.

Based on this groundwork, Part 3 addresses in depth several of the important ethical issues faced by the accounting profession. These are organized under broad categories, including conflicts of interest, ethical dilemmas in professional practice, and potential contributions that can and ought to be made by accountants to the ethical decision-making practices and governance in business. The detailed list of topics covered in this part includes many that are controversial and some that may be surprising, for example, the measurement and analysis of impacts on the environment; corporate social performance, audit, and reporting; and crisis management. All are important areas of business endeavor to which accountants ought to be ready to lend support, if not leadership.

Each chapter begins with an index and concludes with readings, cases, and questions for discussion. Pedagogical notes and helpful annotated bibliographies of more than 220 cases and videos are provided in the Instructor's Manual and on computer diskette.

VALUE-ADDED TO CASEBOOK APPROACHES

Several excellent collections of cases are available for use in accounting curricula, including, for example, that by the American Accounting Association (1993). In comparison, however, the approach adopted in *Professional Ethics for Accountants* significantly enhances casebook collections by providing:

- an orderly development of the ethical purpose and role of professional accountants, within the ethical environment faced by business in general;

- an understanding of professional and corporate codes of conduct;
- in-depth exposure to stakeholder impact analysis, including three approaches to ethical decision making that are useful when the ethical dilemma in question doesn't fit the accountant's code of conduct;
- ethical discussions on the important ethical dilemmas, as well as on several challenges or opportunities facing accountants now and in the future;
- copies of 23 classic and helpful reference articles;
- 20 cases of realistic complexity, organized to move the student along the continuum of maturity of moral reasoning proposed by Lawrence Kohlberg;
- integration of the Arthur Andersen videotapes on ethics; and
- coverage of the relationship between ethics and the law including important legal cases, of environmental responsibility and disclosure, and of the inclusion of ethics in crisis management.

In comparison, the American Accounting Association's (AAA) ethics case materials binder, after providing eight pages of discussion and three readings, refers the reader to other sources. The 51 cases in the AAA's binder have been reviewed and an annotated bibliography and tabulation by topic and Kohlberg stage is provided, along with an annotated classification of cases from other sources, in the Instructor's Manual to *Professional Ethics for Accountants*. Case notes are provided in the Instructor's Manual that augment the AAA approach and build upon the three stakeholder analysis models developed in Chapter 4.

In summary, *Professional Ethics for Accountants* provides the background material and cases to:

- raise ethical awareness of and sensitivity to issues facing business and, in turn, the accounting profession;
- facilitate the understanding of ethical issues and opportunities facing accountants; and
- create the ability to resolve ethical dilemmas without missing important questions or techniques.

Based on my observations of students and qualified practitioners, there is a very real need to increase the capacity of accountants on each of these dimensions, but particularly on the understanding and ethical decision-making dimensions. This is the reason for designing this book with text, readings, and cases, rather than to focus principally on cases.

ACKNOWLEDGEMENTS

I have been fortunate to receive excellent suggestions for improving *Professional Ethics for Accountants* from Graham Tucker, Alex Milburn, Bill Langdon, Peter Jackson, and Michael Deck. But I want to acknowledge specifically the searching and insightful contributions by David Selley and particularly Ross Skinner. To my colleague Max Clarkson I owe a debt of gratitude for providing the platform and encouragement for the development and exercise of my ideas in the classroom and the stimulation to search for new ideas to contribute to our discipline. These contributors should rest easy, however, as I did not accept all of their suggestions and therefore take responsibility for any errors or omissions.

To my wife, Jean, for her continued support, and my children, Catherine, Len, Heather, and John, for their forbearance, I owe my love and respect.

THE END OF THE BEGINNING

No profession can be successful if its members do not understand and properly discharge their role with regard to serving the public and their clients and maintaining a reputation worthy of trust. Awareness of that role and the ethical responsibilities and skills it entails is far too important to be left to osmosis, or to trial and error. *Professional Ethics for Accountants* provides an orderly development of issues, skills, and the understanding necessary to use them effectively, which will hopefully benefit the accounting profession as a whole.

Leonard J. Brooks
Professor of Business Ethics & Accounting
Faculty of Management
University of Toronto

Overview of the Book

For many professional accountants, whether they are auditors, employees, consultants, or directors, good ethical behavior is a very nebulous and disturbing concept. This is because ethical values, which underpin action, have historically been intensely private, rarely discussed, and usually learned in childhood or from senior professionals by osmosis or—at great cost to themselves and their profession—by trial and error. With such skimpy preparation, it is understandable that many professional accountants fail to recognize an ethical dilemma. If they do recognize it, they usually refer to their professional code of conduct for ethical guidance. However, rarely are these codes up to date on new developments faced in today's business world, and even where an ethical dilemma is addressed, interpretations are often necessary before an appropriate course of behavior can be identified. Where codes do not apply, professional accountants are left to their own, often untutored, powers of ethical decision making.

Not surprisingly, except perhaps for the delay in doing so, this state of affairs has come to be recognized as inappropriate, and appropriate ethical behavior is becoming an increasingly important focus for the accounting profession. Unless both business people and accounting professionals learn to integrate modern ethical thinking with traditional economic objectives, the tensions evident in society over the differences in credibility of actions and of expectations of performance will grow until business and the accounting profession as we know them will be further discredited and restricted.

To facilitate the development of sound, balanced ethical decision making by members of the profession, both in audit and nonaudit roles, *Professional Ethics for Accountants* provides an understanding of appropriate values, an awareness of ethical pitfalls, and an understanding of applicable codes of conduct, along with the application of sound ethical reasoning where codes do not apply. As indicated in the preface to this book, the framework developed is orderly and comprehensive, with each chapter beginning with text to put the major issues into perspective, followed by readings from classic and modern sources to enrich the discussion, and cases to deepen the understanding of the issues. This material is organized into five chapters and these, in turn, into three parts, as follows:

Part 1   Developing an Awareness of the Issues

Part 2   Ethical Decision Making

Part 3   An In-depth Treatment of Significant Issues Facing
          Professional Accountants

Pedagogical notes and helpful annotated bibliographies and classifications of cases and videos are included in the Instructor's Manual and on computer diskette to provide contextual background and assist in the development of further study programs.

Developing an Awareness of the Issues

Introduction

Unless professional accountants have developed a rather extraordinary interest in the ethics of their profession, and have been able to pursue that interest continuously and through a variety of daily, periodic, and book-length sources, it is probable that they have not developed an adequate awareness of ethical issues. Remedying that deficiency is the purpose of Part 1. The first chapter begins with a summary of the forces responsible for the changes in the public's expectations for corporate ethical behavior, and in turn in the public's expectations of accountants who audit those corporations as well as those who serve in the management of the corporations. Business has responded, producing further developments in the ethics of business. Chapter 2 examines how these changes have and might affect the role of the professional accountant and the services offered. The importance of judgment and values, and sources of ethical guidance are then discussed to provide a platform for understanding how ethical decisions ought to be made.

CHAPTER **1** The Ethics Environment

CHAPTER **2** The Role of a Professional Accountant

1

The Ethics Environment

Purpose of the Chapter

The professional accountant functions within a framework created for business and other similar organizations by the expectations of the public. This chapter explores the changes that framework has recently undergone, the response of business, and developments produced in business ethics. It also begins to consider what these changes in environment mean for the professional accountant.

Index of Chapter Headings

During the 1980s there has been a growing awareness that business exists to serve the needs of both shareholders and society, and if society's needs are not served then action, which is often painful to shareholders, officers, and directors, usually occurs. As a result, the professional accountant, who serves the often conflicting interests of shareholders directly and the public indirectly, must be aware of the public's expectations for business and other similar organizations. More than just to serve intellectual curiosity, this awareness must be combined with traditional values and incorporated into a professional accountant's framework for ethical decision making and action. Otherwise substandard service will be provided and the organization, the professional, and indeed, the profession will suffer.

What has produced this change in public expectations for business behavior? Several factors appear to share causal responsibility as indicated in Table 1.1.

ENVIRONMENTAL CONCERNS

Nothing has galvanized public opinion about the nature of good corporate behavior more than the realization that the public's physical well-being, and the well-being of some workers, was being threatened by corporate activity. Initially, concern about air pollution centered around smokestack and exhaust-pipe smog, which caused respiratory irritation and disorders. These problems were, however relatively localized so that when the neighboring population became sufficiently irate, local politicians were able and generally willing to draft controlling regulation, although effective enforcement was by no means ensured.

Two other problems associated with air pollution that were slower to be recognized were acid rain, which neutered lakes and defoliated trees, and the dissipation of the earth's ozone layer. In the first case, the sulfur in exhaust gases combined with rain and fell to the ground far away from the source, and often in other legal jurisdictions. Consequently, the reaction by politicians in the source jurisdiction was predictably slow, and many arguments were raised about who was responsible and whether the damage was real or not. Ultimately, however, the level of awareness of the problem became sufficiently widespread to support international treaties and more stringent local regulations.

The dissipation of the earth's ozone layer has been more recently recognized as a serious threat to our physical well-being. The release into the atmosphere of CFCs, once the most common residential and industrial refrigerant,

TABLE 1.1

FACTORS AFFECTING PUBLIC EXPECTATIONS FOR BUSINESS BEHAVIOR

Physical:	Quality of air and water, safety
Moral:	Desire for fairness and equity
Financial malfeasance:	Numerous scandals
Economic:	Weakness, pressure to survive, to falsify
Competition:	Global pressures
Synergy:	Publicity, institutional reinforcement, codification

allows CFC molecules to use up molecules of ozone. At the same time, the cutting down of the rain forests in Brazil, which were a main source for replenishing ozone, has contributed further to the depletion of the ozone layer around our planet, the layer that is our major barrier from the sun's ultraviolet rays, which can produce skin cancer and damage our eyes.

The timing of the recognition of water pollution as a problem worthy of action has paralleled the concern about our depleted ozone layer, partly because of our limited ability to measure minute concentrations of toxins and our inability to understand the precise nature of the risk of wasteborne metals and of dioxins. There were also many assertions by corporations that they did not have the technical solutions for the elimination of air and water pollution at reasonable cost and therefore could not do so and remain competitive. However, once the short- and long-term threats to personal safety were understood, the public, led by special interest groups, began to pressure companies directly as well as governments to improve safety standards for corporate emissions.

Government reaction, often resulting from disasters, has been significant at all levels. Locally, no-smoking regulations have been enacted and local ordinances tightened. Environmental regulation has been the subject of international treaties. In both the U.S. and Canada, environmental protection acts have been put in place which feature significant fines of up to $1–2 million per day for the corporation convicted of environmental malfeasance. In addition, personal fines and/or jail terms for officers and directors have focused the attention of executives on establishing programs to ensure compliance with environmental standards. Nothing has energized executives in the U.S. and Canada more, however than the statement of a judge in regard to the promulgation of the U.S. Sentencing Guidelines on November 1, 1991, to the effect that the "demonstrated presence of an effective program of environmental protection would constitute an adequate 'due diligence' defense which could reduce the level of the fine from $2 million/day to $50,000/day." Although this reaction may be viewed as defensive, the "due diligence" movement should be viewed as only one phase, the codification phase, of the movement toward corporate environmental responsibility.

MORAL SENSITIVITY

During the 1980s, there was also a significant increase in the sensitivity to the lack of fairness and to discrepancies in equitable treatment normally afforded to individuals and groups in society. Several groups were responsible for this heightened social conscience, including the feminist movement and groups advocating for the mentally and physically challenged, for native people, and for minorities. To some degree the public were prepared to entertain the concerns of these groups because unfortunate events had brought the realization that some special interest groups were worth listening to, as environmentalists, consumer advocates, and anti-apartheid supporters had shown. Also, for most of the period from 1960–1990, disposable incomes and leisure time have been sufficiently high to allow the public to focus on issues beyond earning a living. In addition, due to the advances in satellite communications, which have allowed virtually "live" coverage of worldwide problems, the thinking of the North American public has become less inner directed and parochial, and more sensitive to the problems exposed by wide-ranging investigative reporters.

Evidence of public pressure for more fairness and equity is readily available. The desire for equity in employment has resulted in laws, regulations, compliance conditions in contracts, and affirmative action programs in corporations. Pay equity programs have begun to appear to readjust the discrepancy between the pay scales for men and women. Consumer protection legislation has been tightened to the point that the old philosophy of "buyer beware," which tended to protect the large corporation, has been transformed to "vendor beware," which favors the individual consumer. Drug tests for employees have been severely curtailed because the prospect of a false result was significant and therefore unfair. All of these developments are examples in which public pressure has brought about institutional changes through legislatures or courts for more fairness and equity and less discrimination, and therefore will be virtually impossible to reverse. Indeed, the trend is unmistakable.

FINANCIAL SCANDALS: THE EXPECTATIONS GAP AND THE CREDIBILITY GAP

There is no doubt that the public have been surprised, dismayed, and devastated by periodic reports of financial fiascoes. The list of recent classic examples would include Ivan Boesky's use of inside information, the U.S. savings and loan bankruptcies and bailout, the bankruptcy of two Canadian chartered banks, and the bankruptcy of many real estate companies and financial institutions.

As a result of these repeated shocks, the public have become cynical about the financial integrity of corporations, so much so that the term *Expectations Gap* has been coined to describe the difference between what the public think they're getting in audited financial statements and what they are actually getting. The public outrage over repeated financial fiascoes has led, in both the U.S. and Canada, to tighter regulation, higher fines, and investigations (by the Treadway and Macdonald Commissions; see Chapter 3) of the integrity, independence, and role of the accounting and auditing profession.

On a broader basis, continuing financial malfeasance has led to a crisis of confidence over corporate reporting and governance. This lack of credibility has spread from financial stewardship to encompass the other spheres of corporate activity, and has become known as the *Credibility Gap*. Audit committees and ethics committees, both peopled by a majority of outside directors; the widespread creation of corporate codes of conduct; and the increase of corporate reporting designed to promote the integrity of the corporation all testify to the importance being assigned to this crisis.

No longer is it presumed that "whatever company 'X' does is in the best interests of the country" Fiascoes related to the environment, or to dealings with employees, customers, shareholders, or creditors, have put the onus on corporations to manage their affairs more ethically and to demonstrate that they have done so.

ECONOMIC AND COMPETITIVE PRESSURES

While the public's expectations have been affected directly by the factors already discussed, there are a number of underlying or secondary factors that are also at work. For instance, in general, the pace of economic activity has slowed during the late 1980s and early 1990s. This has placed corporations and the individuals in them in the position of having to wrestle with 'no-growth' or shrinking volume scenarios instead of the expansion that had been the norm. Absence of growth has led to downsizing to maintain overall profitability. Whether to maintain their job or volume-incentive-based earnings, or their company, some people have resorted to questionable ethical practices, including falsification of transactions and other records, and the exploitation of the environment or workers. The result has been the triggering of the cases of environmental or financial malfeasance described above.

The concurrent move toward larger free-trading zones, beyond the borders of a single country, has served to produce global competition. This, in turn, has exacerbated domestic economic pressures. In fact, the resulting adjustment has been viewed as a major restructuring that will enable greater productivity with lower rates of employment. Therefore, the pressure on employed individuals to maintain their jobs will probably not abate even as production increases. Nor will greater volume necessarily increase profits, so the pressure on corporations will probably remain. As a consequence, corporations will be unable to rely on a return to profitability to restore the risk of unethical behavior to former levels. It would appear that a return to lower risk levels will depend on the institution of new regimes of ethical-behavior management and governance.

SYNERGY AND REINFORCEMENT AMONG FACTORS

Linkages among the factors affecting public expectations for ethical performance have already been identified, but not the extent to which these linkages reinforce each other and add to the public's desire for action. Few days go by where the daily newspapers, radio, and television do not feature a financial fiasco, plus a product safety issue or an environmental problem or an article on gender inequity. In aggregate the result is a cumulative heightening of the public's awareness of the need for controls on unethical corporate behavior.

In turn, the public's awareness affects politicians, who react by preparing new laws or tightening existing regulations. In effect, the many issues reaching the public's consciousness result in institutional reinforcement and codification in the laws of the land. The multiplicity of ethical problems receiving exposure is focusing thought on the need for more ethical action, much like a snowball gathering speed and mass as it goes downhill.

OUTCOMES

Public expectations have been changed to exhibit less tolerance, heightened moral consciousness, and higher expectations of business behavior. In response to this heightening of expectations, a number of watchdogs and advisers have emerged to help or harry the public and business. Organizations such as Greenpeace, Pollution Probe, and the Sierra Club now monitor business activities that affect the environment. Consultants are available to advise corporations and so-called "ethical" investors on how to screen activities and investments for both profitability and ethical integrity. Mutual funds specializing in ethical investments have sprung up to serve the needs of small investors. Very large investor activity has also become evident as many public-sector and not-for-profit pension funds have taken active interest in the governance of their investee corporations and have presented shareholder resolutions designed to cover their concerns. In the face of all of this interest, politicians have responded by increasing regulations and the fines and penalties (both personal and corporate) involved for malfeasance. The *Credibility Gap* has not favored business organizations.

A New Mandate for Business

The changes in public expectations have triggered, in turn, an evolution in the mandate for business: the laissez-faire, profit-only world of Milton Friedman has given way to the view that business exists to serve society, not the other way around. For some, this may be stating the degree of change too strongly; but even they would concede that the relationship of business to society is one of interdependence where the long-run health of one determines that of the other.

In many forums, Milton Friedman made the following case:

> In a free-enterprise, private property system a corporate executive . . . has [the] responsibility to make as much money as possible while conforming to the basic rules of society, both . . . in law and in ethical custom.
>
> [This is] the appropriate way to determine the allocation of scarce resources to alternative uses.
>
> —*(Friedman, 1970, pp. 32–33)*

Although there are many arguments for and against this position, which are reported in the reading by Mulligan (1986), three critical issues deserve mention. They are (1) that the deviation from a profit-only focus does not mean that profit will fall—in fact, profit may rise; (2) that profit is now recognized as an incomplete measure of corporate performance and therefore a nonaccurate measure for resource allocation; and (3) that Friedman explicitly expected that performance would be within the law and ethical custom.

First, there is the myth that business could not afford to be ethical because too many opportunities would be given up for profit to be maximized, or that executives could not afford to divert their attention from profit or else profit would fall. In fact, research studies exist that show short-term profits increasing as well as decreasing when social objectives are taken into account by executives. However, recently, two long-term perspectives have become available that strengthen the case that social and profit goals can mix profitably. The first is a study by Max Clarkson (1988) that ranked the social performance of 60+ companies on a modified Wartick and Cochran (1985) scale and found that above-average social performance is positively correlated with profits. The second is that the performance of some ethical mutual funds like the Parnassus Fund (U.S.) and the Investors Summa Fund (Canada) has surpassed that of the New York Stock Exchange as measured by the Standard & Poor's (S & P) Index, or the Toronto Stock Exchange 300 Index; and a weighted index of 400 ethically screened U.S. stocks—the Domini Social Index (1993)—often outperforms the S & P 500. These perspectives are neither conclusive nor exhaustive, nor do they clarify causality. They should, however, give some comfort to executives who hear the theoretical argument that the health of society and the business in it are interdependent, but are wavering on the profitability of implementing a multiple-objective structure.

The second aspect of the Friedman argument that has eroded since it was first proposed is the accuracy with which profit guides the allocation of resources to their best use for society. In 1970, when Friedman began to articulate the profit-resource linkage, there was virtually no cost ascribed to the air and water used in the manufacturing process, nor was a significant cost ascribed to the disposal or treatment of wastes. Since the 1980s, the costs of these so-called "externalities" have skyrocketed and yet they are still not fully included, under generally accepted accounting principles, in calculating the profit for the year for the polluting company. Often, pollution costs are borne by and charged against the profits of other companies, towns, or governments, so the original-company profit-maximum-resource-use-for-society linkage is far less direct than Friedman originally envisaged. As the costs associated with these and other externalities rise, the profit-resource use linkage promises to become less and less useful unless the framework of traditional profit computations is modified or supplemented. Perhaps environmental accounting will yield some relief from this dilemma.

Finally, Milton Friedman himself expressed the view that profit was to be sought within the laws and ethical customs of society, a fact not appreciated by many who argue for profit-only in its strongest, laizzez-faire, bare-knuckled form. Obviously, chaos would result if business was carried out in an absolutely-no-holds-barred environment. A minimum framework of rules is essential for the effective, low-cost working of our markets and the protection of all participants. Increased regulation is one response to outrageous behavior, or to the increasing ethical needs of society. What most profit-only advocates fail to see is that the alternative to increasing regulation by government is an increasing self-emphasis on better ethical governance and behavior.

For these reasons, the profit-only mandate of corporations is evolving to one recognizing the interdependence of business and society. Future success will depend on the degree to which business can balance both profit and social goals. This, in turn, will be impossible to manage unless new governance and reporting structures emerge. If ethical and economic objectives cannot be integrated or balanced successfully, and the interests of shareholders continue to dominate those of stakeholders, the tension between business and society will continue to grow.

The Response by Business

The reaction by business to the evolution from a profit-only mandate to one recognizing the interdependence of business and society became more readily observable as the 1980s progressed. In addition, several other important trends developed as a result of economic and competitive pressures, which had and continue to have an effect on the ethics of business and therefore on the professional accountant. These trends included:

- expanding legal liability for corporate directors, and
- management assertions to shareholders on the adequacy of internal controls,

even though significant changes were also occurring in how organizations operate, including:

- delayering, employee empowerment, and the use of electronic data interfaces, and

- increased reliance by management on nonfinancial performance indicators used on a real-time basis.

As a result of these trends and changes, corporations began to take a much greater interest in how ethical their activities were and how to ensure that ethical problems did not arise. It became evident that the traditional command and control (top-down) approach was not sufficient, and that organizations needed to create an environment favorable to ethical behavior, instead of simply imposing an ethical standard. Because boards and management were becoming more interested in ethical issues, and the ability to check and inspect the decisions of others has been diminishing, it has become more and more important that each employee have a personal code of behavior that is compatible with that of the employer. The pathway to these realizations took the following steps.

The initial corporate reaction to a more demanding ethical environment was the desire to know how ethical their activities had been, then to attempt to manage their employees' actions by developing a code of ethics/conduct. After implementing the code, the desire is to monitor activities in relation to it, and to report on that behavior, first internally and then externally.

The desire to know about the appropriateness of its activities led many corporations to undertake an inventory of significant impacts on various aspects of society. Often organized by program, these listings could be used to identify specific issues, policies, products, or programs that were the most problematic and that therefore needed earliest remedial attention.

It quickly became clear that the "inventory and fix" approach leads to a "patched-up" system for governing employee behavior—one that was incomplete and did not offer ethical guidance on all or even most issues to be faced. Employees who had committed a malfeasance, whether voluntarily or not, could still frequently claim that "nobody told me not to do it." In order to reduce this vulnerability and provide adequate guidance, corporations began to develop and implement comprehensive codes of conduct/ethics.

Neither easy to develop nor universally accepted, codes usually had to be refined through a number of revisions. Implementation processes also had to be improved, and even now some executives are uncertain of their role and how to play it most successfully to facilitate strong commitment by employees to the ethical principles involved. (More detailed information on the role, nature, content, and monitoring of performance relative to codes is provided in the next two chapters.) It is evident that codes of conduct will continue to be the touchstone for the ethical guidance of employees for the foreseeable future.

Although codes of conduct offer an essential framework for employee decision making and control, those corporations in highly vulnerable positions due to their products or productive processes found it in their interest to develop early warning information systems to facilitate fast remedial action in the event of a problem. For instance, Occidental Petroleum recognized its capacity to damage the environment and created a three-tier, notification-to-head-office requirement to provide timely information to senior management and experts on cleanup procedures. Depending on the seriousness of the environmental problem, a "significant matter" had to be reported by computer immediately, an "excursion" within 12 hours (i.e., the next business day in New York), or a "reportable incident" within the next reporting cycle (Friedman,

1988). This type of notification system is essential to facilitate crisis management activities and to mobilize response resources on a worldwide basis in an effort to reduce the impact of the problem on the environment and the corporation.

Not content to encourage the use of ethics just through a code of conduct, leading-edge corporations sought ways to include the specific consideration of ethical conduct in operating decisions, in strategic decision making, and in crisis management practices. Mechanisms were developed to ensure that ethical principles were not overlooked, including compliance check-off lists; the encouragement of internal whistleblowing to ombudspersons; training to instill decision frameworks designed to produce sound ethical decisions, mind-focusing scorecards and categorizations for operations and strategies; inclusion of ethical performance as a factor in the determination of remuneration and in continuing internal and external reports; the creation of specific ethical operating goals such as for equity employment levels; and the creation of executive positions like Vice-President for Environmental Affairs, and of specific subcommittees of the Board of Directors to oversee the ethical performance of the corporation.

Although the commitment to these mechanisms grew during the 1980s and early 1990s, nothing galvanized the corporate community more than (1) the promulgation of the U.S. Sentencing Guidelines for environmental offenses on November 1, 1991 (described earlier) which led to widespread concern about "due diligence" procedures, and (2) the realization in the summer of 1992 that General Electric had been sued under the *False Claims Act* in the U.S. for $70 million by a whistleblower too fearful of retribution to report internally to the company (Singer, 1992). The fact that the whistleblower could receive *up to 25 percent* of the outcome was considered shocking, just as the size of the fines in the U.S. Sentencing Guidelines had been a year earlier. In combination, these events matured the realization that corporations ought to create an ethical operating environment in order to protect their interests and those of others with a stake in the activities of the corporation.

Developments in Business Ethics

CONCEPTS AND TERMS

In response to the changes described above, several concepts and terms were developed to facilitate discussion of the evolution taking place in the ethical accountability of business. Two of these developments are particularly useful in understanding business ethics, and how business and the professions can benefit from their application. They are: the stakeholder concept, and the concept of a corporate social contract.

As the ethical environment for business changed, observers and executives realized that many more people than just shareholders had an interest in the corporation or its activities, and that although some of these had no statutory claim on the corporation, they had a very real capacity to influence the corporation favorably or unfavorably. Moreover, as time went by, the claims of some of these interested parties became codified through statute or regulation. By inference, it became evident that the interests of this set of people with a stake in the business or its impacts ought to be considered in corporate plans and decisions. For ease of reference, these people came to be known as *stake-*

holders and their interests as *stakeholder's rights.* Examples of stakeholder groups would include employees, customers, suppliers, lenders, borrowers, host communities, governments, and, of course, shareholders.

The relationship between a corporation and its stakeholders has slowly but steadily broadened over the years. Initially, the corporation was established as a means of gathering large amounts of capital from shareholders, it was accountable only to those shareholders, and its goal was to generate profits. Later, when larger factories appeared, times were such that child labor was prevalent and no cost was ascribed to environmental practices that today would not be condoned. Since that time corporate accountability has broadened to go beyond just shareholders to embrace the reality of stakeholders, and, some would argue, to generate profits but not at any cost to society and preferably in a way that supports society. This evolving relationship between corporations and society has come to be known, in concept, as the *corporate social contract.*

APPROACHES TO ETHICAL DECISION MAKING THROUGH STAKEHOLDER IMPACT ANALYSIS

The evolving accountability to stakeholders within the newer versions of the corporate social contract has made it incumbent on executives to ensure that their decisions reflect the ethical values established for the corporation, and do not leave out of consideration any significant stakeholder's rights. In response, a number of approaches to comprehensive ethical decision making have been developed, three of which will be expanded upon in Chapter 4.

The first, known as the *Five Question Approach,* involves challenging any proposed policy or action with five questions designed to rate the proposal on the following scales: profitability, legality, fairness, impact on the rights of each individual stakeholder, and impact on the environment specifically. The questions are asked in sequence, and options are discarded depending on the degree to which corporate ethical values are offended. Often, options can be modified to be made more ethical as a result of these challenges (Tucker, 1990).

The *Moral Standards Approach,* developed by Professor Manuel Velasquez (1992), focuses on three dimensions of the impact of the proposed action: (1) whether it provides a net benefit to society; (2) whether it is fair; and (3) whether it is right. Although there is some overlap with the first approach, Velasquez's focus is less company-centered, and is therefore better suited to the evaluation of decisions where the impact on stakeholders outside the corporation is likely to be very severe.

The last approach to stakeholder impact analysis to be presented in Chapter 4 is the *Pastin Approach,* created by Professor Mark Pastin (1986), who extends the Moral Standards Approach by taking specific account of the culture within the corporation and of so-called "commons problems." Pastin suggests that any proposed decision be evaluated in comparison to the company's ground rules (he calls this "ground rule ethics"); the net benefit it produces (end-point ethics); whether it impinges on anyone's rights and requires rules to resolve the conflict (rule ethics); whether it is fair ("Social contract ethics"); and finally whether it abuses rights apparently belonging to everyone (problems of the commons). Pastin's approach is quite practically oriented and is best suited to decisions that primarily affect stakeholders directly attached to the corporation, such as employees or customers.

Whether they are involved in the audit function, in management, in consulting, or as directors, professional accountants have been looked upon historically as the arbiters of organizational accountability and experts in the science of decision making. Because we are witnessing a "dramatic and far–reaching change" in corporate accountability with a broadening beyond just shareholders to stakeholders, it is incumbent on accountants to understand this evolution and how it can affect their function. If they do not do so, substandard advice may be given and the legal and nonlegal consequences for ethical shortfalls can be severe.

There is also a very real possibility that the *Expectations Gap* between what users of audits and financial statements thought they had been getting and what they are receiving will be exacerbated if accountants are seen to be out of step with emerging standards of ethical behavior. Studies have been undertaken, such as those by the Treadway Commission in the U.S.A. (1987) and the Macdonald Commission in Canada (1988), which have called for a recognition of new levels of ethical behavior in revisions to professional codes of conduct. Some professional codes have been revised recently in response, but a thorough understanding of the reasons for revision and the underlying principles involved is essential for their proper application and the protection of professionals, the profession, and the public.

An appreciation of the sea change under way in the ethics environment for business is essential to an informed understanding of how professional accountants ought to interpret their profession's code as employees of corporations. At the same time, although the public expects the professional accountant to respect the professional values of objectivity, integrity, and confidentiality that are designed to protect the fundamental rights of the public, the employee-accountant must respond to the direction of management and the needs of current shareholders. Trade-offs are difficult. In the future, there will be less escape from the glare of public scrutiny, and greater danger in greeting problems with a wink and a nod, or sweeping them under the rug. Professional accountants will have to ensure that their ethical values are current, and that they are prepared to act upon them to the best exercise of their role.

The parameters of the role of a professional accountant serving business in its modern ethics environment are examined in the next chapter.

QUESTIONS FOR DISCUSSION

1. Why have concerns over pollution become so important for management and directors?

2. Why are we more concerned now than our parents were about fair treatment of employees?

3. What could professional accountants have done to prevent the development of the *Credibility Gap* and the *Expectations Gap?*

4. Under what circumstances would competitive pressures lead to higher ethical standards in a corporation?

5. Why might ethical corporate behavior lead to higher profitability?

6. Why is it important for the clients of professional accountants to be ethical?

7. How can corporations ensure that their employees behave ethically?

8. Should executives and directors be sent to jail for the acts of their corporation's employees?

9. What are the common elements of the three approaches to ethical decision making that are briefly outlined in this chapter?

10. Why is it important for a professional accountant to understand the ethical trends discussed in this chapter?

CASES

The cases that follow are designed to stimulate an awareness of ethical issues currently facing business and accountants. Specifically, the scenarios covered are as follows:

- The "Bhopal—Union Carbide" case is intended to raise the reader's awareness of ethical issues facing modern corporations. It presents the reader with an event that, while seemingly improbable, happens repeatedly under different circumstances, and offers the reader an opportunity to explore what he or she and others believe to be appropriate levels of corporate responsibility and ethical behavior.

- "Where Were the Accountants?" presents a brief series of scandals and ethical problems upon which management accountants, academic accountants, and auditors could have commented on in time to significantly mitigate the outcome. Why didn't they? Should they have?

- "To Resign or Serve?" introduces the problem of balancing ethical trade-offs in a modern, creative economic world. How far should an auditor go to protect a fellow professional, the profession, or the public?

READINGS

The selection of readings that follows has been chosen to provide background material to enrich the understanding of the issues identified in this chapter. Milton Friedman's article on the proper focus for management being profit only is a classic, and Thomas Mulligan's response raises interesting reservations about it. The two articles on corporate social performance, one by Steven L. Wartick and Philip L. Cochran, and the other by Max B. E. Clarkson, provide an understanding of how a corporation can formally assess, monitor, and improve its interface with society. Both of these articles and the press release on the Domini Social Index suggest that corporate social performance can lead to higher profitability and investment returns on a systematic basis. The final article, by Andrew Singer, reveals the significance of whistleblowing and the impact it may have on corporations. This impact is one of the catalysts that will lead companies to want to develop ethical corporate cultures in the future.

REFERENCES

Clarkson, M. B. E., "Corporate Social Performance in Canada, 1976–86". *Research in Corporate Social Performance and Policy*, JAI Press, Inc., Vol. 10 (1988): 241–265.

Domini Social Index, a market capitalized-weighted common stock index, consisting of 400 U.S. corporations that have passed multiple, broad-based social screens. Maintained by Kinder,

Lyndenberg, Domini & Co., Inc., 129 Mt. Auburn Street, Cambridge, MA 01238.

Friedman, F. B. *Practical Guide to Environmental Management.* Washington, DC: Environmental Law Institute, 1988, p. 34.

Friedman, M. "The Social Responsibility of Business to Increase Profits." *The New York Times Magazine* (September 13, 1970): 32–33.

Macdonald Commission, see *The Report of the Commission to Study the Public's Expectations of Audits,* Canadian Institute of Chartered Accountants, June 1988.

Mulligan, T. "A Critique of Milton Friedman's Essay 'The Social Responsibility of Business Is to Increase Its Profits.'" *Journal of Business Ethics* (1986): 265–269.

Pastin, M. *The Hard Problems of Management: Gaining the Ethics Edge.* San Francisco, CA: Jossey-Bass Publishers, 1986.

Singer, A. W. "The Whistle-Blower: Patriot or Bounty Hunter." *Across the Board* (November 1992): 16–22.

Treadway Commission, see the *Report of the National Commission on Fraudulent Public Reporting,* AICPA, 1987.

Tucker, G. "Ethical Analysis for Environmental Problem Solving." *Agenda for Action Conference Proceedings,* The Canadian Centre for Ethics & Corporate Policy, 1990, 53–57.

Velasquez, M. G. *Business Ethics: Concepts and Cases.* Englewood Cliffs, NJ: Prentice-Hall, 1992.

Wartick, S. L., and Cochran, P. L. "The Evolution of the Corporate Social Performance Model." *Academy of Management Review (1985) Vol 10*(4) (1985): 758–769.

Bhopal–Union Carbide*

On April 24, 1985, Warren M. Anderson, the 63-year-old chairman of Union Carbide Corporation, had to make a disappointing announcement to angry stockholders at their annual meeting in Danbury, Connecticut. Anderson, who had been jailed briefly by the government of India on charges of "negligence and criminal corporate liability," had been devoting all his attention to the company's mushrooming problems. His announcement concerned the complete breakdown of negotiations with officials in the Indian government: They had rejected as inadequate an estimated $200 million in compensation for the deaths of 2,000 people and the injuries of 200,000 others which had been caused in December 1984 by a poisonous leak of methyl isocyanate gas from a Union Carbide pesticide plant located in Bhopal, India.[1] In the wake of more than $35 billion in suits filed against the company's liability coverage, reported to total only about $200 million. The company's stock tumbled. Angry stockholders filed suit charging that they had suffered losses of more than $1 billion because the company's managers had failed to warn them of the risks at the Indian plant. Analysts predicted the company would be forced into bankruptcy. Ironically, the Union Carbide plant in Bhopal had been losing money for several years and Anderson had considered closing it.

The deadly methyl isocyanate gas that leaked from the Union Carbide plant was a volatile and highly toxic chemical used to make pesticides. It is 500 times more poisonous than cyanide, and it reacts explosively with almost any substance, including water. Late on the night of December 2, 1984, the methyl isocyanate stored in a tank at the Bhopal factory started boiling violently when water or some other agent accidentally entered the tank. A cooling unit that should have switched on automatically had been disabled for at least a year. Shakil Qureshi, a manager on duty at the time, and Suman Dey, the senior operator on duty, both distrusted the initial readings on their gauges in the control room. "Instruments often didn't work," Qureshi said later. "They got corroded, and crystals would form on them."

By 11:30 P.M. the plant workers' eyes were burning. But the workers remained unconcerned because, as they later reported, minor leaks were common at the plant and were often first detected in this way. Many of the illiterate workers were unaware of the deadly properties of the chemical. Not until 12:40 A.M., as workers began choking on the fumes, did they realize something was drastically wrong. Five minutes later emergency valves on the storage tank exploded and white toxic gas began shooting out of a pipestack and drifting toward the shantytowns downwind from the plant. An alarm sounded as manager Dey shouted into the factory loudspeaker that a massive leak had erupted and the workers should flee the area. Meanwhile, Qureshi ordered company fire trucks to spray the escaping gas with water to neutralize the chemical. But water pressure was too low to reach the top of the 120-foot-high pipestack. Dey then rushed to turn on a vent scrubber that should have neutralized the escaping gas with caustic soda. Unfortunately, the scrubber had been shut down for maintenance 15 days earlier. As white clouds continued to pour out of the pipestack, Qureshi shouted to workers to turn on a nearby flare tower to burn off the gas. The flare, however, would not go on because its pipes had corroded and were still being repaired.

Panicked workers poured out of the plant, and the lethal cloud settled over the neighboring shantytowns of Jaipraksh and Chola. Hundreds died in their beds, choking helplessly in violent spasms as their burning lungs filled with fluid. Thousands were blinded by the caustic gas, and thousands of others suffered burns and lesions in their nasal and bronchial passages. When it was over at least 2,000 lay dead and 200,000 were injured. The majority of the dead were squatters who had illegally built huts next to the factory. Surviving residents of the slums, most of them illiterate, declared afterward that they had built their shacks there because they did not understand the danger and thought the factory made healthy "medicine for plants."

Union Carbide managers from the United States built the Bhopal plant in 1969 with the blessing of the Indian government, which was anxious to increase production of the pesticides it desperately needed to raise food for India's huge population. Over the next 15 years, pesticides enabled India to cut its annual grain losses from 25 percent to 15 percent, a saving of 15 million tons of grain or enough to feed 70 mil-

Continued

*This case has been adapted from Velasquesz, Manuel, *Business Ethics: Concepts and Cases*, 3/e, © 1992, pp. 3–5.

Reprinted by permission of Prentice–Hall, Inc., Englewood Cliffs, N.J.

Continued

lion people for a full year. Indian officials willingly accepted the technology, skills, and equipment that Union Carbide provided, and Indian workers were thankful for the company jobs, without which they would have had to beg or starve as India has no welfare system. In return, India offered the company cheap labor, low taxes, and few laws requiring expensive environmental equipment or costly workplace protections. In comparison to other factories in India, the Union Carbide plant was considered a model, law-abiding citizen with a good safety record. Said a government official: "They never refused to install what we asked."

At the time of the disaster, the pesticide plant in Bhopal was operated by Union Carbide India Ltd., a subsidiary of the Union Carbide Corporation of Danbury, Connecticut, which had a controlling interest of 50.9 percent in the Indian company. The board of directors of Union Carbide India Ltd. included one top manager from the parent Union Carbide Corporation in the U.S. and four managers from another Union Carbide subsidiary, based in Hong Kong. Reports from the Indian company were regularly reviewed by the managers in Danbury, who had the authority to exercise financial and technical control

over Union Carbide India Ltd. Although day-to-day details were left to the Indian managers, the American managers controlled budgets, set major policies, and issued technical directives for operating and maintaining the plant.

Before the tragedy, the Indian subsidiary had been doing poorly. In an effort to contain annual losses of $4 million from the unprofitable plant, local company managers had initiated several cost-cutting programs. Only a year before the number of equipment operators on each shift had been reduced from twelve to five; morale dropped and many of the best operators quit and were replaced with workers whose education was below that required by company manuals. Although Warren Anderson and other Union Carbide Corporation (U.S.) managers insisted that responsibility for the plant's operations rested with the local Indian managers, they hastened to say that all cost-cutting measures had been justified.

Two years before the disaster, the American managers had sent three engineers from the U.S. to survey the plant and, as a result, had told the Indian managers to remedy 10 major flaws in safety equipment and procedures. The Indian managers had written back that the problems were corrected. "We have no reason

to believe that what was represented to us by Union Carbide India Ltd. did not in fact occur," said the U.S. managers. The U.S. managers had considered closing the failing plant a year earlier, but Indian city and state officials had asked that the company remain open to preserve the jobs of thousands of workers in the plant and in dependent local industries.

Note
1. All material concerning Union Carbide and the Bhopal plant, including all quotations and all allegations, is drawn directly from the following sources: *The New York Times:* December 9, 1984, p. 1E; December 16, 1984, pp. 1, 8; January 28, 1985, pp. 6, 7; January 30, 1985, p. 6; April 25, 1985, p. 34; *San Jose Mercury News:* December 6, 1984, p. 16A; December 12, 1984, pp. 1, 1H; December 13, 1984, p. 1; *Time:* December 17, 1985, pp. 22–31.

QUESTIONS

1. What are the ethical issues raised by this case?

2. Did the legal doctrine of "limited liability" apply to protect the shareholders of Union Carbide Corporation (U.S.)?

3. Were the Indian operations, which were being overseen by the managers of Union Carbide Corporation (U.S.), in compliance with legal or moral or ethical standards?

Where Were the Accountants?

"Sam, I'm really in trouble. I've always wanted to be an accountant. But here I am just about to apply to the accounting firms for a job after graduation from the university, and I'm not sure I want to be an accountant after all."

"Why, Norm? In all those accounting courses we have taken together, you worked super hard because you were really interested. What's your problem now?"

"Well, I've been reading the business newspapers, reports, and accounting journals lately, and things just don't add up. For instance, you know how we have always been told that accountants have expertise in measurement and disclosure, that they are supposed to prepare reports with integrity, and that they ought to root out fraud if they suspect it? Well it doesn't look like they have been doing a good job. At least they haven't been doing what I would have expected."

"Remember, Norm, we're still students with a lot to learn. Maybe you are missing something. What have you been reading about?"

"OK, Sam, here are a few stories for you to think about:

"In this article, 'Accountants and the S & L Crisis,' which was in *Management Accounting* in February 1993, I found the argument that the 200-million-dollar fiasco was due to the regulators and to a downturn in the real estate market, not to accounting fraud. . .but I don't buy it entirely. According to this article, rising interest rates and fixed lending rates resulted in negative cash flow at the same time as a decline in value of the real estate market reduced the value underlying S & L loan assets. As a result, the net worth of many S & Ls fell, and regulators decided to change some accounting practices to make it appear that the S & Ls were still above the minimum capital requirements mandated to protect depositors' funds. Just look at this list of the seven accounting practices or problems that were cited:

- write-off of losses on loans sold over the life of the loan rather than when the loss occurred,
- use of government-issued *Net Worth Certificates* to be counted as S & L capital,
- use of deals involving up-front money and near-term cash flow, which would bolster current earnings at the expense of later,
- inadequate loan loss provisions due to poor loan monitoring,
- write-off of goodwill created upon the merger of sound S & Ls with bankrupt S & Ls over a 40-year period,
- write-ups of owned property based on appraisal values, and
- lack of market-based reporting to reflect economic reality.

The problem, for me, is that many of these practices are not in accord with generally accepted accounting principles [GAAP] and yet the accountants went along—at least they didn't object or improve their practices enough to change the outcome. Why not? Where were the accountants?"

"I am also concerned about the expertise the accounting profession claims to have in terms of measurement and disclosure. For example, recently there have been many articles on the health costs created by smoking, yet there are no accountants involved. For instance, a May 1994 Report by the Center on Addiction and Substance Abuse at Columbia University estimates that "in 1994 dollars, substance abuse will cost Medicare $20 billion in inpatient hospital costs alone," and that tobacco accounts for 80 percent of those hospitalizations. Over the next 20 years substance abuse will cost the Medicare program one *trillion dollars.* No wonder the trustees of the Medicare Trust Fund released a report on April 21 "predicting that the Fund would run out of money in seven years." These are important issues. Why do we have to wait for economists and special interest groups to make these calculations? Shouldn't accountants be able to make them and lend credibility and balance in the process? Wouldn't society benefit? Where were the accountants?

"What about the finding of fraud? Are auditors doing enough to prevent and catch fraudulent behavior? I know what our professors say: that auditors can't be expected to catch everything; that their job is not to search for fraud unless suspicions are aroused during other activities; and that their primary task is to audit the financial statements. But aren't the auditors just reacting to discovered problems, when they could be proactive? Couldn't they stress the importance of using codes of conduct and the encouragement of employees to bring forward their concerns over unethical acts? Why is proactive management appropriate in some other areas

Continued

Continued

like ironing out personnel problems, but reactive behavior appropriate when dealing with fraud? Reactive behavior will just close the barn door after the horse has been stolen. In the case of the Bank of Credit & Commerce International (BCCI), for example, at least $1.7 billion was missing."

"I guess I'm having second thoughts about becoming a professional accountant. Can you help me out, Sam?"

QUESTION

1. What would you tell Norm?

To Resign or Serve?

The Prairieland Bank was a medium-sized, Midwestern financial institution. The management had a good reputation for backing successful deals, but the CEO (and significant shareholder) had recently moved to San Francisco to be "close to the big-bank center of activity." He commuted into the Prairieland head office for two or three days each week to oversee major deals.

Lately the bank's profitability had decreased, and the management had begun to renegotiate many loans on which payments had fallen behind. By doing so, the bank was able to disclose to them as current, rather than nonperforming, as the unpaid interest was simply added to the principal to arrive at the new principal amount. Discussions were also under way on changing some accounting policies to make them less conservative.

Ben Hunt, the audit partner on the Prairieland Bank account, was becoming concerned about the risk associated with giving an opinion on the fairness of the financial statements. During the early days of the audit, it became evident that the provision for doubtful loans was far too low, and he made an appointment to discuss the problem with the CEO and his Vice President of Finance. At the interview Ben was told that the executives knew the provision was too low, but they didn't want to increase it because that would decrease their reported profits. Instead they had approached a company that provided insurance to protect leased equipment, such as earth movers, against damage during the lease, and arranged for insurance against nonpayment upon the maturity of their loans. As a result, they said, any defaults on their loans would be made up from the insurance company, so they didn't see any point to increasing the provision for loan losses or disclosing the insurance arrangement.

When he heard of this, Ben expressed concern to the Prairieland management, but they were adamant.

Because Prairieland was such a large account, he sought the counsel of James London, the senior partner in his firm who was in charge of assessing such accounting treatments and the related risk to the auditing firm. James flew out to confer with Ben, and they decided that the best course of action was to visit the client and indicate their intent to resign, which they did.

After dinner, James was waiting at the airport for his plane home. By coincidence he met Jack Lane, who held similar responsibilities to his own at one of the competing firms. Jack was returning home as well, and was in good spirits. On the flight Jack let it slip that he had just picked up an old client of James' firm, Prairieland Bank.

QUESTIONS

1. Which decision was right: to resign or to serve?

2. What should James do?

The Social Responsibility of Business Is to Increase Its Profits

Milton Friedman
The New York Times Magazine, Sept. 13, 1970

When I hear businessmen speak eloquently about the "social responsibilities of business in a free-enterprise system," I am reminded of the wonderful line about the Frenchman who discovered at the age of 70 that he had been speaking prose all his life. The businessmen believe that they are defending free enterprise when they declaim that business is not concerned "merely" with profit but also with promoting desirable "social" ends; that business has a "social conscience" and takes seriously its responsibilities for providing employment, eliminating discrimination, avoiding pollution and whatever else may be the catchwords of the contemporary crop of reformers. In fact they are—or would be if they or anyone else took them seriously—preaching pure and unadulterated socialism. Businessmen who talk this way are unwitting puppets of the intellectual forces that have been undermining the basis of a free society these past decades.

The discussions of the "social responsibilities of business" are notable for their analytical looseness and lack of rigor. What does it mean to say that "business" has responsibilities? Only people can have responsibilities. A corporation is an artificial person and in this sense may have artificial responsibilities, but "business" as a whole cannot be said to have responsibilities, even in this vague sense. The first step toward clarity in examining the doctrine of the social responsibility of business is to ask precisely what it implies for whom.

Presumably, the individuals who are to be responsible are businessmen, which means individual proprietors or corporate executives. Most of the discussion of social responsibility is directed at corporations, so in what follows I shall mostly neglect the individual proprietor and speak of corporate executives.

In a free-enterprise, private-property system a corporate executive is an employee of the owners of the business. He has direct responsibility to his employers. That responsibility is to conduct the business in accordance with their desires, which generally will be to make as much money as possible while conforming to the basic rules of the society, both those embodied in law and those embodied in ethical custom. Of course, in some cases his employers may have a different objective. A group of persons might establish a corporation for an eleemosynary purpose—for example, a hospital or a school. The manager of such a corporation will not have money profit as his objective but the rendering of certain services.

In either case, the key point is that, in his capacity as a corporate executive, the manager is the agent of the individuals who own the corporation or establish the eleemosynary institution, and his primary responsibility is to them.

Needless to say, this does not mean that it is easy to judge how well he is performing his task. But at least the criterion of performance is straightforward, and the persons among whom a voluntary contractual arrangement exists are clearly defined.

Of course, the corporate executive is also a person in his own right. As a person, he may have many other responsibilities that he recognizes or assumes voluntarily—to his family, his conscience, his feelings of charity, his church, his clubs, his city, his country. He may feel impelled by these responsibilities to devote part of his income to causes he regards as worthy, to refuse to work for particular corporations, and even to leave his job, for example, to join his country's armed forces. If we wish, we may refer to some of these responsibilities as "social responsibilities." But in these respects he is acting as a principal, not an agent; he is spending his own money or time or energy, not the money of his employers or the time or energy he has contracted to devote to their purposes. If these are "social responsibilities," they are the social responsibilities of individuals, not of business.

What does it mean to say that the corporate executive has a "social responsibility" in his capacity as businessman? If this statement is not pure rhetoric, it must mean that he is to act in some way that is not in the interest of his employers. For example, that he is to refrain from increasing the price of the product in order to contribute to the social objective of preventing inflation, even though a price increase would be in the best interests of the corporation. Or that he is to make expenditures on reducing pollution beyond the amount that is in the best interests of the corporation or that is required by law in order to contribute to the social objective of improving the environment. Or that, at the expense of corporate profits, he is to hire "hard-core" unemployed instead of better-qualified available workmen to contribute to the social objective of reducing poverty.

In each of these cases, the corporate executive would be spending someone else's money for a general social interest. Insofar as his actions in accord with his "social responsibility" reduce returns to stockholders, he is spending their money. Insofar as his actions raise the price to customers, he is spending the customers' money. Insofar as his actions lower the wages of some employees, he is spending their money.

The stockholders or the customers or the employees could separately spend their own money on the particular action if they wished to do so. The executive is exercising a

—Continued

Continued

distinct "social responsibility," rather than serving as an agent of the stockholders or the customers or the employees, only if he spends the money in a different way than they would have spent it.

But if he does this, he is in effect imposing taxes, on the one hand, and deciding how the tax proceeds shall be spent, on the other.

This process raises political questions on two levels: principle and consequences. On the level of political principle, the imposition of taxes and the expenditure of tax proceeds are governmental functions. We have established elaborate constitutional, parliamentary and judicial provisions to control these functions, to assure that taxes are imposed so far as possible in accordance with the preferences and desires of the public—after all, "taxation without representation" was one of the battle cries of the American Revolution. We have a system of checks and balances to separate the legislative function of imposing taxes and enacting expenditures from the executive function of collecting taxes and administering expenditure programs and from the judicial function of mediating disputes and interpreting the law.

Here the businessman—self-selected or appointed directly or indirectly by stockholders—is to be simultaneously legislator, executive and jurist. He is to decide whom to tax by how much and for what purpose, and he is to spend the proceeds—all this guided only by general exhortations from on high to restrain inflation, improve the environment, fight poverty and so on and on.

The whole justification for permitting the corporate executive to be selected by the stockholders is that the executive is an agent serving the interests of his principal. This justification disappears when the corporate executive imposes taxes and spends the proceeds for "social" purposes. He becomes in effect a public employer, a civil servant, even though he remains in name an employee of a private enterprise. On grounds of political principle, it is intolerable that such civil servants—insofar as their actions in the name of social responsibility are real and not just window dressing—should be selected as they are now. If they are to be civil servants, then they must be selected through a political process. If they are to impose taxes and make expenditures to foster "social" objectives, then political machinery must be set up to guide the assessment of taxes and to determine through a political process the objectives to be served.

This is the basic reason why the doctrine of "social responsibility" involves the acceptance of the socialist view that political mechanisms, not market mechanisms, are the appropriate way to determine the allocation of scarce resources to alternative uses.

On the grounds of consequences, can the corporate executive in fact discharge his alleged "social responsibilities"? On the one hand, suppose he could get away with spending the stockholders' or customers' or employees' money. How is he to know how to spend it? He is told that he must contribute to fighting inflation. How is he to know what action of his will contribute to that end? He is presumably an expert in running his company—in producing a product or selling it or financing it. But nothing about his selection makes him an expert on inflation. Will his holding down the price of his product reduce inflationary pressure? Or, by leaving more spending power in the hands of his customers, simply divert it elsewhere? Or, by forcing him to produce less because of the lower price, will it simply contribute to shortages? Even if he could answer these questions, how much cost is he justified in imposing on his stockholders, customers and employees for this social purpose? What is his appropriate share of others'?

And, whether he wants to or not, can he get away with spending his stockholders', customers' or employees' money? Will not the stockholders fire him? (Either the present ones or those who take over when his actions in the name of social responsibility have reduced the corporation's profits and the price of its stock.) His customers and his employees can desert him for other producers and employers less scrupulous in exercising their social responsibilities.

This facet of "social responsibility" doctrine is brought into sharp relief when the doctrine is used to justify wage restraint by trade unions. The conflict of interest is naked and clear when union officials are asked to subordinate the interest of their members to some more general social purpose. If the union officials try to enforce wage restraint, the consequence is likely to be wildcat strikes, rank-and-file revolts and the emergence of strong competitors for their jobs. We thus have the ironic phenomenon that union leaders—at least in the U.S.—have objected to government interference with the market far more consistently and courageously than have business leaders.

The difficulty of exercising "social responsibility" illustrates, of course, the great virtue of private competitive enterprise—it forces people to be responsible for their own actions and makes it difficult for them to "exploit" other people for either selfish or unselfish purposes. They can do good—but only at their own expense.

Many a reader who has followed the argument this far may be tempted to remonstrate that it is all well and good to speak of government's having the responsibility to impose taxes and determine expenditures for such "social" purposes

—Continued

Continued

as controlling pollution or training the hard-core unemployed, but that the problems are too urgent to wait on the slow course of political processes, that the exercise of social responsibility by businessmen is a quicker and surer way to solve pressing current problems.

Aside from the question of fact—I share Adam Smith's skepticism about the benefits that can be expected from "those who affected to trade for the public good"—this argument must be rejected on grounds of principle. What it amounts to is an assertion that those who favor the taxes and expenditures in question have failed to persuade a majority of their fellow citizens to be of like mind and that they are seeking to attain by undemocratic procedures that they cannot attain by democratic procedures. In a free society, it is hard for "good" people to do "good," but that is a small price to pay for making it hard for "evil" people to do "evil," especially since one man's good is another's evil.

I have, for simplicity, concentrated on the special case of the corporate executive, except for the brief digression on trade unions. But precisely the same argument applies to the newer phenomenon of calling upon stockholders to require corporations to exercise social responsibility (the recent G. M. crusade, for example). In most of these cases, what is in effect involved is some stockholders trying to get other stockholders (or customers or employees) to contribute against their will to "social" causes favored by the activists. Insofar as they succeed, they are again imposing taxes and spending the proceeds.

The situation of the individual proprietor is somewhat different. If he acts to reduce returns of his enterprise in order to exercise his "social responsibility," he is spending his own money, not someone else's. If he wishes to spend his money on such purposes, that is his right, and I cannot see that there is any objection to his doing so. In the process, he, too, may impose costs on employees and customers. However, because he is far less likely than a large corporation or union to have monopolistic power, any such side effects will tend to be minor.

Of course, in practice the doctrine of social responsibility is frequently a cloak for actions that are justified on other grounds rather than a reason for those actions.

To illustrate, it may well be in the long-run interest of a corporation that is a major employer in a small community to devote resources to providing amenities to that community or to improving its government. That may make it easier to attract desirable employees, it may reduce the wage bill or lessen losses from pilferage and sabotage or have other worthwhile effects. Or it may be that, given the laws about the deductibility of corporate charitable contributions, the stockholders can contribute more to charities they favor by having the corporation make the gift than by doing it themselves, since they can in that way contribute an amount that would otherwise have been paid as corporate taxes.

In each of these—and many similar—cases, there is a strong temptation to rationalize these actions as an exercise of "social responsibility." In the present climate of opinion, with its widespread aversion to "capitalism," "profits," the "soulless corporation" and so on, this is one way for a corporation to generate goodwill as a by-product of expenditures that are entirely justified in its own self-interest.

It would be inconsistent of me to call on corporate executives to refrain from this hypocritical window dressing because it harms the foundations of a free society. That would be to call on them to exercise a "social responsibility"! If our institutions, and the attitudes of the public make it in their self-interest to cloak their actions in this way, I cannot summon much indignation to denounce them. At the same time, I can express admiration for those individual proprietors or owners of closely held corporations or stockholders of more broadly held corporations who disdain such tactics as approaching fraud.

Whether blameworthy or not, the use of the cloak of social responsibility, and the nonsense spoken in its name by influential and prestigious businessmen, does clearly harm the foundations of a free society. I have been impressed time and again by the schizophrenic character of many businessmen. They are capable of being extremely far-sighted and clear headed in matters that are internal to their businesses. They are incredibly short-sighted and muddle headed in matters that are outside their businesses but affect the possible survival of business in general. This short sightedness is strikingly exemplified in the calls from many businessmen for wage and price guidelines or controls or income policies. There is nothing that could do more in a brief period to destroy a market system and replace it by a centrally controlled system than effective governmental control of prices and wages.

The short sightedness is also exemplified in speeches by businessmen on social responsibility. This may gain them kudos in the short run. But it helps to strengthen the already too prevalent view that the pursuit of profits is wicked and immoral and must be curbed and controlled by external forces. Once this view is adopted, the external forces that curb the market will not be the social consciences, however highly developed, of the pontificating executives; it will be the iron fist of government bureaucrats. Here, as with price and wage controls, businessmen seem to me to reveal a suicidal impulse.

—Continued

Continued

The political principle that underlies the market mechanism is unanimity. In an ideal free market resting on private property, no individual can coerce any other, all cooperation is voluntary, all parties to such cooperation benefit or they need not participate. There are no "social" values, no "social" responsibilities in any sense other than the shared values and responsibilities of individuals. Society is a collection of individuals and of the various groups they voluntarily form.

The political principle that underlies the political mechanism is conformity. The individual must serve a more general social interest—whether that be determined by a church or a dictator or a majority. The individual may have a vote and a say in what is to be done, but if he is overruled, he must conform. It is appropriate for some to require others to contribute to a general social purpose whether they wish to or not.

Unfortunately, unanimity is not always feasible. There are some respects in which conformity appears unavoidable, so I do not see how one can avoid the use of the political mechanism altogether.

But the doctrine of "social responsibility" taken seriously would extend the scope of the political mechanism to every human activity. It does not differ in philosophy from the most explicitly collectivist means. That is why, in my book *Capitalism and Freedom,* I have called it a "fundamentally subversive doctrine" in a free society, and have said that in such a society, "there is one and only one social responsibility of business—to use its resources and engage in activities designed to increase its profits so long as it stays within the rules of the game, which is to say, engages in open and free competition without deception or fraud."

SOURCE: *The New York Times Magazine,* Sept. 13, 1970, Copyright © 1970 by The New York Times Company. Reprinted by permission.

A Critique of Milton Friedman's Essay 'The Social Responsibility of Business Is to Increase Its Profits'

Thomas Mulligan
Journal of Business Ethics, 1986

ABSTRACT. The main arguments of Milton Friedman's famous and influential essay are unsuccessful: He fails to prove that the exercise of social responsibility in business is by nature an unfair and socialist practice.

Much of Friedman's case is based on a questionable paradigm: a key premise is false: and logical cogency is sometimes missing.

The author proposes a different paradigm for socially responsible action in business and argues that a commitment to social responsibility can be an integral element in strategic and operational business management without producing any of the objectionable results claimed by Friedman.

In his famous essay, Milton Friedman argues that people responsible for decisions and action in business should not exercise social responsibility in their capacity as company executives. Instead, they should concentrate on increasing the profits of their companies.[1]

In the course of the essay, he also argues that the doctrine of social responsibility is a socialist doctrine.

The purpose of this paper is to assess the merit of Friedman's arguments. I shall summarize his main arguments, examine some of his premises and lines of inference, and propose a counter argument.

FRIEDMAN'S ARGUMENT: CORPORATE EXECUTIVES SHOULD NOT EXERCISE SOCIAL RESPONSIBILITY

Friedman argues that the exercise of social responsibility by a corporate executive is:

a. unfair, because it constitutes taxation without representation;

b. undemocratic, because it invests governmental power in a person who has no general mandate to govern;

c. unwise, because there are no checks and balances in the broad range of governmental power thereby turned over to his discretion;

d. a violation of trust, because the executive is employed by the owners "as an agent serving the interests of his principal";

---

1. Milton Friedman. 'The Social Responsibility of Business Is to Increase Its Profits', *New York Times Magazine*, 13 September 1970, 32 ff. Unless otherwise noted, all quotations are from this essay.

e. futile, both because the executive is unlikely to be able to anticipate the social consequences of his actions and because, as he imposes costs on his stockholders, customers, or employees, he is likely to lose their support and thereby lose his power.

These conclusions are related.

Points (b) and (c) depend on (a), on the ground that "the imposition of taxes and the expenditure of tax proceeds are governmental functions." Point (d) also depends on (a), because it is precisely in imposing a tax on his principal that this executive fails to serve the interests of that principal. Point (e) depends, in part, on (d), since it is the executive's failure to serve the interests of his principal which results in the withdrawal of that principal's support.

Point (a) is thus at the foundation of the argument. If (a) is false, then Friedman's demonstration of the subsequent conclusions almost completely collapses.

Is it true, then, that the executive who performs socially responsible action "is in effect imposing taxes . . . and deciding how the tax proceeds shall be spent"?

To make this case, Friedman argues by depicting how a company executive would perform such action.

He first introduces examples to illustrate that exercising social responsibility in business typically costs money. He mentions refraining from a price increase to help prevent inflation, reducing pollution "beyond the amount that is in the best interests of the corporation" to help improve the environment, and "at the expense of corporate profits" hiring 'hard-core' unemployed.

To establish that such costs are in effect taxes, he argues:

1. In taking such action, the executive expends "someone else's money"—the stockholders', the customers', or the employees'.

2. The money is spent "for a general social interest".

3. "Rather than serving as an agent of the stock-holders or the customers or the employees . . . he spends the money in a different way than they would have spent it".

The first two premises suggest a similarity between this money and tax revenues, which respect to their sources and to the purposes for which they are used. However, an expense is not yet a tax unless it is *imposed* on the contributor,

—Continued

Continued

irrespective of his desire to pay. Only Friedman's third premise includes this crucial element of imposition.

This third premise reveals the essential character of the paradigm on which Friedman bases his whole case.

FRIEDMAN'S PARADIGM

In the above examples of socially responsible action and throughout his essay, Friedman depicts the corporate executive who performs such action as a sort of Lone Ranger, deciding entirely by himself what good deeds to do, when to act, how much to spend:

> Here, the businessman—self-selected or appointed directly or indirectly by the stockholders—is to be simultaneously legislator, executive and jurist. He is to decide whom to tax by how much and for what purpose.

On this paradigm, the corporate executive does not act with the counsel and participation of the other stakeholders in the business. This is the basis of Friedman's claim that the executive is *imposing* something on those other stakeholders—unfairly, undemocratically, unwisely, and in violation of a trust.

But does Friedman's paradigm accurately depict the socially responsible executive? Does it capture the essential nature of socially responsible action in business? Or has he drawn a caricature, wrongly construed it as accurate, and used it to discredit the doctrine it purportedly illustrates?

A COUNTER-PARADIGM

Friedman's paradigm is valid in the sense that it is certainly possible for a corporate executive to try to exercise social responsibility without the counsel or participation of the other stakeholders in the business.

Friedman is also correct in characterizing such conduct as unfair and as likely to result in the withdrawal of the support of those other stakeholders.

Yet Friedman insists, at least with respect to the executive's employers, that the socially responsible executive "must" do it alone, must act in opposition to the interests of the other stakeholders:

> What does it mean to say that the corporate executive has a "social responsibility" in his capacity as a businessman? If this statement is not pure rhetoric, it must mean that he is to act in some way that is not in the interest of his employers.

There is no good reason why this remarkable claim must be true. The exercise of social responsibility in business suffers no diminishment in meaning or merit if the executive and his employers both understand their mutual interest to include a proactive social role and cooperate in undertaking that role.

I propose a different paradigm for the exercise of social responsibility in business—one very much in keeping with sound management practice.

A business normally defines its course and commits itself to action by conceiving a mission, then proceeding to a set of objectives, then determining quantified and time-bound goals, and then developing a full strategic plan which is implemented by appropriate top-level staffing, operating procedures, budgeted expenditures, and daily management control.

Many stakeholders in the business participate in this far-reaching process.

Founders, board members, major stockholders, and senior executives may all participate in defining a mission and in setting objectives based on that mission. In so doing, these people serve as "legislators" for the company.

Top management's translation of these broad directions into goals, strategic plans, operating procedures, budgets, and daily work direction brings middle management, first-line management and, in some companies, employee representatives into the process. This is the "executive branch" of the business.

When the time comes to judge progress and success, the board members and stockholders serve as "jurists" at the highest level, and when necessary can take decisive, sometimes dramatic, corrective measures. However, the grassroots judgment of the court of employee opinion can also be a powerful force. More than one company has failed or faltered because it did not keep a course which inspired and held its talented people.

In sum, a business is a collaborative enterprise among the stakeholders, with some checks and balances. In general, this system allows to any one stakeholder a degree of participation commensurate with the size of his or her stake.

For a business to define a socially responsible course and commit to socially responsible action, it needs to follow no other process than the familiar one described in the preceding paragraphs.

On this paradigm, if socially responsible action is on the corporate executive's agenda, then it is there because the company's mission, objectives, and goals—developed collaboratively by the major stakeholders—gave him license to put it there and provided parameters for his program. Lone Ranger executives are no more necessary and no more wel-

—Continued

come in a socially responsible business than in one devoted exclusively to the maximization of profit.

This paradigm conforms more accurately than Friedman's to the reality of how action programs—socially responsible ones or otherwise—are conceived and enacted in a strategically managed business. The corporate executive in this process, in contradistinction to Friedman's corporate executive, does not impose unauthorized costs, or "taxes," on anyone. On this account, he usurps no governmental function, violates no trust, and runs no special risk of losing the support of the other stakeholders.

THE PROBLEM OF KNOWING FUTURE CONSEQUENCES

The preceding argument addresses most of Friedman's objections to a corporate executive's attempts to exercise social responsibility.

Friedman, however, provides one objection which does not rest on his paradigm of the Lone Ranger executive. This is the objection that it is futile to attempt socially responsible action because the future social consequences of today's actions are very difficult to know.

Suppose, he writes, that the executive decides to fight inflation:

How is he to know what action of his will contribute to that end? He is presumably an expert in running his company—in producing a product or selling it or financing it. But nothing about his selection makes him an expert on inflation. Will holding down the price of his product reduce inflationary pressure? Or, by leaving more spending power in the hands of his customers, simply divert it elsewhere? Or by forcing him to produce less because of the lower price, will it simply contribute to shortages?

The difficulty of determining the future consequences of one's intended good acts has received attention in the literature of philosophical ethics. G. E. Moore, in his early twentieth century classic *Principia Ethica*, writes of "the hopeless task of finding duties"[2] since, to act with perfect certainty, we would need to know "all the events which will be in any way affected by our action throughout an infinite future".[3]

Human life, however, requires action in the absence of certainty, and business people in particular have a bias toward action. They do not wait for perfect foreknowledge of consequences, but instead set a decision date, gather the best

---

2. G. E. Moore, *Principia Ethica*, Cambridge, 1971, p. 150.
3. *Ibid.*, p. 149.

information available, contemplate alternatives, assess risks, and then decide what to do.

Decisions about socially responsible actions, no less than decisions about new products or marketing campaigns, can be made using this "business-like" approach. The business person, therefore, has even less cause than most moral agents to abstain from social responsibility out of a sense of the futility of knowing consequences, since he is more practiced than most in the techniques for making action decisions in the absence of certainty.

SOCIAL RESPONSIBILITY AND SOCIALISM

Some of Friedman's most emphatic language is devoted to his position that the advocates of social responsibility in a free-enterprise system are "preaching pure and unadultered socialism."

He asserts this view in the first and last paragraphs of the essay, and concludes:

The doctrine of "social responsibility" . . . does not differ in philosophy from the most explicitly collectivist doctrine.

Friedman's argument for this conclusion is located roughly midway through his essay, and it too rests on his paradigm of the socially responsible executive "imposing taxes" on others and thereby assuming governmental functions:

He becomes in effect a public employee, a civil servant . . . . It is intolerable that such civil servants . . . should be selected as they are now. If they are to be civil servants, then they must be elected through a political process. If they are to impose taxes and make expenditures to foster "social" objectives, then political machinery must be set up to make the assessment of taxes and to determine through a political process the objectives to be served.

This is the basic reason why the doctrine of "social responsibility" involves the acceptance of the socialist view that political mechanisms, not market mechanisms, are the appropriate way to determine the allocation of scarce resources to alternative users.

I shall raise three objections to this line of reasoning.

First, this argument rests on the paradigm which has already been called into question. If we accept the counterparadigm proposed above as truer to the nature of a socially responsible corporate executive, then there is no basis for saying that such an individual "imposes taxes," becoming "in effect" a civil servant.

—Continued

Continued

Second, it is not apparent how the propositions that, under the doctrine of social responsibility, a corporate executive is "in effect" imposing taxes and "in effect" a civil servant logically imply that this doctrine upholds the view that political mechanisms should determine the allocation of scarce resources.

To the contrary, as Friedman points out, his paradigmatic executive is not a true political entity, since he is not elected and since his program of "taxation" and social expenditure is not implemented through a political process. Paradoxically, it is Friedman who finds it "intolerable" that this agent who allocates scarce resources is not part of a political mechanism. Nowhere, however, does he show that acceptance of such a political mechanism is intrinsic to the view of his opponent, the advocate of social responsibility.

Third, in order to show that the doctrine of social responsibility is a socialist doctrine, Friedman must invoke a criterion for what constitutes socialism. As we have seen, his criterion is "acceptance of the . . . view that political mechanisms, not market mechanisms, are the appropriate way to determine the allocation of scarce resources to alternative uses."

The doctrine of social responsibility, he holds, does accept this view. "Therefore the doctrine is a socialist doctrine.[4]

However, this criterion is hardly definitive of socialism. The criterion is so broad that it holds for virtually any politically totalitarian or authoritarian system . . . including feudal monarchies and dictatorships of the political right.

Further, depending on the nature of a resource and the degree of its scarcity, the political leadership in any system, including American democracy, is liable to assert its right to determine the allocation of that resource. Who doubts that it is appropriate for our political institutions, rather than market mechanisms, to ensure the equitable availability of breathable air and drinkable water, or to allocate food and fuel in times of war and critical shortage?

Therefore, Friedman has not provided a necessary element for his argument—a definitive criterion for what constitutes socialism.

---

4. In the concluding paragraph of his essay, Friedman states, "The doctrine of 'social responsibility' taken seriously would extend the scope of the political mechanism to every human activity." Every human activity" certainly seems at least one extra step beyond the set of activities involved in "the allocation of scarce resources to alternative uses." Unfortunately, Friedman's essay contains no explication of the reasoning he used to make the transition from the language of his argument midway through the essay to the grander claim of this concluding paragraph.

In summary, Friedman's argument is unsound: first, because it rests on an arbitrary and suspect paradigm; second, because certain of his premises do not imply their stated conclusion; and, third, because a crucial premise, his criterion for what constitutes socialism, is not true.

Although he complains of the "analytical looseness" and "lack of rigor" of his opponents, Friedman's argument has on close examination betrayed its own instances of looseness and lack of rigor.

CONCLUSION

I have considered Friedman's principal objections to socially responsible action in business and argued that at the bottom of most of his objections is an inaccurate paradigm. In response, I have given an account of a more appropriate paradigm to show how business can exercise social responsibility.

Friedman is right in pointing out that exercising social responsibility costs money. If nothing else, a company incurs expense when it invests the manhours needed to contemplate the possible social consequences of alternative actions and to consider the merit or demerit of each set of consequences.

But Friedman is wrong in holding that such costs must be imposed by one business stakeholder on the others, outside of the whole collaborative process of strategic and operational business management. He presumes too much in intimating through his imagined examples that the business person who pursues a socially responsible course inevitably acts without due attention to return on investment, budgetary limitations, reasonable employee remuneration, or competitive pricing.

My purpose has been to provide a critique of the major lines of argument presented in a famous and influential essay. The thrust has been to show that Friedman misrepresents the nature of social responsibility in business and that business people *can* pursue a socially responsible course without the objectionable results claimed by Friedman. It would be another step to produce positive arguments to demonstrate why business people *should* pursue such a course. That is an undertaking for another occasion.

For now, I shall only observe that Friedman's own concluding statement contains a moral exhortation to business people. Business, he says, should engage in "open and free competition without deception or fraud." If Friedman does not recognize that even these restrained words lay open a broad range of moral obligation and social responsibility for business, which is after all one of the largest areas of human interaction in our society, then the oversight is his.

—Continued

Continued

The Fuqua School of Business,
Duke University.
Durham, NC 27706.
U.S.A.

Thomas Mulligan is an Assistant Professor at The Fuqua School of Business, Duke University, in the areas of Manufacturing Management Systems and Business Ethics. He has a Ph.D. from Northwestern University in the field of Philosophy and has worked as an educator, manager, and consultant in the manufacturing and software industries.

SOURCE: *Journal of Business Ethics* 5 (1986): 265–269. © 1986 by D. Reidel Publishing Company. Reprinted by permission of Klurwer Academic Publishers.

The Evolution of the Corporate Social Performance Model

Steven L. Wartick
Philip L. Cochran
Academy of Management Review, 1985

This paper traces the evolution of the corporate social performance model by focusing on three challenges to the concept of corporate social responsibility: economic responsibility, public responsibility, and social responsiveness. It also examines social issues management as a dimension of corporate social performance. It concludes that the corporate social performance model is valuable for business and society study and that it provides the beginnings of a paradigm for the field.

The term "corporate social performance" (CSP) has been used for several years in the business and society literature. In most cases, CSP has not been defined precisely; it has been used as a synonym for corporate social responsibility, corporate social responsiveness, or any other interaction between business and the social environment. More recently, however, CSP has started to take on a more precise meaning.

As first described by Carroll (1979), CSP is the three dimensional integration of corporate social responsibility, corporate social responsiveness, and social issues. This integrative nature of CSP is what makes it unique. Instead of arguing that economic responsibility and public policy responsibility are inconsistent with social responsibility (Buchholz, 1977; Friedman, 1962; Heyne, 1968; Preston & Post, 1975), the CSP model integrates economic responsibility and public policy responsibility into its definition of social responsibility. Instead of viewing responsibility, responsiveness and issues as separate, alternative corporate concerns (Ackerman & Bauer, 1976; Frederick, 1978; Murphy, 1978; Sethi, 1979), the CSP model reflects an underlying interaction among the principles of social responsibility, the process of social responsiveness, and the policies developed to address social issues. The CSP model relies on this expanded version of social responsibility and this principle/process/policy approach in order to provide a distinctive view of a corporation's overall efforts toward satisfying its obligations to society.

By integrating social responsibilities, social responsiveness, and social issues, the CSP model provides a valuable framework for overall analyses of business and society. CSP has a micro-level dimension: it focuses on the interface between the firm and its environment, rather than on the relationship between business as an institution and the society in which it operates (Jones, 1983; Preston & Post, 1975). However, CSP does retain an emphasis on the macro-level by continuing to use social responsibility as the starting point for corporate social involvement. As such, the CSP model describes the totality of a firm's efforts to meet changing societal conditions, and thus it provides a starting point for the eventual development of a central paradigm for business and society (Preston, 1975).

Whether the CSP model ultimately leads to a central paradigm for business and society is an intriguing question, but a question still largely a matter for the future. Of equal importance for those who are interested in business and society is the historical evolution of the CSP model. In scholarly inquiry, new models do not appear suddenly. They evolve through a process of analysis, debate, and modification. The value of a model therefore is as much a function of its past as its future.

In his 1979 work Carroll covered much of the background literature of his CSP model. However, his review failed to capture the model's dynamic evolution. It failed to capture the process of analysis, debate, and modification that characterizes scholarly inquiry. In the present paper the evolution of the CSP model is traced. The thesis is that the CSP model has grown out of the major scholarly "confrontations" that occurred during the most recent 30-year debate about corporate social responsibility.

TWO BASIC PREMISES

Thirty years ago, H. R. Bowen argued that businessmen have an obligation "to pursue those policies, to make those decisions, or to follow those lines of action which are desirable in terms of the objectives and values of our society" (1953, p. 6). With this simple proposition Bowen touched off what can be called "the modern debate" about social responsibility. As Heald (1970), Eberstadt (1973), and others have shown, this most recent 30-year period is not the only time when social responsibility was a major societal concern. However, social responsibility was most thoroughly examined and vigorously analyzed in the past three decades.

The concept of social responsibility—as suggested by Bowen's emphasis on the *objectives* and *values* of society—rests on two fundamental premises. First, business exists at the pleasure of society; its behavior and methods of operation must fall within the guidelines set by society. Like govern-

—Continued

Continued

ment, business has a social contract—an implied set of rights and obligations. The specifics of the contract may change as societal conditions change, but the contract in general always remains as the source of business legitimacy (Donaldson, 1983). This social contract is the vehicle through which business behavior is brought into conformity with society's objectives.

The second premise underlying social responsibility is that business acts as a moral agent within society (Ozar, 1979; Rawls, 1971). Like states and churches, corporations reflect and reinforce values. As Donaldson argues, corporations have: (a) "the capacity to use moral rules in decision making" and (b) "the capacity to control not only overt corporate acts, but also the structure of politics and rules" (1982, p. 30). Corporations therefore meet the conditions of moral agency and must behave in a manner consistent with society's values. An ethical dimension to business behavior and responsibility is the logical result.

These two ideas—the social contract and moral agency—have provided the basic premises of the social responsibility concept. Yet, they also have provided the two major targets for critics of social responsibility. The arguments of these critics are revealed in three major challenges to social responsibility.

CHALLENGES TO SOCIAL RESPONSIBILITY

Since Bowen's seminal work, both scholars and practitioners have attempted to review and redefine the basic concept of social responsibility. From these efforts have come the three challenges to social responsibility. Each challenge was offered as something more than a mere complement to social responsibility; each was intended as *an alternative* to social responsibility in management thinking. Each challenge attempted to redefine both the scope of corporate responsibilities in society and the criteria for measuring managerial performance in the social arena.

Challenge 1: Economic Responsibility

Although economic responsibility is based on the assumptions of classical economic doctrine, in the context of this debate it was raised as a challenge to corporate social responsibility. Friedman (1962, 1970) is the most ardent proponent of economic responsibility, although others (Haas, 1979; Heyne, 1968) continue to try to clarify and extend the argument. The challenge of economic responsibility begins on the macro-level by attacking both the social contract premise and the moral agency premise of social responsibility; it continues by deriving micro-level implications.

The Criticism. According to Friedman (1962, 1970), the only social responsibility of business is to maximize profits within "the rules of the game." The sole constituency of business management is the stockholders, and the sole concern of the stockholders is financial return. If, through socially responsible acts (e.g., urban investments, philanthropy, or minority purchasing programs), managers reduce the return to stockholders, then they are, in effect, levying taxes on the corporation. By determining how these self-imposed taxes will be spent, managers undermine the market mechanism for allocating resources and they appoint themselves as non-elected public policymakers. In short, social responsibility is a "subversive" doctrine (not a complementary doctrine) in the social contract of business in a free society.

The challenge of economic responsibility argues that corporations cannot be moral agents. Only individuals can have moral responsibilities. If managers, owners, customers, or employees choose to use their personal property (i.e., salaries, dividends, income, or wages) in efforts to resolve society's problems, so be it. But, to the extent that managers use corporate resources to promote socially responsible activities, they are "stealing" from owners' dividends, from customers' wealth, or from employees' wages. Thus, even on ethical grounds, the concept of social responsibility as anything more than profit maximization is inappropriate. In sum, the proponents of economic responsibility contend that improving profitability is the only socially responsible activity of business. The criteria for judging managerial performance is how well managers meet the objective of improving profitability.

The Response. The response to this first challenge has been to point out that the assumptions of economic responsibility are unrealistic. Some who reject economic responsibility focus on the managerial implications. For example, Walters (1977) argues that economic responsibility is not a useful guide for managers because: (a) it neglects the long run consequences of profit maximization and (b) it fails to identify the appropriate relationship between the manager and changing political and legal conditions. A manager who adheres to the economic responsibility concept runs the risk of becoming the target of government regulation but has no clear direction in relation to political involvement. If the manager chooses to stay out of the political process, shareholders' interests may suffer. If the manager chooses to become involved in the political process, then the firm takes on a political dimension and ceases to be strictly an economic institution. The firm's behavior is subjected to politi-

—Continued

Continued

cal evaluation, and its economic justifications for behavior are discounted.

Others who reject the realism of economic responsibility focus on scope and argue that the business community never has adhered strictly to a concept of economic responsibility (McKie, 1974). Philanthropy, community involvement, paternalism, and voluntary codes of ethics are all indicators of a longstanding, pragmatic divergence from the concept. They also argue that economic responsibility ignores the reality of "market failures"—especially in cases in which costs are not paid for and in which the seller has considerably more information than the buyer (Arrow, 1973). Again, the point is that economic responsibility is not realistic.

In general, those who argue that economic responsibility is not the only social responsibility of business are saying that economic responsibility fails to recognize that modern businesses, especially the megacorporations, are no longer mere economic institutions. Through such activities as lobbying, providing Congressional testimony, and establishing political action committees, corporations have added a political dimension. Because corporate behavior is so critical to the realization of social goals such as equal opportunity, worker safety and health, and environmental protection, a social dimension is added to corporate performance. Because corporations are the major societal entities that develop and apply new technologies, a dimension of their performance rests with technology assessment. To view the modern corporation in a strict economic sense is to ignore reality, and to suggest that its responsibilities include only economic obligations is myopic.

Challenge 2: Public Responsibility

Public responsibility is a relatively recent challenge. Its roots, however, seem to go back to Levitt who, in response to Bowen, argued:

> Business should recognize what government functions are and let it go at that, stopping only to fight government where government directly intrudes itself into business. It should let government take care of the general welfare so that business can take care of the more material aspects of welfare (1958, p. 49).

Preston and Post (1975, 1981) and Buchholz (1977, 1982), extending this notion of separation of responsibilities, offer public responsibility as a substitute for social responsibility. These advocates of public responsibility focus more on the social contract of business and less on the question of moral agency. They maintain an emphasis on macro-level concerns, but they also try to move the discussion to more of a micro-level by addressing organizational responses.

The Criticism. Preston and Post (1975, 1981) begin by arguing that business and society are interpenetrating systems. The systems are linked through the market process and the public policy process. Public responsibility comes from the recognition of a corporation's primary and secondary involvements. Primary involvements are the essential economic tasks of the firm; secondary involvements are the consequential effects resulting from the performance of those primary functions. The market provides direction for the corporation in relation to primary involvements, and the public policy process provides direction for secondary involvements. The organization should "analyze and evaluate pressures and stimuli coming from public policy in the same way it analyzes and evaluates market experience and opportunity" (Buchholz, 1982, p. 435). Corporations therefore have a dual responsibility—a responsibility to the market (similar to economic responsibility as discussed above) and a responsibility to the public policy process. The criteria for measuring managerial performance rest with how well managers respond to both sets of responsibilities. Thus, public responsibility provides a construct for clarifying relevant and irrelevant corporate concerns, and it offers guidelines for implementing and evaluating managerial action. It is based on an orientation that integrates micro-level and macro-level considerations.

In the public responsibility concept, public policy extends beyond the traditional understanding that "public policy equals the law." In this concept public policy refers to "widely shared and generally acknowledged principles directing and controlling actions that have broad implications for society at large or major portions thereof" (Preston & Post, 1975, p. 56). Public policy includes "the broad pattern of social direction reflected in public opinion, emerging issues, formal legal requirements, and enforcement or implementation practices" (Preston & Post, 1981, p. 57). When public policy is considered in this broader context, public responsibility goes beyond the Friedmanian (1962) dictum of maximize profits within the rules of the game. Managers are encouraged to participate in the public policy development process.

The problem that advocates of public responsibility are attempting to address relates to perceived ambiguity of the social responsibility concept. Preston and Post argue that social responsibility is "vague and ill-defined," and that it:

—Continued

Continued

provides no basis for dealing concretely with possible conflicts between traditional corporate goals and social objectives; and it suggests no boundary between the genuine responsibilities of business management and the entire range of activities within the host society (1975, p. 52).

They therefore offer public responsibility as a replacement for social responsibility. Buchholz (1977) suggests that two major problems with social responsibility make this replacement necessary. They are: (a) allocating resources to be used in dealing with social issues and (b) developing accountability when business makes social decisions. Preston and Post, as well as Buchholz, have argued that the use of public responsibility eliminates these problems associated with social responsibility.

The Response. For those who argue against substituting the concept of public responsibility for social responsibility, the major concern is how public policy is defined. If, for example, public policy is defined as broadly as Preston and Post suggest (widely shared and generally acknowledged principles of society or public opinion, emerging issues, formal law, and enforcement practices), then nearly all environmental change is included as public policy. Because the public policy process is the major societal mechanism for articulating changing social conditions, the difference between public policy development and social change are difficult, at best, to distinguish. Also, the differences between public policy and Bowen's "societal values and objectives" are less clear. Effectively, public responsibility and social responsibility become synonymous.

If public policy is defined in the more traditional sense (as governmental legislative development), then public responsibility is too narrowly conceived. This is Jones' point when he argues that using the public responsibility concept is too restrictive because:

1. Public policy does not address many issues that confront corporations in social policy areas.

2. Conflicting statements or expressions of public policy exist at the same level in many areas of corporate social involvement.

3. Statements of public policy emerge from several levels of government, "whose public policy should be heeded?"

4. Public policy can conflict with "higher laws" or "higher moral codes" (1980, p. 64).

Perhaps Jones' points merely reflect the "real-world" difficulties that affect any normative approach to corporate social involvement (Preston & Post, 1981). Yet, the fact remains that this narrower conceptualization of public policy is too restrictive for operationalizing the business and societal interaction.

In short, the critics argue that because of ambiguity in defining public policy, public responsibility adds little as an alternative to social responsibility. If public policy is defined in the broader sense, it is hard to distinguish from social responsibility. If public policy is defined in the narrower sense, it is too restrictive in terms of the scope of corporate responsibilities in society. The challenge of public responsibility does call for increased discussion of how corporate responsibilities may be realized, and in that sense it adds to the debate about corporate social involvement. However, public responsibility as a substitute for social responsibility is still lacking.

Challenge 3: Social Responsiveness

The third challenge to social responsibility comes in the form of social responsiveness. Social responsiveness is intended to shift the emphasis away from social obligations and to social response processes. As such, social responsiveness is targeted at both the social contract and the moral agency of business.

The Criticism. Like those critics before them, the advocates of social responsiveness find social responsibility to be operationally dysfunctional. Ackerman and Bauer, for example, argue that social responsibility "gives little guidance as to the content of what is to be done beyond "something more,' and it deflects our attention from much that is important" (1976, p. 7). They base their judgment on three concepts that they believe underlie social responsibility—the conscience of the executive, costs of foregone profits, and voluntary discretion. All of these concepts are difficult, if not impossible, to assess, and each contributes to the ambiguity surrounding social responsibility.

Two other scholars place social responsiveness in a position beyond social responsibility in an evolutionary pattern of corporate social involvement. Sethi (1979) argues that a broadening conception of legitimacy has moved corporate social involvement from social obligation (a rough equivalent of economic responsibility), to social responsibility (with its prescriptive orientation), to social responsiveness. Murphy (1978) suggests that the current period of social responsiveness (1974 to the present) has been preceded by periods of issue emphasis (1968–1973); awareness development, that is social responsibility (1953–1967); and philanthropy (to the early 1950s). Both of these works imply that social responsiveness is an *advanced* way of thinking about corporate social involvement.

—Continued

Continued

As the replacement for social responsibility, social responsiveness takes on more of a means orientation. Social responsiveness "refers to the *capacity* [italics added] of a corporation to respond to social pressures" (Frederick, 1978, p. 6). Whereas social responsibility is a noun, social responsiveness is a verb. Whereas social responsibility leans toward philosophical discourse, social responsiveness "shuns philosophy in favor of a managerial approach" (Frederick, 1978, p. 7). In all, the advocates of social responsiveness see it as a more tangible, achievable objective than social responsibility, and they see it as "a genuine replacement of the idea of 'responsibility' and . . . not simply one of those fashionable changes in phraseology that occasionally takes the scholarly community by storm" (Frederick, 1978, p. 6).

The Response. Concern with social responsiveness is not, as is the case with economic responsibility, a matter of the usefulness of the point of view. Social responsiveness is a valid concept that leads managers to a clearer emphasis on implementation and policy development. The concern here is similar to the question raised about public responsibility, that is, is social responsiveness a valid replacement for social responsibility? If social responsiveness replaces social responsibility in management thinking, what is lost and what is gained in terms of some of the most important questions of corporate social involvement?

First, it can be argued that to replace social responsibility with social responsiveness eliminates or at least dramatically deemphasizes considerations of business ethics and social *irresponsibility*. Social responsiveness tends to be guided by prevailing social norms; social responsibility attempts to determine fundamental ethical truths. There can be ethical problems and irresponsible actions without public outcry, awareness, and pressure. To attempt to determine what is fundamentally right or wrong is not a frivolous exercise. As most critics of social responsibility point out, ethical analysis does not always provide strong, empirically testable, pragmatic results. But that does not necessarily diminish the value of the concept. Consider such concepts as "self-actualization" in organizational behavior or "competition" in economics; these concepts suffer from similar empirical and pragmatic deficiencies, but still they have provided valuable insights into the workings of human and economic systems. Social responsibility adds a similar dimension to corporate performance, and whether social responsiveness by itself maintains an adequate level of ethical inquiry is doubtful.

Second, social responsiveness does not require continual evaluation of the relations between corporate objectives and societal objectives. Without some sense of social responsibilities to guide activities, the corporation is left with a potpourri of demands all of which are impossible to meet. As a result, social responsiveness by itself is likely to lead to reaction rather than the proaction that many advocates of responsiveness call for.

Third, social responsiveness seems to ignore what Davis (1973) called the Iron Law of Responsibility—if an institution has social power, that institution must use its power responsibly or the power will be taken away by society. Being responsive does not necessarily mean the same thing as being responsible. As Epstein (1979) has argued, social responsibility relates to outcomes or products, whereas social responsiveness relates to process; these two perspectives have significantly different implications for the firm. Suppose, for example, that a multiproduct firm's social responsibility is to produce reasonably safe products. Similarly, the same firm is responsive every time it produces an unsafe product: it withdraws the product from the market as soon as the product is found to be unsafe. After, say, 10 recalls, will the firm be recognized as socially responsible? Will the firm be recognized as socially responsive? The likely answers to these questions are "no" to the first, but "yes" to the second. Over the long term, the socially responsive firm's existence may be threatened by the Iron Law of Responsibility.

CSP: A SYNTHESIS OF THE CHALLENGES

As noted earlier, the distinctive features of the CSP model are its expanded conceptualization of social responsibility and its integration of responsibilities, responsiveness, and issues through a principle/process/policy approach. In a paper that followed the Carroll model of CSP by four years, Strand (1983) took these two basic features and developed a system paradigm for organizational adjustment to the social environment. Like Carroll, Strand argues that the three dimensions of responsibility, responsiveness and responses are fundamentally linked to form a system of corporate social involvement. Social responsibilities are determined by society, and the tasks of the firm are: (a) to identify and analyze society's changing expectations relating to corporate responsibilities, (b) to determine an overall approach for being responsive to society's changing demands, and (c) to implement appropriate responses to relevant social issues. Whereas Carroll emphasizes the relationship between responsibility and responsiveness. Strand emphasizes the more micro-level concerns of responsiveness and responses. Strand does more than Carroll with the third dimension of CSP—developing responses to issues—by elaborating both internal and external responses to environmental change. However, the two basic features of CSP—an expanded con-

—Continued

Continued

ceptualization of social responsibility and an integration of responsibilities, responsiveness and responses—remain unchanged. Thus, Strand's model can be considered an extension of the principles/process/policies relationship underlying CSP thinking.

As illustrated in Table 1, the first two challenges to social responsibility—economic and public—have been assimilated into a more all encompassing definition of social responsibility found in the CSP model. In addition, the dual level orientation—macro-level along with micro-level concerns—of public responsibility has been adopted by CSP. The third challenge—social responsiveness—has been incorporated into the CSP model as the critical link between social responsibilities and responses to social issues.

The CSP Perspective of Economic Responsibility

The CSP model recognizes and accepts the importance of economic responsibility. However, instead of arguing that economic and social responsibility are mutually exclusive, economic responsibility is identified as a subset of social responsibility. As noted by McGuire, "The idea of social responsibilities supposes that the corporation has not only economic and legal obligations, but also certain responsibilities to society which extend beyond those obligations" (1963, p. 144). The point is that social responsibility includes, but is not limited to, economic responsibility.

To illustrate this integrated view of economic and social responsibilities, consider Carroll's (1979) and Strand's (1983) models. Carroll's model defines social responsibility as consisting of economic, legal, ethical, and discretionary responsibilities. Strand's concept of social responsibility describes four concerns: (a) the cultural and economic environments, (b) material, social, and psychological experience of constituents, (c) social demands and expectations placed on organizations, and (d) the environmental texture of organizations. Both authors incorporated economic responsibility into the principles underlying their models and thus incorporated economic responsibility into the definition of social responsibility.

Other recent research supports the idea that economic and social responsibilities are not mutually exclusive but are parts of some more all encompassing concept of corporate responsibilities. Zenisek (1979), for example, argued that corporate social responsibility is really nothing more than a fourth layer of managerial responsibility resulting from the evolution of American capitalism. Economic responsibility and social responsibility (the first and fourth layers) are not trade-offs but rather components of overall societal responsibilities of business. Tuzzolino and Armandi (1981) have offered a need-

hierarchy framework for corporations that is similar to Maslow's need hierarchy for individuals. In their framework, the lowest level of responsibility (the physiological needs equivalent) is profitability, and the highest level of responsibility (the self-actualization needs equivalent) is social responsibility. As in Maslow's model, prepotency exists such that the need for profitability (economic responsibility) predominates if it is not being satisfied. But, in self-actualizing, the firm appeases all of its claimants (it is socially responsible). Recently, Drucker (1984) reemphasized this position by arguing that capital formation and, thus, profitability is the most fundamental responsibility of the firm. Other responsibilities follow profitability and should not be excluded from management's consideration solely because they decrease profit.

The CSP Perspective of Public Responsibility

The CSP model deals with the second challenge, as it does with economic responsibility, by incorporating public responsibility into the definition of social responsibility. Like economic responsibility, the challenge of public responsibility expands but does not replace social responsibility. In Carroll's model, the legal component of social responsibility covers the narrower definition of public responsibility, and the discretionary component covers the broader definition. In Strand's model public responsibility is implicit in his category of "social demands and expectations placed on organizations." Strand equates these demands and expectations to "legal, economic and social pressures" (1983, p. 92).

Most notable of other recent research supporting the inclusion of public responsibility within social responsibility is Dalton Cosier's (1982) four faces of social responsibility. In fact, this conceptualization of social responsibility addresses the major criticism of public responsibility by integrating the narrow definition of public policy with the broad definition of public policy. Dalton and Cosier's framework is based on four types of corporate activities: (a) illegal and irresponsible acts, (b) illegal but responsible acts, (c) legal but irresponsible acts, and (d) legal and responsible acts. The narrow notion of the public responsibility concept exists in the legal/illegal dimension of the framework. The broader definition exists in the linkage between the legal/illegal dimension and the responsible/irresponsible dimension.

In addition to incorporating public responsibility into the definition of social responsibility, the CSP model accepts the general orientation of pubic responsibility, that is, that macro-level and micro-level concerns exist simultaneously in corporate social involvement. Public responsibility rests on the macro-level notion of interpenetrating systems and on

—Continued

Continued

TABLE 1

THE CORPORATE SOCIAL
PERFORMANCE SYNTHESIS
OF THE THREE MAJOR
CHALLENGES TO SOCIAL
RESPONSIBILITY

CHALLENGE	CSP SYNTHESIS
1: Economic responsibility	Incorporated as one level of corporate social responsibility
2: Public responsibility	Incorporated as (1) one level of corporate social responsibility and (2) the underlying orientation for macro-level and micro-level concerns existing simultaneously.
3: Social responsiveness	Incorporated as (1) the action oriented complement to corporate social responsibility and (2) the underlying approach to the development of responses to social issues.

the micro-level notion of primary and secondary involvements; CSP maintains this dual level orientation through its integration of social responsibility and social responsiveness.

The CSP Perspective of Social Responsiveness

The CSP model argues that social responsibility and social responsiveness are equally valid concepts and that both should be included as separate dimensions of corporate social involvement. For example, in Carroll's model, social responsiveness is comprised of reactive, defensive, accommodative, and proactive approaches. As summarized by Carroll:

> Corporate social responsiveness, which has been discussed by some as an alternate to social responsibility is, rather, the action phase of management responding in the social sphere. In a sense, being responsive enables organizations to act on their social responsibilities without getting bogged down in the quagmire of definitional problems that can so easily occur if organizations try to get a precise fix on what their true responsibilities are before acting (1979, p. 502).

In Strand's model, social responsiveness is comprised of (a) organizational type and characteristics, (b) monitoring and boundary spanning, (c) management social values and goals, (d) social response mechanisms, and (e) decision processes (1983, p. 92). Carroll's model therefore emphasizes the link between social responsibility and social responsiveness, and Strand's model emphasizes the link between social responsiveness and social policy.

Both Carroll and Strand view responsibility and responsiveness as vital, complementary concepts; they argue that

the two concepts merely play different roles in the understanding of CSP. Social responsibility maintains a macro emphasis and social responsiveness provides a micro emphasis. Although neither Carroll nor Strand attempts to differentiate precisely the distinct roles of social responsibility and social responsiveness, such a task is important to the CSP model. Thus, in Table 2, a summary of the differences between social responsibility and social responsiveness is presented.

SOCIAL ISSUES MANAGEMENT: THE THIRD DIMENSION OF CSP?

Although the first two dimensions of CSP—social responsibility (including economic and public responsibilities) and social responsiveness—clearly grow out of the debate involving the three challenges to social responsibility, the third dimension of CSP is still in its formative stage. In Carroll's model, the third dimension consists only of issue areas. In Strand's model, the third dimension is more fully developed around organizational responses to quality of life issues. CSP is moving toward social issues management as its third dimension.

Background of (Social) Issues Management

Issues management has been developing along parallel lines in three different areas—public issues management, strategic issues management, and social issues management. The only difference among these three areas is the type of issue considered—public issues relate to legislative matters, strate-

—Continued

Continued

TABLE 2

DIFFERENCES BETWEEN SOCIAL
RESPONSIBILITY AND SOCIAL
RESPONSIVENESS

	SOCIAL RESPONSIBILITY	SOCIAL RESPONSIVENESS
Major considerations	Ethical	Pragmatic
Unit of analysis	Society	The firm
Focus	Ends	Means
Purpose	"Window out"	"Window in"
Emphasis	Obligations	Responses
Role of the firm	Moral agent	Producer of goods and services
Decision framework	Long term	Medium and short term

gic issues have consequences requiring strategic change, and social issues relate to societal change in values and attitudes. The purpose and process of issues management in each area is substantially the same.

The purposes of issues management are to minimize "surprises" emanating from the turbulent business environment and to prompt systematic and interactive responses to environmental change (Brown, 1979; Gottschalk, 1982; "Issues Management," 1981). The process of issues management varies somewhat from organization to organization, but in general it consists of three stages: (a) issues identification, (b) issues analysis, and (c) response development (Johnson, 1983). The formalization of the issues management process was an attempt to address the myriad of issues that emerged in the late 1960s and early 1970s. Issues management was intended to fill the void between the short term, reactive perspective of public relations and the long term, futuristic perspective of corporate planning. In reality, issues management is a misnomer: responses, not issues, are managed.

In the public affairs area, issues management grew out of the work of Chase (1977). Primarily, Chase proposed a five stage process that leads to a more systematic approach to issues identification and response development. In strategic management, Ansoff (1975, 1980) and King (1982) have been most involved in the development of issues management. Beginning with Ansoff's idea that responses to "weak signals" are needed, the continuing emphasis has been on identifying and responding to issues of strategic importance. In the social issues area, Jacoby (1971), Ackerman (1973), Sethi (1975), Post (1978), and Fleming (1981) have led the way in issues management theory. Using expectational gaps as their basic conceptual tool, this group has

focused on: (a) how social issues are defined and differentiated from social trends, (b) what common patterns exist in the development of social issues, and (c) what responses appropriately address the identified issues.

Current Status of (Social) Issues Management

Issues management—whether public, strategic or social—is still suffering from problems associated with a new area. In practice, issues management continues to have problems with issues overload, quantification of analyses, policy program evaluation, and organizational credibility (Johnson, 1983). Even so, issues management has become an established component of public affairs management in several major corporations (Gollner, 1983; Post, Murray, Dickie, & Mahon, 1983).

In theory, the current status of issues management is more promising. The life cycle of social issues is firmly established as a valuable analytical tool (Arcelus & Schaefer, 1982; Post, 1978; Starling, 1984); and issues analysis, the critical linkage between issues identification and effective response development, is being significantly enhanced by "stakeholder analysis" (Freeman, 1984) and social cognition theory (Dutton, Fabey, & Narayanan, 1983; Kiesler & Sproul, 1982).

Social Issues Management and CSP

To the extent that social issues management matures, it will provide the essential third dimension to CSP. Social issues management is a direct extension of social responsiveness. Out of necessity, it follows from the firm's understanding of social responsibility. It provides method to an area that has

—Continued

Continued

been continually criticized as "soft" and tangential to the true purpose of the corporation. In short, social issues management provides the final necessary ingredient to CSP.

CONCLUDING COMMENT

During the past thirty years, the CSP model has grown out of an initial admonishment that firms need to be more socially responsible and into an integrative, three dimensional model of corporate social involvement. Social responsibility—the first dimension—has been an extremely resilient concept. It has assimilated much of the criticism that has been levied against it. Yet, the two fundamental premises of social responsibility—the social contract and moral agency—remain as the ethical component of social responsibility. Social responsiveness—the second dimension—provides the approach to realizing social responsibility. It has become the general means to the ends of satisfying corporate social obligations. Social issues management—the third dimension—is now being developed as the method for operationalizing social responsiveness. Figure 1 extends from Carroll (1979) to provide a summary of the CSP model. As shown in Figure 1, the CSP model suggests that corporate

social involvement rests on the *principles* of social responsibility, the *process* of social responsiveness and the *policies* of issues management. Each of the components has its distinctive direction and orientation; yet, in total, they provide an integrated conceptualization of corporate social involvement as it currently exists.

Clearly, CSP is the result of the analysis, debate, and modification that characterizes scholarly inquiry. Whether CSP becomes the central paradigm for business and society is still an open question, but two points illustrate its potential. First, CSP comes close to meeting what Jones has identified as the three descriptive characteristics of a paradigm: "(1) a unifying or integrating theme, (2) substantial orthodoxy in the basic parameters of research—theory, methods, and values, and (3) predictive or explanatory capability" (1983, p. 559). The unifying theme centers around the principle/process/policy approach; the substantial orthodoxy is consistent with what already exists in the theoretical and empirical work of the business and society field; and the predictive or explanatory capability at this point rests mainly with explanation rather than prediction. Second, the CSP model does pull together the three dominant orientations of those in the field of business and society (Preston, 1975): the philosophical orienta-

FIGURE 1

THE CORPORATE SOCIAL PERFORMANCE MODEL.

PRINCIPLES	PROCESSES	POLICIES
Corporate Social Responsibilities	*Corporate Social Responsiveness*	*Social Issues Management*
(1) Economic	(1) Reactive	(1) Issues Identification
(2) Legal	(2) Defensive	(2) Issues Analysis
(3) Ethical	(3) Accommodative	(3) Response Development
(4) Discretionary	(4) Proactive	
Directed at:	*Directed at:*	*Directed at:*
(1) The Social Contract of Business	(1) The Capacity to Respond to Changing Societal Conditions	(1) Minimizing "Surprises"
(2) Business as a Moral Agent	(2) Managerial Approaches to Developing Responses	(2) Determining Effective Corporate Social Policies
Philosophical Orientation	*Institutional Orientation*	*Organizational Orientation*

—Continued

Continued

tion relates primarily to the principles of social responsibility, the institutional orientation relates primarily to the process of social responsiveness, and the organizational orientation relates primarily to the policies of social issues management. In sum, the past, healthy discourse that led the development of the CSP model makes its future very promising.

Reprints of this article may be obtained from Steven L. Wartick, 321 Carpenter Building, Pennsylvania State University, University Park, PA 16802.

SOURCE: *Academy of Management Review* 10(4) (1985): 758–769. Reprinted with permission.

Steven L. Wartick is Assistant Professor of Business Administration and Coordinator of the Issues Management Research Program, Pennsylvania State University.

Philip L. Cochran is Assistant Professor of Business Administration, Pennsylvania State University.

REFERENCES

Ackerman, R. W. (1973) How companies respond to social demands. *Harvard Business Review,* 51(4), 88–98.

Ackerman, R. W., & Bauer, R. A. (1976) *Corporate social responsiveness.* Reston, VA: Reston.

Ansoff, I. (1975) Managing Strategic surprise by response to weak signals. *California Management Review,* 18(2), 21–33.

Ansoff, I. (1980) Strategic issue management. *Strategic Management Journal,* 1, 131–148.

Arcelus, F., & Schaefer, N. (1982) Social demands as strategic issues. *Strategic Management Journal,* 3, 347–357.

Arrow, K. (1973) Social responsibility and economic efficiency. *Public Policy,* 21 303–317.

Bowen, H. R. (1953) *Social responsibilities of the businessman.* New York: Harper & Row.

Brown, J. K. (1979) *This business of issues: Coping with the company's environment.* New York: The Conference Board, No. 758.

Buchholz, R. A. (1977) An alternative to social responsibility. *MSU Business Topics,* 25(3), 12–16.

Buchholz, R. A. (1982) *Business environment and public policy.* Englewood Cliffs, NJ: Prentice-Hall.

Carroll, A. B. (1979) A three-dimensional conceptual model of corporate social performance. *Academy of Management Review,* 4, 497–506.

Chase, H. W. (1977) Public issue management: The new science. *Public Relations Journal,* 33(5), 25–26.

Dalton, D. R., & Cosier, R. A. (1982) The four faces of social responsibility. *Business Horizons,* 25(3), 19–27.

Davis, K. (1973) The case for and against business assumption of social responsibilities. *Academy of Management Journal,* 16, 312–322.

Donaldson, T. (1982) *Corporations and morality.* Englewood Cliffs, NJ: Prentice-Hall.

Donaldson, T. (1983) Constructing a social contract for business. In T. Donaldson & P. Werhane, (Eds.), *Ethical issues in business* (2nd ed., pp. 153–165). Englewood Cliffs, NJ: Prentice-Hall.

Drucker, P. (1984) The new meaning of corporate social responsibility. *California Management Review,* 26(2), 53–63.

Dutton, J. E. Fahey, L., & Narayanan, V. K. (1983) Toward understanding strategic issue diagnosis. *Strategic Management Journal,* 4, 307–324.

Eberstadt, N. (1973) What history tells us about corporate responsibilities. *Business and Society Review,* 7, 76–81.

Epstein, C. M. (1979) Societal, managerial, and legal perspectives on corporate social responsibility. *The Hastings Law Journal,* 30, 1287–1320.

Fleming, J. E. (1981) Public issues scanning. In L. Preston (Ed.). *Research in corporate social performance and policy* (Vol. 3, pp. 154–174). Greenwich, CT: JAI Press.

Frederick, W. C. (1978) *From CSR1 to CSR2: The maturing of business and society thought.* Working Paper No. 279, Graduate School of Business, University of Pittsburgh.

Freeman, R. E. (1984) *Strategic management: A stakeholder approach.* Boston: Pitman.

Friedman, M. (1962) *Capitalism and freedom.* Chicago: University of Chicago Press.

Friedman, M. (1970, September 13) The social responsibility of business is to increase its profits. *New York Times Magazine,* pp. 33+.

Gollner, A. B. (1983) *Social change and corporate strategy.* Stamford, CT: Issue Action Publications.

Gottschalk, E. C., Jr. (1982, June 10) Firms hiring new type of manager to study issues, emerging trends. *Wall Street Journal,* p. 27.

Haas, P. F. (1979) The conflict between private and social responsibility. *Akron Business and Economic Review,* 10(2), 33–36.

Heald, M. (1970) *The social responsibilities of business: Company, community, 1900–1960.* Cleveland, OH: Case Western Reserve University Press.

Heyne, P. T. (1968) *Private keepers of the public interest.* New York: McGraw-Hill.

Issues management: Preparing for social change. (1981, October 28) *Chemical Week,* pp. 46–51.

Jacoby, N. (1971, July-August) What is a social problem? *Center Magazine,* pp. 35–40.

Johnson, J. (1983) Issues management—What are the issues! *Business Quarterly,* 48 (3), 22–31.

Jones, T. M. (1980) Corporate social responsibility revisited, redefined. *California Management Review,* 22(3), 59–67.

Jones, T. M. (1983) An integrating framework for research in business and society: A step toward the elusive paradigm? *Academy of Management Review,* 8, 559–564.

Kiesler, S., & Sproul, L. (1982) Managerial response to changing environments: Perspective on problem sensing from social cognition. *Administrative Science Quarterly,* 27, 548–570.

King, W. (1982) Using strategic issue analysis. *Long Range Planning,* 15(4), 45–49.

Levitt, T. (1958) The dangers of social responsibility. *Harvard Business Review,* 36(5), 41–50.

McGuire, J. W. (1963) *Business and society.* New York: McGraw-Hill.

McKie, J. W. (1974) *Social responsibility and the business predicament.* Washington, DC: Brookings Institution.

Murphy, P. E. (1978) An evolution: Corporate social responsiveness. *University of Michigan Business Review,* 6(30), 19–25.

Ozar, D. (1979) The moral responsibility of corporations. In T. Donaldson & P. Werhane (Eds.). *Ethical issues in business* (1st ed., pp. 294–300). Englewood Cliffs, NJ: Prentice-Hall.

Post, J. E. (1978) *Corporate behavior and social change.* Reston, VA: Reston.

Post, J. E., Murray, E. A., Jr., Dickie, R. B., & Mahon, J. F. (1983) The public affairs function. *California Management Review,* 26(1), 135–150.

Preston, L. E. (1975) Corporation and society: The search for a paradigm. *Journal of Economic Literature,* 13, 434–453.

Preston, L. E., & Post, J. E. (1975) *Private management and public policy.* Englewood Cliffs, NJ: Prentice-Hall.

Preston, L. E., & Post, J. E. (1981) Private management and public policy. *California Management Review,* 23(3), 56–62.

Rawls, J. (1971) *A theory of justice.* Cambridge, MA: Harvard University Press.

Sethi, S. P. (1975) Dimensions of corporate social responsibility. *California Management Review,* 17(3), 58–64.

Sethi, S. P. (1979) A conceptual framework for environmental analysis of social of issues and evaluation of business response patterns. *Academy of Management Review,* 63–74.

Starling, G. (1984) *The changing environment of business.* Boston: Kent.

Strand, R. (1983) A systems paradigm of organizational adjustment to the social environment. *Academy of Management Review,* 8, 90–96.

Tuzzolino, F., & Armandi, B. R. (1981) A need-hierarchy framework for assessing corporate social responsibility. *Academy of Management Review,* 6, 21–28.

Walters, K. D. (1977) Corporate social responsibility and political ideology. *California Management Review,* 19(3), 40–51.

Zenisek, T. J. (1979) Corporate social responsibility: A conceptualization based on organizational literature. *Academy of Management Review,* 4, 359–368.

Corporate Social Performance in Canada, 1976–86

Max B. E. Clarkson
Research in Corporate Social Performance and Policy, 1988

This paper describes a research project, begun in 1983, the purpose of which was to develop a methodology for the evaluation of corporate social performance (CSP) which could be used by MBA students and applied by them to corporations. Prior to that date, there had been only one significant empirical study of CSP in Canada and the situation in the United States was very much the same: "actual empirical research designed to test the multitude of definitions, propositions, concepts, and theories that have been advanced has been scarce" (Aupperle, Carroll, Hatfield, 1985).

ORIGIN OF THE STUDY

A Canadian research project had been undertaken in 1976 on behalf of the Royal Commission on Corporate Concentration (RCCC), a major inquiry ordered by the Government of Canada, as a result of a series of major takeovers and attempted takeovers which had aroused considerable public concern about concentration of corporate power in fewer hands in Canada. The terms of reference of the Commission included "the economic and social implications for the public interest in such concentrations." In its final report the Commission admitted that "We found the social area the most difficult part of our mandate" (RCCC, 16). The Royal Commission contracted for separate research studies of several large corporations, both Canadian and foreign-controlled, which provided data relevant to the subject of corporate concentration. Several of these studies included sections about social involvement and performance.

The Commission also engaged researchers for a series of special studies, one of which was "Corporate Social Performance in Canada" (RCCC Study 21, 1977). Conducted by the Niagara Institute for the commission, this represented the first serious study in Canada of the attitudes, policies and actions of a wide range of corporations in regard to the then ill-defined area called 'Corporate Social Responsibility.' The researchers used a mail survey directed towards 1083 companies with sales in excess of $10,000,000, in order to ascertain the current state of awareness, analysis, and response to social issues. The 284 usable responses yielded a significant amount of valuable data. Case studies were also commissioned for nine large companies, who undertook to respond in depth to questions about social responsiveness and the management of social issues.

These self-studies, which had been included in the final report on "Corporate Social Performance in Canada" (Study 21), formed the basis for a research project initiated in 1983 for MBA students in the second year elective course on "Cor-

porate Social Responsibilities" at the University of Toronto. The first objective of this project was to evaluate what changes, if any, had taken place in the strategies, policy-making and actions of the companies involved in the original studies in terms of their social performance. Small groups of students were formed, classroom discussion of Study 21 and its methodologies were held, and the field studies began.

The analytic framework used was the Corporate Social Response Matrix, developed by Preston, academic consultant for the Niagara Institute study (Study 21), and implemented using survey instruments and guidelines developed by Kelly and McTaggart (1979). It was based on defined stages of the process of social involvement and the management of social issues:

1. awareness or recognition of an issue

2. analysis and planning

3. response in terms of policy development

4. implementation

Classroom discussion of Daniel Bell's essay on the post-industrial society (1970) led to conceptualisation of a scale between the "economizing" and "sociologizing" modes of management. Some student groups found this approach helpful and evaluated the subject company's position on such a scale, both in 1976 and currently. Hay and Gray's (1974) typology of management styles was also found to be useful in analysis and evaluation. A scale was conceptualized for identifying the management styles and values classified by Hay and Gray as profit maximization, trusteeship and quality of life. The companies' positions on this scale were evaluated in terms of various issues.

Following the publication of Wartick and Cochran's (1985) Corporate Social Performance Model, the decision was made to use this model as the framework for further analysis and evaluation. This model, first presented by Carroll (1979), is described by Wartick and Cochran as follows:

> This integrative nature of CSP is what makes it unique. Instead of arguing that economic responsibility and public policy responsibility are inconsistent with social responsibility (Buchholz, 1977; Friedman, 1962; Heyne, 1968; Preston and Post, 1975), the CSP model integrates economic responsibility and public policy responsibility into its definition of social responsibility. Instead of viewing responsibility, responsiveness and issues as separate, alternative corporate concerns (Ackerman and Bauer,
> —*Continued*

Continued

EXHIBIT 1

THE CORPORATE SOCIAL
PERFORMANCE MODEL

SOURCE: Wartick and Cochran (1985), with
'Implementation' added by the author as the
fourth stage of Social Issues Management

PRINCIPLES	PROCESSES	POLICIES
Corporate Social Responsibilities	*Corporate Social Responsiveness*	*Social Issues Management*
(1) Economic	(1) Reactive	(1) Issues Identification
(2) Legal	(2) Defensive	(2) Issues Analysis
(3) Ethical	(3) Accommodative	(3) Response Development
(4) Discretionary	(4) Proactive	(4) Implementation
Directed at:	*Directed at:*	*Directed at:*
(1) The Social Contract of Business	(1) The Capacity to Respond to Changing Societal Conditions	(1) Minimizing "Surprises"
(2) Business as a Moral Agent	(2) Managerial Approaches to Developing Responses	(2) Determining Effective Corporate Social Policies

1976; Frederick, 1978; Murphy, 1978, Sethi, 1979), the CSP model reflects an underlying interaction among the principles of social responsibility, the processes of social responsiveness, and the policies developed to address social issues. The CSP model relies on this expanded version of social responsibility and this principle/process/policy approach in order to provide a distinctive view of a corporation's overall efforts toward satisfying its obligations to society.

The framework of the model is shown in Exhibit 1.

The single most important feature of this model is that it recognizes and incorporates economic performance as the first among the principles of social responsibility, without excluding the other and necessary legal, ethical and discretionary responsibilities. Once this conceptual step, and it is a major one, has been taken, there is no need to engage in the fruitless and sterile debates which have been the result of the separation of economic from social responsibilities. "The distinction between the 'economic' and 'social' roles of a business organization is mostly a false one" (The Royal Bank, 1985). As soon as this distinction can be seen for what it is, theoretically convenient but realistically false, we can revise a well-known dictum by stating that "the business of business is business in society," and proceed about our business. If the first cannot fulfill its economic responsibilities, clearly it cannot fulfill any social responsibilities, no matter how these are defined.

A business organization fulfills its social contract by being profitable over an extended period of time and by responding to changing values, conditions and expectations in society by implementing effective policies, both in the markets in which it is competing and in the society of which those markets are a part.

THE FIELD STUDIES

One does not need to be unnecessarily sceptical in order to raise questions about the ability of organizations to mislead student researchers. Students themselves tend to be sceptical, however, when studying corporate social performance. The media expose assiduously most cases of misbehavior, perceived or actual, and the natural bias against business and its social performance, as shown by many polls and opinion surveys, is certainly evident in the classroom. The students are strongly urged to seek data and opinions from outside the corporation, using such sources as unions, government departments and data bases, and municipalities in company towns. Finally the completed studies themselves are presented in class and discussed, with representatives of the companies present if they choose to attend.

Reliability and replicability of evaluations is clearly a matter of concern in empirical studies. The difficulties inherent in even defining corporate social responsibility and performance have acted as a major constraint for researchers in

—Continued

Continued

this area. The research project under discussion provided the means by which the value and usefulness of the conceptual model developed by Carroll, Wartick, and Cochran could be tested in the field.

As the project progressed and the reports were studied and discussed, it was clear that certain characteristics of corporate behavior and performance could be identified, described and evaluated, that evaluations could be made about the social orientation of particular organizations, and that these evaluations could be objectively examined and questioned.

These characteristics of corporate behavior and performance have now been organized to conform with the components and classifications of the CSP model, Exhibit 1: Principles, Processes, Policies. The field studies provide relevant data on these characteristics which can then be evaluated.

THE PRINCIPLES OF CORPORATE SOCIAL RESPONSIBILITIES

Economic Responsibilities

"Economic responsibilities of business reflect the belief that business has an obligation to be productive and profitable and to meet the consumer needs of society" (Carroll, 1979).

In fulfilling its economic responsibilities, a corporation must be evaluated primarily by comparison with its own industry. A bank's economic performance cannot reasonably be compared with that of an integrated energy company or a manufacturer of chemicals. The criteria of economic performance should be those appropriate to that industry. Thus the researcher avoids the trap of so many studies examining CSR and profitability. The shortcomings of all these approaches were demonstrated by Aupperle, Carroll, Hatfield (1985) and need no further elaboration here, except to point out that their own use of adjusted Return on Assets (ROA) provided little additional illumination on this hitherto dark subject. Economic performance must be evaluated on a disaggregated, industry-specific basis, over a reasonably long period of time. When we are dealing with the creation of wealth, profitability, return on assets, return on shareholder's equity, financial soundness or long-term investment value, the results of last year or the last quarter provide an inadequate basis for evaluation.

In our studies a company's economic performance, within its industry's competitive context during the last five years, was measured and then classified as: loss, below average, average, or above average.

Legal Responsibilities

"Legal responsibilities of business indicate a concern that economic responsibilities are approached within the confines of written law" (Carroll, 1979).

The students search appropriate information data bases for evidence of past legal actions concerning alleged kickbacks, wrongful dismissals, unfair labor practices, discrimination, environmental pollution and so on, which may reveal a pattern of legal problems sufficient to justify comment and evaluation in the report. Checks are also made with appropriate government departments to determine whether there have been serious problems or complaints in terms of laws concerning the environment, safety, health, labor, consumer protection, etc.

Ethical Responsibilities

"Ethical responsibilities of business reflect unwritten codes, norms, and values implicitly derived from society; ethical responsibilities go beyond mere legal frameworks and can be both strenuously undertaken and nebulously and ambiguously ignored" (Carroll, 1979).

Students searches of information data bases usually reveal major problems that could be considered ethical in nature. These may involve, besides those described above under legal responsibilities, such additional matters as sudden large lay-offs; plant, mine or head office closings without adequate preparation or notice; false advertising; inadequate disclosure, etc.

Discretionary Responsibilities

"Discretionary responsibilities of business are volitional or philanthropic in nature, and, as such, also difficult to ascertain and evaluate" (Carroll, 1979).

The data in the reports relate to the record of the company in terms of donations and of support for community activities. The focus of this element of the research is the question: What is the corporation putting back into the communities from which it is deriving its revenues and profits?

THE PROCESS OF CORPORATE SOCIAL RESPONSIVENESS

In evaluating corporate social responsiveness, the research is focused on finding out how an organization responds to changing values, issues and conditions in the society of which it is a part. What are the processes by means of which corporations identify social and public policy issues as distinct from market issues? What is the corporation's stance or posture with reference to social and public policy issues?

Wartick and Cochran's model identifies four categories of social responsiveness: (1) reactive, (2) defensive, (3) accommodative, and (4) proactive. The research objective in this context is to obtain sufficient relevant data to form the basis for evaluation. In order to provide guidance in this area,

—Continued

Continued

completed reports were analyzed in order to identify those characteristics which were examples of "best practice." Companies that were clearly high performers in terms of social performance were analyzed and the characteristics which follow were derived from those studies.

1. Clear, explicit, widely-circulated statements of mission, strategic goals or purpose, which include references to social and ethical, as well as to economic or competitive, goals.

2. The existence of scanning systems which extend beyond the core economic and market activities of the company to social and political trends and issues.

3. The integration of the output of such extended scanning systems with the processes of corporate strategic planning and goal setting.

4. Linkages between statements of mission, strategic goals or purpose and the processes of policy formulation, operational planning, budgeting, performance appraisal and compensation/reward systems.

5. Meaningful involvement in public policy issues.

In order to evaluate a corporation's processes of social responsiveness as proactive, the students search for evidence of these characteristics. When there is little or no evidence of their presence, an evaluation will be made that the responsiveness processes of the company in question are at best accommodative or else defensive or reactive.

THE MANAGEMENT OF SPECIFIC SOCIAL ISSUES

In all cases the research objective is to find out how the subject company has actually responded to social and public policy issues, how current policies in these areas are developed and implemented, and how the company analyzes and develops responses to new issues. Questionnaires are developed for each company and hard data are sought. Researchers know that there can be a gap between words and action, between policy development and actual implementation, between what Argyris has called "espoused theory" and "theory in action."

Four principal areas are selected for detailed analysis:

1. *Human Resource Issues.* Communication with employees, training and development, career-planning, retirement and termination counselling, lay-offs, redundancies and plant closing, stress and mental health, absenteeism and turnover, health and safety, employment equity and discrimination, women in management, performance appraisal, day care, etc. Are these issues being actively managed? Are relevant data on these issues available and used?

2. *Environmental Issues.* Responses to legal requirements; evidence that compliance is managed and that, for example, incidents of spills, emissions, and pollution infractions are promptly reported to the appropriate authorities; responses to issues relating to the internal environment, such as noise, smoking, VDTs, etc. Are relevant environmental assessments an integral part of the system for capital expenditure proposals and budgeting? Are policies related to energy conservation in effect where relevant?

3. *Community Relations.* Have enternal stakeholder and interest groups been identified? Are contributions policies defined and managed? Is employee involvement in community activities encouraged?

4. *Ethics.* Is there evidence of an environment or culture in which the ethical values of the corporation are clear or explicit, whether or not in the form of a code? Is there careful consideration of the effects of actions taken, contemplated or planned on all important stakeholders?

EVALUATING CORPORATE SOCIAL PERFORMANCE

Each case study evaluated the performance of the subject company based on the data obtained and on analysis using current methodologies. As the studies completed by each class were analyzed, additional learning took place the following year. The characteristics of high performing companies were identified in terms of the processes of Corporate Social Responsiveness for use by the student researchers in their projects. The identification of current social and public policy issues was also derived from analyzing the studies. Key questions were developed and difficulties and problem areas were identified in order to assist students in distinguishing between "what they say" and "what they do," between stated values and policies and actual behavior. In some organizations, it was not easy to get access to those who could or would provide hard answers to hard questions. In others, access to several levels of the organization was facilitated, and in one case the student researchers were allowed to send out their own confidential questionnaire to employees, using company facilities.

One major difficulty, as this project grew in scope, was to provide access to the ever larger body of data represented by the field studies. After reproducing for three years key extracts from the studies in order to serve as a "case book," and making all the studies available in the library, it became clear that another approach was needed. Consequently, in order to be prepared for the course in the fall term of 1987, an index to 32 of the studies was prepared. Exhibit 2 shows the outline of this index, which reflects the CSP model in

—Continued

Continued

EXHIBIT 2

INDEX FOR CSP STUDIES IN
COMPUTER DATABASE

1	**Company Name**	23	Health & Safety Policy
2	Year of Study	24	Stress & Mental health
3	Contents or Index	25	Employment Equity, Discrimination
4	Introduction		
5	Recommendations	26	Women in Management
6	**Social Responsibilities**	27	Performance Appraisal
7	Economic Performance	28	Daycare
8	Legal Responsibilities	29	Other HR Issues
9	Ethical Responsibilities	30	*Environmental Issues*
10	Discretionary Responsibilities	31	External Environment Policies
11	**Social Responsiveness**	32	Energy Conservation
12	Mission Statement	33	Internal Environment Policies
13	Scanning Systems	34	*Community Relations*
14	Internal Linkages	35	Donations Record
15	Public Policy Involvement	36	Contributions Policy
16	**Management of Social Issues**	37	Employee Involvement
17	*Human Resource Issues*	38	Community Relations
18	Training & Development	39	*Ethics*
19	Career Planning	40	Codes of Conduct/Ethics
20	Retirement & Termination Counseling	41	*Customer Relations*
21	Layoff & Redundancy Policy	42	*Other Items*
22	Employee Communication	43	*Other Items*

Exhibit 1. (Not all studies covered every outlined point, of course.) All 32 original studies were then made accessible through data storage in the school's computer system, which is available to all students. Floppy discs were also made available, at cost, for those students who preferred to use their own personal computers. The discs are available for most word-processing packages, such as Wordperfect, Multimate, Wordstar, MacWrite, Microsoft Works, etc. for use with either Macintosh or IBM type systems. Hard copy printouts of each report are also available in the library. Data accessibility has been achieved.

Exhibit 3 identifies the 32 companies in the computerized data base. Three studies were omitted because the companies had requested confidentiality. Two were omitted for reasons of quality. Eleven new studies will be added to the data base in early 1988. Ten studies of government departments, agencies, and nonprofit organizations were also excluded. Exhibit 3 also identifies with (R) nine companies originally studied in 1975/76 for RCCC.

Another problem was presented as a result of the changing methodologies that the students had been using as the project progressed from year to year. In the case studies of 1975/76, mostly self-studies, the use of "methodology" is clearly inappropriate. It was necessary, therefore, to construct a revised and uniform system of evaluation, which could be applied to all existing case studies, using data and the preliminary evaluations of the student researchers as guidance for the senior researchers. The system of evaluation

—*Continued*

Continued

EXHIBIT 3

CASE STUDIES IN C.S.P.
DATABASE

Abitibi Price (R)	Manufacturers Life Insurance
Bank of Montreal	McDonald's Canada
Bell Canada	Molson (R)
Canada Trust	Moore Business Forms
Canada Wire and Cable	Noranda
Canadian National (R)	Northern Telecom
Carling O'Keefe	Ontario Hydro
CIL	Petrocan
Esso Petroleum	Royal Bank (R)
Gulf Canada	Shoppers Drug Mart
Hudson's Bay Co. (R)	Stelco
IBM Canada (R)	Suncor
Inco (R)	Toronto Dominion Bank
Labatt (R)	Wardair
Maclean Hunter	Westinghouse Canada
Magna International	Xerox Canada (R)

which has been developed is based on the Wartick and Cochran model shown in Exhibit I, and makes use of the evaluation system that is an implicit part of this model. The system is explained in the balance of this section. The output of this approach is shown in Exhibit 4. The companies selected for display are the nine companies studied in 1975/76 for RCCC. In order to avoid presenting an excess of data in Exhibit 4, the evaluations of the 1975/76 data are not shown, but comments on the comparisons with the earlier data follow in a later section.

Types of Responsibilities

The first and most important social responsibility is *economic performance* (line 2), which is also, of course, the easiest to measure, for individual companies and their industry group. The evaluation scale is:

1. loss or negative results;
2. below average for the industry group;
3. average for the industry group;
4. above average for the industry group.

Legal and *ethical* responsibilities (line 27) are evaluated in terms only of significant legal or ethical problems in the recent history of the corporation. If no problems have been identified, there is no entry. An 'X' indicates that the reader must refer to the relevant study in order to determine its nature. Codes of Conduct/Ethics are evaluated on line 28. This evaluation is based on the values explained below in the section on Evaluating the Management of Social Issues. *Discretionary* responsibilities are evaluated under the heading of 'Community Relations' which includes data about donations records, contribution policies, and policies about employee involvement and community relations (lines 22–25).

Evaluating Social Responsiveness

The evaluations in this section (lines 4–7) are based on the data about the presence or absence of the characteristics identified and defined in the section above on social responsiveness. Conforming with the model in Exhibit 1, an evaluation is made whether the subject corporation's processes are:

1. reactive;
2. defensive;
3. accommodative;
4. proactive.

—Continued

Continued

EXHIBIT 4

EVALUATIONS OF CORPORATE SOCIAL PERFORMANCE

NAME	ABITIBI	CN	HUDSON BAY	INCO	IBM	LABATT	MOLSON	ROYAL BANK	XEROX
1. Year of Study	83	84	83	85	85	83	84	84	83
2. Economic Performance	3	2	1	1	4	4	3	3	4
3. Social Responsiveness									
4. Mission Statement	4	0	0	4	4	4	4	4	4
5. Scanning Systems	1	1	1	3	4	4	4	4	4
6. Internal Linkages	2	1	1	0	4	4	4	4	4
7. Public Policy Involvement	4	1	1	4	4	4	4	4	4
8. Mgm't Social Issues									
9. Human Resource Issues									
10. Training & Development	4	4	4	4	4	4	4	4	4
11. Career Planning	4	N	N	3	4	4	4	4	4
12. Ret. & Termination Couns.	N	N	N	4	4	4	N	N	N
13. Employee Communication	3	1	N	4	4	4	N	N	N
14. Heath & Safety Policies	4	4	4	4	4	4	4	4	4
15. Stress & Mental Health	N	0	0	4	4	4	4	N	N
16. Employ Equity Discrim.	2	2/3	4	4	4	2	3	4	4
17. Women in Management	1	1	3	1	4	2	1	4	4
18. Environmental Issues									

CONTINUED

—Continued

Continued

EXHIBIT 4

EVALUATIONS OF CORPORATE SOCIAL PERFORMANCE—*Continued*

NAME	ABITIBI	CN	HUDSON BAY	INCO	IBM	LABATT	MOLSON	ROYAL BANK	XEROX
19. External Env. Policies	4	4	4	4	4	4	4	N	4
20. Energy Conservation	4	4	N	4	4	4	4	N	N
21. *Community Relations*									
22. Donations Record	4	2	4	4	4	4	4	4	4
23. Contributions Policy	2	4	4	4	4	4	4	4	4
24. Employee Involvement	4	4	4	4	4	4	4	4	4
25. Community Relations	4	4	4	4	4	4	4	4	4
26. *Ethics*									
27. Legal/Ethical Problems		X							
28. Code of Conduct/Ethics	3	0	0	0	4	N	4	4	4
Summary									
29. Economic Performance	3	2	1	1	4	4	3	3	4
30. Economic Orientation	4	3	4	4	4	4	4	4	4
31. Social Orientation	3	3	3	3	4	4	4	4	4
32. Visibility	2	4	4	3	4	4	4	4	4
33. Ownership	C	G	C	F(60%)	F(100%)	C	C	C	F(79%)
34. Sales Revenue-$B	2.8	5.0	5.7	2.0	2.9	3.17	1.7	9.8	0.865
35. Assets-SB	2.2	8.1	4.3	4.1	1.9	1.8	1.1	100	1.3
36. Employees-M	16.2	61	41	20	12	15.5	11	38	4.2

—Continued

Continued

If there is no evidence of the existence of the characteristics of Social Responsiveness, this absence is indicated by 'O', 'N' signifies that there were no data in the report.

Evaluating the Management of Social Issues

The evaluations in this section (lines 9–25) are based on the stage of development of responses to a wide range of current social issues. The stages are defined again to conform with the model in Exhibit 1:

1. issue awareness and identification;

2. issue analysis;

3. response and policy development;

4. implementation.

An entry of (4) indicates that the stage of implementation has been reached, but does not necessarily imply that the quality of implementation is similar to that of other companies. If the issue has not been identified, or there is no evidence of awareness, the evaluation cell will show "O", 'N' signifies that there were no data in the report to indicate that this issue had been explored by the researchers.

It should be noted here that it is important to recognize that the value '4' in this section connotes 'implementation of policy,' whereas the volume '4' in terms of Social Responsiveness connotes 'Proactive.' The value '4' under economic performance connotes 'above average' performance when compared with the industry group.

Summary

The Summary section (lines 29–36) in Exhibit 4 has several components. The objective of this section is to fulfill two principal functions: first, to provide values that summarize both economic and social performance data, and, secondly, to display data about size and ownership.

Economic Performance (line 29) simply repeats the entry shown in line 3. Economic Orientation (line 30) represents an evaluation of the "orientation" of the organization towards economic performance, as this concept was developed by Aupperle (1984), based on the original Carroll construct (1979). The distinction between economic and social orientations provided the conceptual framework for the integration of economic performance into the definitional model of social responsibilities, along with legal, ethical and discretionary responsibilities. Inherent in this construct were different weightings, or values, for each of these components. Aupperle's empirical test of the construct supported its validity and also determined that "there are four empirically interrelated, but conceptually independent, components of CSR." He further concluded that while corporations

clearly placed more emphasis on the economic component, the noneconomic components taken together are of much greater weight than the economic component alone . . . . In addition, there are strong negative correlations between the economic and each of the three noneconomic components which suggests that the more economically motivated a firm is, the less emphasis it places on ethical, legal and discretionary issues.

Since the data in these case studies supported Aupperle's findings, it was clear that the evaluation of economic and social orientation was a worthwhile objective. The following proposition, based on completed studies, was developed: There is, in the high performing company, a balance between its economic orientation and its social orientation; the presence of this balance does not inhibit emphasis on economic performance, but this emphasis is not at the expense of its social performance; when this balance is not present, economic performance, as Aupperle wrote, will be at the expense of social performance.

It should be noted here that in nonprofit and governmental organizations, economic responsibilities will not be considered as the most important. Legal responsibilities will usually be the focus of attention, with economic performance being evaluated on a basis appropriate to the organization, that is in terms of the effectiveness with which funds provided are administered and spent. The point is that the Wartick and Cochran model is applicable to organizations other than profit-oriented corporations. For this latter group, their economic orientation will normally be very important.

It seems wise to avoid the trap of over-precision in these matters, although it is clearly possible, given the body of data available in this project, to discriminate between 'average' and 'above-average' economic performance, between 'reactive' and 'proactive' processes, between 'important' and 'very important' orientations. Economic orientation (line 30) therefore has been evaluated on the following scale:

1. absent

2. not important

3. important

4. very important

With one exception, all of the market-oriented corporations in the sample to date have been evaluated as having a 'very important' orientation (4) towards economic performance. This evaluation does not apply, however, to all the government and nonprofit organizations which have also been stud-

—Continued

Continued

ied, including CN (the exception referred to above), owned 100% by the government of Canada, whose economic orientation is evaluated as 'important' (3), but not 'very important' (4).

In evaluating the social orientation of a company, it is helpful to recall Frederick's description of social responsiveness, as quoted by Carroll (1979, p. 501).

> Corporate social responsiveness refers to the capacity of a corporation to respond to social pressures. The literal act of responding, or of achieving a generally responsive posture, to society is the focus. . . . One searches the organization for mechanisms, procedures, arrangements and behavioral patterns that, taken collectively, would mark the organization as more or less capable of responding to social pressures.

Principal objectives of the studies in this project have been to identify and describe (1) these "mechanisms (and) procedures," the characteristics of which were described above as the Processes of Social Responsiveness, and (2) the "arrangements and behavioral patterns" described above as the Management of Social Issues. Since the awareness and identification of social issues requiring managerial attention are an outcome of the processes of social responsiveness, the evaluation of a company's social orientation is based on the same scale as that used for social responsiveness:

1. reactive
2. defensive
3. accommodative
4. proactive

The evaluations of the company's management of social issues must also be reviewed, together with relevant data and observations in the case studies, in order to arrive at an objective assessment of the company's philosophy, posture, or orientation. This managerial approach can also be expressed in terms used by McAdam (1973) and quoted by Carroll (1979, p. 502):

1. Fight all the way (reactive)
2. Do only what is required (defensive)
3. Be progressive (accommodative)
4. Lead the industry (proactive)

Visibility is another concept explored by Aupperle (1984) in order to determine whether high visibility firms were more or less concerned about CSP. Visibility is evaluated (line 32) using the following scale of values:

1. very low

2. low
3. average
4. high

This evaluation is somewhat impressionistic since data on advertising expenditures and media coverages, as used by Aupperle, were not available. The market orientation of the firm was used as a surrogate, using 'industrial orientation' and 'consumer orientation' as opposite ends of the scale. Clearly companies like Abitibi and Inco have high visibility in company towns, but, given their orientation towards industrial markets, their overall visibility is 'low' (2) and 'average' (3), respectively.

Ownership or control of a controlling block of voting shares (line 33) is identified as Canadian (C), Government (G) or Foreign (F). This information is included in order to explore, as the number of studies increases, whether there are any corrections between ownership and social performance.

The last three lines of the Summary section contain data about sales, assets, and number of employees (lines 34–36).

ANALYSIS OF THE DATA

Social Orientation and Economic Performance

The three firms is Exhibit 4 with profit levels above average for their respective groups are evaluated as having Social Orientation of level 4-proactive. The five companies with proactive Social Orientation are shown to have profits of at least average levels. These results are consistent with the observation of RCCC Study 21 that superior profits and social responsiveness tend to be associated. Further confirmation is found by examining the data for the 32 companies in the computerized data base, 17 of which show social orientation as proactive and have above average economic performance. Exhibit 5 summarizes the results.

No company whose social orientation was evaluated as proactive (4) had economic performance below average or at a loss. No company in the sample showed economic performance above average unless its social orientation was evaluated as proactive.

Comparisons between 1976 and 1986

Exhibit 4 shows that the Social Responsiveness of IBM, Labatt, Molson, Royal Bank and Xerox is evaluated as 'proactive' (4).

The criteria that provide the basis of three evaluations were described above. The essence of these criteria is the integration by the company of data about values, social and

—Continued

Continued

EXHIBIT 5

SOCIAL ORIENTATION AND
ECONOMIC PERFORMANCE

Social Orientation	ECONOMIC PERFORMANCE		
	Above Average (4)	Average (3)	Below Average (2) or Loss (1)
Proactive (4)	17	6	—
Accommodative (3)	—	1	8

public policy trends and issues, derived from the external environment, with strategic and operational planning, and the linkage of this planning with the day-to-day management of the company.

The data for these five companies on the Management of Social Issues in Exhibit 4 (lines 9–28) show that they were at the implementation stage (4) in most cases. Four of the five companies had widely-circulated codes of conduct of ethics (line 28). All had high visibility (line 32). These companies are very diverse. Three were Canadian-owned and two were foreign-controlled. Assets ranged from 1–100 billion, and employees from 4–38,000 (lines 33–36). Three of the five companies had above average economic performance (4), and two were average (3) (line 29). But since 1976 the social orientation of these five companies has remained proactive (4). Despite the difficult economic and turbulent social environment of the last decade, the data show a continuing proactive stance towards social responsiveness and continuing attention to the management of social issues. Policies had been developed and implementation was under way about such issues as employment equity, women in management and stress and mental health.

The social orientation of Abitibi-Price, CN, Hudson's Bay and Inco is evaluated as "accommodative' (3) (line 31). In 1976 the evaluation of social orientation was "defensive' (2) for Abitibi-Price, CN and Inco and accommodative (3) for Hudson's Bay. Exhibit 4 shows that the evaluation of Social Responsiveness is reactive (1) for CN and Hudson's Bay, whereas with Abitibi-Price and Inco the trend is towards a proactive (4) position (lines 4–7). This trend, or movement, towards a proactive stance is made clearer by referring to the 1976 studies, when the social responsiveness of these two firms was evaluated as defensive (2) or reactive (1). In terms of Social Responsiveness both Abitibi-Price and Inco have made significant progress since 1976.

None of the four companies had widely circulated codes of conduct or ethics, so that the evaluation of Codes of Con-

duct or Ethics (line 29) is zero for all but Abitibi-Price, which was at the policy development (3) stage. In 1986 CN published a code of conduct covering Conflicts of Interest. CN has encountered serious legal and ethical problems concerning discrimination against women, a situation not without irony for a crown corporation, controlled 100% by the Federal government since its founding over 60 years ago. Hudson's Bay has encountered severe losses and major reorganization since the study in 1983.

Since 1976 more attention has been paid to the elements of social responsiveness (lines 4–7) at Abitibi-Price and Inco. An increasing number of social and public policy issues have been identified and analyzed at all four companies, and policy development and implementation have taken place on such issues as employee communication, retirement and termination, health and safety, stress and mental health and employment equity (lines 10–28). Awareness of the issue of women in management has not yet, however, been developed into policies or implementation at these companies (line 17).

Ten years ago, in the group of companies that were studied, Labatt and Xerox were both identified as "the only two companies which appear to have consciously attempted to weave social concerns into their long-term, strategic planning cycle." These two companies provided:

the most evidence of what has been described as 'institutionalization.' In other words, there has been a conscious and careful attempt to ensure that social performance is built into the whole organization, its policies and day-to-day practices, rather than restricted to the Chief Executive Officer, a small circle of senior managers, or a specific department of public affairs. . . . Both companies appear to have adopted a 'philosophy' of corporate responsibility which enjoys the approval and support of the management group as a whole, and both firms have clearly identified the key issues they feel obligated to act

—Continued

Continued

upon. These include employee relations, environmental protection, corporate philanthropy and community involvement (RCCC, Study 21, p. 79, 1977).

These conclusions are corroborated by the data in Exhibit 4, which confirm the proactive stance of these two companies in terms of Social Responsiveness and the Management of Social Issues.

By 1986, however, the data now show that many other companies can also be described in similar terms. In 1976 the summary of Study 21 (p. 87) stated that:

> we find an evolutionary process underway in Canada, particularly among large corporations. This evolution embraces a number of critical factors including the recognition of social impacts caused by the basic economic activities of the firm, the assumption by management of at least some responsibility to deal with these impacts and the development of approaches and tools which make this management task more realizable.

It is clear from the data in the research project that this evolutionary process has indeed been underway and was not wishful thinking. The data also confirm another important conclusion in Study 21 (p. 44) from the survey data of ten years ago that "higher levels of corporate social involvement activity among the respondent companies appear to be generally associated with above-average levels of corporate profits." It can now be stated unequivocally that this is so. 17 companies, out of a total of 32 in the sample, with proactive social orientation showed above-average profits (Exhibit 5). This may be the most important finding in the research project. Substantiation of this finding is shown by comparisons within the same industry, in the section which follows.

Comparisons within Industry Groups

Evaluations for the three largest brewery conglomerates in Canada are shown in Exhibit 6, as well as for three of the five largest banks.

Social orientation (line 31) is evaluated as accommodative (3) for Carling O'Keefe, but not proactive (4) as it is for Labatt and Molson. Carling O'Keefe's economic performance is below average, while the other two are average or above. In terms of Social Responsiveness (lines 4–7), Carling O'Keefe is at the reactive stage (1), while Labott and Molson are evaluated as proactive (4). In the management of social issues Carling O'Keefe is at a lower level of awareness, identification and policy development on a wide range of issues. It is a company with a strong economic orientation (line 30) and "the bottom line" is stressed at the expense of what are

perceived to be extraneous social responsibilities. The company was recently taken over by Elders of Australia.

Of the five largest banks in Canada, the Bank of Montreal has had the lowest return on assets and net margin over the last five years. It ranked fourth in return on equity. The Toronto Dominion Bank has ranked first by these measures. The Royal Bank has an average ranking, slightly above the midpoint (Exhibit 6). Social orientation (line 31) for the Toronto Dominion and Royal is proactive (4). For the Bank of Montreal it is evaluated as accommodative (3). Like other companies whose economic performance is below average, its processes of social responsiveness are not evaluated as proactive (4), but as accommodative (3), and in its management of social issues it is not as far along in its progress towards implementation as the other two higher performing banks (lines 10–28). Its "bottom-line" orientation has been more important than its social orientation. In 1986 the Bank of Montreal published a statement of commitment or purpose, and devoted substantial coverage in its annual report to it. It appears that the bank is moving from an accommodative towards a more proactive stance in terms of its social responsiveness.

CONCLUSIONS

The data from the studies supports the following concluding observations:

- The social performance of the 17 companies, with above average economic performance and a social orientation which is proactive can be described as 'satisfactory.'

- The social performance of the 7 companies, with average economic performance and a social orientation which is proactive or accommodative can also be described as 'satisfactory.'

- The social performance of the remaining 8 companies, whose economic performance was below average and whose social orientation was accommodative can be described as 'unsatisfactory.'

- Firms with 'satisfactory' social performance are, by definition, profitable at average or above-average levels of their industry. Firms with 'unsatisfactory' social performance are less profitable, or below average for their industry.

- In the less-profitable firms, with 'unsatisfactory' social performance, the economic orientation of the company outweighs the social orientation. In these less-profitable firms there exists an imbalance between economic and social orientation, which is accompanied by reactive or accom-

—Continued

Continued

EXHIBIT 6

EVALUATIONS OF CORPORATE SOCIAL PERFORMANCE

	BREWERY CONGLOMERATES			BANKS		
Name	*Carling O'Keefe*	*Labatt*	*Molson*	*Bank of Montreal*	*Royal Bank*	*Toronto Dominion*
1. Year of Study	84	83	84	86	84	84
2. Economic Performance	2	4	3	2	3	4
3. **Social Responsiveness**						
4. Mission Statement	0	4	4	0	4	4
5. Scanning Systems	1	4	4	3	4	4
6. Internal Linkages	0	4	4	3	4	4
7. Public Policy Involvement	0	4	4	4	4	4
8. **Mgm't Social Issues**						
9. *Human Resource Issues*						
10. Training & Development	3	4	4	4	4	4
11. Career Planning	0	4	4	4	4	4
12. Ret. & Termination Couns.	0	4	N	0	N	4
13. Employee Communication	2	4	4	3	4	4
14. Health & Safety Policies	4	4	4	N	N	4
15. Stress & Mental Health	2	4	4	4	N	4
16. Employee Equity/Discrim.	0	2	3	3	4	4
17. Women in Management	0	2	1	4	4	4

CONTINUED

—*Continued*

Continued

EXHIBIT 6

EVALUATIONS OF CORPORATE SOCIAL PERFORMANCE—*Continued*

	BREWERY CONGLOMERATES			BANKS		
Name	*Carling O'Keefe*	*Labatt*	*Molson*	*Bank of Montreal*	*Royal Bank*	*Toronto Dominion*
18. *Environmental Issues*						
19. External Env. Policies	4	4	4	N	N	N
20. Energy Conservation	4	4	4	N	N	N
21. *Community Relations*						
22. Donations Record	4	4	4	4	4	4
23. Contributions Policy	2	4	4	4	4	4
24. Employee Involvement	1	4	4	4	4	4
25. Community Relations	4	4	4	4	4	4
26. *Ethics*						
27. Legal/Ethical Problems						
28. Code of Conduct/Ethics	N	N	4	3	4	4
Summary						
29. Economic Performance	2	4	3	2	3	4
30. Economic Orientation	4	4	4	4	4	4
31. Social Orientation	3	4	4	3	4	4
32. Visibility	4	4	4	4	4	4
33. Ownership	C	C	C	C	C	C
34. Sales/Revenue-$B	0.6	3.17	1.7	8.3	9.8	5.2
35. Assets-SB	0.6	1.8	1.1	87	100	51
36. Employees-M	4.8	15.5	11	33	38	20

—Continued

Continued

modative (but not proactive) social responsiveness. This means that, to repeat the words of Study 21, there has not been a conscious attempt "to weave social concerns into their long-term, strategic planning . . . (or) to ensure that social performance is built into the whole organization, its policies and day-to-day practices." There is, in these less-profitable companies, a lower level of awareness and analysis of social and public policy issues, and consequently of policy development and implementation. Emphasis on the bottom-line (economic orientation) at the expense of social orientation is shown to be related to economic performance which is below-average within an industry group.

- The findings of this research study confirm Aupperle's statement that "there are strong negative correlations between the economic and each of the three noneconomic components which suggests that the more economically-motivated a firm is, the less emphasis it places on ethical, legal and discretionary issues." (Aupperle, 1984, p. 49). Not only is less emphasis placed on ethical, legal and discretionary issues, but economic performance itself is below average, resulting in unsatisfactory social performance. The economic component of corporate strategy and action, in these companies, has not been integrated with social and ethical goals and issues from either strategic or operational viewpoints. Examination and analysis of past performance, of the processes of social responsiveness and the management of social issues, show clearly that the economic component is the responsibility on which these companies have placed so much emphasis that there is little evidence of concern for the ethical and discretionary components. Their orientation is economic, not social, and they have not integrated economic issues with social and ethical issues in their processes or their policies.

- The Wartick and Cochran model, based on Carroll's construct, provides a usable and relevant framework for analyzing and evaluating CSP. As a result of this approach, economic responsibility and public policy responsibility are integrated into the definition of social responsibility. No longer is it possible to view economic responsibility as being inconsistent with, or in opposition to, social responsibility. Economic responsibility is complementary to, and also the first and most important, social responsibility, but it is not the only one. Business does not carry on its affairs in a compartment labeled "economic," separate from the society of which it is a part. Average or above-average economic performance, in an industry group over several years, is related to the integration of social, ethical and discretionary responsibilities and goals with the strategic

planning of the company, which is, in turn, linked with management performance and decision-making at the operating level. To be socially responsible is to be ethically responsible and profitable.

- Empirical case studies of social performance are time-consuming, but can be undertaken successfully by students who have received adequate classroom exposure to the theories underlying the evaluation of CSP, CSR, Social Issues Management and ethical analysis.

- Additional research is necessary in the United States and Canada to validate the initial conclusion of this project. Since the case studies provide an excellent means for 'action learning' on the part of students, the adoption by other business schools of this approach to learning about CSP would generate significant volumes of data in a relatively short period of time. Computerisation of such data with consequent accessibility does not represent a major problem.

- Refinement and reassessment of the systems of evaluation used in this project are necessary. A means by which the quality of social issues management can be evaluated is also necessary. At this stage, evaluation is basically limited to levels of awareness and implementation.

- The focus of additional research should not be restricted only to the market-oriented, profit-making sector. The Wartick Cochran model can be applied to government departments and agencies, to non-profit organizations, and to voluntary associations. Eleven such case studies have been completed to date. Legal responsibilities replace economic responsibilities as the most important for these organizations. When the component of legal responsibility, however, is emphasized at the expense of economic, ethical and discretionary responsibilities, social performance is less than satisfactory. When legal orientation outweighs social orientation, there is a lack of concern for ethical issues and for public policy issues outside or beyond the legal mandate, the processes of social responsiveness are reactive or defensive, and the management of social issues is at a low level of awareness.

ACKNOWLEDGMENTS

I am indebted to my colleague A. Isenman, PhD. for his constructive advice and for teaching the course and supervising the case studies in 1985.

This project would not have been possible without the willing, and often enthusiastic, co-operation, diligence and skills

—Continued

Continued

of so many students who have written the case studies. Lloyd Smith, B. Com. PhD. provided invaluable assistance in developing the index to the case studies, in evaluating independently all numerical values, and in conceptualizing the computerized data base. Ray Lum, B. Com. assumed total responsibility for the organisation, input and verification of all data to the data base and delivered on budget and on time.

REFERENCES

Aupperle, K. E. "An Empirical Measure of Corporate Social Orientation." *Research in Corporate Social Performance and Policy,* Vol. 6, 1984: 27–54, JAI Press.

Aupperle, K. E., Carroll, A. B., Hatfield, J. D. "An Empirical Examination of the Relationship between Corporate Social Responsibility and Profitability." *Academy of Management Journal* 28(2) (1985): 446–463.

Bell, D. "The corporation and society in the 1970s." *The Public Interest* (Fall 1970): 5–32.

Carroll, A. B. "A Three-Dimensional Conceptual Model of Corporate Performance," *Academy of Management Review* (4) (1970): 497–505.

Hay, R., Gray, E. "Social Responsibilities of Business Managers," *Academy of Management Journal* (March 1974).

Kelly, D., McTaggart, T., *Research in Corporate Social Performance and Policy,* Vol. 1, 1979, JAI Press.

McAdam, T. W., "How to put corporate responsibility into practice." *Business and Society Review/Innovation* 6 (1973): 8–16.

The Royal Bank of Canada, "Banking . . . and More." 1985.

The Royal Commission on Corporate Concentration, *Report,* 1978. *Corporate Social Performance in Canada, Study No. 21,* 1977. Ministry of Supply and Services, Ottawa.

Wartick, S. L., Cochran, P. L. "The Evolution of the Corporate Social Performance Model," *Academy of Management Review* (4) (1985): 758–769.

SOURCE: Research in Corporate Social Performance and Policy, Vol. 10, pages 241–265.
ISBN: 0–89232–915–7

Press Release

Kinder, Lyndenberg, Domini & Co., Inc.

129 Mt. Auburn Street Cambridge, MA 01238 (617) 547–7479

THIRD ANNIVERSARY OF THE DOMINI SOCIAL INDEX

Contract: Steven D. Lydenberg **FOR**
Director of Research **IMMEDIATE RELEASE**
May 19, 1993

April 30th marked the 3rd anniversary of the creation of the Domini Social Index. Since its inception three years ago, the DSI has had a total return of 56.38% compared with 46.54% for the S&P 500. The returns on the Domini 400 Social Index (DSI) in April showed a loss of 4.55% on a total-return basis, however. For the same period, the Standard & Poor's 500 Index lost 2.42% on a total-return basis. The value of the DSI stood at 145.85 on a price-only basis at month's end and at 156.38 on a total-return basis.

The performance of the DSI relative to the S&P 500 was helped by the strong performance of Atlantic Richfield. The weak performance of Philip Morris did the most to hurt the S&P relative to the DSI. The strong performance of Dupont, General Motors and Ford did the most to help the S&P relative to the DSI. The weak performance of Wal-Mart, Intel, and Pepsico did the most to hurt the DSI relative to the S&P.

The Domini Social Index is a market capitalization-weighted common stock index, consisting of 400 corporations that have passed multiple, broad-based social screens. The DSI is maintained by Kinder, Lyndenberg, Domini & Co., Inc. (KLD), and is intended to serve as a proxy and benchmark for the universe of stocks from which social investors might choose. The DSI was set at a value of 100 as of May 1, 1990. Since its inception, fewer than one change per month has been made in the DSI, primarily due to takeovers and acquisitions. KLD is an investment advisory firm specializing in social investment research.
DSI Total Return:

April 1 through April 30, 1993	-4.55%
January 1 through April 30, 1993	-0.24%

Revisiting the Performance Debate

On the 3rd anniversary of the Domini Social Index, we thought it appropriate to briefly review the debate on the performance of social investing. The argument that there is a cost to social investing persists, but does not appear to be supported by the facts.

Since the Domini Social Index went live three years ago, it has consistently outperformed the S&P 500 on both a nominal and risk-adjusted basis. This is true even after the DSI's poor relative performance this April. Backtests from the beginning of 1986 yield similar results.

Some have argued that socially screened mutual funds must underperform the stock market averages. These arguments usually focus on a short time period, and, crucially, fail to take different risk profiles into account. For example, two large social funds, Pax and Calvert Managed Growth, hold bonds as well as stocks, making direct comparisons to the stock market averages difficult.

We address these problems by analyzing the quarterly performance of a market-weighted portfolio of socially screened mutual funds in existence from January 1987 to December 1992, and using two widely accepted risk measures to establish comparability. We checked the results against those of the Vanguard Index 500 fund (which mimics the S&P 500).[1]

RISK ADJUSTED PERFORMANCE
BASED ON QUARTERLY RETURNS

	Social Funds	Vanguard Index 500
Sharpe Method	.262	.238
Treynor Method	.0215	.0198

The social funds outperformed on both measures of risk-adjusted performance. It is true that nominal quarterly performance for the social funds was lower, but that is attributable to their lower risk profile, not their social screens. In fact, after adjusting for risk, there has been no cost to owning socially screened mutual funds.

Other data confirms this finding. U.S. Trust of Boston, which has managed both screened and unscreened portfolios since 1982, reports that there has been virtually no difference in long-term performance between the two groups, although short-term performance has varied. Other money managers report similar outcomes.

---

1. Performance as reported by *Morningstar*. The funds were Calvert Managed Growth, Calvert Ariel Growth, Parnassus, Pax, and New Alternatives. We also compared the social funds with a fund portfolio consisting of 70% stocks and 30% bonds, with similar results. In March 1993, Tom Desmond of *Morningstar* wrote that "although creating opportunity risk, these [social] limitations have not really put [Calvert Managed Growth] or Pax World at a disadvantage to the [balanced] fund group."

—Continued

Continued

In view of these long-term, risk-adjusted results, we believe the burden of proof has now shifted to those who assert that there must be a cost to social investing.

TOTAL RETURN FOR DOMINI SOCIAL INDEX AND S&P 500

Annual	DSI	S&P
1990	-4.75%	-3.38%
1991	37.81%	30.56%
1992	12.07%	7.63%
1993 YTD	-0.24%	1.84%
Quarterly	DSI	S&P
1990 Q1	-3.85%	-3.03%
1990 Q2	7.52%	6.29%
1990 Q3	-16.97%	-13.78%
1990 Q4	10.96%	8.95%
1991 Q1	17.86%	14.55%
1991 Q2	-0.96%	-0.20%
1991 Q3	6.67%	5.39%
1991 Q4	10.67%	8.37%
1992 Q1	-1.91%	-2.54%
1992 Q2	-0.09%	1.96%
1992 Q3	5.36%	3.05%
1992 Q4	8.56%	5.10%
1993 Q1	4.52%	4.29%

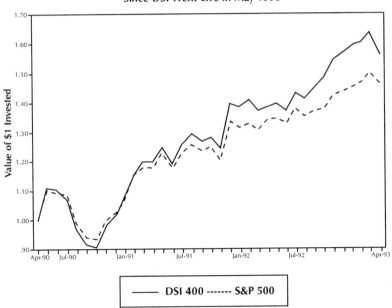

**DSI 400 vs. S&P 500
Since DSI Went Live in May 1990**

——— DSI 400 ------- S&P 500

The Whistle-Blower: Patriot or Bounty Hunter?

Andrew W. Singer

Across the Board, November 1992

The False Claims Act provides financial incentives for employees to report their companies' transgressions to the government. Does that debase their motives?

While serving in Vietnam, Emil Stache had the misfortune to stumble onto a booby-trapped Viet Cong bomb. The explosion killed several of his fellow soldiers, and Stache himself suffered severe shrapnel wounds to his left arm and shoulder. He later learned that the trap had been made from a defective U.S. bomb—one that never exploded.

Years later, Stache was manager of quality engineering and reliability at Teledyne Relays, a subsidiary of Teledyne, Inc. He suspected that Teledyne Relays falsified tests on the electromagnetic relays (electronic components used in missiles, planes, rockets and other military hardware) the company manufactured for the U.S. government.

Stache felt it his ethical duty to report the matter: He knew only too well the price of defective hardware. "It was the only thing he could do," explains his lawyer, John R. Phillips. "He complained about it. He got fired."

Stache brought a lawsuit against Teledyne Relays under the federal False Claims Act: he was later joined in the action by the Department of Justice. The suit claims that Teledyne Relays' failure to properly test the relay components defrauded the government of as much as $250 million. If found guilty, the Los Angeles-based čompany could be liable for as much as $750 million in damages, treble the amount that the government claims it was defrauded.

Who is Emil Stache? A patriot who just did his duty? That certainly is how Phillips and others see him. But if Stache's lawsuit succeeds, he stands to become a very rich patriot, indeed. According to provisions of the amended False Claims Act. Stache and his co-plaintiffs in the suit—another Teledyne Relays employee named Almon Muehlhausen and Taxpayers Against Fraud, a nonprofit organization founded by Phillips—could get 15 percent to 25 percent of any money recovered by the government. Stache himself theoretically could receive as much as $62 million.

(Contacted for comment on the case, Teledyne spokesperson Berkley Baker said, "We have no comment to make. It's in the legal system now.")

Creating Market Incentives

The amended False Claims Act grew out of public outrage in the mid-1980s over reports of fraud and abuse on the part of military contractors—of $600 toilet seats and country-club memberships billed to the government. Congress decided to put some teeth into its efforts to reduce contracting fraud. In 1986, it passed the False Claims Act amendments, whose *qui tam* provisions allow employees who bring forward information about contractor fraud to share with the government in any financial recovery realized by their efforts. (*Qui tam* is Latin shorthand for, "He who sues for the king as well as himself.")

Those market incentives are now bearing fruit. In July, the government recovered $50 million in a case brought by a whistle-blower against a former division of Singer Co. And a week later, the government recovered the largest amount ever in such an action: a $59.5 million settlement with General Electric Co. (GE). That case, a scandal involving the sale of military-jet engines in Israel, was brought initially by the manager of a GE unit.

U.S. Rep. Howard L. Berman of California, a cosponsor of the 1986 amendment, expects recoveries from *qui tam* actions, most of which are against defense contractors, to reach $1 billion in the next two to three years. The Teledyne Relays suit looms as one of the largest cases, but Phillips speaks of two others in the pipeline, one against Litton Industries Inc. and another that is under court seal, that could bring the government "staggering" amounts.

Undermining Voluntary Efforts?

Not surprisingly, many of the defense industry are aghast at the new False Claims Act—and, specifically, its *qui tam* provisions. The law has created "enormous concern in the defense industry," says Alan R. Yuspeh, a government-contracts attorney and partner in Howrey & Simon in Washington, D.C. Some fear that cases may proliferate and people with essentially technical disagreements may bring suits in the hope of reaping payoffs from an out-of-court settlement.

The *qui tam* provisions encourage "bounty hunting" and undermine voluntary ethics efforts, add critics. Why should an employee report wrongdoing to his company when he can hold out and earn millions from the government? And from the larger ethical perspective: Shouldn't people report fraud because it's the right thing to do, and not because they hope to reap a windfall profit?

"I think personally that the provision of bounties is misguided," said Gary Edwards, president of the Ethics Resource Center, a nonprofit education and consulting organization based in Washington, D.C. "It creates an incentive for indi-

—Continued

Continued

viduals in companies that are trying to do a better job—not to report wrongdoing, but to gather data so as to participate in the reward."

"Encouraging tittle-tattles is destructive," declares Charles Barber, former chairman and CEO of Asarco, Inc., a *Fortune* 500 company that produces nonferrous metals. "The integrity of the organization has to be built another way," such as with corporate ombudsman offices. "You can't run a defense company if everyone is being watched."

"I deplore the way we have developed into such a litigious society in which everyone is jumping on the bandwagon to sue about anything that comes up," says Sanford N. McDonnell, chairman emeritus of McDonnell Douglas Corp., the nation's largest defense contractor.

"If We All Lived in An Ideal World . . ."

Phillips, who is generally credited with drafting the amended False Claims Act, responds: "If we all lived in an ideal world, where all did the right thing on principle, we would have no need for such a law. But we don't live in such a world." People who bring charges against their companies take great risks—to their jobs, their families and their careers, he says.

Most agree that the plight of the corporate whistle-blower has historically been a bleak one. A survey of 85 whistle-blowers by the Association of Mental Health Specialties (now Integrity International) in College Park, Md., in the late-1980s found that 82 percent experienced harassment after blowing the whistle, 60 percent got fired, 17 percent lost their homes, and 10 percent reported having attempted suicide. "You can't expect them to [report fraud] when there is nothing but risk and heartache down the road," says Phillips. Sharing in the recovery of damages is one way to right the balance.

Yuspeh, for one, isn't convinced. It is an "unsound piece of legislation. It almost invites disgruntled former employees who may have had some technical disagreement to go out and file a lawsuit." (It should be added that in recent years, large contractors have increasingly reported instances of wrongdoing or fraud to the government voluntarily, before evidence came to public light.)

Congressman Berman says the law works precisely as intended: By providing marketplace incentives, it encourages people to protect the government and the public from waste, fraud and abuse. "I'm not only happy with the law, I'm proud of it," he tells *Across the Board.*

Morally problematic"? "You mean like: If you have any information about a wanted criminal, we'll pay a reward?" asks Berman, rhetorically.

Those companies that commit fraud don't like the Act, suggests Berman, while those in compliance with the law

aren't troubled by it. And he is skeptical of detractors who claim that these are merely technical disputes. "The test here is commission of fraud," he says.

Harks Back To The Civil War

The original False Claims Act dates back to the Civil War, where it was used to prosecute manufacturers who substituted sawdust for gunpowder in Union army supplies. Employees who exposed contractors who overcharged the government could, theoretically, earn 10 percent of the amount recovered. But under the old law, federal prosecutors who took over cases had the option of removing private plaintiffs, leaving whistle-blowers high and dry.

"Very few people were willing to do it under the old system," either through fear of losing their jobs, being black-balled within their industry, or shunned by their friends, says Phillips, a partner in the Los Angeles law firm of Hall & Phillips. It took a kind of heroic figure to blow the whistle, he says.

The amended False Claims Act aimed to fix some of those problems, "We tried to rebuild the law, to give it some teeth," explains Berman. "Where the government is not privy to information about fraud, the taxpayers are represented by private parties."

Even more important than the sheer amounts of money recovered, says Phillips, is the preventive effect of the statute on corporations. "The law has shaken up their internal practices. People who were previously inclined to go along with questionable practices are now doing the right thing," he says.

But companies say the statute undermines their voluntary ethics efforts. "I know their argument," replies Phillips. "But there's no basis to it. They're saying, 'We have a whole system set up. You should come to us first,' "With fraud, he says, the government has an interest in being the first to know. "The government is saying, 'We want information to come directly to us in cases of fraud.'"

"It will enhance corporate efforts, because companies can get socked with treble damages for fraud," says Berman. "Companies will become more vigilant."

Does he know of any contractors who support the amendments? "The goal of the act is not to please government contractors," snaps Berman. "The goal is to protect the government and the public."

The GE Case

The case involving General Electric's aircraft-engine division is one of the more interesting False Claims Act actions to arise. Employees in the division conspired with an Israeli

—Continued

Continued

PORTRAIT OF A WHISTLE-BLOWER

Corporate whistle-blowers have traditionally been treated as malcontents, troublemakers and misfits. And many have paid a steep price for their actions.

A 1987 survey of 87 whistle-blowers by Dr. Donald Soeken, president of Integrity International in College Park, Md., noted: "All but one respondent reported experiencing retaliation which they attributed to their whistle-blowing. And that one individual merely indicated that 'nothing could be proved.'"

Soeken, who was a government whistle-blower himself, compares the whistle-blower to a cross between a blood-hound and a bulldog. "He will track it down [i.e., the wrongdoing] and stand his ground. . . . His conscience is very strong, unwavering. He's the first one to feel guilty when something happens."

That certainly applies to Richard Walker, a whistle-blower in the era *before* the amended False Claims Act. A scientist with a Ph.D. in physics. Walker worked for 27 years at American Telephone & Telegraph Co.'s (AT&T) prestigious Bell Laboratories.

In 1971, as head of a team of scientists working on a high-level military project for the U.S. Navy, he discovered serious errors in Bell Labs' computer projections. He informed his superior of the errors, and said they had better report them to the Navy. When his boss refused, Walker took matters into his own hands.

He decided to give a corporate seminar within Bell Labs, which was his prerogative as a manager. Walker spent an hour exposing the errors he had found and explaining how the company had overestimated the effectiveness of the project. "The way to avoid corruption is to get it out in the open," he told *Ethikos* in a 1987 interview, recalling his thinking at the time.

The immediate response within the company to his seminar seemed positive. "I thought, in view of his feedback, that I had gotten through to these people," said Walker.

He was mistaken. Several months later, Walker's boss wrote a letter to a high Bell Labs officer questioning Walker's technical competence. "On the basis of that criticism, I was moved out of that area and put into a totally inappropriate assignment. It was just a way of getting rid of me."

There was a succession of increasingly demeaning and meaningless assignments. He spent three-and-a-half years in a marine-cable engineering department, followed by a supervisory appointment at a "planning" center in which "for three-and-a-half years, they wouldn't tell me what my responsibilities were."

In 1979, Bell Labs fired Walker for allegedly not taking an active interest in his assigned work. In 1982, Walker brought suit against AT&T, charging that he had been fired without good cause. Walker devoted himself full time to his case. He had an entire room in his apartment set aside to store depositions and other evidence relevant to his case. He spent $50,000 of his own money pressing the litigation. During this time, his wife divorced him and he was forced to sell the house he designed in affluent Mendham, N.J., where he raised his four children.

On March 23, 1987, *Walker vs. Bell* came to trial. Eight days later, the new Jersey judge dismissed the case that Walker had brought.

According to AT&T, justice was served. "Dr. Walker had ample opportunity to prove his allegations before the court, and the court rejected those allegations as being totally unfounded," the AT&T attorney who tried the case commented.

Walker took the defeat hard. Despite the advice of people like Soeken and others, he refused to let the matter rest. For years he tried to interest journalists, government officials and employee-rights organizations in this case. He barraged AT&T officers and directors with letters seeking redress for the wrong he felt he had suffered. All to no avail.

Eventually, Walker moved back to his home state of Michigan, where he remarried and is now working to establish a retreat for whistle-blowers.

Walker may have been ahead of his time. New Jersey has since passed legislation to protect whistle-blowers. AT&T now has an excessive network of corporate ombudsman to handle cases like his. An the amended False Claims Act has since been enacted.

John Phillips, an attorney who has represented other whistle-blowers and a principal author of the amended False Claims Act says that one key effect of the amended Act is that it no longer requires a "heroic" figure to blow the whistle. The Act could also bring forth a higher order of whistle-blower, he suggests. In the past, whistle-blowers "were not always the most stable people," noted Phillips in a 1989 interview with *Ethikos*. Many, he said, had a "need to confess" or to "point the finger at someone."

The people whom Phillips sees coming forward now to report wrongdoing by government contractors are still idealistic in some ways, but in many ways they are "far more credible, substantial, senior people than whistle-blowers, from the pre-[False Claims Act] amendment era."—**A.W.S.**

Continued

general, Rami Dotan, to submit fraudulent claims for work done for the Israeli Air Force. General Electric eventually pleaded guilty to four federal criminal-fraud charges. It agreed to pay the Justice Department $9.5 million in fines for the criminal charges and $59.5 million for the civil case brought under the False Claims Act.

The Justice Department said the company's employees helped divert as much as $40 million to Dotan and others, money that ultimately came from the U.S. government. The scheme became known through a lawsuit filed by Chester Walsh, who served as general manager of the aircraft-engine division's Israeli unit from 1984 to 1988.

What irks General Electric is that Walsh reported the matter first to the government instead of the company, despite the fact that Walsh, like others at GE, signed an ethics statement each year affirming that he would report wrongdoing to the company if and when it was discovered.

"The man involved decided not to report wrongdoing," says Bruce Bunch, a GE spokesman. "He took no steps to stop it. "He participated in it, and all the time he signed our written statement each year that he would report any improprieties to management." It is General Electric's position that Walsh gathered information from 1986 to 1990 and then filed his lawsuit, from which he hoped to gain personally. Walsh could receive 25 percent of the nearly $60 million recovered by the government as a result of the civil suit. (A hearing that will determine the exact amount is set to begin in November in Cincinnati.)

If he had reported the corruption immediately, the case would have come to light, continues Bunch. "We had an ombudsman telephone number at the corporate office, outside of the business loop. Additionally, he could have called the Department of Defense ombudsman."

A case of bounty hunting? "That clearly appears to be what happened here," says Bunch.

Phillips, who represents Walsh, claims that General Electric has smeared his client. "They claim Walsh is a money grubber. That's their party line." (GE Chairman John F. Welch, Jr. had been quoted in the *Corporate Crime Reporter,* a weekly legal publication, labeling Walsh as "a money-grubbing guy who sat back and waited in the weeds so the damages would mount." Bunch declines to comment on the accuracy of that quote.) Phillis tells a different story: "It was his dream job. It was very painful for him to do this."

Walsh feared for his job and even his life, Phillips says. He worried that anything he told GE would get back to Dotan, whom Phillips characterizes as a ruthless, violence-prone individual. His superiors at the aircraft-engine division were

all aware of the arrangement with Dotan, Walsh believed, "He says that Dotan had people removed from their jobs at GE. The idea that he would go back and write a letter to Cincinnati [where the aircraft-engine division is based] about what he had seen was imply not credible," says Phillips.

As proof that Walsh's suspicions were well-founded. Phillips points to the fact that Dotan is now serving 13 years in prison in Israel. The general was charged by the Israeli government with kickbacks, theft, fraud, obstruction of justice and conspiring to kidnap and harm a fellow Israeli Ministry of Defense official.

Couldn't Walsh have gone to General Electric's corporate ombudsman, who is based in Fairfield, Conn., and is presumably outside the aircraft-engine division loop? "He doesn't know who's on the other end," answers Phillips. For all Walsh knew, Phillips says, the ombudsman might just get on the phone with Cincinnati to find out what was going on.

But couldn't he have called anonymously? "It's an 800 number. They can find out where it came from. There was no way he could protect his anonymity." Or so Walsh believed, Phillip says.

"The idea that people will call up blindly some number is ludicrous," Phillips says. "I don't think people have confidence in the GE program." (Subsequent to this interview, *The Wall Street Journal* ran a front-page story on the company headlined: "GE's Drive to Purge Fraud is Hampered by Workers' Mistrust," which appeared to support many of Phillips' assertions.)

"A Detrimental Effect"

Whatever the whys and wherefores of the GE case, it seems clear that the *qui tam* provisions are causing havoc among those in charge of compliance at some defense companies. "Pandemonium" was how the ombudsman at one large defense company characterized the provisions and the large suits now being filed.

"I've heard from some company representatives who believe the availability of the *qui tam* rewards have had a detrimental effect, that they have caused people not to use their internal systems," says the Ethics Resource Center's Edwards.

"No company can be happy with *qui tam* procedures," says John Impert, director of corporate ethics policy and assistant general counsel at The Boeing Co., even though his company has been virtually untouched by the False Claims Act. "It

—Continued

Continued

provides incentives to employees to take an adverse position. This is illustrated graphically in the GE case."

It's important that people report matters of ethical concern, says McDonnell of McDonnell Douglas, "But I don't think they should receive remuneration for that," he says.

FALSE CLAIMS SUITS GROWING

How does the government view the False Claims Act? "It is hardly a secret that the Act is critical to the government's anti-fraud effort," Stuart Gerson, assistant attorney general, acknowledged last year, Gerson added, however, that the statute's *qui tam* provisions, which allow private citizens to bring actions on behalf of the government, have been controversial, affecting as they do "the climate of government contracting and the dynamics of a corporation's relationship with its employees."

As of April 1, six years since the amendments passed, 407 *qui tam* suits had been filed. The government took over 66 of these cases; it is currently litigating 29 cases and has settled or obtained judgments in 37 others. The total recoveries of $147 million from *qui tam* suits under the Act comprise about 13.5 percent of the government's total fraud recoveries for the six-year period. Individuals who brought suits had won $14.5 million as of April, but 75 cases were still under investigation. (The dollar amount doesn't include the large recoveries in July from the General Electric Co. case reported in the main story.)

The number of *qui tam* suits has grown steadily since 1986, notes Gerson, and it is expected to rise further. Thirty-three were filed in all of fiscal-year 1987, for example, while 78 were filed in the first eight months of fiscal-year 1991 alone. Cases involving the Department of Defense are by far the most numerous, but now actions being taken in other areas, including health care, agriculture, and the Department of Housing and Urban Development.

"In short, as attention is focused on the whistle-blower suits, and significant recoveries have been reported, this form of action is proliferating," said Gerson.

However, some government officials recently have expressed second thoughts about the potentially large awards to individual whistle-blowers. In the GE fraud case, Gerson said he had reservations about just how much credit and money the whistle-blower and his lawyers should receive. It remains to be seen whether attempts will be made to curb such awards.—**A.W.S.**

Won't this help eliminate the steep price whistle-blowers have paid for coming forward?" "I'm sure it will stimulate more action, more people coming forward, but I'd rather see it come from individuals who take it to the company ombudsman, and report it without attribution," says McDonnell.

Deputizing Citizens

Attorney Yuspeh and others are fundamentally at odds with the notion that individuals should being lawsuits on the part of the U.S. government. "The role of initiating [lawsuits] on the part of the government is a role for the officer of the U.S. government. I have a big problem with individuals who have a personal profit motive, who have inside information, and who may be disgruntled because of downsizing, having the power of the government to advance a personal agenda.

Yuspeh notes that plaintiffs' lawyers tend to profit from the amended False Claims Act and its controversial *qui tam* provisions: "There's a lot of money for them to make." He would prefer an arrangement where informants would get some money from the government, but would not bring suit themselves. "At least the government is then deciding whether to bring a suit." This would also cut out the plaintiffs' legal fees.

"The problem with *qui tam* suits is that someone who would otherwise do this as part of their normal duties might now wait until they are no longer employed, or until they have an opportunity to enrich themselves," says LeRoy J. Haugh, who is vice president for procurement and finance of the Aerospace Industries Association, an organization based in Washington, D.C.

"Our biggest concern with *qui tam* proceedings is that someone who wants to bring a suit is at no risk at all," Haugh says. "If they can get a lawyer to handle it on a contingency basis and they win, they stand to win a great deal of money. And if they lose, they haven't lost anything, except the lawyer's time."

Answers Congressman Berman: "The situation here is that no one gets anything unless fraud is committed. Lawyer's won't take cases if they're not legitimate."

Still, Haugh says, the negative publicity generated from such suits—even if the company accused of wrongdoing is eventually found to be not guilty—"often overshadows efforts over the last seven or eight years on the part of many companies to comply with Defense Industry Initiative guidelines [a set of voluntary guidelines developed by the nation's largest defense contractors to promote ethical business conduct] and to put into place adequate checks and balances."

—Continued

Continued

Importance Of Building Trust

"I'm not saying that every suit that is brought is a frivolous suit," says Yuspeh, who served as coordinator of the Defense Industry Initiative (DII) steering committee. (He makes clear that he is speaking only for himself in making these comments, not the DII companies.) "Clearly some cases are meritorious. But it makes more sense to have officials of the U.S. government handle them."

Ethics Resource Center's Edwards doesn't quarrel with the notion that whistle-blowers have historically been treated very badly. But he points out that today they have protection under the law against retaliation, and that many excellent voluntary corporate programs have been initiated since the amendments were passed. Many companies today have ethics hotlines, ombudsman offices, extensive ethics-training programs and ethics committees. "Maybe several years ago it was necessary to entice them to blow the whistle," he says. But that isn't the case in many major American corporations today. "A well-developed ethics program should obviate the need for that," he adds.

Even Phillips concedes that voluntary corporate ethics efforts could be effective. "But you've got to convince people that the corporation wants you to do this, and that the corporation will reward you," he says.

Phillips may have hit on something there. Or to put the problem in quasi-dialectical terms: If the *thesis* back in the 1980s was egregious defense-industry waste and abuse, and the *antithesis* was the punitive (at least, from the industry perspective) bounty-hunting provisions of the False Claims Act, the *synthesis* could well be voluntary corporate ethics efforts that enjoy the full confidence of employees—and that really work.

"It takes time, no doubt about it," says McDonnell, referring to building trust within a company. "You can't just mandate it. It has to be built up by actual cases, and it's difficult to advertise it, because that [confidentiality] is the sort of thing you're trying to protect. But when it's done right, it gets the desired result."

Andrew W. Singer is editor and publisher of *Ethikos,* a New York based publication that examines ethical issues in business.

SOURCE: *Across the Board,* November 1992, pp. 16–22. Reprinted with permission.

2

The Role of a
Professional Accountant

Purpose of the Chapter

Building upon the understanding of the ethics environment for the business organizations served, this chapter explores public expectations for the role of the professional accountant. This leads to the consideration of the implications for services to be offered, and of the key "value-added" or competitive edge that accountants should focus their attention on to maintain their reputation and vitality. Sources of ethical guidance for professional accountants fulfilling their role are also introduced.

Index of Chapter Headings

Understanding the Role of a Professional Accountant Is Critical

Unless professional accountants clearly understand their role, they cannot consistently answer important questions in an ethically responsible way, and as a result will probably offer questionable advice and make decisions that leave them and their profession exposed to criticism or worse. For instance, a clear understanding of role is essential to respond appropriately to questions about ethical trade-offs encountered, proper services to offer, and at what levels, such as:

- Who really is our client—the company, the management, current shareholders, future shareholders, the public?
- In the event I have to make a decision with ethical ramifications, do I owe primary loyalty to my employer, my client, my boss, my profession, myself, or the public?
- Am I a professional accountant bound by professional standards, or just an employee?
- Is professional accounting a profession or a business? Can it be both?
- When should I not offer a service?
- Can I serve two clients with competing interests at the same time?
- Is there any occasion when breaking the profession's guideline against revealing confidences is warranted?

The Public's Expectations

PUBLIC EXPECTATIONS OF ALL PROFESSIONALS

There is little doubt that the public have different expectations of behavior for a member of a profession like a doctor or lawyer than they do for a non-professional such as a sales or personnel manager. Why is this? The answer seems to have to do with the fact that members of a profession often work with something of real value where trust in how competently they will function or how responsibly they will conduct themselves is particularly important. Ultimately, the way which the public regard a particular profession will govern the rights it enjoys: to practice, frequently with a monopoly on the services offered; to control entry to the profession; to earn a relatively high income; to self-regulation or to be judged by one's peers rather than government officials. If a profession loses credibility in the eyes of the public, the consequences can be quite severe, and not only for the offending professional.

What makes a profession? In the final analysis, it is a combination of features, duties, and rights all framed within a set of common professional values—values that determine how decisions are made and actions are taken.

The thoughts of Bayles (1981) and Behrman (1988), which are summarized in Table 2.1, are useful in focusing on the important features. Professions are established primarily to serve society. The services provided to society are so important that high levels of expertise are required which, in turn, call for extensive educational programs focused primarily on intellectual rather than mechanical or other training and skills. Almost always, the most highly regarded professions are licensed to practice on the public, and the degree of auton-

TABLE 2.1

WHAT MAKES A PROFESSION

Essential Features: (Bayles)

- Extensive training
- Provision of important services to society
- Training and skills largely intellectual in character

Typical Features:

- Generally licensed or certified
- Represented by organizations, associations, or institutes
- Autonomy

Foundation of Ethical Values: (Behrman)

- Significantly delineated by and founded on ethical considerations rather than techniques or tools

omy accorded a profession from government regulation, with its "red tape," is evident by the degree of control exerted over the education and licensing programs by the organization representing the profession.

It is worth noting the importance of autonomy to a profession. Autonomy, or freedom from government regulations and regulators, allows members of a profession to be judged by their informed, objective peers, rather than by politically appointed regulators, and sanctions to be meted out without raising the attention of the public. This allows a profession to manage its affairs efficiently and discretely so that the public have the impression that the profession is responsible and able to discharge its duties to members of the public properly. If, however, the public become concerned that these processes are not fair or objective, or that the public interest is not being protected, the government will step in to ensure that protection. Here, as it is in dealings with clients, the maintenance of the credibility of the profession is extremely important.

The services provided by a profession are so important to society that society is prepared to grant the profession the rights outlined above, but it also watches closely to see that the corresponding duties expected of the profession are discharged properly. In general terms, the duties expected of a profession are: the maintenance of *competence* in the field of expertise; the maintenance of *confidentiality* with regard to client matters; the maintenance of *integrity* in client dealings; the maintenance of *objectivity* in the offering of service; and the maintenance of *discipline* over members who do not discharge these duties according to the standards expected.

These duties are vital to the quality of service provided, a condition made more significant because of the *fiduciary relationship* a professional has with his or her clients. A fiduciary relationship exists when service provided is extremely important to the client, and where there is a significant difference in the level of expertise between the professional and the client such that the client has to trust or rely upon the judgment and expertise of the professional. *The maintenance of the trust inherent in the fiduciary relationship is fundamental to the role of a professional*—so fundamental that professionals have traditionally been expected to make personal sacrifices if the welfare of their client or the public is at stake.

In the past, it was argued that to be a true professional, the individual had to offer services to the public—that a person serving as an employee in an organization therefore did not qualify as a true professional and could be excused from following the ethical code of the profession involved. For these individuals it was presumed that the need to serve the employer was dominant. Unfortunately, the failings of this limited perspective were exposed in cases such as buildings and other structures that collapsed due to shoddy construction practices, and the disclosure of financial results favorable to current management instead of current and future shareholders. In both instances, the professions involved—engineering and accounting—lost credibility in the eyes of the public, and some engineering and accounting professions consequently decided to make their responsibility to the public explicit in their code of conduct. The concept of *loyal agency* just to an employer has been refuted by philosophers, and is clearly out of step with the expectations of today's public. The conditions of a fiduciary relationship—the necessity to trust or rely on the judgment and expertise of a professional—are as applicable to professionals who serve within organizations as employees as to those who offer services directly to the public. The public view the provision of services within organizations as indirectly for their benefit in any event.

In order to support this combination of features, duties, and rights, it is essential that the profession in question develop a set of values or fundamental principles to guide their members, and that each professional possess personal values that dovetail with these. Normally, desired personal values would include: honesty, integrity, objectivity, discretion, courage to pursue one's convictions, and strength of character to resist tempting opportunities to serve themselves or others rather than the client. Without these values, the necessary trust required to support the fiduciary relationship cannot be maintained, so efforts are usually made by the profession to assess whether these values are possessed by candidates for the profession, and by its members. Such screening is usually undertaken during the prequalification or internship period, as well as by a discipline committee of the profession. Usually, criminal activity is considered cause for expulsion, and failure to follow the standards of the profession that are expressed in its code of conduct can bring remedial measures, fines, suspension of rights, or expulsion.

PUBLIC EXPECTATIONS OF A PROFESSIONAL ACCOUNTANT

A professional accountant, whether engaged in auditing or management, or as an employee or a consultant, is expected to be both an accountant and a professional. That means professional accountants are expected to have special technical expertise associated with accounting and a higher than layperson's understanding of related fields such as management control, taxation, and information systems. In addition, they are expected to adhere to the general professional duties and values described above and to also adhere to those specific standards set forth by the professional body to which they belong. Sometimes a deviation from these expected norms can produce a lack of credibility for or confidence in the whole profession. For example, when an individual or a profession puts personal interests before those of the client or the public, a lack of confidence can develop which can trigger public inquiries into the affairs of the profession in general. Such was the case with the Treadway Commission (1987) in the U.S. and the Macdonald Commission (1988) in Canada.

Recommendations from such inquiries for the revision of professional accounting are difficult to ignore.

Not surprisingly, professional accounting conforms quite well to the combination of features, duties, rights and in a framework of values as described above for professions in general. These have been summarized specifically for professional accounting in Table 2.2.

DOMINANCE OF ETHICAL VALUES RATHER THAN ACCOUNTING OR AUDIT TECHNIQUES

Many accountants, and most nonaccountants, hold the view that mastery of accounting and/or audit technique is the *sine qua non* of the accounting pro-

TABLE 2.2

FEATURES, DUTIES, RIGHTS, AND VALUES OF THE ACCOUNTING PROFESSION

Features:

- Provision of important fiduciary services to society
- Extensive knowledge and skill are required
- Training and skills required are largely intellectual in character
- Overseen by self-regulating membership organizations
- Accountable to governmental authority

Duties essential to a fiduciary relationship:

- Continuing attention to the needs of clients and other stakeholders
- Development and maintenance of required knowledge and skills
- Maintenance of the trust inherent in a fiduciary relationship by behavior exhibiting responsible values
- Maintenance of an acceptable personal reputation
- Maintenance of a credible reputation as a profession

Rights permitted in most jurisdictions:

- Ability to hold oneself out as a designated professional to render important fiduciary services
- Ability to set entrance standards and examine candidates
- Self-regulation and discipline based on codes of conduct
- Participation in the development of accounting and audit practice
- Access to some or all fields of accounting and audit endeavor

Values necessary to discharge duties and maintain rights:

- Honesty
- Integrity
- Objectivity
- Desire to exercise due care
- Competence
- Confidentiality
- Commitment to place the needs of the public, the client, the profession, and the employer or firm before the professional's own self-interest

fession. But relatively few financial scandals are caused by methodological errors in the application of technique. Most are caused by *errors in judgment* about the appropriate use of a technique or the disclosure related to it. Some of these errors in judgment stem from misinterpretation of the problem due to its complexity, while others are due to lack of attention to the ethical values of honesty, integrity, objectivity, due care, confidentiality, and the commitment to the interests of others before oneself.

Examples of placing too much faith in technical feasibility rather than proper exercise of ethical values or judgment are readily available. For example, a conceptually brilliant accounting treatment will lack utility if it is biased or sloppily prepared. Suppression of proper disclosure of uncollectible accounts or loans receivable prior to bankruptcy is often not a question of competence but of misplaced loyalty to management, to a client, or to oneself rather than to the public who might invest in the bank or savings and loan company.

It should be noted, however, that sometimes a disclosure problem is so complex or the trade-offs so difficult to accept that suppression of disclosure seems a reasonable interpretation at the time the decision is made. For example, accountants are often confronted with the decision of when and how much to disclose about a company's poor financial condition. It is possible that the corporation may work out of its problem if sufficient time is allowed, but to disclose the weakness may trigger bankruptcy proceedings.

Particularly in these situations of uncertainty, accountants must take care that their decisions are not tainted by failing to observe proper ethical values. At the very least, ethical values must be considered on a par with technical competence—both qualify as *sine qua non*. However, the edge in dominance may be awarded to ethical values on the grounds that, when a professional finds a problem that exceeds his or her current competence, it is ethical values that will compel the professional to recognize and disclose that fact. Without ethical values, the trust necessary for a fiduciary relationship cannot be sustained, and the rights allowed the accounting profession will be limited—probably reducing the effectiveness an independent profession can bring to society.

From time to time other members of other professions have made the mistake of doing something that is technically possible without regard for the ethical consequences of doing so. This is referred to as the *technological imperative,* meaning if something can be done, it should be done. When this imperative arises in accounting, it is usually because existing accounting standards do not prohibit the practice, and therefore it is presumed to be permitted. However, there are many examples of practices that have been employed, such as pooling of interests, or renegotiation of overdue mortgage loans which were then disclosed as current, only to be reversed, constrained, or changed when they were found not to satisfy the public interest fairly and objectively—in other words in accord with fundamental ethical principles. Consequently, even though technical feasibility may govern the short-term decisions of some accountants, in the longer term, ethical considerations should dominate. Whether the interest of the profession is well served by adopting technical methods without thoroughly exploring their potential consequences is a question worth examining—conceivably the problems associated with pooling-of-interest merger consolidations could have been foreseen and constraints devised if an "ethical screen" had been explicitly in place.

PRIORITY OF DUTY, LOYALTY

Who should be the real client of a professional accountant? If the primary role of the professional accountant is to offer important fiduciary services to society, then the performance of those services often involves choices that favor the interests of one of the following at the expense of the others: the person paying the fee/salary, the current shareholder/owner of the organization, potential future shareholder/owners, other stakeholders (including employees, governments, lenders). A decision will have differing impacts in the short and long terms, depending on the interest and situation of each stakeholder, and each should be examined carefully where a significant impact is anticipated. The intricacies of stakeholder impact analysis are discussed in depth in Chapter 4, but several general observations are worthy of mention for auditors and accountants.

Auditors are appointed by shareholders or owners as their agents to examine the activities of the organization and to report upon the soundness of the financial systems and the reasonableness of the annual statements. This is done to protect the interests of the shareholders/owners from a number of problems, including the unscrupulous conduct of management. It is significant to note that audited financial reports are used by both existing and prospective shareholders and creditors, as well as by governments. To the extent that prospective shareholders/owners, creditors, and governments can be considered as "the public," auditors have a fiduciary relationship with the public that requires the exercise of the same duties and values as would a more direct relationship. This means that a choice of accounting or disclosure treatment that maximized current income at the expense of future income would breach the trust required for the fiduciary arrangement with the public—an outcome that could lead to charges of misrepresentation and loss of reputation for the auditor and the profession as a whole. Accordingly, an auditor's loyalty to the public should not be less than the loyalty to existing shareholders/owners, and certainly not primarily to the management of the organization.

Although this analysis of the responsibility of auditors is based upon fiduciary principles, it is interesting to note that the trend identified in the Appendix to this chapter is supportive. "Trends in the Legal Liability of Accountants and Auditors and Legal Defenses Available" indicates that a broadening of the responsibilities of auditors is in progress, from strict "privity of contract" with existing shareholders to "foreseeable parties" who might use the financial statements. Although there is a very recent case apparently counter to this trend, most observers believe that it is a temporary diversion in a process of change toward broader liability which, while slow, is to be expected. Safe-harbor or limited liability provisions may be forthcoming for auditors, but these will probably only limit the dollar value of legal damages, not to whom liability is owed.

In the case of accountants employed by organizations or by audit firms, there is no statutory or contractual duty to shareholders or the public. However, in the performance of their duties to their employer, they are expected to exercise the values of honesty, integrity, objectivity, and due care. Moreover, because adherence to these values would prohibit a professional accountant from being associated with a misrepresentation, improper acts by an employer should cause a professional accountant to consider his or her responsibility to other stakeholders, including those who would be disadvantaged by the act, and their professional colleagues whose reputations would be tarnished by association. From this perspective, the paramount duty of a professional accountant employee is really to ensure the accuracy and reliability of his or her work for the benefit of the end user—the public. It is not surprising that professional codes of conduct require disassociation from misleading information and misrepresentations. Unfortunately, some current codes do this with the requirement of silence or confidentiality, thus leaving unsuspecting stakeholders to their fate. Logic would dictate that maintenance of the trust required in specific fiduciary relationships be based on the broader trust between the public and the profession as a whole; in the long term codes should be changed to protect the public at large rather than a specific stakeholder.

If the interest of the public at large is not the prime motivator of actions by both professional accountants in public practice and those who are employees, and the codes of conduct of the profession were seen to permit this, the confidence in and support for that profession would be eroded. Government pressure would be brought to bear to reform the profession or to create a new group free of bias and loyal to the public's interest. The Treadway and Macdonald Commissions are examples of such pressure, and each has offered suggestions for change.

Although duty to the public is paramount for professional accountants, how should duty to client/employers, the profession, and the individual professionals be ranked? If the primary goal of the profession is to ensure the provision of fiduciary services to society, then the profession's long-term interests ought to be congruent with those of the public. On the other hand, keeping information from the public is not in the public's interest, it is usually self-interest and should be seen to represent duty to an individual professional.

The ranking of a professional accountant's duty to a client or an employer is conditioned by a real or implied contract for services. On first examination this would imply that the accountant could not serve other masters, including himself or herself, before serving the client/employer. However, the contract is one where the client/employer has contracted with an individual who, by virtue of his or her professional status, is understood to be answerable to the ethical codes of that profession. Thus expecting absolute loyalty to the client/employer rather than to the profession, and ultimately to the public, is unreasonable. It *is* reasonable for the client/employer to expect that a professional accountant will place the client/employer interest before that of the professional's self-interest. To do otherwise would undermine the trust required for a fiduciary arrangement to work. Legitimate confidences would not be shared for fear the interest of the client would be subverted or obviated by premature release, so the professional would not be able to work effectively or on sensitive matters. As a result, the scope of an audit could be constrained to the detriment of the auditor, the profession, and the public. To prevent the release of client/employer confidences, most codes of conduct require that confidences not be divulged except in a court of law or when required by the discipline process of the profession. Based on this analysis, a professional accountant facing a difficult choice should consider that loyalty is owed to affected stakeholders in the following order of priority: the public, the profession, the client/employer, and finally, the individual professional. In order not to undermine the trust necessary for a fiduciary arrangement to work, this order might be revised for practical purposes to place the client/employer first, subject to being overridden by the interests of the public and the profession in circumstances where the impact of concern would warrant such treatment by not being in the public interest either legally or ethically.

CONFIDENTIALITY: STRICT OR ASSISTED

The analysis presented so far places professional accountants in the unenviable position of having to keep confidential those aspects of their clients/employers with which they might not agree, but which may not affect the financial activities of the company sufficiently to be of concern to the public. If, for example, the professional is dismissed for refusing to misrepresent the receivables as current, he or she would have to seek other employment but could not discuss the reason for the dismissal. He or she could not discuss client/employer problems with anyone not bound by a code of confidentiality (e.g., someone in the accounting firm or a lawyer hired specifically for the purpose). Unless the accountant's professional society has an ethics adviser (some now do) who could be called upon, he or she is left in a disadvantaged position from many perspectives. The confidentiality edict also gives unscrupulous client/employers a corresponding opportunity to get away with wrongdoing. Perhaps professional societies will recognize that this strict level of confidentiality is not in the interest of several stakeholders, including the public, and introduce limited confidential, consultative services to ensure that the professional has cost-free help to make the right decision, to call for a response from the client/employer and perhaps resolve the problem, and to reassure prospective employers.

Implications for Services Offered

SERVICES/FUNCTIONS OFFERED

Professional accountants have developed fiduciary services in the following areas:

- accounting and reporting principles, practices, and systems
- auditing of accounting records, systems, and financial statements
- financial projections: preparation, analysis, and audit
- taxation: preparation of tax returns and advice
- bankruptcy: trustee's duties and advice
- financial planning: advice
- decision making: facilitation through analysis and approach
- management control: advice, and design of systems
- corporate and commercial affairs: advice

These services are all bounded by the professional accountant's primary area of competence, accounting. Recently, however, there has been a recognition that management (and indeed other stakeholders) need nonfinancial information to manage and make decisions effectively. For example, nonfinancial indicators of quality have become an important part of control systems which are far more timely than traditional financial reports. Accountants have become involved in the provision of such nonfinancial data because it is a vital part of the managerial decision-making system and because they have exper-tise in the measurement and disclosure and interpretation of data. Indeed, that expertise includes evidence gathering and evaluation skills, skepticism, objectivity, independence and integrity, and reporting skills as well as the understanding of accounting frameworks and practices in which these skills are to be deployed. Consequently, although the core of an accountant's raison d'être remains oriented to financial reports, there is evidence to suggest that the expertise developed in measurement, disclosure, and interpretation of information will present opportunities for the development of other services.

CRITICAL VALUE-ADDED BY A PROFESSIONAL ACCOUNTANT

Viewing the core of a professional accountant's expertise to be the measure-ment, disclosure, and interpretation of information suggests that the profes-sional accountant's competitive advantage over other information systems pro-fessionals will involve higher quality of service on these dimensions. Competence is, of course, a fundamental factor, and high levels of competence can and do provide a competitive advantage. However, it is apparent that high competence can be acquired by nonprofessionals and is therefore not, by itself, the critical value-added by a professional accountant.

The distinguishing feature of a professional from a nonprofessional accountant lies in the professional values adhered to and the expectations those create in the persons being served. In particular, the critical value-added by a professional accountant lies in the expectation that whatever services are offered will be based on integrity and objectivity, and these values, in addition to an ensured minimum standard of competence, lend credibility to the report or activity. These individual ethical values, reinforced by the standards of the profession, provide a competitive advantage to professional accountants and ensure that their services are in demand. In the words of Stanton Cook, president of the (Chicago) Tribune Company, "accountants, entrepreneurs, manufacturers, salespeople and even lawyers all say: 'The product we are ulti-mately selling is credibility'" (Priest, 1991).

STANDARDS EXPECTED FOR BEHAVIOR

The public, and particularly a client, expect that a professional accountant will perform fiduciary services with competence, integrity, and objectivity. Although not obvious, integrity is important because it ensures that whatever the service it will be performed fairly and thoroughly. No detail that would cloud the truth will be omitted, understated, or misstated, nor would an analy-sis be put forward that misleads users. Honesty is implied in all aspects of data gathering, measurement, reporting, and interpretation. Similarly, objectivity implies freedom from bias in the selection of measurement bases and disclo-sure, so as not to mislead those served.

Integrity and objectivity are essential to the proper discharge of fiduciary duties. They are, with competence, the critical value-added from belonging to a profession and therefore must be protected by the profession in order to ensure its future. Consequently, professional accounting organizations take pains to investigate and discipline members whose conduct is questionable, with regard to these ethical values.

IMPORTANCE TO VALUE-ADDED

The proper discharge of the ethical values of competence, integrity, and objectivity relies substantially, if not primarily, upon the personal ethical values of the professional accountant involved. If the profession itself has high standards, the individual professional can choose to ignore them. Often, however, a professional is simply not sufficiently aware of potential ethical dilemmas or the appropriate values to properly discharge his or her duties. Or a professional may err in judgment about the potential outcome of an ethical dilemma, or about the seriousness of the outcome for those who must bear the impact. The credibility of the profession, therefore, rests on the values it espouses, the personal and professional ethical values of each individual member, and the quality of judgment exercised.

DEVELOPMENT OF JUDGMENT AND VALUES

How do professional accountants develop the judgment they must apply to ethical dilemmas? In the past, trial and error has been the established mode—largely experienced when growing up, or on the job, or by learning from others who have faced similar problems and are willing to pass on their own experience. But the limitations of trial and error are obvious as significant costs may be born by the learner, the client, society, and the profession. In addition, an orderly framework for thinking about future problems may never be developed, nor may the level attained by a professional be adequate to safeguard the profession's stakeholders, including the individual himself or herself.

Trial and error can never be entirely supplanted by organized training or educational experiences, but many of the deficiencies noted above can be remedied by a well-ordered, stimulating program that deals with the major issues to be faced and suggests practical, ethical approaches to their resolution. In this regard, it is helpful to consider how far a student's ethical reasoning capacity has progressed and how to advance that capacity. A model developed by Lawrence Kohlberg is helpful in this regard (Kohlberg, 1984, 1989; Colby & Kohlberg, 1987).

Kohlberg argues that individuals pass through six progressive stages of moral development (described in the Ponemon (1992) excerpt "Ethical Reasoning and Selection-Socialization in Accounting" in this chapter). These six stages and the motivation that leads individuals to make decisions at each can be helpful, as is pointed out by Shenkir (1990), in designing an educational program to expose students to the six levels. Such exposure can enable students to develop their awareness, knowledge, and skills for dealing with ethical problems and may, through understanding the motivations involved, shift their moral reasoning to higher stages.

The motivations that influence people at each of Kohlberg's stages of moral reasoning are identified in Table 2.3.

Researchers have found that students in business facing ethical decisions are largely in cognitive stages 2 or 3, so there is quite a bit of growth that is possible and desirable (Weber & Green, 1991). Other researchers have found that business students believe that their success is more dependent on questionable ethical practices than do nonbusiness students, so orderly ethics education

STAGE	MOTIVE FOR DOING RIGHT
Preconventional	*Self-interest*
1.	Fear of punishment and authorities
2.	Self-gratification
Conventional	*Conformity*
3.	Role expectation or approval from others
4.	Adherence to moral codes, or to codes of law and order
Post conventional, autonomous, or principled	*Interests of others*
5.	Concern for others, and broader social welfare
6.	Concern for moral or ethical principle

would appear desirable lest these attitudes pervade the students who enter the ranks of professional accounting (Lane & Schaup, 1989). Leaving the cognitive development of students for the accounting profession to trial and error, rather than significant thought and formal training could, in itself, be unethical. Exposure to educational material, linked traditional course work and particularly to realistic cases should provide students and graduate practitioners with a better understanding of the ethical issues, dilemmas, approaches to their resolution, and values necessary to make good ethical judgments than would the vicissitudes of trial and error.

Sources of Ethical Guidance

CODES OF CONDUCT

There are several sources of guidance available to the professional accountant; certainly the codes of conduct or ethics of their professional body and of their firm or employer rank as important reference points. Other codes may also exist that are relevant such as those involving trade associations, governmental agencies, or special interest groups such as environmentalists. How these work, and what to do if they conflict, is the subject of the next chapter.

LAWS AND JURISPRUDENCE

Professional accountants can also refer to legal cases and lawyers for interpretations of their legal liability and potential defenses. To assist the reader, an analysis of trends and a synopsis of important legal decisions are included in the appendix to this chapter, "Trends in the Legal Liability of Accountants and Auditors and Legal Defenses Available."

Caution should be exercised in applying legal standards to ethical problems, however, for three reasons. First, although the law appears to offer timeless wisdom, in reality it is continuously changing as it tries to catch up to the positions society believes are reasonable. In other words, the law generally lags behind what society views as ethically desirable. Second, and more important, *what is legal is not always ethical.*

According to former U.S. Supreme Court Justice Potter Stewart, ethics is "knowing the difference between what you have the right to do and what is right to do." There are plenty of examples of this difference between legal standards, moral standards and ethical standards. For example, a company may be able to pollute in a way that is harmful to the health of its workers in a Third World country because the local standards are less stringent than at home in North America. Sometimes the legal standard is clear, such as in tax matters or bribery, for example, but large portions of society do not adhere to it, so the mores or norms expected are different: What behavior is right? Legal , moral, and ethical standards are different and should be recognized as such.

The third reason for caution in placing too much reliance on legal interpretations and remedies is that they appear not to be highly relevant to the launching of or final disposition of lawsuits, particularly in the United States. Of 800 allegations of audit failure during the period 1960–1990 against the 15 largest audit firms in the US, only 64 were tried to a verdict (Palmrose, 1991, p. 154). Although some cases were still underway, fewer than 10 percent were submitted to judge or jury, a rate that drops to 2.1 percent for the 1985–89 period.

By far the highest percentage of cases cited in the Palmrose study were settled to reduce legal bills, free up management time and for other practical considerations, rather than both sides realizing the legal merits of their case. Usually, audit firms found it cheaper to settle rather than fight in court. *The cost to their pocketbook in legal fees and lost billable time, and particularly to their reputation, rarely made recourse to the courts a sensible option, even where lawsuits were without legal foundation.*

The reasons for this bizarre situation are outlined in a position statement authored by the Big 6 audit firms in August 1992 entitled "The Liability Crisis in the United States: Impact on the Accounting Profession," which appears in the "Readings" section at the end of this chapter. This statement indicates that several quirks that have developed in the legal framework and process are responsible for an intolerable level of liability for audit professionals: a level that has resulted in individuals who have been offered partnerships hesitating or declining the offer, and in the bankruptcy in 1990 of one of the largest audit firms, Laventhol & Horwath.

As the heads of the Big 6 say: "To restore equity and sanity to the liability system and to provide reasonable assurance that the public accounting profession will be able to continue to meet its public obligations requires substantial reform of both federal and state liability laws" (p. 6). Several reforms are suggested in the statement, but they are not likely to appear quickly because of the multiple jurisdictions involved, and the entrenchment of the practice of contingent legal fees and of the principle of joint and several liability.

Given this scenario, in which the legal "cure" for a problem is unpalatable, the preferred option is "preventative medicine"—not to get into the dilemma in the first place, if at all possible. Instilling high standards of professional ethics into the values and culture of accounting professionals and their organizations can prove to be a significant safeguard against getting into such predicaments. Even in legal jurisdictions such as Canada or the United Kingdom, where the liability crisis is not quite as alarming, high ethical standards and skill in their application can eliminate or reduce professional exposure.

WHEN CODES AND LAWS DON'T HELP

Frequently professional accountants find themselves facing situations that are not covered explicitly in codes of conduct, nor sufficiently related to jurisprudence to benefit from those sources of guidance. Sometimes a professional accounting body will provide its members with consultation services through a so-called Director of Ethics. Most often, however, professional accountants are left to their own devices. They may hire their own adviser from the ranks of legal or ethical experts, but ultimately they will have to rely upon their own knowledge, values, and judgment to decide what is right. Chapter 3 explores in greater detail to what extent codes of conduct may help the professional accountant.

QUESTIONS FOR DISCUSSION

1. Refer to the seven questions in the opening section of this chapter.

2. What is meant by the term *fiduciary relationship?*

3. Why are most ethical decisions that accountants face complex rather than straightforward?

4. When should an accountant place his or her duty to the public ahead of his or her duty to a client or employer?

5. Why is maintaining the confidentiality of client or employer matters essential to the effectiveness of the audit or accountant relationship?

6. Where, on the Kohlberg framework, would you place your own usual motivation for making decisions?

7. Why don't codes of conduct or existing jurisprudence provide sufficient guidance for accountants in ethical matters?

CASES

The following cases have been selected to expose situations that shed light upon the role of auditors and management accountants as they discharge their fiduciary duties. Specifically, the issues covered are as follows:

- "The Lang Michener Affair" shows how legal professionals can take to the slippery slopes of shady deals, conflicts of interest, self-interest, passing the buck, and failing to step forward when they should to protect themselves, their firm, and their profession. It also illustrates the frustrations of a whistleblower, and the workings of a self-regulating profession.

- "Dilemma of an Accountant" portrays an auditor who is caught between his principles and the desire of his superior to have a clean file and a clean opinion. What is he to do?

- "To Qualify or Not?" introduces the real-life dilemma of an accountant who wants to qualify an audit opinion, but realizes that doing so might cause the company to become insolvent.

- "Societal Concerns" asks the reader to consider how realistic and short-sighted our traditional financial statements and reports are. Can accountants go beyond this traditional framework to take on environmental and other issues? Should they?

- "Management Choice" focuses on a management accountant who has a choice of accounting policy and practice to make—a choice that, even if unethical or illegal, she can probably get away with. Should she?

READINGS

The article by J. Michael Cook provides an excellent historical account of the issues behind the evolution of the professional code of the American Institute of Certified Public Accountants in its quest to serve the public and to deserve its trust. Professor L. A. Ponemon's comments on the most widely accepted perspective on the development of an individual's capacity for moral reasoning are put forward to guide the reader in assessing his or her own stage of development, to anticipate and get on with future stages of growth, and to provide a framework for developing the competency of students studying professional ethics. Finally, the position statement of the six largest accounting firms in the U.S. on the legal liability crisis highlights the reality faced by the accounting profession and underscores the value of ethical behavior as an approach to the minimization of vulnerability to the legal process. The purpose of the Appendix on trends in legal liability and defenses available is evident.

REFERENCES

Bayles, M. D. *Professional Ethics.* Belmont, CA: Wadsworth Publishing Company, 1981, p. 7, 8.

Behrman, J. N. *Essays on Ethics in Business and the Professions.* Englewood Cliffs, NJ: Prentice-Hall, 1988, p. 96.

Colby, A., & Kohlberg, L. *The Measurement of Moral Judgment: Theoretical Foundations and Research Validations, and Standard Scoring Manual, Volumes 1 and 2.* Cambridge, England: Cambridge University Press, 1987.

Cook, J. M. "The AICPA at 100: Public Trust and Professional Pride." *Journal of Accountancy* (May 1987): 307–379.

Kohlberg, L. *Essays in Moral Development, Volume I: The Philosophy of Moral Development.* New York: Harper & Row, 1981.

Kohlberg, L. *Essays in Moral Development, Volume II: The Psychology of Moral Development.* New York: Harper & Row, 1984.

Lane, M. S., & Schaup, D. "Ethics in Education: A Comparative Study." *Journal of Business Ethics* 8 (12) (December 1989): 58–69.

"The Liability Crisis in the United States: Impact on the Accounting Profession," Arthur Andersen & Co., Coopers & Lybrand, Deloitte & Touche, Ernst & Young, KPMG Peat Marwick, Price Waterhouse, August 6, 1992.

Macdonald Commission, see *The Report of the Commission to Study the Public's Expectations of Audits,* Canadian Institute of Chartered Accountants, June 1988.

O'Malley, S. F. "Legal Liability Is Having a Chilling Effect on the Auditor's Role." *Accounting Horizons* 7 (2) (June 1993): 82–87.

Palmrose, Z-V. "Trials of Legal Disputes Involving Independent Auditors: Some Empirical Evidence." *Journal of Accounting Research* 29 (Supplement 1991): 149–185.

Ponemon, L. A. "Ethical Reasoning and Selection-Socialization in Accounting." *Accounting, Organizations & Society,* 17 (3/4) (1992): 239–258, 239–244.

Priest, S. "Perspective: The Credibility Crisis." *Ethics in the Marketplace.* The Centre for Ethics and Corporate Policy, Chicago, June 1991, p. 2.

Shenkir, W. G. "A Perspective from Education: Business Ethics." *Management Accounting* (June 1990): 30–33.

Treadway Commission, see the *Report of the National Commission on Fraudulent Public Reporting,* AICPA, 1987.

Velasquez, M. G., *Business Ethics: Concepts and Cases.* Englewood Cliffs, NJ: Prentice-Hall, 1992.

Weber, J., & Green, S. "Principled Moral Reasoning: Is It a Viable Approach to Promote Ethical Integrity?" *Journal of Business Ethics* 10 (5) (May 1991): 325–333.

The Lang Michener Affair*

Martin Pilzmaker was a young, aggressive lawyer from Montreal who was invited in 1985 to join the law firm Lang Michener in Toronto. It was expected that his immigration law practice "could enrich the (firm's) coffers by $1 million a year catering to the needs of Hong Kong Chinese already starting to panic over the crown colony's 1997 return to China's control."

Although rumors of Pilzmaker's questionable practices began to surface and were reported to the firm's Executive Committee in December, it wasn't until early February 1986 that a senior colleague, Tom Douglas, "drew aside Ament and Wiseman (Pilzmaker's junior colleagues) and grilled them on their boss's activities. They told him that Pilzmaker not only smuggled regularly but that he was running a double-passport operation. . . The scam involved the false reporting of lost Hong Kong passports by his clients, which in fact would be kept by Pilzmaker in Canada. On their replacement passports, the clients could travel in and out of the country at will. When the time came to apply for citizenship—which requires three years' residence—they could supply the original "lost" passports to show few if any absences from Canada."

Douglas told the Executive Committee of this activity, by memo, on February 10. The Executive Committee "speculated that Pilzmaker's admissions may have constituted only knowledge of wrongdoing on the part of certain clients and not active complicity. The committee decided to send (two members) Don Wright and Donald Plumley back to Pilzmaker to ask him, in the words of Farquharson's instructing memo, 'if he would be willing to agree' not to participate in any client violation of the Immigration Act."

Early in June 1986, angered that Pilzmaker had not been expelled, Tom Douglas sought advice from Burke Doran, "a colleague he regarded as a personal friend but moreover, one who was a bencher, or governor, of the Law Society. Doran went on to advise him to keep his head down and his mouth shut—a caution Doran later said he had no recollection of giving."

While mulling over this advice and some from another lawyer, Brendon O'Brien, a foremost authority on professional conduct, a further problem came to Douglas's attention. "This was a proposal by Pilzmaker to Brian McIntomny, a young associate lawyer, who was in the market to buy a house. The idea was that McIntomny would put up $50,000 for a $200,000 house, the balance supplied by a Pilzmaker client in Hong Kong. The client would officially own the house, have the phone and utilities registered in his name, while McIntomny lived in it and held a secret deed. After three years, he would pay the client the interest-free $150,000, register the deed to place title in his own name and benefit from the accrued increase in value. The client, meanwhile, would have 'proof' of having resided in Canada for the three years required for citizenship." Douglas arranged for Bruce McDonald, a member of the firm's new Executive Committee now consisting of McDonald, Don Wright, Albert Gnat, Donald Plumley, and Bruce McKenna, to be informed.

An investigation was begun and "at a July 28th Executive Committee meeting, a vote was taken on whether or not to expel Pilzmaker." The vote was three to two in favor of his stay-

ing. Douglas was allowed to address the meeting only after the vote was finalized, and he was enraged.

"On August 6, the night before McKenna's report was submitted but in partial knowledge of what it would likely contain, Douglas had dinner with Burke Doran again, this time in the company of a mutual colleague, Bruce Drake. Drake and Douglas subsequently claimed that when he was asked whether the firm had an obligation to report at least Pilzmaker's double-passport scam to the Law Society, Doran said no, "because no white men have been hurt." (Neither man took this as a racist remark but as meaning it was a victimless crime, with the clients knowingly involved.) The following morning at the office, Drake said he asked Doran if his remarks of the night before could be taken as official advice from the chairman of the Law Society. Doran said yes.

Doran has always denied that, confining his explanation to the dinner and not the morning after: "It's far-fetched to say I was sitting at a social dinner in my capacity as chairman of discipline." Don Wright would later testify, however, that it was Doran's view throughout the period "that we did not have any obligation to report to the Society."

On August 7, McKenna filed a scathing 15-page report to the executive committee listing 15 breaches of unethical behavior both inside and outside the firm by Pilzmaker, noting that "I am not aware of any material statement of fact made by him to me that I have checked out and has proven to be true." Furthermore, "I am concerned that I now have a personal responsibility, as a member of the Law Society and an

Continued

Continued

officer of the court, to report the situation. If each of you review the facts closely, you will have similar concerns about your own obligations." 'On August 20, the executive committee did finally decide Pilzmaker had to go, subject to confirmation by the entire partnership.'

After this, events proceeded at a faster pace:

September 4: Brendon O'Brien, now hired to counsel the firm, advised that "they couldn't afford not to report to the Society."

September 5: A general meeting of the firm's partners is called to review the matter.

September 18: The requisite two-thirds of the 200 votes was obtained to force expulsion.

September 26: Pilzmaker's files were secured at the firm.

October 1: Executive Committee debated impact on the reputation of the firm and of high-profile partners "such as Jean Chretien (who is now the Prime Minister of Canada) and Burke Doran."

November 6: Douglas wrote Don Wright urging the firm to report to the Society.

November 18: Pilzmaker's lawyer filed suit to have Pilzmaker's files transferred to him.

November 21: The Law Society received a report from O'Brien "that (a) Pilzmaker had been expelled, (b) that he had been wrongly billing into the general, not trust, account and (c) that there was more than $300,000 in unpaid fees where Pilzmaker had either not done the work or had not even been retained in the first place."

The Society's investigator, Stephen Sherriff, began his investigation and subsequently called for a fuller report from the firm.

December 5: Pilzmaker's request for his files was granted by Justice Archibald Campbell who "was given no hint that the files contained evidence that at some point might need to be looked at by the Law Society."

December 8: A fuller report is presented to the Law Society.

Twenty-five months later, "(i)n January, 1989, Sherriff filed a lacerating 138-page confidential report that recommended a professional misconduct charge be laid against Burke Doran for placing himself in a conflict-of-interest situation in which he chose the interests of the firm over his responsibility as the Society's then chairman of discipline. Separate charges of professional misconduct were recommended against eight others in the firm. Sherriff contended that (a) they had failed to inform clients that Pilzmaker had likely given them unethical advice and to seek independent counsel and (b) they had failed to report in a timely manner what they knew about his behavior, indeed they reported only when Pilzmaker's lawsuit gave them no alternative."

An Ottawa lawyer, David Scott, was retained to help the Society by analyzing what to do about Sherriff's recommendations. His report of March 2, 1989, was presented to Paul Lamek, the new chair of discipline for the Society. "The ball was now in Lamek's court. He says he saw his job as twofold: To define who Scott meant by 'Managing partners and/or group' and to decide whether a charge could be made against Doran on a basis different from Sherriff's—namely, that as a bencher and chair of discipline, Doran had a 'higher duty' to report than did his colleagues. Although it wouldn't be officially disclosed until this spring, Lamek initially did opt to charge all eight, subject to clarifying just who exactly was on the executive committee from the crucial time on—a period Lamek pinned at June, 1986. That clarification consequently dropped several senior people out of the picture. As for Doran, 'after agonizing analysis' Lamek concluded that no complaint of any kind should be issued."

What was the outcome of these charges/events:

"In the Spring of 1989, when it became obvious that Douglas would have to testify against his colleagues that fall, he finally did resign—three years after he'd first threatened to."

"On October 31, without waiting for the panel's ruling, a disillusioned Sherriff resigned from his job: 'What could have been a testament to the integrity of the Society had ended up sullying it. I had no choice but to quit.'" His departure, coupled with growing media speculation that there might be a "whitewash of a cover-up" in process, had many other members of the Society adding to the chorus of concern.

At a convocation meeting of the benchers last September [1989], lawyer Clayton Ruby, who'd been given a copy of the investigation report by Sherriff, presented a motion that Lamek's decision be set aside and the original recommendations adopted. Ferrier ruled the motion out of order. 'Douglas and Sherriff

Continued

Continued

are right-wingish, not my kind of guys,' [said] the notoriously left-leaning Ruby. "But I really felt that Lamek's decision to charge only five made it look as if we (the Society) were covering something up."

At a general members meeting the following month, former bencher Paul Copeland tried to table a motion demanding simply an explanation for why only five had been charged. He says he too was 'cut off' by Ferrier."

"On January 5 of this year [1990], the five who'd been charged were found guilty of professional misconduct for not reporting their concerns about Pilzmaker three months earlier than they did, specifically at the time McKenna made his damning report. The panel, however, found that the same concerns had not "imposed a duty on them" to inform clients that Pilzmaker had been expelled or that he might have given them unethical advice or that they should get independent legal advice."

Due to the ensuing controversy, on February 7, "the Society hired retired Manitoba former Chief Justice Archibald Dewar to review its handling of the entire affair." But his findings didn't please everyone. "Dewar did not find any evidence of impro-

priety or favouritism in Lamek's charges. The Doran decision was a judgment call, he wrote, and while debatable, to proceed with a charge now would only satisfy critics but "Not be seen as adding lustre to the discipline process."

What he did find, however, was a catalog of complaints against Sherriff. Sherriff was incensed. "The big deal, first,' says Sherriff, 'is that the real bad guy (Pilzmaker) almost went free. The big deal, second, is that the self-governing ability of this profession was compromised. 'Lawyers have special privileges, therefore, special responsibilities. Protecting the public is chief among them. That's the big deal. If you're a man of principle, you won't walk away from it.'"

QUESTIONS

1. Are professionals bound to meet a higher standard of ethical behavior than nonprofessionals? If so, why?

2. In what respects were the actions of the lawyers involved in the Lang Michener Affair not up to the ethical standard you would expect? Consider:

   a. Pilzmaker's conduct.

   b. the conduct of members of the executive committee at Lang Michener, in particular, Burke Doran, and

   c. the investigation and proceedings by the Law Society,

   What obligations did each owe to:

   clients; the legal profession; the Law Society; the public;

3. Do the same considerations apply to other professionals, as to lawyers?

4. Is the self-regulation of a profession on ethical matters effective from the perspective of:

   a. the members of the profession?

   b. the public?

   c. clients?

5. Would you agree with the argument, which was used to exonerate members of the management team, that "when a professional makes a serious mistake, the error is of no consequence, if it is honestly made." (Jorgensen, Bud, *Globe & Mail*, Feb. 5, 1990, p. B9.)

---

* Martin Pilzmaker was disbarred by the Law Society of Upper Canada in January 1990. Five other partners of his firm, Lang, Michener, Lash, Johnston, were also found guilty and reprimanded. But the scandal refused to die, culminating in a major article in the "Insight" section of the *Toronto Star* on Sunday, July 22, 1990. The quotations in the case are from that article.

Postscript: Martin Pilzmaker committed suicide.

Dilemma of an Accountant

In 1976 Senator Lee Metcalf (D-Mont.) released a report on the public accounting industry which rocked the profession. Despite a decade of revisions in rules and regulations (variously established by the Securities and Exchange Commission, Accounting Principles Board, and Financial Accounting Standards Board), public accounting firms were still perceived by many on Capitol Hill as biased in favor of their clients, incapable of or unwilling to police themselves, and at times participants in coverups of client affairs. Senator Metcalf even went so far as to suggest nationalizing the industry in light of these activities.

Just prior to the Metcalf report, Daniel Potter began working as a staff accountant for Baker Greenleaf, one of the Big Eight accounting firms. In preparation for his CPA examination, Dan had rigorously studied the code of ethics of the American Institute of Certified Public Accountants (AICPA), and had thoroughly familiarized himself with his profession's guidelines for morality. He was aware of ethical situations which might pose practical problems, such as maintaining independence from the client or bearing the responsibility for reporting a client's unlawful or unreasonably misleading activities, and he knew the channels through which a CPA was expected to resolve unethical business policies. Dan had taken the guidelines very seriously: they were not only an integral part of the auditing exam, they also expressed to him the fundamental dignity and calling of the profession—namely, to help sustain the system of checks and balances on which capitalism has been based. Daniel Potter firmly believed that every independent

auditor was obligated to maintain professional integrity, if what he believed to be the best economic system in the world was to survive.

Thus, when Senator Metcalf's report was released, Dan was very interested in discussing it with numerous partners in the firm. They responded thoughtfully to the study and were concerned with the possible ramifications of Senator Metcalf's assessment. Dan's discussions at this time and his subsequent experiences during his first year and a half at Baker Greenleaf confirmed his initial impressions that the firm deserved its reputation for excellence in the field.

Dan's own career had been positive. After graduating in Economics from an Ivy League school, he had been accepted into Acorn Business School's accountant training program, and was sponsored by Baker Greenleaf. His enthusiasm and abilities had been clear from the start, and he was rapidly promoted through the ranks and enlisted to help recruit undergraduates to work for the firm. In describing his own professional ethos, Dan endorsed the Protestant work ethic on which he had been raised, and combined this belief with a strong faith in his own worth and responsibility. A strong adherent to the assumptions behind the profession's standards and prepared to defend them as a part of his own self-interest, he backed up his reasoning with an unquestioning belief in loyalty to one's employer and to the clients who helped support his employer. He liked the clear-cut hierarchy of authority and promotion schedule on which Baker Greenleaf was organized, and once had likened his loyalty to his superior to the absolute loyalty which St. Paul advised the

slave to have towards his earthly master "out of fear of God" (Colossians 3:22). Thus, when he encountered the first situation where both his boss and his client seemed to be departing from the rules of the profession, Dan's moral dilemma was deep-seated and difficult to solve.

The new assignment began as a welcome challenge. A long-standing and important account which Baker had always shared with another Big Eight accounting firm needed a special audit, and Baker had reason to expect that a satisfactory performance might secure it the account exclusively. Baker put its best people on the job, and Dan was elated to be included on the special assignment team; success could lead to an important one-year promotion.

Oliver Freeman, the project senior, assigned Dan to audit a wholly-owned real estate subsidiary (Sub) which had given Baker a lot of headaches in the past. "I want you to solve the problems we're having with this Sub, and come out with a clean opinion (i.e., confirmation that the client's statements are presented fairly) in one month. I leave it to you to do what you think is necessary."

For the first time Dan was allotted a subordinate, Gene Doherty, to help him. Gene had worked with the project senior several times before on the same client's account, and he was not wholly enthusiastic about Oliver's supervision. "Oliver is completely inflexible about running things his own way—most of the staff accountants hate him. He contributes a 7:00 A.M. to 9:00 P.M. day every day, and expects everyone else to do the same. You've *really* got to put out, on his terms, to get

Continued

Continued

an excellent evaluation from him." Oliver was indeed a strict authoritarian. Several times over the next month Dan and Oliver had petty disagreements over interpretive issues, but when Dan began to realize just how stubborn Oliver was, he regularly deferred to his superior's opinion.

Three days before the audit was due, Dan completed his files and submitted them to Oliver for review. He had uncovered quite a few problems but managed to solve all except one: one of the Sub's largest real estate properties was valued on the balance sheet at $2 million, and Dan's own estimate of its value was no more than $100,000. The property was a run-down structure in an undesirable neighborhood, and had been unoccupied for several years. Dan discussed his proposal to write down the property by $1,900,000 with the Sub's managers, but since they felt there was a good prospect of renting the property shortly, they refused to write down its value. Discussion with the client had broken off at this point, and Dan had to resolve the disagreement on his own. His courses of action were ambiguous, and depended on how he defined the income statement: according to AICPA regulations on materiality, any difference in opinion between the client and the public accountant which affected the income statement by more than 3% was considered material and had to be disclosed in the CPA's opinion. The $1,900,000 write-down would have a 7% impact on the Sub's net income, but less than 1% on the client's consolidated net income. Dan eventually decided that since the report on the Sub would be issued separately (although for the client's internal use only), the write-

down did indeed represent a material difference in opinion.

The report which he submitted to Oliver Freeman contained a recommendation that it be filed with a subject-to-opinion proviso, which indicated that all the financial statements were reasonable subject to the $1.9 million adjustment disclosed in the accompanying opinion. After Freeman reviewed Dan's files, he fired back a list of "To Do's," which was the normal procedure at Baker Greenleaf. Included in the list was the following note:

1. Take out the pages in the files where you estimate the value of the real estate property at $100,000.

2. Express an opinion that the real estate properties are correctly evaluated by the Sub.

3. Remove your "subject-to-opinion" designation and substitute a "clean opinion."

Dan immediately wrote back on the list of "To Do's" that he would not alter his assessment since it clearly violated his own reading of accounting regulations. That afternoon Oliver and Dan met behind closed doors.

Oliver first pointed out his own views to Dan:

1. He (Oliver) wanted no problems on this audit. With six years of experience he knew better than Dan how to handle the situation.

2. Dan was responsible for a "clean opinion." Any neglect of his duties would be viewed as an act of irresponsibility.

3. Any neglect of his duties would be viewed as an act of irresponsibility.

4. The problem was not material to the Client (consolidated) and the

Sub's opinion would only be used "in house."

5. No one read or cared about these financial statements anyway.

The exchange became more heated as Dan reasserted his own interpretation of the write-down, which was that it was a material difference to the Sub and a matter of importance from the standpoint of both professional integrity and legality. He posited a situation where Baker issued a clean opinion which the client subsequently used to show prospective buyers of the property in question. Shortly thereafter the buyer might discover the real value of the property and sue for damages. Baker, Oliver, and Dan would be liable. Both men agreed that such a scenario was highly improbable, but Dan continued to question the ethics of issuing a clean opinion. He fully understood the importance of this particular audit and expressed his loyalty to Baker Greenleaf and to Oliver, but nevertheless believed that, in asking him to issue knowingly a false evaluation, Freeman was transgressing the bounds of conventional loyalty. Ultimately a false audit might not benefit Baker Greenleaf or Dan.

Freeman told Dan he was making a mountain out of a molehill and was jeopardizing the client's account and hence Baker Greenleaf's welfare. Freeman also reminded Dan that his own welfare patently depended on the personal evaluation which he would receive on this project. Dan hotly replied that he would not be threatened, and as he left the room, he asked, "What would Senator Metcalf think?"

A few days later Dan learned that Freeman had pulled Dan's analysis

Continued

Continued

from the files and substituted a clean opinion. He also issued a negative evaluation of Daniel Potter's performance on this audit. Dan knew that he had the right to report the incident to his partner counselor or to the personnel department, but was not terribly satisfied with either approach. He would have preferred to take the issue to an independent review board within the company, but Baker Greenleaf had no such board. However, the negative evaluation would stand, Oliver's arrogance with his junior staff would remain unquestioned, and the files would remain with Dan's name on them unless he raised the incident with someone.

He was not at all sure what he should do. He knew that Oliver's six years with Baker Greenleaf counted for a lot, and he felt a tremendous obligation to trust his superior's judgment and perspective. He also was aware that Oliver was inclined to stick to his own opinions. As Dan weighed the alternative, the vision of Senator Metcalf calling for nationalization continued to haunt him.

To Qualify or Not?

Jane Ashley was a staff accountant at Viccio & Martin, an accounting firm located in Windsor, Ontario. Jane had been a co-op student while in college and during her first work term with the firm, she had the privilege of being on several audits of various medium sized companies in the Windsor area where she picked up some valuable audit experience. Fresh out of her final academic term, she felt ready to put her scholastic knowledge to work and show the seniors and partners of Vicco & Martin her stuff.

In her first assignment, Jane was placed on an audit team consisting of herself and a senior. This senior, Frankie Small, had been a qualified accountant for five years and had been on staff for over ten. He was well respected within the company and was known for his ability to continually bring engagements in under budget.

The client, Models Inc., which was Viccio & Martin's largest, was a private corporation which made their business in the distribution of self-assembly, replica models, toys and other gaming products. They operated from a central warehouse in Windsor but also distributed from a small warehouse in Toronto and had a drop-off point in Michigan as they purchased merchandise from companies in the United States. Their year-end was April 30. Since Jane had joined the firm on May 15th, she had not been present for the year end inventory count which was taken on the year end date. Frankie S. was present along with another co-op student, who, incidently, had returned for her final academic term on May 11th. Jane asked Frankie how just two people could simultaneously be present for an inventory count at 3 locations.

Frankie responded by telling her that, since the inventory balances at the Toronto warehouse and Michigan drop-off sites were of immaterial amounts (based on representations by management, company records and from audits in prior years) therefore, audit staff had only been present at the Windsor warehouse count. Models Inc. was on a periodic inventory system.

Since she had not been on this engagement before, the evening before her first day of fieldwork, Jane stayed at work late to review the previous year's audit files, this year's audit programs and the notes on this year's inventory count so she could gain a knowledge of the client's business. After an hour or so of reviewing the information, Jane gained a knowledge of the client but she couldn't quite understand what was happening with the inventory section because the working papers were messy and disorganized. Upon reviewing the inventory sheets from this year's count, she found that many of the items were unfamiliar and were referenced only by general product names: there were no serial numbers, no order numbers, etc.

The first day of fieldwork arrived and Jane was given the responsibility of Accounts Payable Cut-off. Upon tracing invoices to the master accounts payable ledger, Jane found that she was having a hard time locating many of them. She brought this matter to the attention of the Accounts Payable Clerk who provided the explanation that invoices received after the year end date were not yet entered in the current year but should have been. Jane was provided with this list and traced it to the Journal entry made to pick up the extra payables. Jane then performed audit procedures on this extra list.

She again found that it was incomplete. The total cut-off problem was, in her estimation (of sample to population figures) in excess of $400,000. She also noted that many of the invoices received had invoice dates after April 30 but title to these goods had changed hands (F.O.B. shipping point) prior to April 30.

The financial statements originally provided by management showed healthy profits of $150,000. The current accounts payable (trade) balance was $1.4 million, which was up over a half a million from last year. The current receivables balance was $800,000 which was up about $100,000 from the previous year. Sales had jumped from $8 million in 1988 to $10 million this year. The company had an operating (demand) line of credit with a lending institution of $1 million dollars. The company owned its two warehouses which had a net equity of approximately $1,600,000 at fair market.

Jane brought the cut-off problem to the attention of Frankie who was perplexed and surprised by the whole issue. The two returned to the office that evening and Jane was asked to prepare a memorandum explaining her findings. It was reviewed by the partner in charge, Mr. Viccio, who contacted the appropriate level of management of Models Inc. to explain the discrepancy.

The Accounts Payable clerk recorded the transactions Jane had found left out, and the audit testing was again performed on the accounts payable cut-off and the rest of the accounts payable section to the satisfaction of the auditor's with respect to all financial statement assertions. The total correc-

Continued

Continued

tions made to accounts payable were in the order of $350,000. The impact of the adjustments were partially to inventory, where traceable, and partly to cost of goods sold. The total affect on the profit figure was $300,000. The financial statements now showed a loss of $150,000.

The head manager and 50% shareholder of the corporation, Mrs. Hyst, was astonished and panic stricken by the entire situation. She was sure something was wrong and that this problem would be rectified at some point throughout the remainder of the audit.

No problems were encountered throughout the remainder of the audit fieldwork however Jane did notice, when she was in the Accounts Payable Clerk's office, that the clerk spent a great deal of time on the phone with suppliers discussing how Models could pay down their over 90-day payables such that the company would not be cut off from purchasing further goods.

Towards the finalization of the audit, Mrs. Hyst came to the auditors and told them that there was most likely inventory that had been left out of the count. She provided a listing which amounted to approximately $200,000. In this listing were material amounts of inventory in the Toronto warehouse, the Michigan drop-off point, goods in transit and goods stored at other locations.

The auditors, who were surprised by the list, decided to perform tests on it and found that it was very difficult and often impossible to track the inventory given the poor system used by the company. Jane telephoned all of the companies that appeared on the list under "goods stored at other locations" and, in all cases, found that no inventory was being kept on behalf of Models.

Suppliers in the U.S. were telephoned for exact shipment dates and, based on the evidence of how long it usually takes to bring goods across the border, it was determined that those goods were included in the year-end inventory count. As for the "extra" inventory stored in the Toronto and Michigan sites, there was no reliable evidence that anything not already accounted for was there. However, there was no way to tell for sure. From the items on this extra list, $50,000 was accounted for as either already counted in inventory as of the year-end date or included in costs of goods sold. The whereabouts of the other $150,000 was not determinable.

Mrs. Hyst was asked to come in to discuss this listing. At the meeting, Mr. Viccio, Frankie and Jane were all present. Mrs. Hyst stated that, if she showed these sorts of losses, the bank would surely call the company's operating loan of $1 million and it would "go under." Mr. Viccio asked the client whether there was any way of determining where the other $150,000 was. She explained that it was hard given their inadequate inventory system but she was pretty sure that it was not counted in the year-end inventory count.

After the meeting, Mr. Viccio explained that there was no reason to doubt management's good faith and that the $150,000 most likely should be added to inventory and taken out of costs of goods sold. Frankie went along with this. Jane however was astonished. She felt that, since there was no evidence backing up the claims made by the client, the firm should be conservative. She also related her experience to the other two concerning the problems the company was having with keeping up with their trade

payables. Mr. Viccio explained to her that the $150,000 should be added to back inventory and that even if it was the cost of goods sold, the client will most likely recover in the near future anyway. "In these situations, we must help the client, we cannot be responsible for their downfall. Who are we to say that there isn't an extra $150,000 in inventory-we're just guessing." Frankie added to this by saying that, if the loan was called, there would be plenty of equity in the buildings of the company to pay it off.

Jane went home that day very distraught. She felt that Mr. Viccio's decision was based on audit fees and that a poor picture on the financial statements would result in the loan being called and Mr. Viccio would not get his fees. Jane was also disappointed with the level of responsibility shown by Frankie, the senior. Jane couldn't believe what was happening given the fact that the original reason for the audit was because the bank had requested it several years ago as the operating loan was increasing. Jane was also aware that Model's major suppliers were requesting the year-end statements as well and, based on them, would make a decision whether or not to extend the company any more credit.

The next day Jane expressed her opinion in a morning meeting held in Mr. Viccio's office. Frankie was also present. She was told that the $150,000 would be added back to inventory.

QUESTION

1. What should Jane do? Why?

This case was adapted from an assignment submitted by Phil Reynolds, an MBA (Accounting) student at the University of Toronto, in the Summer of 1994.

Societal Concerns

Two accounting students, Joan and Miguel, were studying for their final university accounting exam.

"Miguel, what if they ask us whether the accounting profession should speak out about the shortcomings in financial statements?"

"Like what, Joan? We know they don't show the value of employees or the impact of inflation, or the economic reality or market value of many transactions—is that what you mean?"

"No, I mean the advocacy of disclosures which will lead to a better world for all of us. For example, if we could only get companies to start disclosing their impacts on society, and particularly our environment, they would be induced to set targets and perform better the next year. We know that lots of externalities, like pollution costs, are not included in the financial statements, but we could speak out for supplementary disclosures."

"Joan, you go right ahead if you like. But I'm going to stick to the traditional role of accountants—to the preparation and audit of financial statements. It got us this far, didn't it?"

"Yes, but do medical doctors refrain from commenting on health concerns, or do lawyers refrain from creating laws that govern our future? Why should we shy away from speaking out on issues that we know something about that mean a lot to our future?"

QUESTION

1. Is Joan or Miguel right? Why?

Management Choice

Anne Distagne was the CEO of Linkage Construction Inc. which served as the general contractor for the construction of the air ducts for large shopping malls and other buildings. She prided herself on being able to manage her company effectively and in an orderly manner. For years there had been a steady 22–25% growth in sales, profits and earnings per share, which she wanted to continue because it facilitated dealing with banks to raise expansion capital. Unfortunately for Sue Fault, the Chief Financial Officer, the situation has changed.

"Sue, we've got a problem. You know my policy of steady growth—well we've done too well this year. Our profit is too high: it's up to a 35% gain over last year. What we've got to do is bring it down this year and save a little for next year. Otherwise it will look like we're off our well-managed path. I will look like I didn't have a handle on our activity. Who knows, we may attract a takeover artist. Or, we may come up short on profit next year."

"What can we do to get back on track? I've heard we could declare that some of our construction jobs are not as far along as we originally thought, so we would only have to include a lower percentage of expected profits on each job in our profit this year. Also, let's take the $124,000 in R & D costs we incurred to fabricate a more flexible ducting system for jobs A305 and B244 out of the job costs in inventory and expense them right away."

Now listen Sue, don't give me any static about being a qualified accountant, and subject to the rules of your profession. You are employed by Linkage Construction and I am your boss, so get on with it. Let me know what the revised figures are as soon as possible.

QUESTIONS

1. Who are the stakeholders involved in this decision?

2. What are the ethical issues involved?

3. What should Sue do?

The AICPA at 100: Public Trust and Professional Pride

Michael Cook

Journal of Accountancy, May 1987

From one perspective, the American Institute of CPA's centennial marks a very short time in the history of accounting. Five thousand years ago, Babylonians and Assyrians kept records of cash receipts and disbursements on clay tablets. Roman bookkeepers reviewed government accounts under contingent fee arrangements 3,000 years later. Double-entry bookkeeping was invented 500 years ago and "audits" started to take place. By those measures, the AICPA and the organized profession are infants; the past 100 years, but a page in a long history.

But from a more useful perspective, the AICPA's centennial marks the end of an important and dramatic era. In a short 100 years we have evolved from bookkeepers and clerks to members of a recognized, respected profession, and the AICPA has become a truly national organization of CPAs.

In these past 100 years we have gained the public's trust in our profession's objectivity and integrity. The words of the president of the Institute, Colonel Robert H. Montgomery, at our 50th anniversary ring as true today as they did in 1937: "We are here today because there was and is a need for us. That demand will continue as long as people feel a need to know the truth, whether or not it hurts.... Our profession always has had a vision—this urge to find and to tell the truth—and we should cling to it and continue to strive for its accomplishment."

We have earned the public's trust by keeping ourselves adaptable and sensitive to its changing needs, anticipating those needs when possible and taking a proactive stance on them. We have dealt successfully with a practice environment that has changed markedly, and continues to change, in its social, economic, governmental and legal aspects.

The AICPA now has a century of professional responsiveness and responsibility of which to be proud; these qualities are at work today in the Institute and will continue indefinitely into the future. That's why I've given this article its subtitle—"Public Trust and Professional Pride." These past 100 years demonstrate that we, as a profession, have tackled the tough issues—we've earned the public's trust. Because of this I have, and I believe I share with my fellow members, a strong sense of confidence in our ability to handle present problems and future challenges. We may not be infallible as a profession, but our overall track record is most impressive. And we keep on trying. With the trust of the public and confidence in ourselves, we will have the strength to handle what the future brings.

100 YEARS AT A GLANCE

A short look at the past quickly demonstrates the Institute's responsiveness in meeting the challenges we have faced in the last century.

1887. One hundred years ago corporate leaders did not have a clear idea of the capabilities of accountants. As James T. Anyon wrote in 1925, on the "Early Days of American Accountancy," a great many executives "had very mixed ideas as to just what the business of the expert accountant was and exactly what he professed to do. Some considered that he was an experienced bookkeeper and no more; others looked upon him as a man whose business it was to detect fraud, embezzlement and stealing, and that his employment was of value only in this direction; while many had a vague idea that he was merely a man of figures, a rapid and unerring calculator who could add up two or three columns of figures at a time, and who could tell you immediately the square or cube root of any given number."

Our predecessors, men such as Edwin Guthrie and James Anyon, British accountants who arrived in New York in the early 1880s, and native Americans such as Charles Waldo Haskins and Charles E. Sprague, changed those perceptions; they also changed the members of the accounting profession in the process. Together, these men set out to see that competence and professionalism were encouraged among practicing accountants and that accountants' capabilities were recognized. They formed in 1887 (by a December 1886 resolution) the American Association of Public Accountants, now the AICPA.

1896. Although the AICPA is not the accounting profession, it is impossible to separate the development of the profession from that of the AICPA. Indeed, the AICPA began with only 31 members, but James Anyon reported that those 31 men constituted almost all the accountants in the United States. And that small group—united in a professional association—began to work toward setting standards and instituting state licensing.

In 1896 New York became the first state to license public accountants. Certification required passage of an examination in accounting theory and practice, auditing, and commercial law. Thus was born the CPA examination. Other states quickly adopted legislation to license CPAs; by World War I, legislation had been enacted in 45 jurisdictions, with the rest adopting legislation in the 1920s or shortly thereafter.

—Continued

Continued

1913. I doubt that the framers of the 1913 federal income tax legislation could have dreamt of its effect on business practices and individuals or of its ultimate effect on the national economy. When it comes to describing this legislation's impact on members of our profession, I can do no better than to quote from the November 1913 issue of this *Journal:*

". . . it is indubitable that the income tax law is to have a more far-reaching effect upon public accountants than upon any other profession or business in the country. Hundreds of [people] who have never seen the necessity for a correct system of accounting now find themselves compelled to prepare statements of income and expenditure; and the work in nine cases out of ten will fall upon the shoulders of the public accountants.... The corporation tax law in its administration vastly increased the labors of public accountants, but the work arising from the enactment of that law was far less than that which will result from the new income tax act...."

1916. In 1916, aware that the interstate practice of public accounting was being impeded by the diversity of state licensing requirements, the Institute published its first Model Accountancy Bill. The model bill has proved to be so useful that it has been revised and reissued seven times, with the latest issued in 1984.

1917. Our profession attained two milestones in 1917. First, the Institute issued an official audit procedure in the form of a *Federal Reserve Bulletin* entitled *Approved Methods for the Preparation of Balance-Sheet Statements.* The Institute revised this bulletin in 1929 and 1936. Additional efforts in this standard-setting area will be discussed later.

As the second milestone in 1917, the Institute began to develop the Uniform CPA Examination, which is now required by the boards of accountancy of all 50 states, the District of Columbia, Puerto Rico, Guam and the Virgin Islands. As mentioned earlier, starting with the first CPA exam in New York in 1896, each state offered its own CPA examination as its licensing statute went into effect. The exam's subject matter and level of difficulty varied from state to state, however, which raised doubts that CPAs were meeting comparable licensing requirements.

In response to requests from the states, the Institute made its admission examination available starting in June 1917, when some 250 CPA candidates took the Institute's examination in the states of New Hampshire, Kansas and Oregon. Gradually other states, seeing the merit and practicality of a uniform test, began using the Institute's exam. By 1952 all jurisdictions had adopted the Uniform CPA Examination. Although originally achieved through only an examination, entrance into the profession now requires demonstrated competence, an academic degree and experience in the field.

1932. In the wake of the 1929 stock market crash, the Institute appointed a special committee on the development of accounting principles. In 1932 this committee issued its "basic principles" of accounting, which dealt with unrealized profits, capital surplus, treasury stock, and notes or accounts receivable from officers or employees. The committee also recommended to the New York Stock Exchange that audit certificates for listed companies should state that the financial statements were prepared in accordance with these "accepted principles of accounting."

By 1959 the committee had issued 51 accounting research bulletins. Established as the Accounting Principles Board in 1959, this committee came under heavy attack from federal and business sectors in the mid-1960s. A central theme to the criticism was whether a private professional organization had the right to create accounting standards and to impose them on the public business community.

In 1972 an Institute group appointed to study the establishment of financial accounting standards (the Wheat committee) recommended that an independent foundation and standard-setting board be established outside the Institute to be financed by organizations with a strong interest in accounting. Consequently, the Financial Accounting Foundation, the Financial Accounting Standards Advisory Council and the Financial Accounting Standards Board were founded in 1973.

1934. Aided by information provided in the testimony of Colonel Arthur H. Carter, president of the New York State Society of CPAs and later managing partner of Haskins & Sells, Congress passed the Securities Act of 1933 and the Securities and Exchange Act of 1934, which established the Securities and Exchange Commission and increased the accounting and auditing work required by publicly traded companies. At the time, members of Congress had been contemplating using government auditors for all publicly traded companies, and Carter's testimony was instrumental in persuading them of the benefits of using independent accountants instead.

1936. The American Society of CPAs, which had splintered off from the Institute in the 1920s, merged back into the main group during this year. The differing opinions on policies and programs that had prompted this split were reconciled, and the profession once again presented a united front.

—Continued

Continued

1939. In 1939, in response to concerns arising from the McKesson & Robbins case, the Institute established a committee on auditing procedure. This committee developed recommendations on the examinations of inventories and receivables, the appointment of independent auditors and the form of the accountant's report. The substance of the proposals was published in Statement on Auditing Procedure no. 1, *Extensions of Auditing Procedure.*

At the same time, the SEC was gathering evidence and hearing testimony in the McKesson & Robbins matter. After hearing about the Institute's initiatives, the SEC commended the profession for adopting the new audit requirements that had been set forth in *Extensions of Auditing Procedure* and indicated that it would rely on the profession to adopt further extensions of auditing procedures.

A significant outcome of the McKesson & Robbins matter was the Institute's creation of the committee on auditing procedure. In 1948 the Institute adopted 10 generally accepted auditing standards. Since that time, through this committee, which became the auditing standards executive committee in 1972 and then the auditing standards board in 1977, the Institute has published the most comprehensive body of auditing standards in the world.

1957. The Institute adopted its current name, altering its title from the American Institute of Accountants.

1959. During this year the Institute organized its continuing professional education division, which has grown through the years to become a major Institute function.

In 1971, on the recommendation of the committee on CPE, the AICPA council passed a resolution urging state boards of accountancy to adopt a mandatory CPE requirement for all practicing CPAs. As of 1987, 48 states have mandatory CPE requirements, and the other jurisdictions either mandate CPE as a state CPA society requirement or are in the process of implementing such a requirement.

Late 1960s—early 1970s. The Institute's standard-setting efforts have not always satisfied the profession's critics in Congress, the media and elsewhere. Criticisms come to the boiling point whenever there is a spate of business failures, as there was with some large companies that had attracted considerable investor interest in the late sixties and early seventies. The profession was the subject of hearings in both the House of Representatives and the Senate, hearings that led to the introduction in the House of legislation intended to regulate the accounting profession.

The profession responded to these criticisms and legislative proposals with alacrity. New auditing standards were issued on errors and irregularities and on illegal acts by clients, and an independent Commission on Auditors' Responsibilities (the Cohen commission) was established.

1977. By vote of council at a heated meeting in Cincinnati in 1977, the AICPA established the division for CPA firms.

The division had been gradually evolving at the Institute during the 1970s. In 1971 a voluntary quality review program for local firms had been formed; reviewers were from out of state, and no written reports were issued on the results of the reviews. In 1974 the Institute enlarged this effort to encompass a voluntary multioffice quality control review, which supplemented the program for local firms.

The division for CPA firms is divided into two sections: one for SEC practice and one for private companies practice. Requirements for membership in the division include, among others, CPE and periodic peer reviews.

The formation of the division was a major step in the program of self-regulation. It enabled the Institute for the first time to deal with firms, not just individual members, and recognized quality control compliance reviews—peer reviews—as an essential part of an effective self-regulatory program. It acknowledged that the public had a legitimate need for more information about CPA firms and the quality of their practices and provided for even more oversight by the SEC. And it placed in the hands of the division the power to sanction member firms.

A FINAL HISTORICAL OBSERVATION

The above thumbnail sketches obviously demonstrate a concerned, responsive organization. The AICPA has its flaws and foibles, but overall it is made up of people who are responsible, serious and concerned about their profession and its place in the business world.

The history of our profession has included many challenges, and we have responded to each one. Just think of a few—the crisis in confidence in 1929 and the massive McKesson & Robbins fraud. Each time we responded with measures to ensure that these problems would be avoided in the future. It may be true that those who don't learn from history are doomed to repeat it; if so, we should be all right because we've learned a lot in the past century. We've learned from our challenges, we've responded to them and they've made us grow. We've earned the public's trust in our integrity and professionalism.

Ours is a profession striving to contribute to the public interest; a profession with high standards and even higher ideals. These ideals, which have governed our activities over the past century, are encapsulated and summarized in the Institute's mission statement, adopted by council in 1986.

—Continued

Continued

The statement merits reproduction, because it defines our activities today and charts the course of our future.

OUR MISSION IN TODAY'S ENVIRONMENT

We have to interpret and apply our mission statement in a very complex business environment in which there are somewhat conflicting views of our effectiveness as a profession.

On the one hand, according to a recent Louis Harris survey, "certified public accountants emerge strong with the general public, those who are 'knowledgeable' about accounting, stockowners, and the special publics surveyed." Indeed, a majority of the general public agrees that we have and follow high ethical and moral standards, which is gratifying in an era when trust in established institutions is fragile at best. And strong majorities of both general and special publics rank us highly on attributes such as competence, reliability and objectivity. So we have clearly established a positive public perception of CPAs.

On the other hand, we have our share of critics with an interest in auditing and financial reporting who do not fully share that positive perception. The quality of our audits and the effectiveness of our financial reporting system have been challenged in congressional hearings over the past two years. These hearings have been influenced by a number of highly publicized business failures, and our critics continue to pose the question "Where were the auditors?" that was originally asked by Senator Lee Metcalf and Congressman John Moss in the 1970s. At that time the profession responded in three ways:

- A voluntary program to monitor practice and to improve compliance with performance standards—the division for CPA firms—was set in motion.

- New auditing standards were issued on errors and irregularities, illegal acts, planning and supervision, communicating weaknesses in internal accounting control and more.

- The Cohen commission made an extensive study of the audit process and public expectations and issued a comprehensive report with far-reaching recommendations.

These action were the first steps of an evolving process that continues today.

In 1986 concerns about business failures and undetected fraud led Congressman Ron Wyden to introduce legislation requiring auditors to search for financial fraud and bring possible irregularities and illegal acts to the attention of corporate management and audit committees, which would be expected to report these acts to regulatory and law enforcement authorities. Congressmen John Dingell, Wyden and

others are concerned about the adequacy of regulation of the profession.

We are dealing with these congressional concerns on several levels, all expansions on the three responses initiated in the 1970s:

- The report of the special committee on standards of professional conduct for CPAs (the Anderson committee) proposes numerous changes in the Code of Professional Ethics, recommends a program (required for all AICPA members) to monitor practice and to improve compliance with performance standards, and requires all members who audit SEC registrants to belong to the SEC practice section (SECPS).

- The ASB has addressed a whole range of "expectation gap" issues and has issued 10 exposure drafts proposing significant revisions of existing auditing standards.

- An independent commission, the National Commission on Fraudulent Financial Reporting, is studying ways for all participants in the financial reporting process to improve the prevention and detection of fraud.

AICPA MISSION STATEMENT

The American Institute of Certified Public Accountants is the national professional organization for all certified public accountants. The mission of the AICPA is to act on behalf of its members and provide necessary support to ensure that CPAs serve the public interest in performing quality professional services. In fulfilling its mission, the AICPA gives priority to those areas where public reliance on CPA skills is most significant.

To achieve its mission, the AICPA:

1. Promotes uniform certification and licensing standards for CPAs.

2. Sets requirements for maintaining members' professional competence.

3. Assists members in the continuing development of professional expertise.

4. Provides standards of professional conduct and performance.

5. Monitors professional performance to enforce professional standards.

6. Promotes public confidence in the integrity, objectivity, competence, and professionalism of AICPA members and the services they perform.

—Continued

Continued

7. Encourages highly qualified individuals to become CPAs and promotes the availability of appropriate educational programs.

8. Unites CPAs—whether in public practice, industry, education, or government—in their efforts to serve the public interest.

9. Serves as the national representative of CPAs to government, regulatory bodies, and other organizations.

10. Assists members in understanding and adjusting to changes in the economic, political, and technological environment.

OUR CHALLENGES TODAY

Some would ask why we face the concerns of the late 1970s again, just 10 years later.

In part this situation arises because we will be investigated and criticized whenever there are significant business failures. We know auditors cannot prevent business failures; we also know that business failures are inevitable in a dynamic, volatile and competitive business environment. Consequently, we must be prepared to answer without apology the questions and criticisms that always accompany such business failures. Even though we realize this, we seem to be in a principally defensive position lately. Why is this so, and what should we be doing to strengthen our performance and our ability to answer our critics?

First, as a profession, our communications with our clients and the public have not been as effective as they could be. Our reporting standards and formats need to be clarified. The Cohen commission noted that the standard auditor's report was not read for its information content and that it is an often-unread symbol, a "seal of approval." Can we convincingly deny a responsibility to insure against business failures when our audit report is regarded as a confirmation of the sound financial health of the entity—as a seal of approval?

Consequently, it is particularly important that the ASB's proposal to revise the audit report receive the support of the profession. We must effectively convey what an audit is and is not, what it can and cannot reasonably be expected to accomplish and the meaning of our opinion on the financial statements.

Second, the profession, with some justification, has been reluctant to accept expansion of the auditor's role and responsibilities in the financial reporting process. Yet we must recognize that professional services that do not evolve to meet the changing needs of the users of those services will decline in value and others will seek to fill the resulting void,

often in unsatisfactory ways. Can we deny government's initiatives for us to assume greater responsibilities if we fail to meet the reasonable expectations of the users of our services?

For example, as the ASB has proposed, auditors must become more concerned about the *total* control structure and environment, not just "internal accounting controls." An additional proposal would require auditors to perform certain analytical procedures that would provide a better understanding of the overall business environment. And it is particularly desirable that the profession work to enhance the relevance, reliability and understandability of financial statements. ASB proposals dealing with matters such as continued existence, reporting on management discussion and analysis, and auditing client judgments and estimates are important in that regard.

Third, there is disagreement about the degree of our responsibility for the detection of material errors and irregularities. According to the Louis Harris survey, the general public believes that uncovering material errors and irregularities is the most important function of the independent audit. This is not an easy challenge to accept in today's environment for legal liability, but it can be accepted if we can effectively communicate the distinctions between "responsibility" and "liability" and between an "auditor" and a "guarantor."

The ASB's exposure draft on errors and irregularities makes those distinctions and provides useful guidance on the conduct of an audit. It emphasizes that professional skepticism is crucial to an effective audit. The profession needs to embrace that document and its companion document on illegal acts. A failure to do so will be seen as evidence of an unwillingness to serve the public interest.

Finally, I believe it is essential that we act affirmatively on the Anderson committee recommendations. In considering the Anderson report, a key question is whether we are to accept the role and responsibilities of a self-regulatory organization committed to monitoring the quality of our professional work and responding to the needs of the public on an equal footing with the needs of our members.

The party I favor is for us to stand up for quality—to require CPE and quality reviews and to require all firms that engage in SEC practice to participate in the programs of the SECPS.

Equally important, I believe we must have a strong code of ethics that we are prepared to live by and to enforce vigorously. The decisions the profession makes in this area will have a significant impact on our future.

—Continued

Continued

WHAT LIES AHEAD?

We face many problems and challenges. In addition to those mentioned previously, there are, for example, criticisms of the quality of audits of governmental units and federal financial assistance programs; concerns about the scope of services we provide to audit clients; concerns about the confidentiality that surrounds certain of our self-regulatory activities; and, as we all are so painfully aware, burgeoning legal liability and difficulty in obtaining adequate insurance at a reasonable price. The courts, Congress and the SEC continue to challenge our role and seek to redefine our responsibilities. All of these factors and others discussed in this article will affect our profession in ways we cannot fully comprehend today.

When I consider the upcoming changes and challenges to our profession, I see two different facets of the future—the short term and the long term—that will have to be analyzed and handled in different ways. Dealing with the short-term future requires a practical, pragmatic grasp of the problems and needs in our purview today; analyzing the long-term future lends itself more to the rhetorical, to the visionary questions.

At this noteworthy moment in our professional history, we must grapple with both aspects of our future. The next few years are critical—serious choices must be made that will affect the very essence of our professional lives. Is the AICPA to be regarded as a professional "club," with initial entry requirements and yearly dues, whose principal emphasis is on serving the needs of its members? Or will it be a serious, self-regulatory body, intent on monitoring and demonstrating the quality of our professional services and responding to the needs of the public on an equal footing with the needs of our members? Will we commit ourselves to a communicative, proactive stance on the "expectation gap" issues, or will we continue a defensive posture, seeking to maintain the status quo?

These issues are at the heart of the questions we must come to grips with in the short term, and our decisions in these areas will have an enormous impact on our long-term future. The long term will also be influenced by factors that we cannot identify today.

Who can really predict what our profession will be like in 10 years? I don't think I can. I hope and expect that the AICPA will continue to be a growing, healthy, dynamic organization. Our membership doubled in the decade before 1976 and again in the 10 years between 1976 and 1986, growing from about 60,000 members to over 240,000 members in 20 years.

I see this growth continuing. But as to predicting the nature of an accountant's daily work, and the way in which it will be performed—who really knows? With all of the changes resulting from greater computerization, advances in EDP and the continuous stream of information that these will provide, will we be performing continuous audits? When our markets have a continuous flow of financial information, will they function the same way they do today? What will be the effects of advances in expert systems and artificial intelligence? No one can tell for sure.

Changes are occurring in our profession at a phenomenal rate. For example, who could have predicted 10 years ago, when a small minority of people entering our profession were women, that today that number would approach 50 percent? And the changes we're seeing now are really only the beginning. I believe, as awesome as it might sound, that the next 10 years will bring more changes to our profession than the last 100 have.

But change is not something to fear. The words of the committee on scope and structure are as true today as they were in 1975:

"Every profession is continually changing or being changed. It is changed by the aspirations of its own members—not only by those who cherish its old traditions, but by those who are inspired by a new vision of its function in society. It is changed by the emergence of additional opportunities for service which, if accepted, can stimulate its growth and, if neglected, may reduce its prestige. It is changed by the need to develop new skills—a requirement which may often entail the enlistment of those trained in different disciplines or an apparent incursion into other realms of knowledge. It is changed by the impact of new social and moral values and by the influence of political decisions reflecting those values. It is changed by the spectacular advance of technological innovation. It is changed by the mounting demand for a constantly higher level of competence—not only in terms of a wider span of knowledge, but also a greater depth of knowledge in specialized areas. And a profession successfully adapts to its altered environment or it runs the risk of extinction. For no calling has a valid claim to eternal professional status. It must constantly justify its retention of that privilege by responding, in a creative and responsible manner, to the changing needs of society."

I believe that change and challenge are really just other names for opportunity. And we'll be there, taking advantage of every new opportunity to work with and be responsive to the public, which has vested its trust in us.

The future will bring many challenges, and we must meet them in a positive frame of mind—alert and adaptable, responsive and responsible. I have no doubt that we will do this. All we have to do is look at the caliber of the people

—Continued

Continued

around us, at the people who are attracted to accounting as a profession; you never cease to impress me.

Although we may not be able to predict the future, we know that we will always be able to rely on the integrity and professionalism of our fellow members. These really are the greatest qualities we can celebrate during our centennial year, and let's be sure that we do pause to appreciate our two greatest assets—the confidence that we have in ourselves and in the value of our profession, and the honor of the public's trust in our objectivity and integrity. We have much to be grateful for and to be proud of, and this will give us the ability, enthusiasm and resilience to cope with whatever challenges are ahead of us. I'm certain that our successors will view our second hundred years with the same pride and confidence that we feel today as we look back over the first hundred years of our great organization.

J. Michael Cook, CPA, *is chairman of Deloitte Haskins & Sells and 1986–87 chairman of the AICPA board of directors. A former chairman of the AICPA SEC regulations committee, he has also served on council, the auditing standards board, the future issues committee and the executive and peer review committees of the SEC practice section of the division for CPA firms. He serves on the advisory committee of the University of Florida's School of Accountancy and has testified before the House Subcommittee on Oversight and Investigations in defense of self-regulation for the accounting profession.*

Ethical Reasoning and Selection-socialization in Accounting

(Extract of pp. 239–244 only)

Lawrence A. Ponemon

Accounting Organizations and Society, March 1992

ABSTRACT *This paper extends the work of researchers who have examined the ethical reasoning of CPAs in professional practice. Its purpose is to explore the influence of accounting firm socialization upon the individual CPA's level of ethical reasoning. Based on cognitive-developmental theory, and using a well-known measure of ethical reasoning, two hypotheses regarding selection-socialization are explored. To test these hypotheses, a triangulated research design was incorporated, employing cross-sectional, longitudinal and experimental methods. Findings of all three studies corroborate the existence of ethical socialization whereby those progressing to manager and partner positions within the firm tend to possess lower and more homogeneous levels of ethical reasoning. Experimental findings also suggest that firm managers' promotion decisions are biased in favor of individuals possessing ethical reasoning that is closer to their own capacity. This implies that the ethical culture of the accounting firm stymies an individual's development to higher levels of ethical reasoning.*

Our profession's image is largely the sum of our individual attitudes and actions. Each failure tarnishes the image of the profession. Each of us is a professional, and each responsible for maintaining high standards. We cannot rationalize questionable actions by hiding behind our firms (Walters, 1986, p. 72).

Recently, the ethical core of the accounting profession in the United States has been under close scrutiny due to a rash of bad press caused, in part, by a litigious business environment, recession in financial markets and crisis in the national Savings and Loan industry. To overcome a potentially soiled reputation, the profession is now striving to modify and improve the ethical behaviors of individual accounting professionals (CPAs) in the practice of auditing, tax and consulting. Essential to developing an effective mechanism for change is an understanding of the individual practitioner's abilities to reason and behave ethically.

Recently completed empirical studies have explored the underlying ethical reasoning processes of accountants in professional practice (Armstrong, 1984, 1987; Ponemon, 1988, 1990; Ponemon & Gabhart, 1990; Ponemon & Glazer, 1990; Shaub, 1989; Tull, 1982). Findings of these works suggest that accountants are not reaching their potential for higher levels of ethical judgment or behavior. Further, Ponemon's (1990) cross-sectional study of 52 CPAs shows a markedly negative association between position level within the firm and level of ethical reasoning. In that study it was

concluded that (1990, p. 209), "This work suggests that differences in ethical behavior are likely to reflect differences in socialization; thus different positions in a firm's hierarchy are likely to engender different ethical proclivities."

This paper extends prior work by examining the process of ethical socialization in the public accounting profession. Relying upon cognitive-developmental theory, and using a well-known psychometric of ethical reasoning, it provides the results of cross-sectional, longitudinal and experimental studies, all corroborating the socialization phenomenon in public accounting firms. That is, the ethical reasoning levels of accountants, on average, decrease and become more homogeneous as they progress to higher positions in the firm hierarchy. Findings also provide evidence of selection-socialization, whereby the management of accounting firms hire and promote only those individuals who share a common set of ethical values and beliefs.

The remainder of this paper is organized as follows. In the next section, the relevant literatures on the psychology of moral reasoning and socialization in public accounting firms are reviewed. Two hypotheses are then advanced. The first hypothesis examines the influence of accounting firm socialization as a determinant to the ethical reasoning levels of individuals entering and remaining in the profession. The second hypothesis examines selection-socialization. To test these hypotheses, three empirical studies were undertaken. The first was a random, cross-sectional study of professional accountants at various position levels in public firms throughout the United States. The second was a two-year longitudinal study of auditors at various position levels within one international firm. The third study was based on a field experiment involving audit managers' judgments regarding the promotion potential of actual audit seniors within the same firm. The implications of this research are discussed in the last section of the paper.

THEORETICAL DEVELOPMENT AND HYPOTHESES

Psychology of Ethical Reasoning

Drawing from the field of cognitive development, the psychology of ethical reasoning provides a theory that explains the human decision-making process prior to ethical behavior. It is concerned with the process that individuals follow in making

—Continued

Continued

a decision. It is not concerned with the moral philosophy of what is right or wrong. The psychology is a well-developed field of research based on the work of the noted child psychologist Jean Piaget ([1932], 1966). From this early work, Lawrence Kohlberg developed a model of ethical cognition that includes a series of developmental equilibria present in individuals. Kohlberg (1969) advanced a stage-sequence model defining a series of cognitive levels and stages somewhat akin to the rungs of a ladder. That is, all individuals move upwardly through these developmental levels beginning at what is termed "pre-conventional morality", to the second level termed "conventional morality" and sometimes to the final and highest level called "post-conventional morality".

To paraphrase Kohlberg (1984, pp. 624–639), one way to understand the three levels is to think of them as three different types of relationships between the self and society's rules and expectations. To a pre-conventional person, rules and social expectations are something external to the self; a conventional person identifies self in relation to others; a post-conventional person differentiates the self from the rules and expectations of others and defines his or her values in terms of self-chosen principles. Accordingly, to the pre-conventional person, resolution of an ethical dilemma is simply based upon the immediate cost and/or benefit of ethical action. To the conventional person, resolution is based upon the avoidance of harm to others belonging to one's social institution. The post-conventional person frames an ethical judgment based upon an internalized and self-chosen set of principles.

Within each of the three levels of ethical judgment are two developmental stages, producing a total of six discrete equilibria. For example, pre-conventional behavior consists of a lower order belief system termed "stage 1" where an individual chooses to do right if he or she can avoid punishment, and a higher order belief system termed "stage 2" where an individual choses to do right only when it serves one's own immediate interest (e.g., expected benefits exceed expected costs). Table 1 presents a summary of the three levels and six stages.

To illustrate this model, consider the ethical motivations of an individual accountant at different levels of ethical reasoning. The preconventional person is not cognizant of differences among individuals. Such individuals view their actions in physical terms and are not conscious of the psychological interests of others. An accountant at stage 2, for example, would choose to comply with professional standards, ethical codes or law only if he or she deemed that ethical behavior was less harmful or costly than unethical behavior. Conversely, if the accountant could benefit from unethical actions, and there is no possibility of getting caught, he or she would probably choose to do so.

The conventional individual is aware of shared feelings, agreements and expectations which take primacy over individual interests. At the conventional level the accountant has a need to be a *good* person in the eyes of co-workers, management and the profession as a whole. At stage 3, he or she desires to maintain rules and authority which support stereotypical good behavior. At stage 4, the individual feels obligated to keep the system of rules and conventions going, and seeks ways to avoid breakdown in the system. The stage 3 accountant, at times, may feel pressure to abide by peer group norms, even though such behavior would result in a blatant violation of firm policy. However, at stage 4 the accountant feels obligated to the policies of the firm or the standards of the profession, and is better able to withstand peer pressure.

The post-conventional individual follows self-chosen ethical principles, in which case particular laws or social agreements are usually valid because they rest on such principles. However, when laws or rules violate these principles, one acts in accordance with the principle rather than abiding by the rule. For example, the stage 5 individual's social perspective is that of a rational individual aware of values and rights prior to social attachments and contracts. The accountant believes that the rules and laws governing moral action in the profession are based on some rational calculation of overall utility (i.e. the greatest good for the greatest number of people). Here the individual recognizes that moral and legal points of view sometimes conflict, but has learned to balance moral principles with the rules and expectations of the profession and society. Hence, the accounting practitioner makes a choice to do right if it is consistent with his or her self-chosen ethical principles.

It is important to note that the model is cognitive in that it attempts to explain how a person thinks; it is structural in that it describes an underlying innate mental process; it is developmental in that the structure develops within an individual over time; it is sequential in that the development progresses in order and only in one direction (i.e. one only goes up the ladder and only one step at a time) and consists of six discrete identifiable stages. Further, Rest (1979a) posits that while one stage might dominate an individual's reasoning, he or she is never simply at one stage of cognition.

Since the inception of the stage-sequence theory, researchers have set out to construct reliable psychometric instruments to assess an individual's level of ethical reason-

—*Continued*

Continued

TABLE 1

SIX STAGES OF MORAL
REASONING*

Pre-conventional level: focus is self	
Stage 1	Obedience: you do what you're told primarily to avoid punishment.
Stage 2	Instrumental egotism and simple exchange: let's make a deal or only consider the cost and/or benefits to oneself.
Conventional level: focus is relationships	
Stage 3	Interpersonal concordance: be considerate, nice and kind and you'll get along with people. Focus is on cooperation with those in your environment.
Stage 4	Law and duty to the social order: everyone in society is obligated and is protected by the law. Focus is on cooperation with society in general.
Post-conventional level: focus is personally held principles	
Stage 5	Societal consensus: you are obligated by whatever arrangements are agreed to and by due process and procedure. Focus is on fairness of the law or rule as determined by equity and equality in the process of developing the rule.
Stage 6	Nonarbitrary social cooperation: how rational and impartial people would organize cooperation is moral. Focus is on fairness of the law or rules derived from general principles of just and right as determined by rational people.

*Adopted from Rest, J. (1979a).

ing (Colby & Kohlberg, 1987; Rest, 1979b). Two commonly used instruments are the Moral Judgment Interview (MJI) and the Defining Issues Test (DIT). Kohlberg and colleagues developed the MJI, a series of standardized paradigms requiring the individual to resolve a moral dilemma. Each individual's verbal protocol to the resolution of dilemmae is analyzed according to an elaborate scoring method, resulting in a single (global) stage score. Rest developed the DIT, a self-administered questionnaire that provides an objective measure of ethical reasoning. While DIT results are consistent with Kohlberg's stage-sequence model, its primary measures are based on a distribution of ethical capacities rather than a single stage score.

While much research has been conducted to validate the stage-sequence model of ethical development, criticisms about the developmental hierarchy and the stability of moral reasoning stages have been raised (Gibbs, 1977; Kuhn, 1980; Kurtines & Greif, 1974). As a result, refinements and exten-

sions to the moral development model, with fewer restrictive requirements on equilibrium stages, were advanced by Kohlberg *et al.* (1983) and Rest (1979a). Others have been concerned with the justice orientations that define moral stages, resulting in possible cultural and gender biases in psychometric tests (Gibbs, 1977; Gilligan, 1977; Lyons, 1982; Murphy & Gilligan, 1980). A final area of concern has been the relationship between moral reasoning and ethical action (Blasi, 1980).[1]

---

1. Kohlberg (1984) and Rest (1986) provide a summary of the results of hundreds of studies in this area and also address the most salient critiques to the theory including the stability of moral judgment stages, the existence of possible gender bias and the possibility of measurement error in psychometric methods.

—Continued

CHAPTER 2 *The Role of a Professional Accountant*

Continued

Despite these issues, the theory of ethical reasoning and development has been shown to be of consequence in applied psychological research, including studies of criminal behavior (Kohlberg *et al.*, 1972), moral atmosphere within organizations (Higgins *et al.*, 1984), whistle-blowing judgment (Brabeck, 1984) and ethical decision making in the business environment (Carmella, 1985; Trevino, 1986; Trevino & Youngblood, 1990). Several studies have examined public accounting professionals' ethical reasoning and development (Armstrong, 1984, 1987; Ponemon, 1988, 1990; Ponemon & Gabhart, 1990; Ponemon & Glazer, 1990; Shaub, 1989; Tull, 1982).

Findings of these studies suggest that accountants do not develop ethical reasoning capacities commensurate with individuals having similar socio-economic and educational backgrounds. For example, based on a study of accounting students and practitioners, Armstrong (1987, p. 33) writes, "CPA respondents appear to have reached the moral maturation level of adults in general, instead of maturing even to the level of college students, much less to the level of college graduates. In other words, their college education may not have fostered continued moral growth". Ponemon (1990), in a study of accounting practitioners at various position levels in public firms, reported a marked negative association between accountants' position or rank and their level of ethical reasoning as measured using the MJI. Ponemon & Gabhart (1990) experimentally investigated the influence of ethical reasoning on auditors' independence judgment. In this study, auditors at lower levels of ethical reasoning were sensitive to factors relating to penalty (personal harm) resulting from misconduct when framing an independence judgment. Auditors at higher levels of ethical reasoning, however, were sensitive to affiliation (harm to others) when framing their judgment. Finally, Ponemon & Glazer (1990) examined the ethical development of accounting students and alumni from a small liberal arts college and large state university. They found accounting seniors and alumni of the liberal arts college achieving, on average, a significantly higher level of ethical reasoning than comparable students and alumni from the state institution.

In summary, the psychology of ethical reasoning has been shown to be of consequence to the study of behavior in accounting and auditing because many professional judgments are conditioned upon the beliefs and values of the individual. While these studies report significant and consistent results, they are limited in two major respects. First, findings were based on small, regional or non-randomly generated samples of accounting practitioners. Second, because studies were cross-sectional rather than longitudinal, socialization processes could only be inferred rather than explicit-

ly tested. Despite limitations, the present research is motivated by (and attempts to extend) prior work in this area. It explores and attempts to explicitly test the influence of accounting firm socialization on the ethical reasoning and development of individuals remaining in the accounting profession.

Socialization in Accounting Firms

Researchers have long been concerned with explaining how individuals become successful in their chosen careers (Forbes, 1987; Hall, 1976; Lawrence, 1990; Rosenbaum, 1979, 1984; Whyte, 1956). Career success or individual attainment within organizations has been explained by psychological and sociological processes (Nystrom & McArthur, 1989). Much of this work suggests that promotion serves as an employee screening and signaling mechanism. That is, employees who get a promotion are likely to be perceived by management as having personal characteristics commensurate with the culture and philosophy of the organization. Several studies indicate the importance of symmetry in the perceptions of subordinates and superiors in terms of selection and promotion (Lockheed, 1980; Smircich, 1983; Weick, 1979). As a result, management is more likely to promote subordinates who share common views of the organization and its people. Other studies suggest that as employees assume greater managerial responsibilities within an organization they tend to develop homogeneous cognitive traits, including their level of ethical reasoning (Avolio & Gibbons, 1988; Fisher *et al.*, 1987).

Studies of socialization in the accounting profession have typically focused upon the work-related behaviors, attitudes or perceptions of individuals employed by large public firms (cf. Dillard & Ferris, 1989). One common theme in this literature is the existence of an underlying and often deliberate process of socialization at work within the accounting firm, resulting in the acculturation and assimilation of all members entering and remaining in the profession (cf. Blank, 1984). Early studies revealed organizational conflict emerging from socialization pressures resulting in systematic differences between the perceptions of newly hired versus highly experienced accounting practitioners (Rhode *et al.*, 1976, 1977; Sorensen, 1967; Sorensen & Sorensen, 1974). Other studies also found a widening gap between high-level and low-level accountants in terms of career goals and objectives (Sorensen *et al.*, 1973; Sorensen & Sorensen, 1972). At the center of such conflict are often discordant values brought about by an individual's career aspirations versus the bureaucratic demands of the firm. Those who maintain

—Continued

Continued

a low regard for bureaucratic details will typically become dissatisfied with their career and leave the firm.

Later studies examined determinants of an individual's career success and upward mobility in public firms. In general, these studies show that individuals who are able to adapt into the firm's culture or work ethic will more likely progress. Those unable to do so will quickly become disillusioned with their careers and leave the firm (Aranya & Ferris, 1984; Benke & Rhode, 1980; Blank, 1984; Bullen & Flamholtz, 1985; Dean *et al.*, 1988; Dillard & Ferris, 1979; Ferris, 1977). In a related field, other researchers have examined organizational processes or control mechanisms employed to motivate and convince employees to think and behave in the best interests of the firm (Dirsmith & Covaleski, 1985a, Hofstede, 1968; McNair, 1991; Merchant, 1982; Ouchi, 1980; Wilkins & Ouchi, 1983; Rockness & Shields, 1984). According to Ouchi (1980), two implicit mechanisms are termed clan control and selection-socialization. Davidson (1990) suggests that the selection-socialization process in accounting firms can occur two ways. That is, the individual, being unable to fit into the culture of the firm, may voluntarily choose to leave, or firm management may seek to hire and promote only certain types of individuals from the population of eligible personnel.

Like other organizations, the culture of an accounting firm can have a profound effect on the beliefs and values of its personnel (Dillard, 1981; Otley & Berry, 1980). Accounting firms may have self-perpetuating organizational cultures because their managements tend to select and promote individuals who are perceived to be similar to themselves (Benke

& Rhode, 1984; Rhode *et al.*, 1976). An "up or out philosophy", and the lack of diversity among individuals in the partner ranks, strengthen a firm's culture and its influence on the socialization of auditors at all positive levels (Davidson, 1988; Dirsmith & Covaleski, 1985b). A strong culture may be beneficial to the accounting firm because it can reduce deviant (undesirable) behavior (Neimark & Tinker, 1986). On the other hand, such a culture may demand too much social conformity—reducing creative activities within the firm and ultimately weakening its competitive edge (Ouchi, 1980; Wilkins & Ouchi, 1983).

A strong organizational culture may cause those individuals who are unable to conform to the ethical norms or values espoused by accounting firm management to be weeded out of the firm. In support of this theory, studies of accountants' ethical behavior show individuals at higher position levels having a stronger sense of commitment or obligation to the profession (Aranya & Ferris, 1984; Aranya *et al.*, 1982; Armstrong, 1984; Loeb, 1970; Norris & Niebuhr, 1983; Schilit, 1981; Yerkes, 1975). Indeed, the ethical socialization process itself may serve as the principal catalyst for Ponemon's earlier findings (1990) of an inverse relationship between position within the firm and the individual accountant's ethical reasoning. As a result, individuals with too high a level of ethical reasoning may experience difficulty progressing to upper echelons in the accounting firm's formal hierarchy.

SOURCE: *Acounting Organizations and Society,* Volume 17, No. March 4, 1992, pp. 239–258 Copyright © 1992 Elsevier Science Ltd. Reprinted with permission.

The Liability Crisis in the United States: Impact on the Accounting Profession A Statement of Position

Arthur Andersen & Co., Coopers & Lybrand, Deloitte & Touche, Ernst & Young, KPMG Peat Marwick, Price Waterhouse

The tort liability system in the United States is out of control. It is no longer a balanced system that provides reasonable compensation to victims by the responsible parties. Instead, it functions primarily as a risk transfer scheme in which marginally culpable or even innocent defendants too often must agree to coerced settlements in order to avoid the threat of even higher liability, pay judgments totally out of proportion to their degree of fault, and incur substantial legal expenses to defend against unwarranted lawsuits.

The flaws in the liability system are taking a severe toll on the accounting profession. If these flaws are not corrected and the tort system continues on its present inequitable course, the consequences could prove fatal to accounting firms of all sizes. But a liability system seriously lacking in logic, fairness and balance is not just the accounting profession's crisis. It is a business crisis and a national crisis.

This position statement describes these matters in more detail, as well as needed reforms that the American Institute of CPAs (AICPA) and the six largest accounting firms are advocating. In seeking these reforms, the firms are not attempting to avoid liability where they are culpable. Rather, the firms seek equitable treatment that will permit them and the public accounting profession to continue to make an important contribution to the U.S. economy.

AN EPIDEMIC OF LITIGATION

The present liability system has produced an epidemic of litigation that is spreading throughout the accounting profession and the business community. It is threatening the independent audit function and the financial reporting system, the strength of U.S. capital markets, and the competitiveness of the U.S. economy.

The principal causes of the accounting profession's liability problems are unwarranted litigation and coerced settlements. The present system makes it both easy and financially rewarding to file claims regardless of the merits of the case. As former SEC Commissioner Philip Lochner recently pointed out in *The Wall Street Journal*, plaintiffs may simply be seeking to recoup losses from a poor investment decision by going after the most convenient "deep pocket"—the audi-

tor.[1] In too many cases, moreover, claims are filed with the sole intent of taking advantage of the system to force defendants to settle.

The doctrine of joint and several liability makes each defendant fully liable for all assessed damages in a case, regardless of the degree of fault. In practical terms this means that, even with no evidence of culpability, a company's independent auditors are almost certain to be named in any action filed against that company alleging financial fraud, for no reason other than the auditors' perceived "deep pockets" or because they are the only potential defendant that is still solvent. A particularly egregious example of the abuses encouraged by joint and several liability is the common practice of plaintiffs' attorneys settling with the prime wrongdoers, who don't have a defense or money, at a fraction of what these parties should pay. The attorneys then pursue the case against the "deep pocket" professionals, who as a result of joint and several liability are exposed for 100 percent of the damages even if found to be only one percent at fault.

Other elements in the system also act as incentives for unwarranted litigation leading to forced settlements. For example, American judicial rules make no effective provision for recovery of legal costs by prevailing defendants, even if the plaintiff's case is meritless. In addition, judicial restrictions on the types of cases in which punitives damages may be awarded have been significantly relaxed in recent years, making solvent professional and business defendants a prime target. The prospect of having to pay all damages as a consequence of joint and several liability, the high costs of defense, and possible punitive damages are persuasive factors in coercing settlements.

Abusive and unwarranted litigation is a problem not just for the accounting profession, but for business and the economy generally. A small group of attorneys is reaping millions of dollars by bringing federal securities fraud claims (under SEC Rule 10b-5) against public companies whose only crime

---

1. Philip R. Lochner, Jr., "Black Days for Accounting Firms," *The Wall Street Journal*, May 22, 1992, page A10.

—Continued

Continued

has been a fluctuation in their stock price. These attorneys use the threat of enormous legal costs, a lengthy and disruptive discovery process, protracted litigation, and damage to reputation to force large settlements.

The CEO of a high tech company that has been the target of 13 specious Rule 10b-5 suits calls these actions "legalized extortion" and their effects go far beyond the "payoffs" demanded. These meritless suits siphon off funds needed for research and development, capital investment, growth and expansion. They divert management's time, talent and energy from the principal mission of running the business. They send liability insurance premiums skyrocketing. Ultimately, the direct and indirect costs of these suits are borne by shareholders, along with employees, customers, and all of a company's stakeholders.

Joint and several liability encourages the inclusion of "deep pocket" defendants such as independent accountants, lawyers, directors and underwriters in these suits in order to increase the prospect and size of settlements. Prohibitive legal costs, the unpredictable outcome of a jury trial, and the risk of being liable for the full damages compel even blameless defendants to race each other to the settlement table. And they do this despite the realization that, to the uninformed public, "agreeing" to settle is seen as an admission of wrongdoing.

A survey by the six largest accounting firms of the cases against them involving 10b-5 claims which were concluded in fiscal year 1991 showed that: (i) the average claim subjecting the accounting firm to joint and several liability was for $85 million; (ii) the average settlement by the firm was $2.7 million, suggesting there might have been little or no merit to the original claim against the accountant; yet, (iii) the average legal cost per claim was $3.5 million. It is not surprising that an accounting firm would agree to settle a case for less than what it had already spent in legal fees and, therefore, avoid the risk of liability of over twenty times the settlement by a jury that may be hostile to a business with "deep pockets." However, controlling risk by settling where you did nothing wrong becomes a very expensive strategy for "winning" the liability game.

FINANCIAL CRISIS FOR THE ACCOUNTING PROFESSION

The financial impact of rampant litigation on the six largest accounting firms has been well-publicized. Numerous headlines and articles resulted from the firms' own disclosure that, in 1991, total expenditures for settling and defendant

lawsuits were $477 million—nine percent of auditing and accounting revenues in the United States. This figure, a multiple of what other businesses spend on litigation, does not even include indirect costs. It covers only costs of legal services, settlements and judgments, and liability insurance premiums, minus insurance reimbursements. The 1991 figure represents a substantial increase over the 1990 figure of $404 million or 7.7 percent of audit and accounting revenues. And based upon reported settlements through June 30, 1992, there appears to be no end to the continuous upward spiral.

The litigation explosion has affected the entire accounting profession. It has been estimated that there are about $30 billion in damage claims currently facing the profession as a whole. A recent survey by the AICPA indicates that claims against firms other than the six largest rose by two-thirds between 1987 and 1991. Ninety-six percent of those firms having more than 50 CPAs reported an increase in exposure to legal liability. The same group has experienced a 300 percent increase in liability insurance premiums since 1985. Smaller firms must now carry far more coverage, and high deductibles force them to pay even medium-sized claims out-of-pocket. The median amount for deductibles is now $240,000—nearly six times the 1985 median of $42,000. Forty percent of all the firms surveyed are "going bare," largely because liability insurance is simply too expensive.[2]

For the largest firms, the increase in insurance premiums was dramatically higher than that reported by the smaller firms, coupled with drastically reduced policy limits. Deductibles also have risen dramatically and now exceed $25 million for a first loss. The higher rate of increase in liability insurance for the largest firms generally reflects the larger proportion of audit work for publicly-held companies, thereby subjecting them to a greater liability risk.

IMPACT ON CORPORATE ACCOUNTABILITY AND ECONOMIC COMPETITIVENESS

The heavy financial burden placed on accounting firms by runaway litigation affects business and the economy in two major ways: first, through the actual and threatened failure of accounting firms; and, second, through the "survival tactics" firms are forced to employ.

In 1990, Laventhol & Horwatyh, the seventh-largest firm, collapsed—the largest bankruptcy for a professional organi-

---

2. Survey of accounting firms (excluding the six largest), American Institute of Certified Public Accountants, 1992.

—Continued

Continued

zation in U.S. history—necessitating that its former partners agree to pay $48 million to avoid personal bankruptcy. While other factors contributed to the firm's demise, the overriding reason was the weight of its liability burden. According to former CEO Robert Levine, L&H, like other accounting firms, was included as a defendant because of the perception of being a "deep pocket" rather than deficiencies in the performance of its professional responsibilities. "It wasn't the litigation we would lose that was the problem," he asserted. "It was the cost of winning that caused the greatest part of our financial distress."

The consequences of L&H's failure reverberated throughout the capital markets. Audits in process were interrupted. New auditors had to be found, with the inevitable time lag that occurs for start-up. Special rules had to be adopted by the SEC to deal with public companies whose prior year financial statements reported on by L&H had to be reissued in connection with public offerings and periodic public filings. Companies whose financial statements were audited by L&H were placed under a cloud through no fault of their own.

Furthermore, the failure undermined confidence in the ability of the profession to carry out its public obligations by creating concerns about the financial viability of other firms. It also created a deep sense of apprehension throughout the accounting profession that has only grown worse. During 1992, another prominent firm, Pannell Kerr Foster, closed or sold about 90 percent of its offices and opted to reorganize its offices as individual professional corporations. *Accounting Today* quoted a former PKF partner who indicated that liability was one of the reasons for this massive restructuring.

The magnitude of the six largest accounting firms' liability-related costs, as well as the size of some highly-publicized judgments and settlements, has fueled speculation about their survival. This is not surprising. A grim precedent has been set, and without decisive action the liability crisis will grow worse and the six firms' collective liability burden, enormous as it is, will increase.

This potential long-term threat to the survival of the six firms has serious implications for the independent audit function, the financial reporting system and the capital markets. As a group, the six largest accounting firms audit all but a handful of the country's largest and most prominent public companies in every category:

- 494 of the *Fortune* 500 industrials;
- 97 of the *Fortune* 100 fastest growing companies;
- 99 of the *Fortune* 100 largest commercial banks;
- 92 of the top 100 defense contractors; and

- 195 of the 200 largest insurance companies.

In each of these categories, at least one of the six firms audits more than 20 percent of the companies. According to figures from *Who Audits America,* the six firms audit 90 percent (4,748 of 5,266) of the publicly-traded companies in the U.S. with annual sales of one million dollars or more.[3]

The detrimental effects on auditing, financial reporting, and our capital markets are already very much in evidence. They are a natural consequence of the risky and uncertain practice environment which the litigation epidemic has created not only for the six largest firms, but for the entire accounting profession.

The "Tort Tax"

One obvious effect is what the media has called "the tort tax"—that is, the increased cost of goods and services caused by runaway litigation. To quote SEC Chairman Richard C. Breeden, "Accounting firms, in particular, pay substantial and increasing costs to litigate and settle securities cases. At some point, these increasing litigation costs will increase the cost of audit services and tend to reduce access to our national securities markets."[4] If companies must pay higher costs for services provided not only by auditors, but by underwriters, attorneys and other frequent "deep pocket" defendants, it will be more expensive for them to raise needed capital. Opportunities for investors will be reduced, and U.S. businesses will be placed at a competitive disadvantage *vis-a-vis* companies in countries with more rational liability systems—virtually every other country in the world.

The Impact of Risk Reduction

The liability burden cannot be measured only in dollars and cents. Other effects are less easy to detect, but are no less costly. For example, groups targeted by frequent litigation now practice risk reduction as a matter of professional survival. Doctors, for instance, are avoiding such fields as gynecology and obstetrics. The result is a scarcity of practitioners in crucial specialties.

Accountants are also practicing risk reduction. The six largest firms are attempting to reduce the threat of litigation by avoiding what are considered high-risk audit clients and

---

3. *Who Audits America,* 25th Edition, Data Financial Press, Menlo Park, California, June 1991, pp. 393–396.
4. Letter from SEC Chairman Richard C. Breeden to Rep. John D. Dingell (D-MI), Chairman, Committee on Energy and Commerce, U.S. House of Representatives, May 5, 1992.

—Continued

Continued

even entire industries. High risk categories include financial institutions, insurance companies, and real estate investment firms. Also considered "high risk" are high technology and mid-size companies, and private companies making initial public offerings (IPOs). These companies are a ready target of baseless Rule 10b-5 suits because their stock prices tend to be volatile. Unfortunately, they are also the companies that most need quality professional services, are a key source of innovation and jobs, and play a crucial role in keeping this country competitive.

Risk avoidance is not confined to only the largest accounting firms. Smaller and medium-sized firms are dropping their public clients or abandoning their audit practices altogether. A recent survey of California CPA firms showed that only 53 percent are willing to undertake audit work. This creates serious problems for smaller companies (and their shareholders) that need viable alternatives to the major firms. Additionally, the survey showed that thirty-two percent of the reporting CPA firms are discontinuing audits in what they consider as high risk sectors. Another survey by Johnson & Higgins found that 56 percent of the mid-sized firms surveyed will not do business with clients involved in industries they consider high risk.

Impact on Professional Recruitment and Morale

Another troubling effect of the litigation explosion on the accounting profession, its clients and the public is one that cuts across all industries and services. The litigious practice environment is making it increasingly difficult to attract and retain the most qualified individuals at every level. The *Atlantic Monthly* has reported that fewer top business students are choosing to go to public accounting firms to do audit work because, among other things, they perceive it as risky.

It is likely that the most serious impact on recruitment and retention of qualified people is yet to be felt, since widespread media and public attention have only recently begun to focus on the accounting profession's liability plight. Recruiters from the six largest firms report that they are encountering more awareness, more questions and more apprehension about the liability risk on college campuses across the country. Transforming public accounting from a secure and respected career to one in which becoming a partner carries with it the threat of personal financial ruin, is no way to ensure the profession's ability to meet its responsibilities to investors and the public.

NEEDED REFORMS

To restore equity and sanity to the liability system and to provide reasonable assurance that the public accounting pro-

fession will be able to continue to meet its public obligations requires substantive reform of both federal and state liability laws.

Proportionate Liability

While other serious problems must also be addressed, the principal cause of unwarranted litigation against the profession is joint and several liability, which governs the vast majority of actions brought against accountants at the federal and state levels.

In arguing for an end to joint and several liability, the profession is in no way attempting to evade financial responsibility in cases where accountants are culpable. The profession is merely asking for fairness—the replacement of joint and several liability with a proportionate liability standard that assesses damages against each defendant based on that defendant's degree of fault. SEC Chairman Richard Breeden recently acknowledged that joint and several liability can lead to unfair results by forcing marginal defendants to settle even weak claims. He has also expressed support for reducing the coercive "effect of allegations of joint and several liability in cases of relatively remote connection by the party to the principal wrongdoing."[5]

Proportionate liability will help restore balance and equity to the liability system by discouraging specious suits and giving blameless defendants the incentive to prove their case in court rather than settle. By creating overwhelming pressure on innocent defendants to settle, joint and several liability gives plaintiffs' lawyers a strong incentive to bring as many cases as possible, without regard to the relative merits, include as many defendants as possible without regard to their degree of fault, and to settle these cases at a fraction of the alleged damages. Thus victims of real fraud receive no more (on average 5 to 15 percent of their alleged damages) than so-called "professional" plaintiffs and speculators trying to recoup investment losses. On the other hand, the lawyers bringing these suits typically receive 30 percent of the settlement plus expenses. If plaintiffs' lawyers were not able to use the threat of joint and several liability to compel innocent defendants to settle meritless cases, they would have to focus all of their efforts on meritorious claims. That, in turn, would result in more appropriate awards for true victims.

---

5. Letter from SEC Chairman Richard C. Breeden to Sen. Terry Sanford (D-NC), June 12, 1992.

—Continued

Continued

Current Reform Efforts

The six largest firms have joined with the AICPA and concerned businesses in calling for federal securities reform to curb unwarranted litigation brought under Rule 10b-5. Proposed remedies include replacing joint and several liability with proportionate liability and requiring that plaintiffs pay a prevailing defendant's legal fees if the court determines that the suit was meritless.

Curbing baseless Rule 10b-5 actions will, however, ease but not solve the liability problem. Of the total cases pending against the six largest firms in 1991, only 30 percent contained Rule 10b-5 claims. Of that 30 percent, less than 10 percent were exclusively 10b-5 claims.

The greatest liability exposure resides in the states. Reform of state liability laws affecting accountants is of critical importance to the future viability of the profession. The 10b-5 effort, if successful, will certainly serve as an important precedent for further reform. Beyond proportionate liability, reasonable limitations on punitive damages, as well as disincentives to filing meritless claims ought to be enacted. Reforms could be accomplished either through federal preemption or state-by-state modification of their statutes governing legal liability. The accounting profession will continue to participate in various state liability reform initiatives.

No less important is the need for the accounting profession to remove legislative, regulatory and professional restrictions on the forms of organization that may be used by accounting firms. Accountants must be free to practice in any form of organization permitted by state law, including limited liability organizations. The accounting profession is not seeking special treatment. Importantly, public accountants only seek to practice in forms of organization that are available to the vast majority of American businesses. Such changes will not relieve culpable individuals of legal responsibility for their own actions, but simply end the current inequity of full personal liability on all partners for all judgments against their firms resulting from the actions of others. The six largest firms will continue to aggressively pursue needed state-level liability reform.

The six largest firms are exploring all possible alternatives for reducing the threat that liability poses to their ability to meet their public obligations and to their survival. In this pursuit, the firms cannot support any legislative or regulatory proposal that increases the responsibilities of the profession unless these increased responsibilities are accompanied by meaningful and comprehensive liability reform. The firms will support initiatives at both the federal and state levels that will restore balance to the current system of justice.

August 6, 1992

J. Michael Cook
Chairman and Chief Executive Officer
Deloitte & Touche

Ray J. Groves
Chairman
Ernst & Young

Shaun F. O'Malley
Chairman and Senior Partner
Price Waterhouse

Eugene M. Freedman
Chairman
Coopers & Lybrand

Jon C. Madonna
Chairman and Chief Executive
KPMG Peat Marwick

Lawrence A. Weinbach
Managing Partner-Chief Executive
Arthur Andersen & Co., S.C.

Appendix: Trends in the Legal Liability of Accountants and Auditors and Legal Defenses Available

Leonard J. Brooks and Richard Leblanc
University of Toronto, 1994

TRENDS IN THE LEGAL LIABILITY OF ACCOUNTANTS AND AUDITORS

Contract experts contend that stakeholders (including employees, suppliers, customers, creditors) and their interests are protected adequately through explicit and implicit contracts with a business enterprise. However, there has been a progressive trend over the last 30 years, reflected through changes in the law, that has been predicated on the notion that contracts may be insufficient to protect the interests of certain stakeholders who rely upon the conduct of and statements made by governors of a corporation and the professionals associated with it. Public and stakeholder knowledge, expectations, and sophistication have been heightened, and the law has changed to reflect a third-party duty (foreseeable) owed beyond contract by virtue of the position held within the company and the standard of conduct expected of a professional such as an auditor or an accountant. A precedent-setting Canadian case, *R v. Bata Industries Ltd.* (1992), 70 C.C.C. (3d) 394 (Ont. Prov. Ct.), established that the courts will in fact pierce the corporate veil to determine the controlling mind and, more particularly, not merely what someone in a position of authority, such as a director, did do or know but what that director could or ought to have done or known under the circumstances.

This broadening trend from that of contractual privity to a duty owed to foreseeable stakeholders is reflected in the common law for auditors and accountants. Both auditors and accountants are now being sued by stakeholders without privity of contract, such as investors, shareholders, suppliers, and creditors. This is sometimes referred to as a "foreseeability" or "fairness" principle and is actually one part of a test of negligence that courts will use in determining whether an accountant or auditor's conduct has been negligent.

In very general legal terms, in order to establish auditor or accountant negligence, a duty of care must be owed by virtue of the relationship that is recognized in law; that standard of care must have been breached; that breadth of duty owed must have caused in a proximate and not remote way the actual damage to a third party (plaintiff) who relied to its detriment on the audit statements; the resultant damage must have been reasonably foreseeable (hence the "foreseeability" test) and, lastly, the conduct of the plaintiff must not be such so as to bar recovery; that is, the plaintiff must not have voluntarily assumed the risk, must not have contributed to the negligence and must be able to show that he or she attempted to mitigate damages.

A significant increase in auditor and accountant litigation has occurred as a result of this trend in the law that broadens standing among third-party stakeholders, who may sue auditors for negligence if the above requirements are met. So now, in addition to the auditor or accountant being bound by contract and fiduciary duty of trust to the client, he or she must, as a result of the above-mentioned foreseeability or fairness principle, assume additional duties to third-party stakeholders.

The trend along the continuum between contractual privity on one end and stakeholder fairness and foreseeability on the other can be demonstrated by a review of how the common law has developed in Canada, England, and the U.S. on this issue. Both the high courts in Canada and England have spoken on the foreseeability test of auditor liability, suggesting that the U.S. Supreme Court may soon speak on this point as well.

The leading Canadian case on auditor liability to foreseeable parties is *Haig v. Bamford et.al.* (1976) 72 D.L.R. (3d) 68. The Supreme Court of Canada held in *Haig* that where an accountant has negligently prepared financial statements and a third party relies on them to his or her detriment, a duty of care in an action for negligent misstatement will arise in the following circumstances:

(i) the accountant knows that it will be shown to a member of a limited class of which the plaintiff is a member and which the accountant actually knows will use and rely on the statements;

(ii) the statements have been prepared primarily for guidance of that limited class and in respect of a specific class of transactions for the very purpose for which the plaintiff did in fact rely on them;

(iii) the fact that the accountant did not know the identity of the plaintiff is not material as long as the accountant was aware that the person for whose immediate benefit they were prepared intended to supply the statements to members of the very limited class of which the plaintiff is a member.

—Continued

Continued

In short, *Haig v. Bamford* stands for the proposition that an accountant will be found liable to a third party where the accountant had actual knowledge of the limited class of which the third party is a member and that third party will use and rely on the statement.

In England, in a landmark case establishing the modern role governing liability for professional advisers whose negligence gives rise to economic loss, the House of Lords in *Hedley Byrne & Co. Ltd. v. Heller & Partners Ltd.* [1964] A.C. 562 (H.L.) held that a professional adviser has an implied duty of care in making an oral or written statement to another person whom he or she knows or should know will rely on it in making a decision with economic consequences.

The "foreseeability" test in the above-mentioned Canadian *Haig* case was narrowed recently in *Caparo Industries plc. v. Pickman et. al.* [1991] 2 W.L.R. 358 (H.L.). Although an English case, *Caparo,* which came down from the House of Lords, is of precedential value to Canadian jurisprudence and has been followed in both Ontario and British Columbia courts. *Caparo* narrows the scope of the foreseeability doctrine by focusing on whether the auditor knew the "purpose" for which the third party was to use the financial statements. The *Caparo* foreseeability test is as follows: A duty is said to arise only where the auditor knew the *purpose* for which the financial statements were to be used by the person relying on them and knew that the statements would be communicated to that person either as an individual or as a member of an identifiable class, specifically in connection with a particular transaction or a transaction of a particular kind. The duty extends only to the particular transaction for which the accountants knew their accounts were to be used. Moreover, the advisee must reasonably suppose that he or she was entitled to rely on the advice or information communicated for the very purpose for which it was required. No duty arises in respect of statements put into general circulation and relied on by strangers to the maker of the statement for a purpose that the maker had no reason to anticipate, such as non-shareholders contemplating investment in a company.

Therefore, although both Canada and England have moved from contractual privity to a stakeholder foreseeability test of auditor liability, the British decision *Caparo* restricts *Haig*'s primary emphasis on foreseeability to that of knowledge of purpose. In other words, an auditor may be liable to a foreseeable third party under *Haig* where the accountant had actual knowledge of the third party and that party's intention to rely on the statement. An auditor may be liable to a foreseeable third party under *Caparo* where the accountant knew the purpose for which the third party was to rely upon and use the financial statements. The point is that the trend in auditor and accountant liability toward being liable

to foreseeable third parties has been established in both Canada and England and has resulted in increased litigation for auditing firms.

Unlike Canada and England, the United States Supreme Court has never ruled on the duty owed to foreseeable third parties. In fact, state supreme courts are split between considering contractual privity (often termed *intended beneficiary)* versus foreseeable third parties as the required grounds for suit. Two cases are noteworthy here. *Ultramares Corporation v. Touche* 174 N.E. 441 (1931) stands for the proposition that experts who prepare statements or reports for a third party who is not a client will not be held accountable in negligence for any misstatement or misreport to that third party (nonclient). In other words, an immediate legal relationship (contractual privity) must exist between the parties in order for one to be liable in negligence to another.

The trend away from this contractual privity requirement in *Ultramares* to that of foreseeability was apparent in *Credit Alliance Corp. v. Arthur Andersen & Co.* 493 N.Y.S. 2d 435 (1985). In this case, the court reaffirmed yet relaxed the *Ultramares* principal. The court said that a legal relationship approaching that of a contract must exist for an auditor to be held liable in negligence to a nonclient. The court, however, stated that an auditor will meet the "contractual privity" test where the auditor was aware that his or her statement would be used for a particular purpose and that a known party was intended to rely on it. In addition, some evidence must exist demonstrating a relationship between the auditor and the nonclient third party and demonstrating that the auditor knew that nonclient third party was relying on the auditor's statement.

Despite the fact that the trend from contractual privity to foreseeable third parties is still not being applied uniformly in the U.S., the foreseeability doctrine for auditors and accountants is now good law in both Canada and England as the high courts have spoken. The result of this trend has been "joint and several" liability exposure by auditors and accountants to third-party plaintiffs. Joint and several liability means that all codefendants, including the auditors, must account for all damages. If the client is insolvent, the audit firm's and its partners' assets are exposed regardless of the degree of fault. This is often the case as lawyers are trained to sue "deep pockets"—those entities believed to be most able to bear the burden of the loss, such as an accounting firm.

LEGAL DEFENSES AVAILABLE

This litigation exposure has had a chilling effect on the auditing profession and has resulted in a reluctance to pur-

—Continued

Continued

sue risky engagements such as environmental or social audits; exorbitant legal bills; increases in professional liability insurance premiums; increasing opportunity costs of the litigation; and adverse publicity for the profession as a whole.

Nevertheless, a number of defensive and proactive measures can be offered to auditors and accountants to limit their liability to foreseeable third-party litigants. These defenses include:

1. Due diligence and due care
2. Contributory negligence
3. Engagement letter provisions
4. Documentation and recordkeeping
5. Legal counsel

A cursory overview of each of these will be provided.

1. Due Diligence and Due Care

The defense of due diligence exists both in common law and statute. Due diligence entails a thorough and proper examination (reasonable investigation) of all relevant financial records prior to the rendering of an opinion, advice, or conclusion. Due care includes the application of auditing and financial analysis models and techniques to the existing subject matter. Due diligence is the principal means by which an accountant or auditor can defend against a negligence claim by a client for an alleged breach of a duty of care and skill.

In common law, there is no definitive law defining the standard of due diligence for an auditor or accountant. Each case is fact-dependent. However, due diligence for an auditor is generally meant to be understood as requiring an auditor to make a complete examination of the matter to be audited before issuing any report or giving any advice.

To illustrate the judicial reasoning in this due diligence defense and the degree to which the courts will intervene in applying the law to the facts, the recent precedent-setting Canadian case *R. v. Bata Industries* (1992), 70 C.C.C. (3d) 394 (Ont. Prov. Ct.) hinged on the due diligence defense. Although the conduct involved applied to a company director, the judicial reasoning and degree of intervention illustrates profoundly the leaning of the courts in evaluating the due diligence defense; this reasoning could and likely would be as applicable in evaluating whether an auditor acted with due diligence. At page 427, Justice Ormstrom, addressed effectively the issue of due diligence:

I ask myself the following questions in assessing the defense of due diligence:

(a) Did the board of directors establish a pollution prevention "system" as indicated in *Regina v. Sault Ste. Marie,*

i.e., Was there supervision or inspection? Was there improvement in business methods? Did he exhort those he controlled or influenced?

(b) Did each director ensure that the corporate officers have been instructed to set up a system sufficient within the terms and practices of its industry of ensuring compliance with environmental laws, to ensure that the officers report back periodically to the board on the operation of the system, and to ensure that the officers are instructed to report any substantial non-compliance to the board in a timely manner?

I reminded myself that:

(c) The directors are responsible for reviewing the environmental compliance reports provided by the officers of the corporation but are justified in placing reasonable reliance on reports provided to them by corporate officers, consultants, counsel or other informed parties.

(d) The directors should substantiate that the officers are promptly addressing environmental concerns brought to their attention by government agencies or other concerned parties including shareholders.

(e) The directors should be aware of the standards of their industry and other industries which deal with similar environmental pollutants or risks.

(f) The directors should immediately and personally react when they have noticed the system has failed.

Within this general profile and dependent upon the nature and structure of the corporate activity, one would hope to find remedial and contingency plans for spills, a system of ongoing environmental audit, training programs, sufficient authority to act and other indices of a proactive environmental policy.

Applying the preceding judicial reasoning in the due diligence defense, auditors as well may limit their liability by adopting proactive and defensive measures to support a due diligence defense. These measures may include but are not limited to:

- educating and communicating with personnel as to the technical, regulatory, legal, and ethical standards required by the profession and the firm and having reporting procedures implemented to ensure that this occurs;

- ensuring that all personnel are properly trained and supervised and having reporting and information systems to facilitate prompt identification and bottom-up flow of difficulties, problems;

—Continued

Continued

- maintaining confidentiality and independence, and avoiding conflicts of interest and judgment; conforming with one's fiduciary duty of trust to the client;
- understanding industry standards and familiarity with the client's business and reputation for integrity;
- obtaining the necessary engagement letter provisions;
- proper documenting and record keeping; and
- supporting senior managing partners and partners and rewarding and compensating the above-desired behaviors.

2. Contributory Negligence

Contributory negligence exists as a defense for the auditor in a negligence claim for a breach of a duty of care and skill. The auditor, in using this defense, submits to the court that the client (often company management) contributed to the breach through an act (or acts) of commission or omission. In other words, the client did or failed to do something, and this contributed to the loss. The contributory negligence defense by auditors exists notwithstanding the policy argument against it; namely, that the auditor should not be permitted to use this defense to reduce liability, for doing so would defeat the purpose of having an auditor act as a check on the conduct of managers of a company through the analysis of financial documents.

3. Engagement Letter Provisions

An engagement letter is an agreement between the auditor and the client identifying whether the audit and/or other services will be provided, due dates, and fees. To mitigate liability and potential litigation, auditors should attempt to include provisions in the engagement letter that:

- narrow the scope of services to be provided in specific, rather than broad, general, terms. This limits liability to failure to perform the terms of the engagement letter.
- indemnify the auditor for third-party claims arising from services rendered by the auditor to the client in accordance with the engagement letter.
- enable the auditor to modify or withdraw the opinion or conclusion should circumstances warrant, such as, for example, the subsequent discovery of a material misstatement.
- permit liability claims against the auditor to be released completely should litigation claims against the indemnitor be settled.
- enable the auditor to participate fully in the preparation of a public offering document insofar as his or her opinion

or conclusion is used or summarized in the final document. This participation would include the right to limit and qualify the scope of the opinion or conclusion prior to it reaching public investors via the public disclosure documents and/or the disclaiming of any fiduciary or agency relationship with shareholders should a public offering not be contemplated but the auditor's opinion or conclusion still used.

4. Documentation and Recordkeeping

Due diligence, due care, and a reasonable investigation can be more effectively demonstrated to a court by an auditor during litigation when he or she has a documentary or computerized record of all working papers, tests, and procedures performed that preceded the opinion or report and all written communications with the client. Also, the auditor should not agree in advance to release original copies of confidential client information to third parties without first seeking legal counsel, for retaining copies of the original document for record-keeping purposes could aid in litigation defense and regulatory purposes.

5. Legal Counsel

Auditors and accountants should not wait to be sued but should take a proactive approach and seek legal counsel concerning their legal rights, exposure, and obligations. Competent and experienced legal counsel educates, communicates, limits exposure to client and third-party liability and costly litigation, and also aids in establishing due diligence evidence should litigation commence. More particularly, auditors should seek legal counsel in preparing and reviewing engagement and representation letters; developing the due diligence reviews; and reviewing the legal implications impacting and flowing from preliminary and final versions of the auditor's opinions and conclusions.

A REVIEW OF CASES

Ultramares Corporation v. Touche 174 N.E. 441 (1931)

In *Ultramares*, the creditors of the insolvent Ultramares corporation sued the accountants for negligence in relying on the financial statements to their detriment. Particularly the accounts receivable had been inflated $700,000. The New York Court of Appeals held that the accountants had been negligent but were not liable to the creditors because of privity of contract. Only the contracting parties could sue the accountant for negligent services. At page 444, Justice Cardozo held that "to hold the maker of the statement to be

—Continued

Continued

under a duty of care in respect of the accuracy of statement . . . is to find liability in an indeterminate amount for an indeterminate time to an indeterminate class." This case stands for the proposition that contractual privity is required in order to sue an accountant or auditor in negligence for any misstatement or misreport.

Hedley Byrne & Co. Ltd. v. Heller & Partners Ltd. [1964] A.C. 562 (H.L.)

In *Hedley Byrne,* the National Provincial Bank telephoned and wrote to Heller & Partners on behalf of Hedley Byrne to find out whether Easipower Ltd., a customer of Heller & Partners, was of sound financial position and thus a company with which Hedley Byrne would want to do business. Heller & Partners, disclaiming all responsibility to both inquiries by National Provincial Bank, said Easipower Ltd. was of sound financial shape. Hedley Byrne, in reliance on those statements, entered into a contract with Easipower Ltd., who subsequently thereafter sought liquidation.

The House of Lords, in deciding that Heller & Partners Ltd. would have been liable except for the disclaimer established the modern role governing liability for professional advisers whose negligence gives rise to economic loss. A professional adviser has an implied duty of care in making an oral or written statement to another person whom he or she knows or should know will rely on it in making a decision with economic consequences.

Haig v. Bamford et. al. (1976) 72 D.L.R. (3d) 68

In *Haig,* the Saskatchewan Development Corporation agreed to advance a $20,000 loan to a financially troubled company in part based on the conditional production of satisfactory audited financial statements. The company engaged Bamford's accountants to prepare the statements. The accountants knew that the statements would be used by Saskatchewan Development Corporation. Relying on the accountant's information, Saskatchewan Development Corporation advanced $20,000 to the company. Later investigation disclosed that a $28,000 prepayment on two uncompleted contracts had been treated as if the contracts had been completed, thereby showing a profit instead of a loss, and the accountants failed to spot the error. The court held that where an accountant has negligently prepared financial statements and a third party relies on them to his or her detriment, a duty of care in an action for negligent misstatement will arise in the following circumstances: The accountant knows that it will be shown to a member of a limited class of which the plaintiff is a member and which the accountant actually knows will use and rely on the statements; the state-

ments have been prepared primarily for guidance of that limited class and in respect of a specific class of transactions for the very purpose for which the plaintiff did in fact rely on them; the fact that the accountant did not know the identity of the plaintiff is not material as long as the accountant was aware that the person for whose immediate benefit they were prepared intended to supply the statements to members of the very limited class of which the plaintiff is a member.

Credit Alliance Corp. v. Arthur Andersen & Co. 493 N.Y.S. 2d 435 (1985)

The contractual privity requirement in *Ultramares* was broadened somewhat by the same New York Court of Appeals, but has not approached in scope the stakeholder foreseeability test of *Haig* in Canada and *Caparo* in England. The court held that in order for a relationship to approach that of privity the auditor must have been aware that the financial statement would be used for a particular purpose by a party known to the auditor and the auditor must have had subjective knowledge that the third party had intended to rely upon the statement. Also, evidence, such as the auditor's conduct, must be presented demonstrating the above requirements and the third-party plaintiff carries this burden.

Caparo Industries plc. v. Pickman et. al. [1991] 2 W.L.R. 358 (H.L.)

Caparo, in its takeover of Fidelity plc, had Touche Ross & Co. audit the financial statements of Fidelity. Caparo later alleged that its purchase of shares and subsequent takeover were made in reliance on the accounts which they claimed were misleading and inaccurate in that they showed a pre-tax profit of £1.3 million instead of a loss of £400,000. Caparo sued Touche Ross for negligence, maintaining that Touche Ross owed them a duty of care as shareholders and potential investors with respect to the audit and certification of the accounts.

The House of Lords decided that Touche Ross owed no duty of care to Caparo either as a potential investor before it was registered or as a shareholder thereafter for the following reasons:

> While there is no general principle that will determine the existence and scope of a duty of care in all cases, in order for a duty of care to arise, there must be: the harm said to result from the breach of duty must have been reasonably foreseeable; there must be a relationship of sufficient "proximity" between the party said to owe the duty and the party to whom it is said to be owed; and the situ-

—*Continued*

Continued

ation must be one in which, on policy grounds, the court considers it fair, just and reasonable that the law should impose a duty of a given scope on the part of one party for the benefit of the other.

In the case of negligent misstatements made by such professional advisers as accountants, a relationship of proximity sufficient to give rise to a duty of care typically arises where the advice is required for a purpose which is made known to the advisor when the advice was given; the adviser knows that his or her advice will be communicated to the advisee, either specifically or as a member of an ascertainable class in order that it should be used by the advisee for that purpose; it is known that advice so communicated is likely to be acted upon for that purpose without independent inquiry; and it is so acted upon by the advisee to his or her detriment.

The duty extends only to the particular transaction for which the accountants knew their accounts were to be used. Moreover, the advisee must reasonably suppose that he or she was entitled to rely on the advice or information communicated for the very purpose for which it was required. No duty arises with respect to statements put into general circulation and relied on by strangers to the maker of the statement for a purpose which the maker had no reason to anticipate, such as a nonshareholder contemplating investment in a company.

PART *II*

Ethical Decision Making

Introduction

The two chapters of Part 1 have provided an awareness of ethical issues business and professionals are facing which are already shaping the future of both. Within the ethics environment, the appropriate role for a professional accountant was examined and the priorities, judgments, and values that provide the basis for decisions and ethical choices were addressed.

Part 2 extends the awareness developed in Part 1 into an understanding of the techniques of ethical decision making. Chapter 3 presents information on both professional and corporate/employer codes of conduct, which serve as a first source of guidance when making decisions. Because many issues are not covered explicitly in these codes, Chapter 4 provides several practical approaches to making ethical decisions.

CHAPTER 3 Codes of Conduct

CHAPTER 4 Approaches to Ethical Decision Making

3

CHAPTER

Codes of Conduct

Purpose of the Chapter

As the business environment in which professional accountants function continues to evolve at rapid rates, the possibilities for making ethical mistakes multiply and put a premium on the development of sound processes for ethical decision making. The first source of guidance for making ethical decisions to which professional accountants should turn is the code of conduct of their professional society, and then to the code of their employer, firm, or corporation. So important have these codes become, they are now regarded as an important part of the internal control system of the firms and corporations. In order to use these codes effectively, a professional accountant should understand why and how they are constructed, and what their pitfalls are. Codes of conduct, however, cannot be exhaustive, so many issues may not be covered fully or satisfactorily. Because of this, several of these codes are examined here in order to develop a workable, comprehensive understanding so that professional accountants can play a leadership role in the assessment, revision, implementation, monitoring, and operation of effective codes of conduct.

Index of Chapter Headings

Introduction

When an individual faces an ethical dilemma, or any decision that requires the assessment of tradeoffs between persons likely to be affected, the decision maker's values and judgment will have to be employed. When that decision maker is also a member of a profession, and/or a member or employee of a firm or corporation, the individual's values and judgment should reflect the ethical culture and expectations of the profession, firm, or organization. In order to guide their members or employees, professions and organizations have developed explicit codes of conduct to be consulted as the first step in making ethical decisions. The failure to make ethical decisions can stem from lack of understanding of these codes, inability to interpret and extend them or the principles involved, or flaws in their construction.

Stake and Role of Professional Accountants

Concern for the implementation and operation of an effective corporate code of conduct may seem tangential to the role and responsibility of a professional accountant. However, if the employees of the company engage in unethical behavior, the company is put at risk and the accounting summaries of its activities are likely to be misstated. In fact, the ethical fabric of a company is essential to the internal control system that underlies the reporting and other functions of the enterprise. *Nothing could therefore be more fundamental to the interests of professional accountants than the ethical culture spawned by properly implemented codes of conduct.* Consequently, the implementation and operation of ethical codes should be well within the purview of the professional accountant.

The importance of developing an effective code of conduct and its place within the system of internal control was recognized by the Treadway Commission (1987), which recommended that:

> Public companies should develop and enforce written codes of corporate conduct. Codes of conduct should foster a strong ethical climate and open channels of communication to help protect against fraudulent financial reporting. As part of its ongoing oversight of the effectiveness of internal controls, a company's audit committee should review annually the program that management establishes to monitor compliance with the code. (p. 35)

In response, in 1988 the American Institute of Certified Public Accountants (AICPA) issued two Statements of Auditing Standards (SAS), SAS 55 and 60, which incorporated the review of codes of conduct into the review of internal controls—the process by which a corporation seeks to ensure the safekeeping of its assets, the propriety of its activities, and the proper recording of its transactions. Canadian accountants should observe a similar, although less authoritative, recommendation in the form of an Auditing and Related Service Guideline (*CICA Handbook* "Communication with Audit Committees (or Equivalent)", August 1991). Consequently, auditors are required to report material weaknesses caused in internal control by faulty codes of conduct or code compliance, to the audit committee of the organization under audit. Failure to do so effectively could result in legal liability for the auditor.

In both the U.S. and Canada, directors, officers, and employees are particularly interested in effective codes of conduct because of their value in demonstrating "due diligence" in the governance of corporate affairs. This defense is essential to limiting the legal liability of those governing corporations, as well as those individuals who are carrying out what they perceive to be their instructions. Again, the capacity of auditors and accountants to improve the ethical performance of their clients or employers and to reduce their potential legal liability requires an understanding of the reasons for, content, and potential of codes of conduct, both professional and corporate.

Professional Accounting Environment in the U.S. and Canada

The analysis that follows takes into account the various professional accounting organizations found in the U.S. and Canada. Together with standard setters, regulators, the courts, politicians, financial markets, and the public, they create the body of expectations to which professional accountants must respond. These expectations may take the form of written standards, commonly understood standards of practice, generally accepted accounting principles, or even research studies and articles that shed light on a subject. No one organization has a monopoly on the creation of the environment of expectations that a professional accountant in the U.S. or Canada should meet.

There are five national and international professional accounting organizations operating in North America, plus their subsets in each U.S. state or Canadian province (e.g., The Institute of Chartered Accountants of Ontario or a State Society of Certified Public Accountants). They and their functional and geographic mandates are set out in Table 3.1.

The regulatory frameworks of each country occupy an important place in the creation of the professional accounting environment because written stan-

TABLE 3.1

NATIONAL AND INTERNATIONAL ACCOUNTING ORGANIZATIONS OPERATING IN NORTH AMERICA

NAME	DESIG-NATION	PRIME MANDATE(S)	LOCATION
American Institute of Certified Public Accountants (AICPA)	CPA	Auditing, management accounting	U.S. & some Canadian provinces
Institute of Management Accountants (IMA) [Formerly National Association of Accountants (NAA)]	CMA	Management accounting	U.S.
Canadian Institute of Chartered Accountants (CICA)	CA	Auditing, management accounting	Canada
Society of Management Accountants of Canada (SMAC)	CMA	Management accounting	Canada
Certified General Accountants Association of Canada (CGAAC)	CGA	Management accounting, auditing	Canada, some provinces

dards usually flow from them. Table 3.2 provides an overview of the contributions of important organizations to the environment.

It is important to note that although a national body can develop a code of conduct, in all cases the local state or provincial subset organization controls its own members by enacting its own code of conduct (using the national code as a guide, but not always adopting all of its provisions), and policing and disciplining its members. Consequently, the standard of ethical expectation varies somewhat from jurisdiction to jurisdiction, and from organization to organization. Fortunately, the basic principles of ethical conduct apply to all organizations, and the remainder of the analysis in this book will focus on these general principles.

Professional Codes of Conduct

PURPOSE AND FRAMEWORK

Professional codes of conduct are designed to provide guidance about the conduct expected of members in order that the services offered will be of acceptable quality and the reputation of the profession will not be sullied. If that reputation is sullied, some aspect of a fiduciary relationship has been breached and a service has not been performed in a professional manner. Alternatively,

TABLE 3.2

CONTRIBUTIONS TO THE NORTH AMERICAN REGULATORY FRAMEWORK FOR PROFESSIONAL ACCOUNTANTS

ORGANIZATION	CONTRIBUTION GOVERNING ORGANIZATION'S MEMBERS/USERS
AICPA	Statements of Auditing Standards (SAS), research studies, journal articles, code of conduct
IMA	Statements of accounting practice, research studies, journal articles, code of conduct
Financial Accounting Standards Board (FASB)	Financial Accounting Standards (FAS)
Securities & Exchange Commission (SEC)	Regulation with respect to disclosure for companies raising funds in the U.S.
CICA	Accounting and auditing standards in Canada, research studies, journal articles' Codes of Conduct originate from Provincial Institutes.
SMAC	Statements of accounting practice, research studies, journal articles, code of conduct
CGAAC	Statements of accounting practice, research studies, journal articles, code of conduct
Ontario Securities Commission (OSC)	Regulations related to financial disclosure in Canada's principal securities market (Ontario), whose regulations are accepted by the SEC
U.S. and Canadian courts	Common law decisions affecting legal liability

it may mean that a member has violated the rules of society in some way so as to bring the profession's name into disrepute and thereby damage the public trust required for its members to serve other clients effectively.

To be effective, codes of conduct need to blend fundamental principles with a limited number of specific rules. If a code were drafted to cover all possible problems, it would be extremely voluminous—probably so voluminous that few members would spend the time required to become familiar with it and to stay abreast of the constant flow of additions. With practicality in mind, most professional codes have evolved to the framework outlined in Table 3.3.

FUNDAMENTAL PRINCIPLES AND STANDARDS

The fundamental principles and standards described in Table 3.4 are found in most codes.

The maintenance of the *good reputation* of the profession is fundamental to the ability of the profession to continue to enjoy its current rights and privileges, including autonomy in the discipline of its members, the setting of accounting standards, and the recognition by the public and government that new professional organizations need not be created to serve the *public interest.* The phrase *at all times* is significant because the public will view any serious transgression of a professional accountant, including those outside business or professional activity, as a black mark against the profession as a whole. Consequently, if a professional accountant is convicted of a criminal offense or fraud, his or her certification is usually revoked.

Maintenance of standards of care is also imperative to ensure proper service to clients and the public interest. *Integrity,* or *objectivity,* and honesty in the preparation of reports, choice of accounting options, or interpretation of accounting data will ensure that neither the client nor the public will be misled. Sometimes reports or opinions can lack integrity if the professional involved has failed to maintain *independence* from one of the persons likely to benefit or be harmed by the report, and this causes the professional to bias the report, decisions, or interpretations toward the favored party.

Charges of bias are very hard to refute, so professionals are often admonished to avoid any situation or relationship that might lead to the *perception* of bias. This is why, even though in the past many professionals have served successfully as bookkeeper, auditor, shareholder, and director of an organization, modern codes of conduct recommend against situations involving such apparent conflicts of interest. The prospect of an auditor misstating a report for his or her own gain, or that of fellow shareholders, was judged to be too tempting a prospect to allow. Similar reasoning has led to the introduction of the sepa-

TABLE 3.3

TYPICAL FRAMEWORK FOR A CODE OF CONDUCT FOR PROFESSIONAL ACCOUNTANTS

- Introduction and purpose
- Fundamental principles and standards
- General rules
- Specific rules
- Discipline
- Interpretations of rules

PART II   Ethical Decision Making

TABLE 3.4

FUNDAMENTAL PRINCIPLES IN
CODES OF CONDUCT FOR
PROFESSIONAL ACCOUNTANTS

Members should:

- at all times maintain the good reputation of the profession and its ability to serve the public interest
- perform with:
  - integrity
  - objectivity
  - independence
  - professional competence
  - due care
  - confidentiality
- not be associated with any misleading information or misrepresentation

ration of duties within an organization and, wherever possible, between the bookkeeping and audit functions. In simplistic terms, from the profession's viewpoint, why leave freshly baked cookies on the open windowsill to cool if the temptation presented may someday lead someone to sneak one? It is interesting to speculate as to who is more at fault—the person leaving the cookies in a vulnerable position, or the person succumbing to temptation.

It would be impossible for a professional accountant to offer services at the level a client or employer has the right to expect if the professional has failed to maintain *competence* with regard to current standards of disclosure, accounting treatment, and business practice. However, beyond understanding and developing a facility with current standards, a professional accountant must act with due care.

The exercise of *due care* involves an understanding of the appropriate levels and limits of care expected of a professional accountant in different circumstances. For example, a professional accountant is not expected to be all-knowing and all-seeing with regard to incidents of fraud which occur at a client or employer. However, if the professional becomes aware of these, there are expectations for follow-up and reporting that need to be observed. Similarly, audit procedures need not specifically cover 100 percent of an organization's transactions; judgment sampling and statistical sampling may be applied to reduce specific coverage to a level deemed appropriate according to professional judgment. That level will be set with reference to what other professionals regard as providing sufficient evidence for the forming of an opinion based on due care. In a court of law expert witnesses will be called to testify as to what levels of judgment represent the exercise of due care.

Confidentiality is fundamental to fiduciary relationships from several perspectives. First, these relationships are very important to the well-being of the client or employer. They usually involve personal information, or information that is critical to the activities of the organization and that would result in some loss of privacy or of competitive advantage if it were disclosed to specific individuals or to the public. Advice, for example, about a business transaction, could be used in bargaining if it were known by the other party to the transaction. Second, it is not beyond the realm of possibility that such information could be used for the professional's own purposes for profit, or to gain some other advantage. Finally, if it were suspected that a professional accountant were not going to maintain a client's or employer's information in confidence, it is unlikely that full information would be shared. This would put an audit and other services on a faulty foundation, which would lead to substandard and potentially misleading opinions and reports.

Keeping information confidential should not, however, lead to illegal behavior. For example, codes of conduct usually specify that a professional accountant *should not be associated with any misrepresentations*. If the professional cannot induce revision by persuasion, then he or she is usually required by the code to disassociate himself or herself from the misrepresentation by resignation. Professional accountants are also usually prohibited from disclosing the misrepresentation except subject to a disciplinary hearing or in a court of law. That this resignation and nondisclosure of a misrepresentation benefits neither the public, the profession, or the professional is a matter that should be redressed in revisions to professional codes by measures suggested in Brooks (1989).

RULES: GENERAL AND SPECIFIC

Professional accountants are expected to apply the fundamental principles outlined above in order to protect the public interest as well as the interest of the profession and of the members themselves. There are, however, matters that lend themselves to coverage in general or specific rules such as proper relations between members, or the organization and conduct of a professional practice. The appropriate form of advertising would be one of the administrative matters covered in rules rather than fundamental principles.

DISCIPLINE

Customarily, codes of conduct provide information about the operation of the discipline process of the professional association. Members should know how and to whom to report a concern over conduct, what the process is for investigation of the concern, what the hearing process entails, how decisions will be made, what fines and other penalties can be imposed, how results will be reported, and how appeals will be considered. Unless these facts, together with some examples of sanctions levied, are known, a professional is likely to misjudge how important the ethical conduct of the members is to the profession and to society.

Sanctions for unethical behavior can include any of the items listed in Table 3.5.

Not all of the sanctions identified above are levied by each professional accounting body. In fact, in Canada, although efforts are now underway to rectify the oversight, the professional bodies have no means of disciplining the accounting firms for the errors of their partners and employees.

Usually the discipline process begins with a complaint being lodged with the professional organization about the ethical conduct of a member or firm. Alternately, the conviction on a legal charge of consequence (fraud, etc.) may trigger the discipline process. The complaint or legal charge is investigated by staff, and a decision is made whether or not to charge the accused. Charging the accused necessitates a hearing to determine guilt or innocence, a process that can be quite cumbersome. The hearing can be held in camera (the public are not permitted to attend) or in public. It can involve lawyers for the plaintiff (the staff of the professional body) and defendant, and a tribunal or panel,

TABLE 3.5

POSSIBLE SANCTIONS FOR
UNETHICAL BEHAVIOR BY
PROFESSIONAL ACCOUNTANTS
UNDER PROFESSIONAL CODES
OF CONDUCT AND
REGULATORY AUTHORITIES

SOURCE: Distillation of discipline cases from
the professional accounting and regulatory
bodies in the U.S. and Canada (see Table 3.2).

	LEVIABLE ON THE:	
	Professional	Accounting Firm
Caution	Yes	Yes
Reprimand	Yes	Yes
Review by peer	Yes	Yes
Requirement to complete courses	Yes	No
Suspension:		
• for a specified period	Yes	No
• for an indefinite period	Yes	No
• until specific requirements are completed	Yes	No
• from appearing before regulatory bodies (SEC, OSC)	Yes	Yes
Expulsion from membership	Yes	No
Compensation for damage	Yes	Yes
Fine	Yes	Yes
Costs of hearing	Yes	Yes
Ancillary orders		
• for Community work	Yes	No
• for Financial support	Yes	Yes

which often includes an outside layperson to ensure that proper procedures are followed and the public interest is served, to hear the case.

The cost of the hearing can be substantial in terms of both out-of-pocket costs and lost work time that could be billed to clients. In the end, the largest cost involved is the lost reputation of the guilty accountant. In the auditors' world credibility is what professionals strive the most to protect as it is evidence of the value of their audit opinion. Without it, their audit services would be worthless.

When a professional accountant or firm is found guilty of a charge, the details of the case are made public, usually in the newsletter of the professional organization. It is essential that full details be published to warn other members of ethical problems and the sanctions that they might encounter, and to preserve the profession's upstanding image as a profession worthy of policing itself (i.e., worthy of the trust of the public).

A guilty professional can look forward to more than one sanction. For example, he or she might receive a reprimand, a fine, and the bill for costs of the lawyers and hearing. Alternatively, the penalty might be a suspension from membership until a set of required courses are completed and restitution for damages and costs is made. If the professional appears to need supervision for awhile, the penalty might include the review of all work by a peer.

Fines can range in size from less than $1,000 to more than the damage done to the injured party. The amounts are growing over time. If the penalty involves the prohibition from practice, or from appearance before the securities commissions, the lost revenue can be very large indeed. The inability to appear before the SEC appears to be a most powerful sanction to use against accounting firms.

INTERPRETATIONS OF RULES

Sometimes when the profession finds that a concern arises in the profession due to a debate over the proper application of a rule, a clarification is issued in the form of an interpretation. These interpretations often appear as an addendum or appendix to the code, which can be modified as circumstances require.

MOTIVATION FOR RECENT CHANGES IN PROFESSIONAL CODES

The Metcalf investigation, the Treadway Commission (1987), and the Macdonald Commission (1988) were public or quasi-public processes of investigation designed to explore how the members of the AICPA and the CICA were serving the public interest. These investigations would not have been necessary unless some doubt existed about the service being provided. Although there were some specific problems that triggered the formation of these commissions, concern over the credibility of financial reporting was essentially responsible. From the perspective of the accounting profession this manifested itself as an *expectations gap* "between what the public expects or needs and the auditors can reasonably expect to accomplish" (Macdonald Commission, 1988, iii).

In response to the Treadway Commission, a committee of the AICPA was formed, (see page 155) under the chairmanship of G. W. Anderson, with the goal of redesigning the AICPA Professional Standards: Ethics and Bylaws (Anderson, 1985, 1987). Paramount in the revisions proposed to the U.S. and Canadian codes by both the Anderson Committee and the Macdonald Com-

TABLE 3.6

THE MACDONALD COMMISSION: OVERVIEW OF PRINCIPAL RECOMMENDATIONS

SOURCE: The MacDonald Commission: Report of the Commission to Study the Public's Expectation of Audits, June 1988.

Recommendations to strengthen auditor independence/integrity:

    Improvement of auditor relationships (#11 in Commission Report)

    Strengthen professional standards (7)

    Strengthen professional code of conduct (3)

Recommendations to strengthen auditor professionalism:

    Increase responsiveness to public concerns (6)

    Emphasize vital role of professional judgement (4)

    Improve self-regulation (2)

Recommendations to improve financial disclosure:

    Expand accounting standards and improve financial disclosures (13)

    Greater auditor responsibility for those disclosures (2)

Recommendations to lessen public misunderstanding of the auditor's role:

    Publish a statement of management responsibility (24)

    Expand audit report to clarify auditor's role and the level of assurance the audit provides (25)

    Audit committee to report annually to shareholders (3)

The Treadway Commission: Fraudulent Financial Reporting

In June 1985 the Independent National Commission on Fraudulent Financial Reporting, sponsored by the American Institute of CPAs, the American Accounting Association, the National Association of Accountants, the Institute of Internal Auditors and the Financial Executives Institute, was formed at the AICPA's initiative.

The commission's aims have been to determine what factors contribute to fraudulent financial reporting and to develop practical, constructive recommendations for reducing the incidence of this problem.

MULTIDIMENSIONAL PROBLEM

A commission early finding was that fraudulent financial reporting is a multidimensional problem with multiple causal influences.

According to Chairman James C. Treadway, Jr., solutions can be determined only by studying the entire financial reporting process, and everyone involved in it, including management, the audit committee and the independent public accountant as well as internal controls, corporate culture and law enforcement.

In Treadway's view, many approaches have potential for reducing fraud and no simple answers exist. The commission is emphasizing the "big picture" to identify and air the issues, create heightened awareness and offer concrete guidance on how to minimize the incidence of fraud. It has stressed that no single conclusion can be separated from the totality of its recommendations.

MANAGEMENT'S RESPONSIBILITY

The commission's initial conclusions in the exposure draft, issued this month, highlight management's ultimate responsibility for financial statement accuracy and its duty to set a tone of personal and professional ethics within the company.

In addition, numerous recommendations focus on enhancing internal controls with a greater role for the audit committee, the obligation of the public accountant to detect fraud, mandatory auditor involvement is quarterly financial reports, mandatory membership for auditors of public companies in a professional quality assurance program, more public representation of the AICPA auditing standards board, and enhanced law enforcement and stiffer penalties as a deterrent to management fraud.

RETAINING PUBLIC CONFIDENCE

Following a 60-day comment period ending July 1, the commission plans to publish its final report early this fall.

The report will have an impact on issuers, regulators, auditors, educators, directors, law enforcers and professional organizations. The ultimate aim of reducing fraudulent financial reporting is to protect the integrity of the financial reporting system and to retain public confidence in the accounting profession and its ability to regulate itself, thereby reversing the escalation in litigation and liability and avoiding government intervention.

National Commission on Fraudulent Financial Reporting
Chairman
James C. Treadway, Jr.
Commissioners
William M. Batten
William S. Kanaga
Hugh L. Marsh, Jr.
Thomas I. Storrs
Donald H. Trautlein
Executive Director
G. Dewey Arnold
Research Director
Jack L. Korgstad
General Counsel
Catherine Collins McCoy

mission was the desire to restore the public's faith that the profession was serving the public interest. The categorization of the principal recommendations of the Macdonald Commission (refer to Table 3.6) makes this general objective abundantly evident.

CURRENT CODES OF PROFESSIONAL CONDUCT

The codes of professional conduct that have resulted from the concerns, investigations, commissions and committees are summarized below for the representative codes of the American Institute of Certified Public Accountants and the Institute of Chartered Accountants of Ontario. Discussion of the provisions of each code are covered elsewhere in this book. For instance, discussion of the need to keep client information confidential is included in Chapters 2, 3 and 5.

SHORTFALLS WITH AND IN PROFESSIONAL CODES

In the past, most professional accountants have tended to view their codes as being less relevant than the technical material with which they were required to deal. In some cases lack of awareness of the significance of the code was at the root of the problem, while in other instances inability to interpret the general principles and rules was responsible. As our ethics environment has changed and ethical shortfalls have become recognized as serious threats to professional practice, there have been numerous calls for renewed interest, understanding, and commitment on the part of the professionals themselves. One such article, which is included as a reading to this chapter, is by Ken Gunning (1989). Other articles have called for ethics to be part of organized educational programs which now concentrate on technical matters (Brooks [1993]; also a dedicated issue of *Accounting Education* [March 1994]). One of the goals of this book is to rectify the scant treatment given to ethical matters and to foster more serious attention on the part of both student and graduate professionals.

Although it would be theoretically attractive for professional codes of conduct to solve all of the problems professional accountants face, in reality their application requires the use of judgment based upon a full set of principles and rules. In this regard, many codes have the following deficiencies that would call for the use of such judgement:

- No or insufficient prioritization is put forward to resolve conflicting interests;

- Consultation on ethical matters is encouraged for some members, but is inhibited for others;

- A fair reporting/hearing process is not indicated, so members are uncertain whether to come forward;

- Protection is not offered to a whistleblower;

- Sanctions are often unclear, and their applicability is not defined;

- Resolution mechanisms for conflicts between professionals and firms, or employers, or employing corporations are not put forward.

These deficiencies are discussed in the reading by Brooks (1989), which appears later in this chapter. Fortunately, some of these issues have been redressed in several codes, and the best qualities of some codes are finding their way into others. One example of a "best treatment" is to be found in the *Resolution of Ethical Conflict* provisions of the Institute of Management Accountants code, which is reproduced as Schedule 1 in Brooks (1989).

Aside from the flaws mentioned above, there is a tendency for codes of conduct and the training related to them to focus on what may not be done rather than on how to do something positively. This negativistic approach has been recognized, and recent revisions of codes, both professional and corporate, are beginning to stress the fundamental principles that are essential to the maintenance of strong ethical and fiduciary capabilities. The code of conduct, particularly of leading-edge corporations, is being seen as part of a message to employees as to how to proceed, rather than a proscription on how not to act. It is being seen as a motivating document for action and consultation, rather a list of rules. Time will tell how far this trend will go.

SUMMARY OF THE AICPA *CODE OF PROFESSIONAL CONDUCT**

Principles:

Responsibilities: In carrying out their responsibilities as professionals, members should exercise sensitive professional and moral judgments in all their activities. (Article I)

The Public Interest: Members should accept their obligation to act in a way that will serve the public interest, honor the public trust, and demonstrate commitment to professionalism. (Article II)

Integrity: To maintain and broaden public confidence, members should perform all professional responsibilities with the highest sense of integrity. (Article III)

Objectivity and Independence: A member should maintain objectivity and be free of interest in discharging professional responsibilities. A member in public practice should be independent in fact and appearance when providing auditing and other attestation services. (Article IV)

Due Care: A member should observe the profession's technical and ethical standards, strive continually to improve competence and the quality of services, and discharge professional responsibility to the best of the member's ability. (Article V)

Scope and Nature of Services: A member in public practice should observe the principles of the Code of Professional Conduct in determining the scope and nature of services to be provided. (Article VI)

	Rules:	Important interpretations/ issues covered:
101	Independence	• will be impaired by various transactions, relationships and interests, including : direct or material financial interests, common investments, loans; family relationships, or official office such as: director, officer, employee, promoter, underwriter, trustee, or borrower (except under normal terms from a financial institution for auto, home, credit cards); and the threat of litigation.
102	Integrity and objectivity	• no conflicts of interest are allowed • no misrepresentations
201	General Standards	• professional competence • due professional care

		• planning and supervision • sufficient relevant data
202	Compliance with standards	• necessary if service involves auditing, review, compilation, management consulting, tax, or other professional services
203	Accounting principles	• no departures from generally accepted accounting principles, *unless a misleading statement would result,* then must state why a departure is warranted and approximate effects
301	Confidential client information	• no disclosure without consent, except for proper court or CPA proceedings • no use for personal gain
302	Contingent fees	• not allowed for audit, review, compilation, examination of prospective financial information, or tax return or claim for tax refund
501	Discreditable acts	• not permitted; discrimination, deviation from government standards, negligence
502	Advertising and solicitation	• cannot be false, misleading or deceptive, or involve coercion, over-reaching, or harassment
503	Commissions and referral fees	• not allowed for audit, review, compilation, examination of prospective financial information, otherwise requires disclosure • cannot be paid or accepted without disclosure to the client
505	Form of organization and name	• permits up to 33.3 percent non-CPA, active, owners provided: CPA has ultimate responsibility overall and for attest and compilation services, and each engagement; non-CPA's abide by CPA code and CPE requirements, and do not hold themselves out as CPA's

*__Code of Professional Conduct,__ American Institute of Certified Public Accountants, Inc. NY, NY, 1994

One of the unresolved issues in many professional codes is the overlap between professional codes and those of the firm or corporation for which the professional works as an employee. The professional accountant is governed by both, and the internal control system and integrity of the organization

SUMMARY OF *RULES OF PROFESSIONAL CONDUCT AND COUNCIL INTERPRETATIONS** OF THE INSTITUTE OF CHARTERED ACCOUNTANTS OF ONTARIO (ICAO)

Rules:

General

101	Compliance with bylaws and regulations	**Important Interpretations/issues covered:** • is mandatory • details for employing students
102	Conviction of criminal and similar offenses	• may result in a charge of professional misconduct
103	No association with misrepresentation	• on a letter, report, statement or representation, or related to candidacy as a student or member
104	Must reply in writing to Institute correspondence	

Standards Affecting the Public Interest

201	Maintenance of the good reputation of the profession and its ability to serve the public interest	• necessity of licensing to practice public accounting • rules for criticism of a professional colleague or other public accountant • facilitation of client's choice of professional adviser • responses to requests by prospective clients • resignation of auditors
202	Integrity and due care	
203	Maintenance of professional competence	• see rule 206
204	Independence and objectivity	• those who give opinions on financial statements must be free of any influence, interest or relationship which would impair professional judgement or objectivity, or has the appearance of doing so
205	False or misleading statements	• no association even where a disclaimer is given • covers; letters, reports, representations, financial statements, written or oral
206	Disclosure of material facts and misstatements	• covers omissions, material misstatements, non-compliance with generally accepted accounting principles and generally accepted auditing standards as set out in the *CICA Handbook*
207	Informing clients of conflicts of interest	• business connections, affiliations, or interests
208	No unauthorized benefits	• from client or employer
209	Confidential information about a client's affairs	• no improper use
210	Maintenance of confidential information	• no disclosure unless pursuant to the proceedings of lawful authority, the Council, or the Professional Conduct Committee or its subcommittees • responsibility for subcontracted agents
211	Duty to report apparent breaches of members, students of applicants	• of rules of conduct • of competencies, regulation or integrity
212	Handling of trust funds and other property	• in accord with trust and trust law • segregation, records
213	No unlawful activity	• association of person, name, or services
215	Contingent fees, or free services	• none allowed • none, except for charitable, benevolent or similar services
216	No referral fees or compensation	• none allowed, except in sale or purchase of an accounting practice
217	Advertising restrictions	• advertising cannot be false or misleading; in bad taste, or contrary to professional courtesy; or reflect

		unfavorably on competence or integrity, or include unsubstantiated statements
		• no endorsements if member is in public practice
		• mailings only to clients, close associates, requesters
		• limitation of member in practice to educational symposia and seminars
218	Retention of documentation and working papers	• for a reasonable time period

Relations with Fellow Members and Non-members Engaged in Public Accounting

301	Solicitation of professional engagement entrusted to another public accountant	• none allowed
302	Acceptance of appointment where there is an incumbent auditor	• not allowed without asking outgoing auditor if there are circumstances which should be taken into account
303	Response required for Rule 302 enquiry	
304	Joint appointments	• carry joint and several liability
		• must advise other accountant of activities
305	Communication of *special assignments* to incumbent	• must communicate with incumbent unless client makes such a request in writing before the engagement is begun
306	Responsibilities on *special assignments*	• no action to impair the position of the other accountant
		• no services beyond referral terms, except with approval

Organization and Conduct of a Professional Practice

401	Misleading name or style	• not allowed
402	Responsibilities conveyed with use of style	• public accountants must use "chartered accountant(s)" or "public accountant(s)"
		• public accountants are responsible for the failure of non-members associated with the practice to abide by the Rules of Conduct
403	Operation of offices	• offices must be under the charge of a licensed public accountant who is normally in attendance
		• private "offices of convenience" may be used, but not advertised
404	Office by representation	• representation by another accountant does not constitute maintaining an office
405	Attracting clients	• cannot be by bringing disrepute to the profession
406	Sole and firm names	• surnames used in title cannot exceed number of active or deceased partners
		• "& Co." cannot be used unless the number of active partners exceeds the number of surnames used in the title
407	Practice of public accounting in a corporate form	• prohibited in Ontario, except under specific circumstances: refer to current code for recent changes
408	Practice of "related functions" (non-audit, review or compilation work)	• possible through audit firms or other corporate forms
		• related functions include: management consulting, trustee in bankruptcy, etc.
		• members are responsible for the failure of others in the organization performing the related functions to follow the Rules of Conduct
410	Practice of related functions exclusively	• if not engaged in public accounting, a member need not be constrained by Rules 215, 216, 217(d), 301, 403–406 incl.

*As included in the <u>*ICAO Member's Handbook,*</u> ICAO, Toronto, Canada, 1994.

depends upon its code, so an understanding of corporate codes in general, and of their employer's code in particular, is essential to the day-to-day activities of employed professionals. This understanding is the subject of the next section.

Corporate/Employer Codes

PURPOSE AND FOCUS

An effective code is the major organizational structure with which to implement ethical policy (Murphy, 1989; appears as a "Reading" in this chapter), and to communicate behavioral expectations and culture. It is an essential part

---

George Weston Limited Code of Business Conduct

George Weston Limited ("Weston") is dedicated to maintaining its reputation for integrity and good corporate citizenship, and expects all employees to abide by basic principles of ethical and lawful business conduct. The increasingly complexity of law and business life has made it appropriate for Weston to establish formally this Code of Business Conduct.

1. ADHERENCE TO CURRENT LAW

All employees are expected to comply with all laws applicable to the business of Weston. If any employee is in doubt as to whether or not a particular course of action would infringe applicable law, he or she should discuss the proposed activity with management who in turn should seek the guidance of appropriate company legal counsel, if necessary.

2. APPROPRIATION OF COMPANY ASSETS

Employees are not permitted to borrow or to make use of company funds or other assets for their own personal gain or benefit unless such benefits are derived as part of an authorized Western employee compensation or benefit program. The Weston name, property and goodwill must not be used by employees for their personal advantage.

3. MISUSE OF CONFIDENTIAL INFORMATION

Employees shall not use confidential information gained by virtue of their association with Weston for their own personal gain, nor shall they disclose such information for the use of others.

4. CONFLICTS OF INTEREST

All employees should avoid activities which involve conflict of interest with Weston. The transaction of business by West-

on with businesses owned in whole or in part by any employee or any member of his/her family or person from whom the employee would derive direct or indirect benefits is prohibited unless written approval is requested and received from the appropriate Chief Executive Officer.

5. OUTSIDE BUSINESS ACTIVITIES OF EMPLOYEES

Employees are not permitted to engage in outside business activities which deprive Weston of the time and attention required to properly perform their duties or which are in competition with or related to Weston activities.

6. GIFTS FROM CUSTOMERS OR SUPPLIERS

No employee of Weston shall accept gifts, favors or trips other than of nominal nature, from customers or suppliers or prospective customers or suppliers, nor shall they use their status with Weston to obtain personal gain from those doing or seeking to do business with Weston.

7. GIFTS TO CUSTOMERS OR SUPPLIERS

No gifts or favors, other than nominal, are to be made to customers or suppliers or to their employees, nor shall employees of Weston provide excessive entertainment or benefits to other persons.

8. ILLEGAL PAYMENT TO PUBLIC OFFICIALS

In most jurisdictions, Weston is required by law to report immediately to the proper authorities any corroborated instance where a public official at any level of government attempts to obtain money or property or favors from West-

–Continued

---

of a modern system of internal control. Unless employees are told, in writing, how they are expected to behave, managers, executives, and directors are vulnerable to charges that they failed to provide adequate guidance to their workers. If so, the company and its officers and directors can be fined heavily, and in some jurisdictions the officers and directors can go to jail. More importantly, it has been suggested that the fines and court costs involved in ethical dilemmas are usually smaller than the lost sales and related margin due to disenchantment of the public. Whistleblowing outside the corporation may also be prevented by implementation of effective ethical codes because they can help to create an ethical culture in which employees believe doing what is right is expected and bringing forward concerns over unethical behavior will not result in ethical martyrdom.

Continued

on by the wrongful use of his official position or as a condition to perform certain duties he is normally obligated to perform. All such incidents should be immediately reported to the appropriate Chief Executive Officer. In no circumstances should any employee agree to solicitation. No employee of Weston shall offer gifts or favors to any public official that could be construed as a payment to influence the official.

9. PROPER MAINTENANCE OF RECORDS

All transactions of Weston must be properly recorded and accounted for on the books of the company. This is essential to the integrity of Weston's governmental and financial reporting obligations. In particular, (i) no unrecorded or inadequately recorded fund or asset of Weston shall be established or maintained; (ii) no false, artificial or misleading entries in the books and records of Weston shall be made; and (iii) no transaction shall be effected and no payment shall be made on behalf of Weston with the intention or understanding that the transaction or payment is other than as described in the documentation evidencing the transaction or supporting the payment.

10. POLITICAL AND CHARITABLE ORGANIZATIONS

All employees are encouraged and entitled, to make political and charitable contributions from their personal time and funds in the exercise of responsible citizenship. Corporate contributions, of any kind, to political organizations should be approved by the office of the Chairman. Involvement of employees in political and charitable organizations should not deprive Weston of the time and attention required to properly perform the employees' duties unless previous approval is requested and received from the appropriate executive officer.

11. HUMAN RELATIONS

All people with whom Weston has business relations, whether customers, suppliers or employees are to be treated in a dignified and understanding manner. Discrimination or harassment of any kind will not be practised. Conformity with legal requirements such as Equal Opportunity laws shall not be regarded as discrimination.

12. CONCLUSION

It is impossible in a document of this nature to cover the full spectrum of employee activities. However, the foregoing are meant to be general guidelines provided to employees of Weston to enable them to understand the type of conduct considered acceptable in the course of the duties on behalf of Weston. Inevitably, circumstances will arise which may cause employees to question whether or not particular activity falls within acceptable behavior, and which are not covered by these guidelines. In these circumstances, employees should discuss their proposed course of conduct with their immediate superior or the appropriate Chief Executive Officer. Any employee who violates this Code of Business Conduct shall be subject to appropriate disciplinary measures which could lead to dismissal or to legal action brought against that employee.

I have read and have been given a copy of the Weston Code of Business Conduct. I understand and will abide by its provisions.

Date _____ Signature _____

Name (Please print) _____

SOURCE: George Weston Limited conducts food processing, food distribution, and resource operations in North America. In 1993 George Weston Limited had sales of $11.9 billion and a total capital investment of $4.5 billion.

TABLE 3.7

PATTERNS OF CORPORATE
CODES OF ETHICS

SOURCE: Brooks, 1986, p. 111; Conference
Board, 1987, p. 15.

FOCUS	CHARACTERISTICS
Stakeholder or constituent	Introduction followed by a discussion, on a stakeholder basis, of principles, objectives, or policies
Strategic policy or professional responsibility	Foreword by chief executive officer, chairman of president; followed, on a companywide basis, by an introduction, purpose, objectives, policies, and management philosophies.
Issues oriented or corporate mission	One issue after another is dealt with but without an overall framework of principles and policies.

The basic foundation block to building an ethical culture to manage or govern corporate behavior is an effective code of conduct. Depending on the choice of the senior executives or owners, codes can be drafted to focus on:

1. the interests of stakeholders;
2. the strategic policies or responsibility of the organization (e.g., refer to the insert in this chapter from George Weston Limited);
3. a specific mission or several issues; or (e.g., see the Johnson & Johnson credo in the reading by Murphy in this chapter), or
4. a composite of the above.

These options are expanded upon in Table 3.7. Successful examples of each type can be cited, but increasingly the most common is focused on stakeholder interests. This approach is discussed more fully in the reading by Clarkson and Deck (1992), which appears later in this chapter.

CONTENTS

There are a number of ways of categorizing the content of corporate codes of conduct, including by stakeholder interest, by specific topic or policy, and by nature, that is, whether the code features principles or rules, etc. On many of these dimensions there has been a difference in emphasis between U.S. and Canadian codes, which is due, in part, to the ethics environment in each country. In the U.S., for example, the regulatory environment has been much more active, thus requiring companies to fashion codes in a more specific manner than in Canada.

Late in the 1970s, just before the period when most U.S. companies were creating codes, a scandal arose involving officers at Lockheed Aircraft Corporation who bribed Japanese government officials to buy jet aircraft. The public outcry in the U.S. resulted in the passage of the Foreign Corrupt Practices Act of 1977, which forbade such activities and required U.S. companies to declare when such payments were made. To avoid possible fines and adverse publicity, U.S. companies began to use codes to make clear to their employees what behavior was expected. Similar desires accounted for the inclusion of proscriptions against behavior likely to lead to antitrust proceedings, conflicts of interest, and inappropriate political contributions. In Canada, on the other hand, the regulatory environment was not as active, and codes adopted a more

TABLE 3.8

COMPARISON OF FREQUENCY
OF STAKEHOLDER'S INTERESTS
ADDRESSED IN CORPORATE
ETHICAL CODES

SOURCE: Brooks, 1986, p. 112; Conference Board, 1987, p. 15.

STAKEHOLDER	CANADIAN CODES	WORLDWIDE CODES
Employees	88%	90%
Host communities and countries	75%	48%
Customers	69%	87%
The public	44%	N/A
Shareholders	44%	40%
Governments	44%	56%
Suppliers	38%	87%
6 Others		

philosophical focus on the broad responsibilities of corporations with particular reference to stakeholder relationships with employees, host communities, and customers. These features, and the general nature of Canadian codes, can be seen in Tables 3.8 and 3.9.

Tables 3.10 documents the topics found in the codes of the mid- and late 1980s. Note the shift in emphasis in U.S. codes referred to above.

In the late 1980s and early 1990s, companies in both countries have been pressured by the public, special interest groups like Greenpeace, ethical

TABLE 3.9

PROFILE OF TOPICS COVERED
IN CANADIAN CORPORATE
CODES OF ETHICS

SOURCE: Brooks, 1986, p. 113.

AREA OF SOCIAL CONCERN	WEIGHTED AVERAGE PERCENT OF ALL STATEMENTS
General:	
Operational objectives	34.8
Financial issues	12.0
Trustworthiness of the company, its personnel and procedures as perceived by insiders and outsiders	11.7
	58.5
Human resources*	19.6
Product of service contributions*	9.9
Community involvement*	5.3
Environment and physical resources*	1.7
	95.0
Introduction to statement	5.0
	100.0

*Major areas of social performance originally identified by the Committee on Accounting for Social Performance of the National Association of Accountants (1974)

TABLE 3.10

MOST IMPORTANT TOPICS IN CORPORATE CODES OF CONDUCT

SOURCE: Brooks (1986), p. 113; White & Montgomery (1980), p. 84; Mathews (1987), pp. 111–113.

TOPIC/RANK (1 IS HIGHEST)	CANADIAN 1986	U.S. 1980	U.S. 1987
General statement of ethics and philosophy		1	2
Corporate citizenship	1		
Planning	4		
Shareholders, duty to	5		
Trust of company name and representatives by public, business community, or employees/integrity	6		8
External communications	8		
Conducrt of personnel	2		
Competence of personnel	7		
Conflict of interest		2	8
Inside information		6	
Gifts, favors, entertainment		7	
Communications, internal	10		
Compliance with applicable laws		4	1
Political contributions		4	
Payments to government officials/political parties		6	5
False entries in books and records		8	
Product or service commentary	3		
Undisclosed or unrecorded funds or assets		9	
Responsibility for dealers or agents actions		10	
Enforcement or compliance procedures			6
Relations with:			
▪ Customers/suppliers	9		5
▪ U.S. government			3
▪ Foreign governments			9
▪ Competitors			10

investors like the staff pension funds of New York and California, and regulators to manage their activities with greater sensitivity to the environment and several other stakeholder concerns. To some extent this pressure has been galvanized by tragedies or increasing social awareness of the plight of specific stakeholders. Codes of conduct have been modified to indicate and clarify responsibilities in these matters. These new issues, which are described in Table 3.11, should be familiar due to the attendant media coverage.

The environmental responsibility/sustainability issue is instructive with regard to the evolution of ethical standards underway. The public perception has grown that our environmental resources are finite and need to be conserved for future generations, and for our own health and survival. Many of the

TABLE 3.11

RECENT ISSUES TO BE
INCLUDED IN CORPORATE
CODES OF CONDUCT

ISSUE	STIMULUS
Environmental	Exxon *Valdez* oil tanker spill: avoidance
responsibility/	Air and water pollution, ozone depletion: avoidance
sustainability	Limits to waste disposal: recycling
Fair treatment of:	Greater social awareness and conscience
Employees	Feminism: sexual harassment, equity in hiring, pay Minorities: discrimination, equity Health and safety: higher standards for all Drug problems: privacy versus safety
Customers	Ethical consumerism: quality Seller beware
Shareholders	Misuse of information, conflicts of interest
Host community	Plant layoffs

seven serious environmental hurdles we face, which were identified by the United Nations's Brundtland Commission (1987), have begun to capture the attention of both the public and politicians. The earth's ozone layer is a case in point, generating global action toward the reduction of chloroflourocarbons (CFC) emissions. More broadly, both the U.S. and Canada have enacted environmental protection acts, which, as mentioned above, can trigger very high fines of up to $2 million a day in the U.S. and $1 million a day in Canada, as well as personal fines and jail terms for executives. In the U.S., when sentencing guidelines were introduced on November 1, 1991, advising of the $2 million per day fine, a judge indicated that this could be reduced to $50,000 per day if an effective *due diligence* program designed to avoid environmental malfeasance could be shown to be in place at the corporation. The interest of many large companies was immediately stimulated to find out about such a program and how to implement it so as to make it effective. Not surprisingly, one of the fundamental elements in this process is the organization's code of conduct, which sets out behavioral expectations for all employees. It is to the effective implementation of these codes that we now turn.

EFFECTIVE IMPLEMENTATION AND USE OF CODES OF CONDUCT

The due diligence requirements referred to above provide a good introduction to the conditions necessary for the effective implementation of a code. However, as was pointed out in the opening section of this chapter, "Stake and Role of Professional Accountants," the primary concern of accountants that the code of conduct be properly implemented and used is to ensure the effectiveness of the system of internal control. Although the list may change as time goes by, that set out in Table 3.12 offers a good start toward ensuring that internal control is adequately dealt with, in this instance, with regard to a company's environmental responsibilities. There are, of course, many other reference sources for appropriate environmental standards including the *Valdez or CERES Principles* (Sternberg, 1989).

TABLE 3.12

ESSENTIAL FEATURES FOR
COMPANIES TO DEMONSTRATE
DUE DILIGENCE/ADEQUATE
INTERNAL CONTROL WITH
REGARD TO THEIR PROTECTION
OF THE ENVIRONMENT

SOURCE: Adapted from a client letter from the
legal firm of Borden & Elliot, Toronto, March
1989.

1. Have a written environmental policy, which is made known to appropriate employees;
2. Develop and implement operating practices that guard against environmental malfeasance, including contingency plans to cover mishaps to ensure full scale, timely cleanup;
3. Brief employees on their duties and responsibilities under the policy as well as their potential personal liability, and the liability of others;
4. Inform employees of legal requirements, including notice to government, complete with a contact list;
5. Make a person primarily responsible for environmental matters and monitoring compliance;
6. Consider an environmental audit or consult an expert to start the protection process and monitor progress;
7. Monitor pollution control systems and report mishaps on a timely basis;
8. Regularly review reports on compliance, potential problems, environmental charges, conviction, and employee training;
9. In addition to the foregoing, management should:
- keep abreast of new legislation;
- internally review compliance and advise directors of the results of that review
- allocate a real and satisfactory budget to achieve these features.

Here we will discuss several critical features for the proper implementation of a code of conduct, all of which are embedded in these environmentally oriented guidelines.

First, *top management must endorse and support the code,* and be seen to act in accord with it, or it will be only be given lip service by middle management and workers. It is critical that management "walk their talk" as the saying goes or the entire program will be a waste of time and money.

The tone and content of the code must be such that *general principles are favored instead of only specific rules,* or else employees will find the code oppressive and hard to interpret. It is also important that *background reasons* for the principles be *given* so that employees can understand the principles sufficiently to interpret them when specific guidelines are not available. Experience has shown that codes designed as extensive rule books are rarely useful because they are too difficult to consult. If the underlying reason for a specific pattern of behavior is given, employees find it easier to understand and they buy into the code rather than fight or dismiss it. Getting the buy-in is essential.

Guidance should be provided for balancing the tradeoffs between short-term profit and social objectives. If employees believe profit is to be earned at all costs, then unethical behavior based on short-term thinking can result, with negative consequences for the company.

When in doubt over the proper conduct, *employees should be encouraged to seek counsel.* Rather than have them act inappropriately, or waste time needlessly, a company should encourage employees to consult their superior, a hot line, or an ethics officer.

A *fair and confidential hearing process should be ensured* or whistleblowers will not come forward. They don't want to risk paying the price for snitching, even though it is in the best interests of the company for them to do so. Nor do they want an accused person to be dealt with in a cavalier way—they want a speedy, fair hearing process with protection for both parties. *Whistleblowing should be legitimized,* and whistleblowers who come forward should be protected.

Someone should be charged with the *ongoing responsibility for updating the code* so that issues can be addressed as they come up. Otherwise many issues will be lost in the pressures of day-to-day activity or because people won't know where to send their suggestions.

The *distribution of the code should be to all employees* so that none will be able to claim they were not told how to behave. It is surprising how many companies believe their line workers don't have responsibility for environmental acts, for actions toward fellow workers, etc. Not only do excellent suggestions come from the plant, but bad actions are noticed, and support for the company's general activities is enhanced by bringing these employees, in addition to management personnel, into the distribution loop.

Training in support of the code is essential. Such training should focus on the awareness of issues, interpretation of the code in accord with top management wishes, approaches to ethical analysis so that decisions not covered by the code can be made, realistic cases for discussion, and legitimization of the discussion of ethical issues and of whistleblowing. Codes are written by committees who spend long hours over each paragraph, so how is each employee supposed to know all the thought that went into its construction just by quickly reading the passage? Training is essential to help understand what is meant by the code, and how the code applies to new problems.

Compliance with the code should be furthered by encouragement; monitoring; and facilitation of the reporting of wrongdoing. These issues should not be left to chance, otherwise the organization might miss an opportunity to head off a disaster or to accomplish an ethical performance objective. Various methods for achieving compliance are listed in Tables 3.13, 3.14 and 3.15, together with an indication of the frequency of their use.

Reinforcement of the code should be undertaken through measuring the code's effectiveness; reporting ethical performance using the avenues listed in

TABLE 3.13

COMPLIANCE MECHANISMS USED

SOURCE: Table G in Brooks, 1990.

MECHANISM	PERCENTAGE OF RESPONDENTS USING	VALID RESPONSES
Awards	2.0%	99
Specific bonuses	1.0%	99
Specific inclusion in:		
• Performance reviews	33.7%	95
• Remuneration decisions	14.7%	95
• Promotion decisions	20.0%	95
Reprimands	77.9%	95
Suspension	56.8%	95
Demotion	33.7%	95
Fines	25.3%	95
Dismissal	61.1%	95

TABLE 3.14

METHODS OF MONITORING
COMPLIANCE

SOURCE: Table H in Brooks, 1990.

METHOD	PERCENTAGE OF COMPANIES USING	VALID RESPONSES
Internal Audits	67.3%	98
Supervisory surveillance	56.1%	98
Reviews by legal department	31.6%	98
Annual sign-off affidavits		
• by some employees	44.9%	98
• by all employees	20.4%	98
Employee surveys	10.2%	98

Table 3.16 below; featuring ethical performance in company publications; and ensuring that other company policies are supportive (such support should include a linkage with the remuneration systems). If you can't measure performance (measurement techniques are discussed in Chapters 4 and 5), it is very hard to manage it. Reporting that performance has the impact of producing a scorecard which people are induced to improve upon for the next report. Publicizing good results can have a salutary effect on subsequent performance as well, and including that performance in the corporation's reward systems will go a long way toward underscoring how important ethical issues are to top management.

In the process of surveying CEOs for the reading titled "A Survey on the Effectiveness/Compliance of Corporate Codes of Conduct in Canada" (1990) Brooks found that Canadian CEOs believed the following aspects of their company codes needed significant improvement: training programs (59.4 per-

TABLE 3.15

METHODS OF FACILITATION OF
REPORTING OF WRONGDOING

SOURCE: Table I in Brooks, 1990.

FACILITATION BY	PERCENTAGE USING	VALID RESPONSES
Absolute confidentiality	62.2%	90
Whistleblower protection plan	1.9%	90
Ombudsman program	5.7%	53
Hotline program	1.9%	53
Monitoring by a Committee of the Board:		
• Ethics or Public Issues Committee	3.8%	53
• Audit Committee	41.5%	53
Non-board Ethics Committee	3.8%	53
Human Resources Dept.	9.4%	53
Auditors	5.7%	53
Combination of items above	15.1%	53

TABLE 3.16

ETHICAL PERFORMANCE
REPORTS

SOURCE: Table J in Brooks, 1990.

INTERNAL REPORTS:	FREQUENCY
To the Board	8
To board Committees (Audit)	1
To Management from:	
Managers	
Annual Conduct Report	2
Absenteeism	1
Manager's Reports	2
Internal Audit Department	2
Legal Department	1
Security Department	1
To employees:	2
Newsletter	1
External Reports:	
Annual Report	10
Audit Report	4
Annual Meeting Report	1
Total	36

cent), reports of performance (52.2 percent), measures of performance (50.6 percent), and compliance mechanisms (31.9 percent).

Finally, it should be understood that it is unlikely that employees will see the merit of ethical behavior in regard to one area of the company's operations, if there are others in which they believe management want or are prepared to tolerate questionable behavior. Whistleblowers will not come forward, for example, unless there is a feeling of trust that they and the parties they accuse will be dealt with fairly and confidentially. Consequently, *the development of a broadly based ethical culture* within the company is an essential precursor for a really effective code of conduct.

Issues Not Resolved in Codes of Conduct

Despite the usefulness of codes of conduct, several issues that could be faced by employees (including professional accountants) are often not resolved in codes of conduct. Accordingly, thought should be given to the following matters when a code is being created or revised:

1. *Conflicts between codes.* Occasionally a professional, or some other employee, will be subject not only to the company/employer's code but also to another code such as a professional code for engineers or accountants. To avoid placing the person in an ethical dilemma of debating which code to follow, at the very least, advise consultation with an ethics officer/ombudsperson.

2. *Conflicts between competing interests or corporate stakeholders.* Sometimes the priority of competing interests can be made clear in training sessions. If not, protected routes for consultation should be available. This subject is discussed at length in Chapters 4 and 5.

3. *When should a professional blow the whistle, and to whom?* A protected, internal route for discussion and reporting should be available for professional accountants. An employer should realize that every professional accountant has a professional duty to uphold, a duty that could supersede loyalty to the employer. It would be helpful if the professional's accounting society were to provide consultation to the professional on a confidential basis to assist in these decisions, as is the case in the United Kingdom.

4. *Adequate protection of whistleblowers.* The most successful arrangements for whistleblowing involve reporting, in confidence, to an autonomous individual of high rank or one who reports to a person of very high rank in the organization: for example, an ombudsperson who will follow up concerns without revealing the informant's name or exposing the informant, and who reports directly to the head of the organization. With this level of apparent support, investigations can be undertaken without interference. The ombudsperson should report back to the informant with the results of his or her investigations.

5. *Service decisions involving judgment.* Codes of conduct should be fashioned so as not to rule out the exercise of a professional's values when those are required for the judgments they must make. In the final analysis, it is the exercise of these values and the judgments based on these that could save the individual, the firm or employer, the profession, and the public from ethical problems. The challenge is to develop codes and cultures that do not force the abandonment of personal values, but rather foster the development and exercise of values and judgment processes that will benefit the stakeholders when they really need them.

Conclusion

Understanding the contributions a professional or corporate code of conduct can make to the internal control and ethical performance of a profession or corporation is essential to the well-being of all stakeholders, but particularly to accounting professionals, directors, executives, and management. Codes are in need of constant improvement and reinterpretation to meet the new challenges of an increasingly complex economy, a growing sensitivity to our environment, and the needs of stakeholders. Each professional has a role to play for his or her firm, profession, or corporation in keeping abreast of developments that call for inclusion, reinterpretation, or improvement in their use. Because not all problems are susceptible to specific treatment in codes of conduct, the process of ethical management should incorporate an orderly exercise of judgment so that professionals can interpret a code of conduct to make decisions about problems beyond the scope of the code. That is the subject of the next chapter.

QUESTIONS FOR DISCUSSION

1. What is the most important contribution of a professional or corporate code of conduct?

2. Are one or more of the fundamental principles found in codes of conduct (see Table 3.4) more important than the rest? Why?

3. Was the "expectations gap" which triggered the Treadway and Macdonald Commissions the fault of the users of financial statements, the management who prepared them, the auditors, or the standard setters who decided what the disclosure standards should be?

4. Why should codes focus on principles rather than specific detailed rules?

5. How can corporations integrate ethical behavior into their reward and remuneration schemes?

6. What should an auditor do if he or she believes that the ethical culture of a client is unsatisfactory?

CASES

- The "Dow Corning Silicone–Breast Implants" case illustrates how a company with an excellent code and a world-class, follow-up monitoring procedure can still have problems with code effectiveness.

- "Playing God" reveals the dilemma of Trish Ohling, who needs to choose a technique for a capital budgeting analysis. What basic ethical values should guide her?

- In "Economic Realities or GAAP," Stan Jones is asking penetrating questions about the fundamental utility of traditional financial reports, and the role of the auditor.

- Confidentiality, and its strange treatment in professional accounting codes, is the subject of "Locker Room Talk," a case drawn from the American Accounting Association collection.

READINGS

The readings attached are divided between articles on professional codes and corporate codes. Articles by Anderson, Brooks, and Gunning are intended to provide the reader with background on the reasons for the current structure of the AICPA code, deficiences that remain in codes, and how to think about, approach, and use codes, respectively. On the corporate side, the article by Murphy provides a broad overview of the role of corporate codes and their impact on corporate culture, with reference to useful examples. Clarkson and Deck describe their work on a useful, modern approach to the framing of corporate codes, and indicate how the approach can be used to analyze and score existing codes. The article by Brooks on effectiveness of codes is presented to raise the awareness of the reader about the various means available to improve the effectiveness of codes. What we are learning is that just having a printed code does not guarantee its use.

REFERENCES

Anderson, G. D. "The Anderson Committee: Restructuring Professional Standards." *Journal of Accountancy* (May 1987): 77.

_____. "A Fresh Look at Standards of Professional Conduct." *Journal of Accountancy* (September 1985): 93–106.

Berenbeim, R. E. *"Corporate Ethics"* a report of the Conference Board, Inc., New York, 1987.

Brooks, L. J. *"Canadian Corporate Social Performance."* The Society of Management Accountants of Canada, Hamilton, May 1986 p. 267.

_____. "Ethical Codes of Conduct: Deficient in Guidance for the Canadian Accounting Profession." *Journal of Business Ethics* Vol. 8, No. (5) (May 1989): 325–336.

_____. "Survey on the Effectiveness/Compliance of Corporate Codes of Conduct in Canada." The Centre for Corporate Social Performance & Ethics, 1990.

_____. "No More Trial and Error: It's Time We Moved Ethics out of the Clouds and into the Classroom." *CAmagazine* (March 1993): 43–45.

Brooks, L. J., and Fortunato, V. "Discipline at the Institute of Chartered Accountants of Ontario." *CAmagazine* (May 1991): 40–43.

Brundtland Commission Report. *Our Common Future.* Report of the World Commission on Environment and Development, Oxford University Press, 1987.

Clarkson, M. B. E., and Deck, M. "Applying the Stakeholder Management Model to the Analysis and Evaluation of Corporate Codes." The Centre for Corporate Social Performance & Ethics, 1992.

Gunning, K. S. "Completely at Sea." *CA Magazine* (April 1989): 24–37.

Macdonald Commission, see *The Report of the Commission to Study the Public's Expectations of Audits,* Canadian Institute of Chartered Accountants, June 1988.

Mathews, M. C. "Codes of Ethics: Organizational Behaviour and Misbehaviour." *Research in Corporate Social Behaviour,* Guest Editor: Frederick W. C., Series Editor: Preston L. E. JAI Press Inc., Greenwich, Connecticut 1987, 107–130.

Metcalf, Lee. Spearheaded a senatorial investigation of the large U.S. accounting firms and the AICPA in the 1970s; in response the AICPA established the Cohen Commission.

Murphy, P. E. "Creating Ethical Corporate Cultures." *Sloan Management Review* (Winter 1989): 81–87.

Singer, A. W. "The Whistle-Blower: Patriot or Bounty Hunter." *Across The Board* (November 1992): 16–22.

Sternberg, K. "New Pressure for Good Conduct" *Chemicalweek* (September 20, 1989): 23.

Treadway Commission, see the *Report of the National Commission on Fraudulent Public Reporting,* AICPA, 1987.

White, B. J., Montgomery, R. "Corporate Codes of Conduct." *California Management Review* (Winter 1980): 80–87.

Dow Corning Silicon-Breast Implants

On January 6, 1992, the "growing controversy over the safety factor led the U.S. Food and Drug Administration to call for a moratorium on breast implants."[1] As January wore on, the crisis deepened until, on January 30, the *Toronto Globe & Mail* carried a New York Times Service report entitled "Dow Corning fumbles in damage control."

Among other critical points, that article stated:

Regardless of whether Dow Corning Inc. ever convinces regulators its silicone-gel breast implants are safe, the company seems likely to be branded as bungling in its handling of the problem, say public relations and crisis management experts.

"It's a textbook case of crisis management," . . . "it looks like the lawyers are in charge, trying to limit their liability." "But the damage is much worse to the corporation if they lose in the court of public opinion than if they lose in the court of law."

Consultants concede that because Dow Corning argues there is little evidence supporting many of the injury claims, it is difficult for the company to act sympathetically without appear-

---

1. Feder, Barnaby. "Dow Corning fumbles in damage control" *Toronto Globe and Mail* (January 30, 1992): 3.

Dow Cancels Implant Line

Rob McKenzie

Financial Post, March 20, 1992
Beseiged Dow Corning Corp quit the breast implant business yesterday, offering money to some women in the U.S. who need their implants removed, but leaving Canadian taxpayers to fund any medical costs here.

Bert Miller, president of subsidiary Dow Corning Canada Inc., said the number of medically necessary removals will not be as high as critics expect.

"I honestly don't think it's a huge amount," he said.

Dow Corning insisted its gel-filled sacs are no health hazard.

"Our reasons for not resuming production and sales, therefore, are not related to issues of science or safety, but to the existing condition of the marketplace," Dow Corning chairman and chief executive Keith McKennon said in a statement.

Miller told reporters in Toronto he was "personally quite convinced

that there's been no unnecessary risk that wasn't worth the benefit."

He added: "We at Dow Corning stand by our product."

Many women say the company's silicone-gel implants maimed them or caused other health problems, either by leaking or bursting.

On Feb. 20, a panel of the U.S. Food and Drug Administration recommended use of the implants be sharply restricted. In Canada the Department of Health and Welfare has imposed a moratorium on their use.

Dow Corning, a Michigan-based joint venture of Dow Chemical Co. and Corning Inc., sold more than 600,000 breast implants, including an estimated 27,000 in Canada.

Besides ceasing production and sales, the company said it will spent US$10 million on research into breast implants. In the U.S., it will offer up to US$1,200 each to women who for medical reasons need their

implants excised, but are not covered by private health insurance.

Miller said such surgery in Canada is covered by health-care programs.

Women who fear their implants will harm them, but as yet show no ill effects, are not eligible for aid.

"If she has no physical manifestation and the implant is not giving any problems, she should be calmed," Miller said.

Bryan Groulx, a manager of business development for the Canadian unit, added: "We're not here to provide unnecessary surgery."

One of Dow Corning's strongest critics, Ottawa consultant and breast-implant expert Dr. Pierre Blais, said yesterday's announcement was "a courageous and an appropriate decision."

Breast implants account for about 1% of Dow Corning's sales.

—Continued

Continued

ing to undermine its legal strategy. (p. B1)

The controversy escalated until, on March 20, one month after the U.S. authorities called for sharply restricted use and their Canadian counterparts opted for a moratorium, Dow Corning canceled its breast implant line. The company also offered up to $1,200 each to women in the U.S. not covered by private insurance who needed to have their implants removed. In addition, $10 million was to be spent by the company on research into breast implants.[2]

Among the issues raised by this unfortunate controversy is how faulty breast implants could come to be sold by Dow Corning, a company that had been lionized for almost a decade in three Harvard cases for its outstanding ethics program. The basic details of this program,* are as follows:

Six managers serve three-year stints on a Business Conduct Committee;

each member devotes up to six weeks a year on committee work.

Two members audit every business operation every three years; the panel reviews up to 35 locations annually.

Three-hour reviews are held with up to 35 employees. Committee members use a code of ethics as a framework and encourage employees to raise ethical issues.

Results of audits are reported to a three-member Audit & Social Responsibility Committee of the Board of Directors.[3]

Interestingly, although the silicone breast implant operation had been audited four times since 1983, and the ethics audit approach had failed to uncover any signs of problems, Jere Marciniak, an area Vice-President who is Chairman of the Conduct Committee, has stated that, "he has no plans to touch . . . the ethics program . . . 'it will still aid and guide us through this difficult time.'"

QUESTIONS

1. Why didn't the Dow Corning ethics audit program reveal any concerns about the silicone-gel breast implant line?

2. What are the critical factors necessary to make such an ethics audit program work effectively?

3. Was the announcement on March 20 well advised and ethical?

4. Are there any other ethical dilemmas raised by the case?

SOURCE: "Dow cancels implant line." *Financial Post* (March 20, 1992).

---

*Further details of the program are discribed in "Dow Corning Corporation: Business Conduct and Global Values (A)", Harvard Business School case #9–385–018. See also pages 200 and 201 of the article by P. E. Murphy which is a reading in this chapter.

2. McKenzie, Rob. "Dow cancels implant line" *The Financial Post* (March 20, 1992): 3.
3. Byrne, John A. "The Best Laid Ethics Programs. . . . *Business Week* (March 9, 1992): 67–69.

Playing God

Trish Ohling was the Controller of South East Converters, Inc., a subsidiary of a small conglomerate in the paper industry, which was owned by Evan Trist, a man in his seventies. She was involved in the preparation of submissions for new capital funding which would go to the owner for his decision along with all of the rest of the submissions from the other subsidiaries. Trist had never created a tightly controlled management structure or specified the form of presentation or analytical techniques to be used in these submissions, because, as he said, "I prefer to hire only fully qualified people and then rely upon them to look after my interests."

"I'm in trouble," Trish began, thinking aloud. "If I use the optimistic estimates my management teammates have developed, we will surely get the capital we want, but we may not be able to achieve the results I forecast. If I use the 'best guess' figures we have developed it will be touch and go as to whether we are successful in getting the money or not. We need this project to maintain our competitive position, otherwise I and many others are ultimately out of a job."

"There is another way, of course. Our project will pay off very quickly, but there will be a big cleanup and storage problem when our sludge by-product gets too large for our current in-ground storage facility, which will happen in about seven years. I could just submit our projections for the first five years, and our project will look terrific. If I just use the payback period method of presentation, the seventh-year problem will never show up. Besides, Evan will be in his late seventies by then and probably won't remember anything about this. I may not even be working here by then."

QUESTIONS

1. Who are the stakeholders in this instance?

2. In this situation, why would Evan Trist's interest be better protected by a fully qualified professional rather than just a knowledgeable bookkeeper employee?

Economic Realities or GAAP

Stan Jones was an investor who had recently lost money on his investment in Fine Line Hotels, Inc., and he was anxious to discuss the problem with Janet Todd, a qualified accountant who was his friend and occasional adviser.

"How can they justify this, Janet? This company owns 19.9 percent of a subsidiary, Far East Hotels, which has apparently sustained some large losses. But these consolidated statements don't show any of these losses, and the investment in Far East hasn't been written down to reflect the loss either. I bought my shares in Fine Line just after their last audited statements were made available but just before the papers reported that the statements didn't reflect any of the losses. What should I do in the future—wait until the papers report the true economic picture? If I can't rely on audited figures, what's the sense of having an audit? And don't tell me that if the ownership percentage had been 20 percent, the consolidated statements would have reported the loss. That's just outrageous."

QUESTION

1. How should Janet Todd respond?

Locker Room Talk

Albert Gable is a partner in a CPA firm located in a small mid-western city which has a population of approximately 65,000. Mr. Gable's practice is primarily in the area of personal financial planning; however, he also performs an annual audit on the city's largest bank.

Recently, Mr. Gable was engaged by Larry and Susan Wilson to prepare a comprehensive personal financial plan. While preparing the plan, Mr. Gable became personal friends of the Wilsons. They confided to him that they have had a somewhat rocky marriage and, on several occasions, seriously discussed divorce. Preparation of the comprehensive personal financial plan, which is nearing completion, has taken six months time. During this period, Mr. Gable also performed the annual audit for the bank.

The audit test sample selected at random from the bank's loan file included the personal loan files of Larry and Susan Wilson. Because certain information in the loan files did not agree with facts personally known to Mr. Gable, he became somewhat concerned. Although he did not disclose his client relationship with the Wilsons, he did discuss their loan in detail with a loan officer. The loan officer is very familiar with the situation because he and Larry Wilson were college classmates, and now they play golf together weekly.

The loan officer mentioned to Mr. Gable that he believed Larry Wilson was "setting his wife up for a divorce." In other words, he was arranging his business affairs over a period of time so that he would be able to "leave his wife penniless." The loan officer indicated that this was just "locker room talk" and that Mr. Gable should keep it confidential.

Mr. Gable's compensation from his firm is based upon annual billings for services. If Mr. Gable resigns as CPA for the Wilsons, it would result in his losing a bonus constituting a substantial amount in annual personal compensation. Mr. Gable is counting on the bonus to contribute to support tuition and expenses for his youngest daughter who will be starting as a freshman in college next fall.

QUESTIONS

1. What are the ethical issues?

2. What should Albert Gable do?

SOURCE: Prepared by Paul Breazeale, Breazeale, Saunders & O'Neil Ltd., Jackson, Mississippi. Drawn from the Ethics Case Collection of The American Accounting Association.

A Fresh Look at Standards of Professional Conduct

The Core of the Proposal: A Goal-oriented, Positively Stated Code and Mandatory Quality Reviews.

George D. Anderson

Journal of Accountancy, September 1985

A crisis of confidence and credibility is confronting the accounting profession. In today's volatile environment, perhaps no other single issue is of greater concern to, or as deeply felt by, CPAs than this one. If it is not, it should be.

This is not, of course, a brand-new problem. Nor is it likely to dissipate soon, for the criticisms of the profession are widespread and harsh.

The American Institute of CPAs responded to the urgency of the situation: In 1983 Rholan E. Larson, then chairman of the AICPA, appointed the special committee on standards of professional conduct for CPAs.

The charge to the committee was indeed an awesome one—no less than a comprehensive evaluation of the relevance of the existing ethical standards to professionalism, integrity and the commitment to quality service and the public interest.

Several elements and themes were part of this evaluation: the changing economic, social and regulatory climate in which the profession functions; the role of the AICPA in the process of establishing standards of professional conduct; and five of the areas explored in *Major Issues for the CPA Profession and the AICPA,* the 1984 report of the future issues committee:

1. The expansion of services and products.
2. Changes in the nature and extent of competition in the profession.
3. The role of self-regulation.
4. Improving the quality of practice.
5. Independence and objectivity.

After extensive research, consultation, and debate—some of it quite heated—the special committee discerned no panacea and identified no easy, "instant" solutions. Rather, the members finally reached a consensus on the broad outlines of a proposal that is considered both relevant and workable. These tentative conclusions and recommendations are the substance of an interim report that was presented to the AICPA's governing council for consideration at its spring meeting this year.

This article highlights the major recommendations of the interim report; conveys the ethical, professional and social considerations that helped to shape it; and contrasts, in concrete terms, the present structure to the proposed one.

With so much at stake for the profession, it is hoped that this broad dissemination of the issues and the special committee's recommendations in the pages of the *Journal of Accountancy* will spur further reflection on the problems by the membership and elicit its invaluable responses.

THE NEED FOR REFORM

Broad and pervasive environmental changes contribute to the need for reform: New concepts and standards of behavior are evolving in society and in the profession; moral and ethical norms are shifting; established institutions are under great stress.

The societal roles of individuals and institutions (and those who make them up) are being redefined. Other contributing factors to this portrait of change are the revolution in information technology; new life-styles and attitudes; the dramatic rise in litigation; the expanding concept of professional responsibility, which translates directly into professional liability; the shift in attitude toward government regulation—all these and more affect the relevance and effectiveness of professional standards in encouraging quality service.

The net result for the profession of these pervasive environmental changes, some would contend, is that self-restraint, conservatism and adherence to basic values, in the interest of being part of a respected profession, are being abandoned at a pace and to an extent that is unprecedented.

For over a decade, the 13 rules of conduct of the AICPA Code of Professional Ethics have been accepted by members as guides to appropriate behavior, and they enhanced the quality of services that members provided to the public. The rules were accepted as the authoritative statement of what the profession stands for.

In short, they were a positive influence because they were perceived as serving the public interest.

In recent years, however, the rules have been strongly challenged by the public sector and by parts of the profession itself, and the special committee has concluded that the

—Continued

Continued

rules no longer sufficiently influence behavior. The causes are numerous: The 1960s saw an explosion of economic activity that was accompanied by unanticipated (and perhaps unintended) applications of accounting principles and a burgeoning demand for an increasing array of services and products from the profession.

The accounting profession had the training and knowledge that uniquely qualified it to respond to this expanding public need. Practice development and the scope of services offered by the profession did indeed change dramatically, but the rules governing performance did not change significantly.

As a result there is a widening gap between public expectations and the level of performance responsive to present ethical norms, and criticism of the profession is increasing. The common thread in this criticism—by Congress, the state legislatures, the media—is that CPAs are believed to have lost the commitment they once had to quality service.

Many of the charges levied against the profession are exaggerated. But more and more observers are voicing legitimate concerns about quality.

The most troubling point is that the code, which should be a strong guide to behavior in a turbulent environment, does not function as such. It does not sufficiently influence, to the extent that it should, how professional services are marketed and rendered.

As many have suggested, the accounting profession is facing a crisis of immense proportions. Public confidence in the profession is eroding, and this erosion can be directly attributed to the alarming amount of work that does not fully meet the profession's standards or the public's expectations.

This gap is evident from several sources. It is evident from the complaints filed by the General Accounting Office and from positive enforcement and quality assurance review programs of state boards of accountancy and state CPA societies. It is also evident from the personal observations of numerous members of the profession.

The fundamental, overriding objective of standards of professional conduct should be the maintenance of high-quality performance and the weeding out of substandard practice. The existing system, the special committee concluded, is not accomplishing this objective.

If the overall quality of the profession's work is perceived as having deteriorated, then whether CPAs are thought of as "professional" or "commercial" is not terribly important. What always is important is whether the public has lost confidence in CPA's ability to provide quality professional services.

Poor-quality work does more to raise questions about accountants' integrity, objectivity and competence than do all the commercial practices, such as advertising and solicitation, that might be adopted by the most aggressive practitioner. Clearly, a way must be found to enhance the quality of the CPA's work product if the profession is to continue to serve the public interest and to merit the public trust.

An excellent perspective of these matters has been offered by Arthur M. Wood, chairman of the Public Oversight Board, which oversees the activities of the SEC practice section of the AICPA division for CPA firms;

"To believe that the crisis exists because Congressman [John D.] Dingell [D-Mich.] is holding hearings about the accounting profession would be a serious error. Congressman Dingell's hearings are a symptom, not a cause. The cause of this crisis is the fact that investors and depositors are losing faith in the ability of the accounting profession to perform the job that has historically been its unique function in our society."[1]

The profession must not be misled by the focus of the current congressional investigations into assuming that the problems relate only to large CPA firms that serve large public companies. On the contrary, the failure of CPAs to meet the profession's standards is a professionwide problem. The appropriate response, therefore, must also be professionwide.

ROLE OF THE AICPA

The Institute, as the national professional association of CPAs, plays a vital role in establishing and maintaining professional standards. Its primary objectives should be to provide leadership to other accounting organizations, to safeguard the public interest, to preserve and strengthen the audit function, and to enhance the quality of professional performance of its members. The Institute should strive to have the members and the public see AICPA membership as a professional designation that means more than the mere possession of a CPA certificate.

The two principal recommendations of the special committee should, then be considered in the context of this AICPA role:

1. That the existing ethical and performance standards be substantially modified (see Exhibit 1).

2. That a mandatory quality assurance review (QAR) program be established to monitor and improve practice (see Exhibit 2).

---

1. For an adaptation of Wood's remarks, made at the spring 1985 meeting of the AICPA's governing council, see Journal of Accountancy. Aug. 85, pp. 142–48.

—Continued

Continued

EXHIBIT 1

PROPOSED ETHICAL AND PERFORMANCE STANDARDS

Goal-oriented code (basic constitution)
- Contains positively stated standards.
- Integrity objectivity due care.
- Establishes basic responsibilities.
- Provides the basis for performance standards.
- Applies equality to all AICPA members.

Structure of performance standards
- Rules of general applicability are in the bylaws.
- AICPA senior technical committees are responsible for interpretation of the rules.
- Standards provide guidance on conflicts of interest.

Role of senior technical committees
- Establish performance standards consistent with the code.
- Determine application to members not in public practice.

Scope of practice
- Code and performance standards provide parameters.

EXHIBIT 2

PROPOSED MONITORING AND IMPROVING OF PRACTICE

1 Mandatory quality assurance review (QAR) program
- Actively and systematically monitors practice–is not complaint-based.
- Focus is on quality of work.
- Is directed at practice in firms (firms must participate in an acceptable program).
- Applies initially only to members in public practice.

2 Structure of QAR program
- AICPA to establish a model program
- State CPA societies to establish QAR committees and conduct the QAR program.

3 Operation of QAR program
- Starts with desk reviews of accounting and auditing practices.
- Takes remedial or corrective actions when deficiencies are found.

4 AICPA sanctions
- Suspension or expulsion.

5 State boards of accountancy
- Complaints filed with boards for pervasive deficiencies and noncooperation.

Mandatory CPE
- An AICPA membership requirement covering all members except those retired or not actively engaged in the profession

ETHICAL AND PERFORMANCE STANDARDS

The existing code, with its 13 rules of conduct, would be replaced by a goal-oriented code. The committee concluded that the profession should have a code that would guide behavior and would inspire members to serve their clients and the public to the best of their abilities. It should set forth the principles on which members could make decisions that would lead them to the optimum, rather than the minimum, standards of conduct and performance.

The code should serve as the basic constitution from which performance and behavioral standards are derived. It would identify the need for integrity, objectivity and due care and would identify basic responsibilities of AICPA members to the public, to clients and to colleagues.

An important departure from the existing code is that the proposed code would apply equally to all members—to those in public practice as well as those not in public practice. (Presently, members not in public practice are governed by only two rules, which require them to avoid acts discreditable to the profession and falsehoods.)

A move to a positively stated, goal-oriented code raises the issue of what would happen to the existing rules of conduct. Under the special committee's proposal, the bylaws would contain a basic requirement that all AICPA members *must* comply with performance standards.

The existing rules designating the bodies authorized to establish performance standards with which members must comply would be included as provisions of the bylaws. The disposition of other rules would depend on whether they are generally applicable to all services equally or whether they require different interpretations for different areas of practice. Rules deemed to have general applicability would be included as bylaw provisions; the Institute's senior technical committees would be expected to develop appropriate interpretations of other rules that pertain to their areas of responsibility.

The responsibility of the senior technical committees to establish performance standards and for members to adhere to these standards would be greatly expanded. These committees would be given responsibility for interpreting standards of general applicability. They would also be assigned responsibility for establishing specific performance standards appropriate to their areas.

The auditing standards board, for example, would interpret the concept of independence as it applies to audit and

—Continued

Continued

other attest services. Because different standards of objectivity might be required for tax and management advisory services, the appropriate executive committees (tax and MAS) would set the objectivity standards for these areas and provide guidance on conflicts of interest.

The senior technical committees would establish performance standards consistent with the code. They would also make clear the extent to which the standards apply to the activities of AICPA members who are not in public practice. This would suggest a much greater involvement by members not in public practice in the work of these committees than has been the case in the past.

The special committee to date has not fully considered the scope of practical issue, but it is envisioned that the performance standards would provide guidance in establishing general parameters for the scope of practice.

MONITORING AND IMPROVING PRACTICE

The centerpiece of the proposed system is a mandatory quality assurance review program, an active, systematic monitoring of practice. The QAR program would focus on the quality of performance and on discouraging and weeding out substandard work. It would be directed toward firms, and all AICPA members in public practice would be required to practice only in those firms that participate in QAR programs acceptable to the Institute.

The special committee has also concluded that the AICPA should adopt a mandatory continuing professional education program covering all its members. This mandatory CPE program, with exemptions for members who are retired or not actively engaged in the profession, would be an integral part of the effort to improve the quality of performance and would be the element that would immediately affect AICPA members who are not in public practice.

The QAR program would be a joint effort of the AICPA and the state CPA societies, analogous to the Institute's existing joint ethics enforcement program (JEEP). The AICPA would establish minimum standards and a model QAR program. The state societies would then be asked to establish QAR committees and to be responsible for conducting the program under the aegis of the Institute. The AICPA would conduct the program should a given state society decide not to participate.

The QAR program would start with desk reviews of audit, review and compilation reports submitted by firms. A field review would be conducted when a serious deficiency is found in the desk review. When a less serious deficiency is encountered, remedial or corrective actions would be required, such as CPE. For a pervasive deficiency, for which

corrective action is inadequate, and for noncooperation, the AICPA would establish sanctions that could lead to suspension of or expulsion from membership. In addition, when such action is necessary, a complaint would be filed with the applicable state board of accountancy, with a view to seeking suspension or removal of the member's license to practice.

The QAR program was developed as a response to the special committee's belief that the existing complaint-based approach has not worked as effectively as it should and that restructuring the system will not solve the basic deficiencies. The special committee believes, rather, that a system must be established to actively monitor compliance with performance standards and with the precepts of the code. Through such an approach, the profession will be able to enhance the quality of practice.

It is not suggested that a QAR will be a comprehensive peer review such as is necessary to meet membership requirements for the division for CPA firms. Rather, the QAR program should entail only minimal costs and minor disruptions. The special committee has not fully addressed as yet the question of who should bear the costs, but those members who benefit from the program should be assessed for it.

COMPARISON OF THE EXISTING AND PROPOSED SYSTEMS

Highlighted in Exhibit 3 are the similarities of and differences between the existing and proposed systems.

The existing system is the AICPA Code of Professional Ethics, consisting of the 13 rules of conduct and the interpretations and ethics rulings derived from them. In contrast, the proposed system would be a positively stated, goal-oriented code of professional conduct. It would be the basic constitution from which all performance standards would be derived.

The existing system assigns to the AICPA's professional ethics executive committee the responsibility for interpreting and enforcing the rules of conduct adopted by the membership, issuing rulings and administering JEEP. In contrast, under the proposed system, rules of conduct of general application would be established and included in the bylaws. The senior technical committees would be given the responsibility for issuing performance standards and specific rules in their areas.

The proposed enforcement philosophy, approach and structure would differ significantly from the existing system, which focuses on specific violations of rules and provides for penalties for such infractions. The existing system is complaint-based in that currently only a complaint or an

—*Continued*

Continued

EXHIBIT 3

A COMPARISON OF THE SYSTEMS

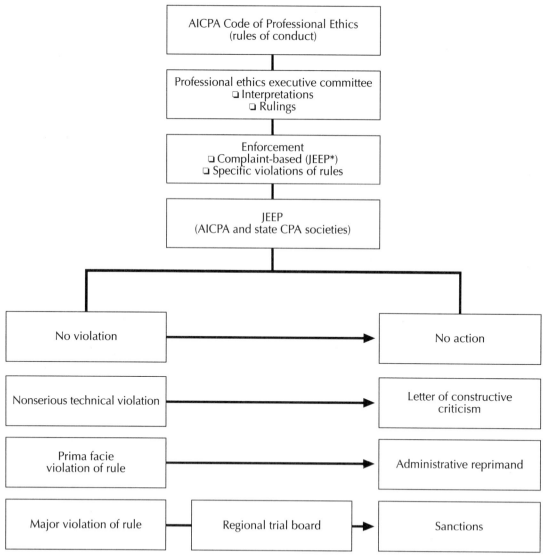

Existing system

AICPA Code of Professional Ethics
(rules of conduct)

Professional ethics executive committee
❑ Interpretations
❑ Rulings

Enforcement
❑ Complaint-based (JEEP*)
❑ Specific violations of rules

JEEP
(AICPA and state CPA societies)

| No violation | → | No action |

| Nonserious technical violation | → | Letter of constructive criticism |

| Prima facie violation of rule | → | Administrative reprimand |

| Major violation of rule | Regional trial board → | Sanctions |

*Joint ethics enforcement program (JEEP)

—Continued

Continued

EXHIBIT 4

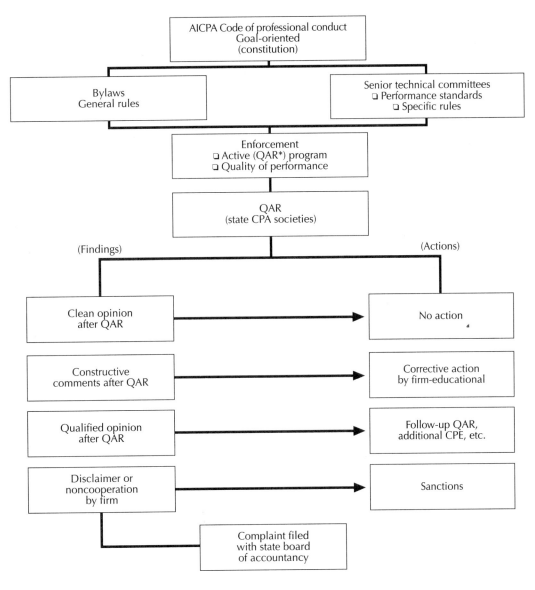

Proposed system

AICPA Code of professional conduct
Goal-oriented
(constitution)

Bylaws
General rules

Senior technical committees
❑ Performance standards
❑ Specific rules

Enforcement
❑ Active (QAR*) program
❑ Quality of performance

QAR
(state CPA societies)

(Findings) (Actions)

Clean opinion
after QAR → No action

Constructive
comments after QAR → Corrective action
by firm-educational

Qualified opinion
after QAR → Follow-up QAR,
additional CPE, etc.

Disclaimer or
noncooperation
by firm → Sanctions

Complaint filed
with state board
of accountancy

*Quality assurance review (QAR)

—Continued

readings

Continued

allegation of a failure to comply with a specific rule triggers a disciplinary procedure. The proposed system focuses on the quality of practice, with the primary objective of improving overall quality through remedial and corrective actions. The imposition of sanctions is reserved for use as a last resort, when all other efforts have failed.

The proposed QAR program and the existing JEEP—both of which contemplate the joint efforts of the AICPA and the state CPA societies—have similar structures and goals.

Findings and actions under the existing JEEP include

1. A finding that no rules were violated leads to no action.

2. A finding that a member has committed a minor technical violation may result in a letter of constructive criticism, which is educational in thrust.

3. A finding that a member has committed a serious violation of a rule could lead to an administrative reprimand, which could call for additional CPE.

4. A finding that a member may have committed a major violation of a rule calls for referral to the appropriate regional trial board, and the outcome of the hearing could be formal sanctions, including suspension or dismissal.

Findings and actions under the proposed QAR program would include

1. A clean opinion after a QAR would lead to no action.

2. A clean opinion after a QAR, with constructive comments, would contemplate corrective action on the part of the firm; here, too, as under JEEP, the thrust would be educational.

3. A qualified opinion because of deficiencies found during a QAR would lead to such actions as a follow-up field review, additional CPE, and so forth.

4. A disclaimer after a QAR or noncooperation on the part of the firm would lead to sanctions and the filing of a complaint with the appropriate state board.

RESPONSIVENESS OF THE PROFESSION

The special committee's proposal calls for dramatic, indeed revolutionary, changes in performance standards and in the approach to monitoring and enforcing compliance with these standards. In view of the sharp contrasts between the existing and proposed systems, the profession will be required to reassess traditional orientations and attitudes and long-held assumptions if the proposed code is to be adopted and a QAR program implemented successfully.

The profession is seen as essentially conservative, perhaps, but it is also innovative. CPAs, in the main, have always been willing to accept demonstrably worthwhile change to serve the public interest.

If substandard work and the trend toward commercialism in the profession is to cease, CPAs must key their actions accordingly. They must see to it that the profession retains respect and independence, that it remains dedicated to serving the public interest.

The desire to practice as one sees fit must be tempered with the realization that individual practitioners' decisions and actions profoundly affect the entire profession. If all CPAs conduct themselves in accordance with the highest ethical and professional standards and provide high-quality services, the overall level of professionalism will be raised.

The single most important challenge to the profession today is to accept—and respond positively to—the currents of complex change in the nation's economic, political and social life. Adopting the more relevant and adequate proposed code, combined with an active approach to monitoring and enforcing compliance with professional standards, would constitute an affirmative response to this multilayered challenge.

Author's note: I wish to acknowledge the valuable assistance of Thomas W. McRae, AICPA vice-president-technical, in writing this article.

GEORGE D. ANDERSON, CPA, is managing partner of Anderson and ZurMuehlen & Co., Helena, Montana. A former chairman of the American Institute of CPAs (1981–82). Mr. Anderson has served on several ethics-related Institute committees and currently is chairman of the AICPA special committee on standards of professional conduct for CPAs. He is a former president of the Montana Society of CPAs and was a member of the Grace Commission's executive committee.

The Anderson Committee: Restructuring Professional Standards

Special Committee on Standards of Professional Conduct for Certified Public Accountants

Journal of Accountancy, May 1987

IN OCTOBER 1983 THE SPECIAL committee on standards of professional conduct for certified public accountants was appointed to study the relevance and effectiveness of professional standards in today's environment.

After three years of analysis, consultation and vigorous debate, the committee issued its final report in July 1986— *Restructuring Professional Standards to Achieve Professional Excellence in a Changing Environment.* The report urges the membership to give thoughtful consideration to the committee's recommendations for sweeping revisions in the American Institute of CPAs Code of Professional Ethics and substantial reforms in a way adherence to professional standards is achieved.

The AICPA leadership initiated the study in response to concerns over the profession's ability to serve the public interest and retain public confidence in a rapidly changing environment. The special committee's basic charge was to consider the changing economic, social, legal and regulatory climate, to thoroughly assess the relevance and effectiveness of existing ethical standards, to evaluate the role of the Institute in establishing standards and to recommend a course of action to be taken.

ROOM FOR IMPROVEMENT

Amid criticism in the profession by Congress, the media, regulators and the public, the committee concluded that some legitimate concerns had been raised about CPAs' behavior and commitment to quality. It found a need for greater flexibility and responsiveness in the existing system and substantial room for improvement in the way the profession identifies and deals with substandard work. The final report includes recommendations for changes in four broad areas:

1. Restructure the Institute's Code of Professional Ethics into two sections, including new standards of professional conduct and completely revised rules of performance and behavior.

2. Provide guidance to practitioners in making judgments regarding the scope and nature of services and adherence to professionalism.

3. Establish a new program for the systematic monitoring of practice to improve the quality of service and to assure compliance with performance standards.

4. Establish mandatory continuing professional education for the AICPA membership and postbaccalaureate education requirements for entry into the profession.

REVOLUTIONARY CHANGES

The revolutionary nature of the report's recommendations is expected to have a profound impact on how the profession functions. The Institute and the state CPA societies are working together to encourage their members' careful consideration of the report. The membership has been urged to recognize the report's implications for the profession's continued ability to regulate itself and to counteract the real threat of intrusive outside regulation.

The special committee's report represents a positive response to changing times and revitalizes the concepts that the profession has always valued: the public interest, integrity, independence and objectivity, and due care. It reaffirms the profession's commitment to the highest attainable level of professional service and conduct.

After implementation proposals have been submitted to and cleared by council, they will be presented to the membership for ballot to put the recommendations into effect. The AICPA is requesting whole-hearted support for all of the committee's proposals. Full endorsement and implementation are expected to send a clear message that the profession intends to achieve and maintain the highest standards of excellence as it meets the challenge of the future.

George D. Anderson
Chairman

Robert L. Bunting	Bernard Z. Lee
Joseph P. Cummings	Herman J. Lowe
James Don Edwards	Archie E. MacKay
Robert C. Ellyson	William L. Raby
Francis A. Humphries	Ralph Saul
Richard Kasten	John P. Thomas
James Kurtz	Kathryn D. Wriston

A Survey on the Effectiveness/Compliance of Corporate Codes of Conduct in Canada

Leonard J. Brooks
Professor of Business Ethics & Accounting
The Centre for Corporate Social Performance & Ethics, University of Toronto, 1990

INTRODUCTION

Several studies have indicated that the majority of large companies in Canada, and indeed worldwide, have issued codes of conduct (Brooks, 1986; Schroeder, 1983; Berenbeim, 1987). These and other studies have provided analyses of the content of the codes and have chronicled the historical trends evident in their development (Brooks, 1989; White and Montgomery, 1980; Hoffman, 1986; Ethics Resource Center, 1990). However, there is a paucity of empirical examination of what makes such codes effective, and how companies ensure compliance with their codes. These were the issues addressed by the survey which was administered in March 1990, the findings of which are the subject of this report.

THE GROWING IMPORTANCE OF EFFECTIVENESS AND COMPLIANCE

Reasons for the growing existence of corporate codes of conduct have been explained elsewhere (Benson, 1989; Brooks, 1989), but recently significant additional legal penalties have become associated with employee misbehavior which codes were designed to guard against. For instance, for an unfavorable environmental impact companies can be fined up to $1 million per day and the executives can be jailed. More importantly, first in Canada and then in the U.S., lawyers have written to their clients and the public advising that in order to defend against negligence, directors and executives would have to be able to demonstrate that they had developed an effective code and had communicated it to the appropriate employees in their organization (Harbell, 1989; Pitt & Groskaufmanis, 1990). The code of conduct has apparently become an accepted and expected means of communicating to employees and in controlling their behavior, at least in the eyes of prominent lawyers in Canada and the U.S. As a consequence, emphasis has shifted from the creation of a code to making the code effective and ensuring compliance with it.

THE INVESTIGATION PROCESS

In order to examine what makes codes effective and how compliance is ensured, in March 1990 a questionnaire (which is available from the author) was sent to 1432 Chief Executive Officers (CEO) of both for-profit and not-for-profit Canadian organizations. CEO's were asked to return a completed questionnaire and a copy of their corporate code for analysis.

The primary purpose of the questionnaire was to identify companies with effective codes of conduct and to gather information on how effectiveness and compliance were achieved. Since the intention was to gather information on exemplary behavior, and not on the state of codes in general, the receipt of only 139 responses is sufficient for the analysis which follows.

It should be noted that the mechanism used to evaluate corporate codes was the self-assessment of the CEO of the corporation involved. Biased results, both favorable and unfavorable, might again be considered a problem, but the guaranty given to survey participants for the confidentiality of their identity, and that of their corporation's, should minimize such tendencies by limiting the rewards involved.

FINDINGS AND ANALYSIS

In total, 139 responses were received. Thirty-eight of the 139 were letters which did not provide answers to the specific questions asked, and 2 questionnaires were received after the final tabulations were completed. Accordingly there were 99 valid responses to the questionnaire. No doubt these 99 respondents exhibit a self-selection bias reflective of organizations with a high social responsibility quotient, but that should serve to make the findings more useful.

Effectiveness: Overall and of Reinforcing Mechanisms

The questionnaire was designed to elicit information about the overall rating of the corporation's code, and then to delve into each of the mechanisms which could have been used to reinforce the code thereby making it effective and encouraging compliance with it. Based on a search of relevant literature and on several hypotheses to be tested, data were collected on the following reinforcing mechanisms: support for the code from senior management, and from middle management; the content of the code; the corpora-

—Continued

Continued

tion's training program; various compliance mechanisms, as well as various measures and reports of performance.

According to Table A, on the favorable end of the overall effectiveness scale only 6.4% of the respondents (94 to this part of question 2) indicated their code was extremely effective whereas 12.8% thought their code needed improvement. An interesting cross check on the unfavorable end of the scale is available from the answer to question 10, where 17.8% of 73 respondents indicated that their corporate code had not reduced the incidence of unethical behavior. Consequently while perhaps 13–18% of codes were not considered effective, roughly 94% could be improved. The question is how to do so.

Review of the rankings in Table A of the effectiveness of reinforcing mechanisms reveals potential for improvement.

Evidently the possibility for improvement exists in each mechanism, with the order of priority for attention being confirmed as indicated, with the caveat that this priority appears to be driven by the percentage of non-existent rankings on each dimension. Subsequent questions explored how each mechanism was or was not being used.

Senior and Middle Management Support

Question 3 elicited information on the degree to which management support was evident during the initial distribution

Reinforcement Mechanism	Based on Percent Ranked			
	Needs Improvement or Non-existent		Not Extremely Effective	
	Percent	Rank	Percent	Rank
Training Programs	59.4	1	95.7	1
Reports of Performance	52.2	2	93.5	2
Measures of Performance	50.6	3	93.5	2
Compliance Mechanisms	31.9	4	92.6	4
Content of Code	9.4	5	84.4	5
Middle Management Support	8.1	6	82.7	6
Senior Management Support	5.1	7	73.5	7

of the code, in subsequent communications and through daily conduct.

89 respondents indicated that the initial distribution of their codes was accompanied by a letter or video from senior or middle management. As might be expected, senior management levels dominated this form of support as follows:

TABLE A: CEO'S RATING OF THE OVERALL EFFECTIVENESS OF THEIR COMPANY'S CODE, AND THE EFFECTIVENESS OF EACH REINFORCING MECHANISM USED

PERCENTAGES OF RESPONSES SHOWN IN EACH CELL

	Extremely Effective	Highly Effective	Effective	Needs Improvement	Non-Existent	Valid Responses
Overall Effectiveness	6.4	37.2	43.6	12.8	N.A.	94
Senior Management Support	26.5	42.9	25.5	4.1	1.0	98
Middle Management Support	17.3	33.7	40.8	6.1	2.0	98
Content of Code	15.6	37.5	37.5	9.4		96
Training Program	4.3	12.8	23.4	20.2	39.4	94
Compliance Mechanisms	7.4	19.1	41.5	17.0	14.9	94
Measures of Performance	6.5	10.8	32.3	18.3	32.3	93
Reports of Performance	6.5	9.8	31.5	20.7	31.5	92

—Continued

Continued

Initial Endorsement of Code by	Percent
Chairman, President or Vice Chair	67
Chairman + senior officer	8
	75
One other senior officer, alone	3
A senior officer + a middle manager	19
A middle manager, alone	3
	100

Only 62 respondents indicated that their company had frequent supportive communications dealing with their code. 14 of these were by way of newsletters or magazines and the rest (77%) used letters or other means of notification. Senior management again dominated these letter/notification communications as follows:

Frequent Supportive Communication By	Percent
Senior management	54
Senior management and others	38
General counsel	6
Other	2
	100

Only 70 of 139 CEO's responded as to whether management supported their corporate code through daily conduct. In 67.1% of these companies, both senior and middle managers provided such daily support, whereas in 20% only senior management did and in the rest (12.9%) only the middle management was considered to do so.

In summary, there appears to be less top management support than expected as indicated by the responses of the CEO's who answered the questions in the topic. The questions were answered by 89, 62 and 70 respectively of 99 respondents, with the lower number of responses being related to ongoing support for their company codes.

Nature of the Code

Question 4A elicited information on the design of the respondent's code. First, with regard to the controversy over whether codes ought to be highly specific in nature or more general thus encouraging employees to interpret a principle to a wide range of situations, the 98 respondents favored a design providing both (70.4%) rather than just general principles (28.6%) or specific rules (1.0%).

In an attempt to discover the depth of ethical reasoning put forward to employees in the codes, 97 respondents indicated that only 49.5% of the codes supplemented assertions of what to do or not do with background reasons. However,

70.1% of the codes were said to provide some ethical reasoning which has rooted in basic values.

Finally, respondents were asked about the comprehensiveness of purpose of their codes, particularly with regard to whether guidance was being provided on economic or ethical/social matters or some attempt was being made to integrate guidance on both dimensions. Interestingly, and contrary to the Friedmanite view that corporations should only pursue profits, 77.8% of the 72 respondents indicated that an attempt was being made to provide guidance integrating economic and ethical purposes and 19.4% of the codes covered just ethical/social matters. Only 2.8% focused on just economic matters.

Use of the Code

The overwhelming majority of codes (73.5%), according to 98 respondents, were distributed to all management and employees. However, some codes were only distributed selectively, as follows: top management only (1%), middle management only (1%), top and middle management only (17.3%), all non-management employees only (7.1%).

As far as the timing of distribution was concerned, regardless of level of management or employee the pattern appears to be approx. 65% when the person joins the corporation, approx. 12% after the person joins, and approx. 23% both upon joining as well as at later intervals.

Governance: Administration and Revision

Ninety-three respondents indicated that the administration of their codes was usually assigned (85% of the time) to one functional group or one person instead of to more than one. Table B reveals that the functional areas most commonly assigned the task were:

	Sole Responsibility	Joint Responsibility	Total
Personnel	31%	8%	37%
Corp. Law/Sec.	15%	4%	19%
General Admin.	11%	3%	14%
Corporate/Public Affairs	8%	1%	9%
Senior Management	6%	3%	9%
Finance, Internal Audit	4%	2%	6%

It is noteworthy that the involvement of the internal audit function is relatively low, as is that of corporate affairs. Many of the corporate affairs departments have performed admirably the years, but their involvement in administering

—Continued

Continued

TABLE B: RESPONSIBILITY FOR ADMINSTERING CODES OF CONDUCT

PERCENT OF 93 RESPONSES SHOWN IN EACH CELL

Department or Individual Assigned Responsibility	Sole Responsibility	Corp. Law/Sec	Gen'l Admin	Corp Affairs	Internal Audit	Other
Personnel/Human Resources	31	2	3	1	1	1
Corp. Law/Secretary	15				1	1
General Administration	11					
Corporate/Public Affairs	8					
Finance, Control, Internal Audit	4					
Board Committees	3					
Chairman, President	3					1
Senior Management	6	2			1	
Other	5					

only 9% of the codes should reduce the charge by critics that corporate codes are more window-dressing than substance.

In the case of assignment of responsibility for revising corporate codes of conduct, a somewhat changed picture emerges from an analysis of Table C. Although only 58 respondents answered the question the following major frequencies of assignment emerged:

	Sole Responsibility	Joint Responsibility	Total
Personnel	23%	17%	40%
Corp. Law/Sec.	19%	12%	31%
Finance, Control, Internal Audit	5%	6%	11%
Chairman, President	10%	–	10%
General Admin.	5%	2%	7%

TABLE C: RESPONSIBILITY FOR REVISING CODES OF CONDUCT

PERCENT OF 58 RESPONSES SHOWN IN EACH CELL

Department or Individual Assigned Responsibility	Sole Responsibility	Corp. Law/Sec	Gen'l Admin	Corp Affairs	Internal Audit	Other
Personnel/Human Resources	23	9	2		3	3
Corp. Law/Secretary	19				3	
General Administration	5					
Corporate/Public Affairs	5					
Finance, Control, Internal Audit	5					
Board Committees	3					
Chairman, President	10					
Senior Management	5					
Other	5					

—Continued

Continued

TABLE D: CEO'S RATING OF TOPICAL COVERAGE OF COMPANY'S CODE						
PERCENTAGES OF RESPONSES SHOWN IN BOXES						
Issues	*Extremely Effective*	*Highly Effective*	*Effective*	*Needs Improvement*	*Non-Existent*	*Valid Responses*
Human Resources	14.3	29.7	41.8	6.6	7.7	91
Community Involvement	8.7	19.6	41.3	10.9	19.6	92
Environment	6.7	15.7	19.1	20.2	38.2	89
Product or Services	11.8	30.1	36.6	9.7	11.8	93
Economic	11.5	29.9	33.3	9.2	16.1	87

Personnel and, to a lesser extent, legal departments continue to dominate the revision process, while general administration and corporate affairs have declined. These changes may represent the fact that only some firms have undergone a process of revision.

Contents of Codes

Each CEO was asked to rate the effectiveness of the topical coverage of their company's code on a five point scale. While the full set of responses is shown on Table D, those topical areas rated most in need of improvement or deemed to be non-existent were:

Topical Area	*Percent of Codes Ranked Needing Improvement or Non-existent*
Environment	58%
Community Involvement	31%
Economic Matters	25%
Product or Services	22%
Human Resources	14%

Presumably this ranking reflects the current strength of public pressure, as well as other factors including the degree to which earlier attention to human resource or product and service issues had resulted in fulsome treatment before the date of the survey. *It is significant that almost 40% of the respondents indicated their code had no coverage of environmental responsibilities, almost 20% offered no coverage of responsibilities in regard to the local community and over 15% had no guidance relative to economic matters.*

These observations were confirmed by questioning the responsibilities covered by the codes. As Table E reveals, relatively few CEO's responded when asked if their code covered responsibilities to the environment (38/99) or to communities (52/99). Several of the other responsibility areas also showed low response rates.

TABLE E: RESPONSIBILITIES COVERED IN THE CODE				
PERCENTAGES OF RESPONSES SHOWN IN BOXES				
Responsibilities To	*By Management*	*By Other Employees*	*By Both*	*Valid Responses*
Shareholders	27.6	0	72.4	76
Fellow employees	14.3	3.9	81.8	77
Customers	9.2	3.4	87.4	87
Suppliers	11.4	2.5	86.1	79
Communities	23.1	3.8	73.1	52
Public in general	12.7	0	87.3	71
Environment	31.6	0	68.4	38

CEO's were also surveyed with regard to the latest revisions to their company's code as well as those they foresaw in the next revision. Those deficiencies identified in the coverage of topics and responsibilities should be evident in the responses which are presented in Table F. However, while it is evident that the lack of coverage of environmental responsibilities is beginning to be remedied, that of community involvement is not, nor is it clear that significant upgrades are expected on economic issues.

A detailed analysis of the topics covered in the codes submitted was not made by this researcher. However, an analysis of a similar set of codes was made by staff at the Centre for Social Performance and Ethics, and will be available from the Centre.

Training in Support of the Code

From the perspective of 97 CEO's who responded, employees were generally judged to be very (28.9%) or moderately (56.7%) familiar with their company's code. Only 13.4% of employees were thought to have very little familiarity and only 1% were judged to be not familiar at all with the codes.
—Continued

Continued

TABLE F: TOPICS UPGRADED IN THE LATEST REVISION OF
CODES AND EXPECTED TO BE UNGRADED IN THE TEXT

Topic	Latest Revision	Next Revision
	Number of Responses	
Human resources		2
Sexual Harassment	3	
Equal opportunity employment/promotion	1	
Conflict between personnel	1	
Health and Safety	2	1
Privacy	2	
Family responsibility	1	
Hiring of relatives		1
Community involvement		2
Environment	8	20
Product of Services		1
Customer rebate guide	1	
Economic	1	
Gratuity guidelines	3	
Competition, international operation	2	
Other		
General revision	22	6
Policy clarification:	5	
Response to legislation, legalities	1	2
Employee sign-off, awareness	1	3
Conflict of interest	3	1
Insider trading	1	
Internal share purchases	5	1
Confidentiality of information	2	
Specification of procedures	5	
Compliance questionnaire	1	
Reporting procedure	1	
Reporting of frauds	1	
Role of the audit committee		1
Computer ethics	1	
Total	74	41

However, *responses to questions on training programs indicated that while 64% of 89 companies were offering courses in support of the code, the sparse details they provided indicated those courses to be* *of very short duration and often non-compulsory.* For example, only 51.2% of 43 respondents indicated their company's courses were given to all management and employees. In a further 28% of the companies, only senior and/or middle management received such training. *Only 21 CEO's provided information on the length of training programs, with 81% indicating courses of one-half day or less.* Only 37.3% of 51 respondents indicated annual training programs, with a further 17.8% offering programs at recurring intervals: 33.3% offer a program once only and 7.8% offer it upon employment. Only 52% of 50 respondents indicated a compulsory program.

Of the 37 CEO's indicating what their training program format was, the overwhelmingly popular (81%) approach was that of discussion groups, followed by a variety of other approaches. Interestingly, none of 46 respondents indicated the use of an outside consultant to mount the course.

Overall, the emphasis on training as a mechanism for reinforcing codes of conduct appears to have considerable scope for strengthening.

Compliance: Encouragement, Monitoring and Reporting of Wrongdoing

A review of the responses to questions on how companies encourage compliance with their codes of conduct indicates how few use positive rather than negative compliance mechanisms. Similarly, few companies have build code compliance into their performance review, remuneration and promotion decisions. The specific frequencies involved are noted in Table G.

TABLE G: COMPLIANCE MECHANISMS USED		
Mechanism	*Percentage of Respondents Using*	*Valid Responses*
Awards	2.0%	99
Specific bonuses	1.0%	99
Specific inclusion in:		
Performance reviews	33.7%	95
Remuneration decisions	14.7%	95
Promotion decisions	20.0%	95
Reprimands	77.9%	95
Suspension	56.8%	95
Demotion	33.7%	95
Fines	25.3%	95
Dismissal	61.1%	95

—Continued

Continued

There are several ways in which the CEOs' companies monitor compliance with their codes, but very few approaches have achieved widespread popularity. The most common are listed in Table H.

TABLE H: METHODS OF MONITORING COMPLIANCE

Method	Percentage of Companies Using	Valid Responses
Internal audits	67.3%	98
Supervisory surveillance	56.1%	98
Reviews by legal department	31.6%	98
Annual sign-off affidavits		
• by some employees	44.9%	98
• by all employees	20.4%	98
Employee surveys	10.2%	98

Several other methods were listed as being used, but with less than 10% frequency. These included: computerized checks; periodic discussion; reviews by auditors, human resources departments, controller's office, security departments and committees of the Board and of management.

Essential to the maintenance of a high degree of compliance with codes of conduct is the possibility of being found out if a mistake is made. In many cases such mistakes will pass unnoticed unless someone reports the wrongdoing. This, however, is unlikely given the cultural bias against whistleblowing and the dire consequences such as loss of merit pay, promotion and often one's job which usually have befallen

TABLE I: METHODS OF FACILITATION OF REPORTING OF WRONGDOING

Facilitation By	Percentage of Companies Using	Valid Responses
Absolute confidentiality	62.2%	90
Whistleblower protection plan	1.9%	90
Ombudsman program	5.7%	53
Hotline program	1.9%	53
Monitoring by a Committee of the Board:		
Ethics or Public Issues Committee	3.8%	53
Audit Committee	41.5%	53
Non-board Ethics Committee	3.8%	53
Human Resources Dept.	9.4%	53
Auditors	5.7%	53
Combination of items above	51.1%	53

the whistleblower. These negatives must be combatted and offset if reports of wrongdoing are to be facilitated. Surprisingly, however, very few companies are taking steps to do so as is indicted by the low frequencies of use shown in Table I.

Similar to the overall conclusion on the use of training, companies have room to improve their use of mechanisms for encouragement of compliance and the reporting of wrongdoing, as well as several methods for monitoring compliance with their codes of conduct.

Measures of Effectiveness

When asked whether their companies employed specific measures of effectiveness only 13 responded in the affirmative. The list of the twelve specific measures reported included:

• Violation reports	6
• Periodic discussions	1
• Annual report to parent	1
• Performance measures	1
• Annual compliance reports	1
• Ad hoc reviews	1
• Sales/longevity of staff	1
	12

Obviously the paucity of specific measures of effectiveness reveals a major area of possible improvement as companies strive to reinforce their codes of conduct. With such a limited response, it is interesting to speculate on whether codes of conduct are really effective or, at least, are effective as far as the CEO's are concerned. Happily, the percentage of 73 respondents answering affirmatively (32.9%) is almost double that reporting negatively (17.8%). The areas in which reductions of unethical behaviour were noted by the CEO's included:

Conflicts of interest	Compliance
Use of company assets	Marketing procedures
Gifts	Environment
Human resources	General
Fraud	

The evidence cited for such reductions of unethical behaviour included:

Employee awareness/responsiveness	Audits
Minimal lawsuits	Signed statements
Reduction of investigations	Staff surveys
No violations	Number of incidents reported

—Continued

Continued

Reporting of Ethical/Social Performance

Forty-two CEO's indicated that their companies reported on its ethical/social performance, as follows:

Internal report	28
External report	6
Both	8
	42 of 99 respondents

These forty-two were then asked about the nature of their reports and the responses of thirty-one who answered are recorded in Table J. Some companies had more than one reporting mechanism thus resulting in 36 different reports being cataloged in Table J.

TABLE J: ETHICAL PERFORMANCE REPORTS	
	Frequency
Internal Reports:	
To the Board	8
To board Committees (Audit)	1
To Management from:	
Managers	
Annual Conduct Report	2
Absenteeism	1
Manager's Reports	2
Internal Audit Department	2
Legal Department	1
Security Department	1
To employees	2
Newsletter	1
Sub-total	21
External Reports:	
Annual Report	10
Audit Report	4
Annual Meeting Report	1
Sub-total	15
Total	36

Given the low response rate of 31% (31/99) to this question, there appears to be scope for more companies to institute reporting mechanisms for their ethical/social performance achievements. To do so would serve to focus the attention of the Board, management and employees on conduct objectives rather than presume them less important than other corporate goals. In the area of environmental performances, many companies will soon have to develop compliance reports in any event. Perhaps these can serve more than one purpose.

CONCLUSION

The Chief Executive Officers surveyed are relatively satisfied with their codes of conduct. However, they indicated improvement can and needs to be made to enhance code effectiveness and compliance. In particular, efforts need to be made to improve code content on environmental and community responsibilities and on training, compliance, evaluation and reporting of ethical performance.

REFERENCES

Benson, G. C. S., "Codes of Ethics," *Journal of Business Ethics,* Vol. 8, No. 5, (May 1989), pp. 305–319.

Brooks, L. J., "Corporate Codes of Ethics," *Journal of Business Ethics,* Vol. 8, (1989), pp. 117–129.

_____, *Canadian Corporate Social Performance,* Society of Management Accountants of Canada, Hamilton, Ontario, 1986.

Berenbeim, R. E., *Corporate Ethics,* A Research Report from The Conference Board, Inc., N.Y., N.Y., 1987.

Ethics Resource Centre, a handbook entitled: *Creating a Workable Company Code of Ethics.* Washington, D.C., 1990.

Harbell, J. "Personal Liability of Directors and Officers for Environmental Matters" in a newsletter to clients from Borden & Elliott, Toronto, Canada, March 1989, pp. 3–6. Reissued in 1990 as a paper of 7 pages by Stikeman, Elliott under the same title.

Hoffman et al., "Are Corporations Institutionalizing Ethics?", *Journal of Business Ethics,* Vol. 5, 1986, pp. 85–91.

Pitt, H. L. and Groskaufmanis, K. A., "Why A Corporate Code May Not Protect You," *Across the Board,* May 1990, pp. 22–25. For a longer version, see "Minimizing Corporate Civil and Criminal Liability: A Second Look at Corporate Codes of Conduct," in *The Georgetown Law Journal,* Vol. 78 (1990), pp. 1559–1654.

Schroeder, H., *Corporate Social Performance in Canada: A Survey Report to Survey Participants,* University of Lethbridge, Lethbridge, Alberta, 1983.

White, B. J. and Montgomery, R., "Corporate Codes of Conduct," *California Management Review,* Winter 1980, pp. 80–87.

Funding for this research project has been received from the Social Sciences and Humanities Research Council of Canada. © 1990 by L. J. Brooks.

Ethical Codes of Conduct: Deficient in Guidance for the Canadian Accounting Profession

Leonard J. Brooks
Professor of Business Ethics & Accounting
Faculty of Management
University of Toronto

Journal of Business Ethics, Volume 8; 1989.

ABSTRACT. *Current trends toward increased pace, more complex substance and lower tolerance of error have caused the financial marketplace to rely more heavily on the integrity of financial data and, therefore, of those who prepare the financial statements. At the same time, these trends place higher challenges before professional accountants and it is essential that they have excellent ethical guidance to live up to modern expectations. However, in view of the current codes of conduct, an accountant may not have a clear understanding of what priority of interests to satisfy, who can be consulted for advice, to whom to report misdeeds, what protection is offered a 'right-doer' and what sanction will be forthcoming for 'doing wrong'. Possible solutions are offered to these problems in ways that ought to strengthen the accounting profession and prevent unscrupulous companies from taking advantage of both members of the profession and the unsuspecting public. To provide the appropriate quality of service to society in the future, the Canadian accounting profession should offer its members the improved guidance and enhanced mechanisms for confidential consultation, assistance and protection outlined herein.*

INTRODUCTION

The Canadian accounting profession is facing an increasingly complex and challenging environment. Rampant corporate growth through takeovers, numerous, new, high-risk means of financing; expansion of accounting standards and securities regulations; and particularly the recent scandals, insolvencies and commissions[1] thereon, testify to changes in the pace, substance and tolerance to be found in the North American financial marketplace. The growing knowledge expectation inherent in these changes is challenging the professional accountant to maintain an adequate level of technical competence, while at the same time the shrinking tol-

erance for error is bringing additional pressure for increasing quality of services provided. It is this last challenge—providing an appropriate quality of accounting services—that is the focus of this article.

The quality of accounting services is a function of technical competence and judgement, where judgement depends in part on the integrity of the accountant making the decisions between accounting alternatives. For example, an accountant providing service must understand the alternatives available (i.e., have technical competence) *and* must also select from among those alternatives, the one(s) which best suit(s) the circumstances. Unless the selection process is absolutely objective, bias can influence the selection decision and downgrade the quality of accounting service provided. If the bias is significant, poor decisions will be made by the user of the accounting services, and wealth may be transferred inappropriately. Consequently the integrity of accountants is of critical importance in the provision of high quality accounting services in the future.

The primary means of ongoing guidance about the integrity of professional accountants lies in their ethical codes of conduct. Unfortunately, as the analysis to follow will show, the codes of professional accountants in Canada have the following significant deficiencies, the majority of which exist because the ethical codes do not treat circumstances where a professional accountant is an employee as thoroughly as is the case for non-employees:

— no prioritization of conflicting interests;

— consultation is encouraged for some, but inhibited for others;

— a fair reporting/hearing process for ethical dilemmas is not indicated;

— protective mechanisms are not outlined for a "right-doer";

— specific sanctions are not linked to offenses.

If society is desirous of the highest possible level of service from the Canadian accounting profession, these deficiencies should be remedied. If they are not remedied, of all the

---

1. The bankruptcies during 1985 of the Canadian Commercial Bank and the Northland Bank, both in Alberta, resulted in the appointment of Justice W. Z. Estey to undertake an Inquiry into the Collapse of the CCB and Northland Banks. *The Report* of the Inquiry is dated August 27, 1986.

During 1987, Principal Trust Co. was declared insolvent and a public inquiry was held which continued into 1988.

—Continued

Continued

stakeholders involved, accounting professionals and the profession itself probably have the most to lose. Several public studies[2] have already been undertaken to examine the profession, and proposals have been put forth for changes in the profession's role, practice and autonomy to make the professional a better servant of society in North America. Ultimately, however, the integrity of financial dealings depends upon the integrity of financial data and, in turn, upon the integrity of its preparers, the accounting profession.

BACKGROUND INFORMATION ON THE CANADIAN ACCOUNTING PROFESSION

There are three professional accounting organizations with significant numbers of members in Canada: The Canadian Institute of Chartered Accountants (CICA), the Society of Management Accountants of Canada (SMAC), and the Certified General Accountants Association of Canada (CGAAC).[3] In general, these Canada-wide bodies oversee research activity, and set standards of disclosure. Provincial bodies, however, handle admittance to the profession by examination through an interprovincial committee and have the power to govern ethical conduct and the related discipline processes, which are now essentially in-camera.[4] More specifically, rather than each provincial body inventing a completely new code of ethics, the tendency has been to follow the example set in Ontario, usually the largest provincial body in Canada. Consequently a reasonably accurate picture of Canadian professional accounting codes can be seen by comparing the codes of the Institute of Chartered Accountants of Ontario (ICAO), the Society of Management Accountants of Ontario (SMAO) and the Certified General Accountants Association of Ontario (CGAAO).

Table I provides the numbers of accountants registered in Ontario and in Canada as a whole. It splits members into those engaged in serving the public directly through audit, accounting, tax and consulting services, and those management accountants who serve the public indirectly through the preparation of financial statements for their employer, etc. While the ratio of employee/non-employee members is difficult to determine accurately, it is probably greater than 1.0 because management accountants are employees and the largest percentage of members listed as serving the public directly are also employees working for the non-employees (partners and principals) who serve the public directly. This information is useful because the ethical codes appear to address non-employee concerns more thoroughly than those of employees.

The last major revision to the ethical codes extant in Ontario occurred fifteen years ago in 1974.[5] Since that time several single-item revisions have been made to cover such matters as appropriate advertising practice, client arrangements on new assignments, etc. Recently, the Macdonald Commission, sponsored by the C.I.C.A., recommended further revisions as a partial answer to the public's false expectations for auditor performance, but it is too early to tell what changes, if any will result.

ETHICAL CODES: PURPOSES AND NATURE

In general, ethical codes of conduct for accountants ought to provide sufficient guidance for accountants to fulfill their role as professionals, and to inform interested observers such as investors, management or government agencies how accountants ought to behave. More specifically, to ensure the accounting profession provides effective service to society, an ethical code of conduct for accountants ought to:

A. Specify the reasons for the general rules related to:

  a. technical competence:

  b. due care:

  c. objectivity: and

  d. integrity.

B. Provide guidance:

  a. for behavior towards various groups in society including:

   — the public (i.e., investors, etc);

   — the accounting profession in general;

   — clients (audit or consulting);

   — employers if the accountant works for an organization; and

---

2. In Canada: *Report of the Commission to Study the Public's Expectation's of Audit's* (The Macdonald Commission). In U.S.A.: *Report of the National Commission on Fraudulent Financial Reporting* (The Treadway Commission). *Report of the Special Committee on Standards of Professional Conduct for Certified Public Accountants* (The Anderson Report).

3. Because of an early merger in which Certified Public Accountants (CPAs) become Chartered Accountants (CAs) in Ontario, the number of CPAs in Canada is not significant.

There is another organization of accountants, The Canadian Academic Accounting Association, (CAAA) whose members are predominantly academic and not involved in the preparation or certification of financial statements for the public or for corporations.

4. Although the process is 'open' in the case of the ICAO, there is no advance notice, so an interested observer has to enter the Building each day to check the notices of meeting.

5. 1975 for the CGA's; 1973 for the ICAO and 1971 for the SMAO.

—Continued

Continued

TABLE I

MEMBERSHIP IN THE CANADIAN
ACCOUNTING PROFESSION,
1988–1989

SERVICE TO PUBLIC	CANADA-WIDE			ONTARIO ONLY		
	CICA	SMAC	CGAAC	ICAO	SMAO	CGAAO
Direct: audit, accounting, tax, consulting	19,606	1,150*	N/A	8,487	500*	697
Indirect: management accountants	13,226	N/A	N/A	8,055	N/A	2,376
Other	12,138	N/A	N/A	4,462	N/A	3,448
Total	44,970	18,987	17,250	21,004	8,985	6,521
Legend: *estimate N/A not available						

SOURCES: *CICA Annual Report 1987–88,* dated March 31, 1988; *ICAO Annual Report 1988,* dated February 29,
1988; CGAAC executive, effective September 1, 1988; CGAAO executive, effective September 30, 1988; SMAC
membership records, effective January 1, 1989; SMAO membership records, effective January 1, 1989; Note 3.

b. for resolving conflicts between these interests, and between these interests and the accountant.

C. Provide support or protection for accountants who wish to "do the right thing" (i.e. comply with their code and report an ethical problem); and

D. Specify sanctions clearly so that the consequences of wrongdoing will be understood.

While the need for guidance about the interaction between the accountant and various groups is self-evident, the need for the resolution of conflicts between these groups requires explanation. Suppose an accountant working for an employer finds a misdeed which, if not clarified, will mislead investors. Should the misdeed be reported to the public if the employer refuses to correct it, or should it be kept confidential within the employer company. The same concern over the priority of interests would be true if a questionable payment were discovered by an auditor. Should it be reported to the public (Canada has no statute requiring such disclosure at present) or be kept confidential to the client's operations. If an employer orders an accountant to misrepresent some fact, does the employee owe a duty to his employer to maintain confidentiality, or to the public and/or his profession to report the problem. Similarly, if accountants are dismissed for questioning the ethics of an act of a superior, do they owe a duty of confidentiality to their ex-employer or can they tell a prospective employer the circumstances of their dismissal thus fulfilling a personal duty to themselves. Just which inter-

est outranks the others? The answer is not clear in the ethical codes for Canadian accountants.

Explanation is also needed to clarify how an ethical code could provide support/protection for an accountant who wants to 'do the right thing" and comply with the code, but is hesitating for a number of reasons. Such a professional would benefit by access to an informed consultation process in order to build an understanding of what he/she ought to do. Secondly, he/she should be assured that his/her concerns will receive a fair hearing and that retaliation will not result if he/she stays within a prescribed reporting system. Third, where unfair retaliation is suspected, a mechanism should be available to protect the accountant who "does right". Fourth, exhortative statements, and explanations of why an accountant should behave properly, are always useful.

SIGNIFICANT PROBLEMS WITH ETHICAL CODES

Unfortunately, Canadian professional accounting codes make no effort to sort out the priority of conflicting interests; a process of consultation is not laid out for accountants and inhibitions may actually be placed in the way of informal consultation; a fair reporting/hearing process is not indicated; protection is not offered to a 'right-doer"; and statements of sanctions are not clear enough to provide effective motivation. These significant problems will be discussed in turn.

—Continued

Continued

No Prioritization of Conflicting Interests

Existing ethical codes do not indicate clearly whether Canadian professional accountants owe their ultimate duty to the public, to their client or employer, or to their profession, or to themselves. In fact, not only is the professional's primary duty not known, the secondary or tertiary orders of priority are not commented on either. The closest the codes come to such prioritizing is to lay down an admonishment that client/employee matters are to be kept confidential.[6]

This admonishment carries a differing impact depending on the position of the accountant involved. For an accountant employed by a corporation or an audit firm, this confidentiality guideline prohibits reporting a wrongdoing to the public. For example, an accountant employed by a corporation would be unable to explain to a prospective employer the circumstances for which his/her employment was terminated. Similarly an accountant employed by an audit firm can report a problem to his superiors, but if they do not report it to the client and to the public, the confidentiality guideline would prevent the employee from doing so. Conceivably an employee accountant could choose to breach the confidentiality guideline and whistleblow to the public. This could be a very disruptive action for the corporation and its shareholders, and would very likely jeopardize the accountant's job or future. Reporting the problem to the accountant's society, presumably because it endangered the profession, would probably generate a reaction from the accountant superiors (if of the same professional body), but since the professional accounting bodies have no disciplinary powers over non-members or the enterprise as a whole, information on the problem might not filter through to the public.

In the case of an auditor appointed by shareholders, the auditor has a contractual relationship to render an audit opinion on the financial statements. A significant problem arising during the audit must be reported to management for proper reflection on the financial statements or qualified audit opinion will be given and the public thereby notified. However, if the problem does not affect the financial statements in a significant way, then no public report or qualification is presently called for in the ethical codes. For example, instances of bribery could go unreported to management and to the public.

According to this analysis, current codes suppress the flow of information to the public and therefore appear to rank the interests of a client's management or an employer higher than those of the public, the profession, or the professional. If this is the intended ranking of priorities, then it indicates the employee professional should be loyal to the management of the client or to the employer rather than to the shareholder owners or future owners (i.e., the public) of the corporation - a relationship which may be at odds with the public's expectation for the accounting profession as a whole. If the intended ranking of priorities is otherwise, why not say so? Speculation about this issue is unlikely to produce effective decision making.

Consultation is Encouraged for Some, but Inhibited for Others

As noted above, all of the ethical codes require that the affairs of a corporation be kept confidential unless disclosures is required by a court of law, or by the disciplinary proceedings of the professional body. Consequently, an accountant employed by a corporation would appear to be prevented from consulting a professional colleague outside the corporation, even one associated with the professional institution to which the accountant belongs, prior to the initiation of a court or disciplinary action. An accountant employed by a corporation could ask another accountant outside the corporation for consultation on a "no names" basis, but the veneer covering the confidence would be so thin that such action would amount to winking at the intent of the confidentiality rule. An accountant could hire a lawyer for counsel because the lawyer could be expected to keep the corporation's affairs confidential, but few lawyers are well versed in accounting technicalities or professional codes of ethics,, to say nothing of the cost.

The same inhibitions do not face auditors or accountants employed in audit firms. Although not explicitly covered in the ethical codes, consultation about audit client problems goes on without problem among the accountants of the audit firm because all are required to keep the confidence inside their firm. Even so, although it is again not mentioned in the

---

6. All professional codes have more or less the same provision as the ICAO rules 210.1 and 210.2 which state: *210.1* "A member or student shall not disclose or use any confidential information concerning the affairs of any client except when properly acting in the course of his duties or when such information is required to be disclosed by order of lawful authority or by the Council, the professional conduct committee or the practice inspection committee in the proper exercise of their duties." *210.2* "A member or student shall not disclose or use any confidential information concerning the affairs of any employer except when properly acting in the course of his duties or when such information is required to be disclosed by order of lawful authority or by the Council, the professional conduct committee or the practice inspection committee in the proper exercise of their duties."

—Continued

Continued

ethical codes, the professional accountants engaged in auditing in Ontario, are encouraged to consult a "Practice Advisor", a professional employed by their provincial body (i.e., ICAO). If informed, effective action is desired, why is consultation inhibited for some professionals but encouraged, outside the ethical code, for others?

A Fair Reporting/Hearing Process is Not Indicated

None of the ethical codes specify to whom, within an employer corporation or audit firm, a professional should report a misdeed, nor do they indicate what role the professional body might play in the process. Professionals are left entirely to their own devices on these dimensions, and consequently may not believe that a fair reporting/hearing process is possible within their employer corporation or audit firm. As a result they may not report the misdeed for fear of retaliation. After all, the risk of losing one's job because someone else might stumble on the misdeed and report it, might be remote compared to the risk of retribution by an aggrieved superior.

Protection is Not Offered to a "Right-Doer"

At present, none of the ethical codes offers any support for a professional who reports a misdeed within his corporation or audit firm and then faces an unfair hearing process and/or retaliation. Absurdly, an employee professional who reports a misdeed to a prospective employer to clear up why they left earlier employment might be prosecuted by the professional body for failing to abide by the confidentiality guideline. Protection for members is a vital attribute of any successful organization, and while efforts should be directed toward counselling members away from wrongdoing, support for members in good standing should not be ignored.

Unclear Application of Sanctions

In the existing codes, sanctions are not linked to offenses. How, then, can a professional accountant fully understand the range of penalty for a wrongdoing? Professionals might therefore underestimate the gravity of their misdeeds and be led astray. Table II presents a list of sanctions found in the three ethical codes under review.

Possible Corporate Consequences

It should be noted that the requirement for confidentiality on client affairs may encourage offending corporations not to take proper remedial action, or not to worry about the ethical scruples of professional accountants in their employ. Since professional codes now require confidentiality, corporate executives know that it is unlikely that either their employees or the professional accounting body will bring a misdemeanor to the attention of the public. Even if a professional is brought before the relevant disciplinary committee of his peers, deferrals may ensue which mean that public disclosure of wrong doing will be long after the event, thereby greatly reducing any impact on the individual, audit firm or corporation involved. In fact, most disciplinary judgements do not explain the wrongdoing in sufficient depth for a reader to attribute any blame or impact to the corporation involved. Thus, except for offenses which concern an external auditor's opinion on the financial statements of a publicly held company, a corporation can now assume that public disclosure of its ethical misdeeds is unlikely. To this extent the Canadian public, if not the members of the professional accounting community, are not being well served by their professional codes of conduct.

POSSIBLE SOLUTIONS

Clarification of Priorities

Disclosure of the relative priority of a professional accountant's duty to himself/herself, his/her profession, client, employer, and the public is necessary to avoid confusion and possible degradation of the profession.

But what is the proper priority for duty to be paid to the professional accountant's stakeholders, and does the priority differ for auditors as opposed to the accountants employed by corporations, or by audit firms?

The first priority of duty among an auditor's stakeholders is settled by the fact that auditors are elected by shareholders as their agents to examine the activities of the corporation owned by the shareholders. However, regardless of whether the shares of the corporation are traded publicly or not, the auditor's report is to be used by both existing, as well as prospective, shareholders and creditors. Consequently, auditors owe duty to the public, at least to those who might become shareholders, creditors or other users of financial statements (i.e., government). Moreover, since auditors are not permitted to favor existing at the expense of future shareholders, and vice versa, shareholders and public may be regarded as paramount in an auditor's priority of duty. It is interesting to note that this order of duty is owed only on matters affecting the financial statements and not on any others such as unethical or questionable acts.

In the case of accountants employed by corporations or by audit firms, they do not owe a statutory or contractual duty to shareholders or the public. As employees, they owe duties of loyalty and of performance to their employer, and only if the employer acts improperly are employees free to

—Continued

Continued

TABLE II

SANCTIONS IN ETHICAL CODES
OF CONDUCT ISSUED BY
CANADIAN PROFESSIONAL
ACCOUNTING BODIES

SOURCES: See references for—CGAAO Certified General Accountants Association of Ontario, pp. 12–14; SMAO Society of Management Accountants of Ontario, p. 5; ICAO Institute of Chartered Accountants of Ontario; By-Law 80, Section 5, pp. 3:30.

	MENTIONED IN CODE OR BY-LAWS		
Sanction for the Professional	*CGAAO*	*SMAO*	*ICAO*
1. Caution		x(a)	x
2. Reprimand	x	x(a)	x
3. Review under the Peer Review program	x		
4. Requirement to complete professional development courses	x	x	x(or exam)
5. Suspension for a specified period	x	x(b)	x
6. Indefinite suspension, specifying conditions for reinstatement	x	x	x
7. Expulsion	x	x	x
8. An order to compensate the aggrieved party	x		
9. Assessment of fine	x	x(to $5,000 max.)	x
10. Assessment of costs	x	x	x(c)
11. Ancillary orders as may be appropriate or requisite	x	x	

Notes: (a) Kept on file or not. (b) Not to exceed two years. (c) Done in practice.

consider their duty to other stakeholders. In that event, since their codes of conduct required them to exercise due care, objectivity and integrity, and to disassociate themselves from misrepresentations,[7] an employee accountant's paramount duty is really to the accuracy of his/her work for the benefit of the end user: the shareholder or the public.

This similarity of ranking for both auditors and employee accountants is not that surprising. If professional accountants were seen to be misleading the public for the gain of their clients' existing shareholders or management, or employer, or themselves and their code of ethics was seen to permit this, the confidence in and support for that profession would be eroded. Government pressure would be brought to bear to reform the profession or create a new group free of bias and loyal to the public's interests. Commissions which have recently studied the North American accounting professions and have offered suggestions for change are evidence of such pressure. The Financial Accounting Standards Board (FASB) was created in response to early charges of bias in the United States.[8] and the effects of the Treadway and Macdonald Commissions are yet to emerge.

---

7. Each code calls for disassociation from misrepresentations in its own way. The ICAO code does so directly in Rule 205.1. The CGAAO code requires that members not lend their names, themselves or their services to any unlawful activity (Sect. 403) or to an act which will discredit the profession (Sect. 404). The SMAO code requires that members shall not discredit the profession (Rule 4(a)) and not engage in or counsel any business incompatible with the society's ethics (Rule 4(b)). Consequently, if a member of any of the professional accounting bodies could not persuade his employer not to make a significant misrepresentation, then that member would have to resign to disassociate him/herself from the problem.

---

8. The Wheat Report, *Establishing Financial Accounting Standards,* from a study group sponsored by the American Institute of Certified Public Accountants (AICPA) recommended the formation of the FASB in 1972. The establishment of the Board in June, 1973 effectively removed the setting of accounting standards from the control of the AICPA whose members were responsible for audits in the U.S.A.

—Continued

Although duty to the public is paramount for professional accountants, how should duty to employers, the profession and the individual professional be ranked. Ethical codes state that confidentiality of client/employer data must be maintained and that a professional accountant must disassociate himself/herself from any misrepresentations of fact. Consequently, a professional must resign to disassociate but cannot tell why. This places the rights of the individual professional below the rights of the client/employer. At the same time the professional's duty to his/her profession should be above that of the client/employer if the individual professional must disassociate from misrepresentations to save the reputation of the profession. As a result of this line of reasoning a professional accountant ought to owe duty to the following in descending order of priority: the public, current shareholders, the accounting profession, employer, and the professional accountant himself/herself.

An alternative ranking might be derived if the act of a professional disassociating from a misrepresentation is interpreted differently. For example, although disassociation is intended to protect the profession and the professional, the fact that the confidentiality guideline prohibits any reason for disassociation from being disclosed could be taken to raise the rights of the management and/or shareholders above those of the public. However, the professions believe that, if management knew that auditors were going to serve as "stool pigeons" outside traditional financial statement matters, then management could "clam up" and refuse to share information which is essential for the traditional audit function. Therefore, although the disassociation and confidentiality rules appear to elevate the rights of existing management and shareholders above that of future shareholders (i.e., the public), that was not the ultimate intent of the profession.[9]

In summary, the problem of confused priorities can be clarified by the inclusion of a reasoned explanation such as that above. While there might be some debate over the accountant's order of priorities in the middle of the range, a consensus ranking should place the public's interest first and the professional's own interest last.

Modification of Confidentiality Guideline to Enhance Consultation

It should be evident that there is a significant difference between consultation/airing a complaint within a corpora-

tion or audit firm, or to a "Practice Advisor," rather than whistleblowing in public; and it is whistleblowing in public that confidentiality rules were primarily designed to control. Consequently, overstrict confidentiality guidelines which inhibit healthy consultation and reporting are counter to the interests of most stakeholders.

A remedy against the currently overstrict confidentiality rules could therefore formally recognize the concept of "confidential consultation" on ethical matters within the ethical codes of the profession. Advice on ethical matters could then be sought without offending the profession's codes from a "Practice Advisor" or other "Ethical Consultant" (EC) designated by the member's professional body.[10] The designated advisor or consultant could be bound by the same client confidentiality rules as the person seeking advice except as noted below. The introduction of an EC would provide parallel treatment for members performing audits as well as those employed in non-audit situations.

If it is believed that the EC's advice might generate excessive legal risk for the professional society as a whole, the EC could work within a tiered system of responsibility where serious problems would be referred for legal advice. However, unless the cost of such advice was mostly covered in members' dues, there would be a continuing tendency not to use the service. Moreover, if members choose not to get advice, for reasons of cost or confusion or difficulty of access, there is a risk that will rebound on the entire profession if members make poor decisions.

It is worth noting that the confidentiality problem may not be resolved even if the professional rule is relaxed sufficiently to allow an EC. Uncertainty and reluctance to consult may still exist if the employer's code of conduct retains its specification of complete confidentiality. The employee will have to decide whether to be loyal to his employer or to his profession. Therefore, in addition to clarifying in the profession's codes that consultation with an EC is not considered to be a breach of corporate confidentiality, corporate codes of conduct should be modified to permit all professionals to consult with ECs who are employed by the professional's association.

Provision For a Fair Reporting/Hearing Process
Unfortunately, neither the ethical codes of conduct of the professional accounting bodies in Canada, nor most corpo-

---

9. For an extended discussion of this issue and the role of the accountant, please see Chapter 7 of the Macdonald Commission, pp. 100–104.

10. The Institute of Chartered Accountants in England and Wales has initiated a similar program called IMACE.

—Continued

Continued

rate codes specify to whom a report of wrongdoing should be made.

An excellent example of the type of guidance which should be incorporated in the Canadian ethical codes can be found in the code of the National Association of Accountants (NAA) in the U.S.A. It is reproduced as Schedule 1.

Some corporations have recognized the need for an objective hearing process and have identified a formal reporting and investigative process in their ethical codes of conduct. The corporation's audit committee, composed of a majority of outside directors who do not rely on the corporation for their livelihood, could provide an interested and objective unit, as might a special subcommittee of the Board of Directors. The audit committee, however, probably has some expertise in accounting matters, has an interest in misdeeds from an audit perspective, and has recourse to the corporation's external auditors. It is conceivable that a reporting and hearing process involving executives or a corporate ombudsman might be defined, but to strengthen the objectivity of the process, all reported cases should be reviewed by the corporation's audit committee.

SCHEDULE 1

SAMPLE FROM THE NAA (NOW IMA) CODE OF CONDUCT

Resolution of ethical conflict

In applying the standards of ethical conduct, management accountants may encounter problems in identifying unethical behavior or in resolving an ethical conflict. When faced with significant ethical issues, management accountants should follow the established policies of the organization bearing on the resolution of such conflict. If these policies do not resolve the ethical conflict, management accountants should consider the following courses of action:

— Discuss such problems with the immediate superior except when it appears that the superior is involved, in which case the problem should be presented initially to the next higher managerial level. If satisfactory resolution cannot be achieved when the problem is initially presented, submit the issues to the next higher managerial level.

— If the immediate superior is the chief executive officer, or equivalent, the acceptable reviewing authority may be a group such as the audit committee, executive committee, board of directors, board of trustees, or owners. Contact with levels above the immediate superior should be initiated only with the superior's knowledge, assuming the superior is not involved.

— Clarify relevant concepts by confidential discussion with an objective advisor to obtain an understanding of possible courses of action.

— If the ethical conflict still exists after exhausting all levels of internal review, the management accountant may have no other recourse on significant matters than to resign from the organization and to

submit an information memorandum to an appropriate representative of the organization.

Except where legally prescribed, communication of such problems to authorities or individuals not employed or engaged by the organization is not considered appropriate.

SOURCE: *Statement Number 1C, June 1, 1983: Standards of Ethical Conduct for Management Accountants,* The National Association of Accountants, p. 3.

An audit committee should be objective because of the interests of its constituents but there is some possibility that it might suppress remedial action if harm would accrue to the corporation or its shareholders. Professionals who are fearful of this may not come forward unless additional assurance is provided through an outside agency such as the professional's accounting society. The additional assurances provided could also serve as a back-stop where no action would be triggered unless the corporation's process was deemed untimely or ineffective. If, for example, the professional filed a statement of complaint both with the corporation (perhaps with the ombudsman) and with the professional association, (perhaps with the EC), then the corporation's process could be monitored. If the corporation did not investigate and deal with the matter within a specified time period, and file a response with the professional body, the latter could send a request for action within a second, short time-period. If no action was forthcoming, and the corporation's shares are traded publicly, the professional body could release the statement of complaint to a public file at the relevant securities commission for investigation. If no action was forthcoming and the corporation is private, the professional body could release the statement of complaint to a government body such as the Exchequer Court of Canada for subsequent release to the public on request. Faced with an investigation and possible notoriety, the corporation would probably respond. A similar process could be followed if the professional and the professional body agreed that the corporation's response was shallow or ineffective.

Protection for the Professional

While these processes should ensure that an investigation and hearing is fair and objective, the professional is unprotected from termination or diminished prospects. In order to forestall discriminatory action, effective protective mechanisms should be in use within the employer corporation or audit firm. For example, the corporate code of conduct could specify that persons raising legitimate complaints

—Continued

could apply to have subsequent discriminatory actions reviewed by the ombudsman or audit committee.

Protective programs within the corporation could be reinforced through the accountant's professional society as an adjunct to the reporting process described above. While professionals are themselves constrained from disclosing a client confidence, the EC who has been involved would be able to indicate to a prospective employer that an unspecified ethical matter had come up, and that the professional in question had acted responsibly. Confirmation of this kind could be helpful as would participation in suits from wrongful dismissal or discrimination. By participating in these processes the professional society would be contributing significantly to the protection of its members, a role espoused by Durkheim[11] as essential for an effective society.

Clarification of Sanctions

To improve a professional's understanding of the penalties for misbehavior, and to offset a corporation's possible reliance on the current confidentiality guideline to avoid remedying ethical wrongdoings, two approaches recommend themselves. For professionals, it would be appropriate to publish a list of the usual range of penalties and fines to be incurred specifically linked to misdeeds. If a range of sanctions for a misdeed in very broad, clarifying examples might be helpful. For corporations, the prospect of and timely publicity of misdeeds would probably be enough to induce them not to attempt to compromise their professional accountants. Once again, the professional accounting body could have an enhanced capacity as a protective institution for its members, and for society as a whole.

CONCLUSIONS

Current trends toward increased pace, more complex substance and lower tolerance of error have caused the financial marketplace to rely more heavily on the integrity of financial data and, therefore, of those who prepare the financial statements. At the same time these trends place higher challenges before professional accountants and it is essential that they have excellent guidance to live up to modern expectations. However, in view of the current codes of conduct, an accountant may not have a clear understanding of what priority of interests to satisfy, who can be consulted for advice, to whom to report misdeeds, what protection is offered a 'right-doer' and what sanction will be forthcoming for 'doing wrong'. Consequently, ethical misdeeds may never be reported to the

public. Even worse, unscrupulous corporation executives could set out to exploit these deficiencies and thus take advantage of both members of the profession and the unsuspecting public.

The deficiencies noted in ethical codes of conduct apparently stem from the Canadian accounting profession's failure to adequately recognize the guidance needed by employee members and the failure to relax an overstrict confidentiality guideline. Pressures are rising, however, for formal ethical codes to be revised to offer clear guidance to employee professionals, and to create and formally recognize within the codes, the concept of confidential consultation for all members. Moreover, it is unlikely that any professional society, once the need is known, can shy away from assisting and protecting its members who have complied with its ethical codes.

The concept of confidential consultation will require leadership from the profession to convince corporations to accept its practicalities and to alter codes of conduct to support it. Farsighted leadership will also be required when the discussion about priority of duties leads to an assessment of the broadening of the profession's role; particularly with respect to non-financial matters, and to whether to become an agent of the government on financial matters as has been suggested recently by the Macdonald Commission.[12] Facing these challenges squarely is vital to the ability of the Canadian accounting profession to continue to offer the appropriate quality of service to society in the future.

REFERENCES

Certified General Accountants Association of Ontario: 1975, *Code of Ethics and Rules of Professional Conduct,* CGAAO.

Durkheim, E.: 1978, 'Professional Ethics', reprinted from *Professional Ethics and Civic Morals* (1957) in *Ethics in the Accounting Profession,* by S. E. Loeb, John Wiley & Sons, New York, pp. 38–48.

Establishing Financial Accounting Standards: 1972, The Wheat Report, AICPA, New York.

Estey, W. Z.: 1986, *Report of the Inquiry into the Collapse of the CCB and Northland Bank,* Supply and Services Canada, Ottawa, Canada.

11. Durkheim (1957), p. 43.

12. In paragraph 9.18 on page 131, The Macdonald Commission "recommended that, to cover the situation where legal obligations to communicate are absent, or deficient, the provincial institutes of chartered accountants relax professional confidentiality requirements to enable the auditor to communicate matters of great moment to the regulator (with notice to the directors) if the institution itself fails to do so."

—Continued

Continued

Report of the Commission to Study the Public's Expectations of Audits: 1988, The Macdonald Commission, CICA, Toronto, Canada.

Report of the National Commission on Fraudulent Reporting: 1987, The Treadway Commission, AICPA, New York.

Report of the Special Committee on Standards of Professional Conduct for Certified Public Accountants: 1986. The Anderson Report, AICPA, New York.

Statement Number IC, June 1983: Standards of Ethical Conduct of Management Accountants, National Association of Accountants, New York, p. 3.

The Institute of Chartered Accountants of Ontario Rules of Professional Conduct: 1973, ICAO, Toronto, Canada (plus revisions).

The Society of Management Accountants of Ontario: 1986, *By-Law No. 1* and *Rules for Certified Members in Public Practice* and *Conflict of Interest Rules,* SMAO, Toronto, Canada.

Leonard J. Brooks is Professor of Business Ethics & Accounting at the Faculty of Management of the University of Toronto. He is the author of Canadian Corporate Social Performance, *published by the Society of Management Accountants of Canada (1986); editor of the* Corporate Ethics Monitor, *and Vice-Chairman of the Canadian Centre for Ethics & Corporate Policy.*

Reprinted by permission of Kluwer Academic Publishers.

Applying the Stakeholder Management Model to the Analysis and Evaluation of Corporate Codes

Max B. E. Clarkson and Michael Deck
The Centre for Corporate Social Performance & Ethics, University of Toronto, 1992

THE STAKEHOLDER MANAGEMENT MODEL

This paper describes how the Stakeholder Management Model has been applied to the analysis and evaluation of corporate codes, to the creation of a database containing sixty corporate codes, and to the development of Corporate Code Profiles.

The Stakeholder Management Model and its methodology provide a systematic approach to the management of a corporation's relationships with its principal groups of stakeholders. Stakeholders are persons or groups which have, or claim, ownership, rights, or interests in a corporation and its activities, past, present or future. Such claimed rights or interests may be legal or moral, individual or collective. A corporation cannot exist without stockholders, but neither can it exist without customers, employees, suppliers, and the society which provides the markets and the necessary infrastructure. A corporation is, from this perspective, a system of stakeholders, a complex set of relationships between interest groups with different objectives.

A corporation may consider that the needs of one stakeholder group are more important than those of another, but the successful operation of the corporate system on a continuing basis depends upon all stakeholder groups being reasonably satisfied and remaining as part of the system. If any one group, such as suppliers or customers, were to become dissatisfied and withdraw from this system, in whole or in part, the corporation would be seriously damaged or unable to continue to operate.

For example, the inability of Dow Corning to keep its customer and public stakeholder groups satisfied with the safety of one of its products has led to complete withdrawal from their leading position in the breast implant market. The stakeholder system for that product division has collapsed. The top managers of A. H. Robins and Manville consistently refused to acknowledge that there was any justification for the concerns of their former customers and employees, and they paid with bankruptcy for their inability to recognize and deal with the ethical imperatives of stakeholder management. In both cases ethical bankruptcy preceded financial bankruptcy and the collapse of their stakeholder systems.

The Stakeholder Management Model was developed as part of a large program of empirical research into the relationship between economic and social performance in organizations. The data showed that:

. . . the concepts of stakeholder management were being applied by corporations to the management of relationships and social issues, even though the term "stakeholder management" may not have been in use. Whether or not stakeholders were classified as internal or external was irrelevant, just as it was irrelevant whether they were described as stakeholders at all. The fact remained and the data showed that all the companies being studied had relationships with the usual list of stakeholders to be found in any textbook on the subject, and that these relationships were being managed in one way or another. The realities of the data that had been collected and analysed corresponded with the concepts and realities of stakeholder management. (Clarkson 1991, p. 334)

The data also showed that in order to achieve average or above average profits in its industry, a corporation must manage its stakeholder relationships in order to satisfy the reasonable needs and expectations of its principal stakeholder groups on a continuing basis. Without such balanced performance the data showed that corporations did not achieve above-average profits in their industry.

THE FUNCTION OF CODES

Codes, which often include statements of mission, purpose, or vision, are part of the control and evaluation system of a corporation. Their function is to provide guidance and direction for the management of the multiplicity of transactions between the company and its stakeholders. In order for codes to be effective, they must be clear, consistent, and congruent with the company's culture, values, policies, and ground rules. The analytical framework based on the Stakeholder Management Model provides a systematic method for analysing and evaluating a code's content and approach. Figure 1 shows the relationship between codes and other systems of evaluation, management's decisions and actions, and the corporation's responsibilities to its stockholders.

There is another important group of stakeholders which has a major stake and interest in the effectiveness of the company's code. This group is comprised of the company's directors and officers. It has now become essential for corporate directors and officers to protect themselves and their companies from the legal liabilities arising out of the multitude of reg-

—Continued

Continued

Figure 1

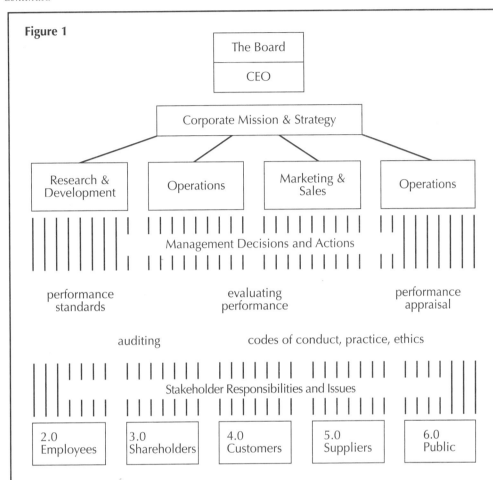

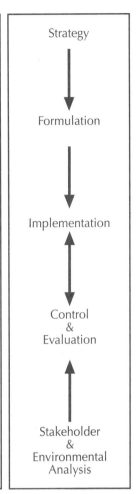

ulations and penalties which have been enacted in recent years relating to the environment, health, safety, and terms and conditions of employment. Negligence, ignorance or carelessness on the part of employees can result in criminal charges, which, if proved, will entail sentences involving fines or jail. Unethical or dishonest behavior can result in civil lawsuits which may lead to bankruptcy for the companies involved, as shown by the examples of Manville and A. H. Robins.

In order to protect themselves against potential liability, directors and officers must now be able to show that they have exercised "a duty of care", which means demonstrating that they have not been negligent. The corporation, on the other hand, must defend itself against strict standards of liability proving "due diligence", whereas directors and officers

must simply prove that they took all reasonable care in the exercise of their corporate responsibilities.

"Due diligence" with reference to environmental regulations may also become a requirement in loan and mortgage agreements. This development is a consequence of the recent experience of some banks and other major creditors that have been unable to foreclose, subsequent to default, on certain properties, such as refineries or chemical plants, which have in curred significant or unknown liabilities owing to the contamination of soil and water.

The formulation and implementation of codes is one way in which corporations and their directors and officers can

—Continued

Continued

demonstrate due diligence and show that they have taken reasonable care in the exercise of their responsibilities. Legal counsel, consequently, are advising corporations to protect themselves and codes are proliferating. Just because a code has been drafted or approved by a lawyer, however, does not ensure that it will be effective.

TYPES OF CODES

The terms "Code of Ethics", "Code of Conduct", and "Code of Practice" are often used interchangeably. It is useful, however, to distinguish among these terms in order to establish a basic typology. Each basic code type has a different intent and purpose. In practice, corporate codes tend to include elements of all three types, but for analytical purposes it is helpful to consider these three basic types as benchmarks.

Codes of Ethics are statements of values and principles which define the purpose of the company. These codes seek to clarify the ethics of the corporation and to define its responsibilities to different groups of stakeholders as well as defining the responsibilities of its employees. These codes are expressed in terms of credos or guiding principles. Such a code says: "This is who we are and this is what we stand for," with the word "we" including the company and all its employees, whose behavior and actions are expected to conform to the ethics and principles stated in the code.

Codes of Conduct are statements of rules: "This is what you must (or must not) do", as distinct from the code of ethics, which is stating: "This is how we expect you to behave." Codes of conduct typically are comprised of a list of rules, stated either affirmatively or as prohibitions. Penalties for transgressions may be identified and systems of compliance and appeal defined. Potential conflicts of interest are often described, with appropriate rules for guidance.

Codes of Practice are interpretations and illustrations of corporate values and principles, and they are addressed to the employee as individual decision maker. In effect they say: "This is how we do things around here." Such a code seeks to shape the expression of the corporation's stated values through the practices of its employees. Codes of practice tend to rely on guidelines for decision making, using such rules of thumb as "act and disclose" or "seek advice".

Each of the three types is useful and each can be appropriate or necessary in particular business and organizational settings. For example, in a divisionalised corporation, it would be appropriate to draft a Code of Ethics in order to enunciate the company's overall purpose and the guiding principles and ethics that govern its actions and behavior. At the divisional and functional area levels, different and divisionalised Codes of Conduct and Practice are appropriate, so long as the rules, examples, and guidelines are not in conflict with the statements of the corporation's guiding principles and ethics.

Authors of codes should be clear about which type of code is intended and for what purpose it is to be used in order to ensure that the types of statements being made are congruent with these intents and purposes. This is particularly important when a single document is being designed to cover the range of ethics, conduct and practice.

CODE AND STAKEHOLDER RELATIONSHIPS

The corporation can be viewed as a system of stakeholders, a complex set of relationships between interest groups with different objectives. The existence of these relationships means that each party, corporation and stakeholder, bears some responsibilities towards, makes some claim upon, and has rights to be considered by the other. The principle of mutual responsibility applies to each stakeholder issue. Whether the issue is the environment (See Figure 2), health, or safety, the corporation has responsibilities to its stakeholders and its stakeholders have responsibilities to the corporation as well as to other stakeholders. A thorough definition and inventory of these mutual responsibilities will result in a framework for comprehensive codes of ethics, conduct, and practice.

The principle of mutual responsibility can be applied usefully to other stakeholder relationships, such as those with customers or suppliers. Its application is particularly clear in the analysis and development of a code directed to employees as a stakeholder group. With this group the mutuality of the relationship is self-evident and the mechanisms for evaluation and compliance are already in place.

DEVELOPMENT OF THE FRAMEWORK

Brooks (1990) collected published codes from sixty Canadian companies as part of his research on effectiveness and compliance. The ETHIDEX software, developed by Deck (Clarkson, 1991 p. 335) was used as the means for applying the Stakeholder Management Model to the analysis and evaluation of the codes collected by Brooks. A rough categorization by industry of the companies studied is as follows:

Industry	# Included	Industry	# Included
Communications	1	Consumer Goods	6
Financial	8	Government	2
High Tech	6	Insurance	4
Manufacturing	5	Misc. Service	3
Petroleum	4	Pharmaceuticals	3
Publishing	2	Resources	5
Retail	3	Transportation	2
Utilities	4		

—Continued

Continued

FIGURE 2

Responsibilities to stakeholders	Customers	eliminate or minimize their risk exposure
		inform about risks
		train in the proper and safe use of the service
	Employees	inform about risks
		train to protect themselves from risks
		train to protect others from risks
		eliminate or minimize their risk exposure
	Communities	inform about risks
		eliminate or minimize risk exposure
		prevent accidents
		minimize impacts of accidents
		where possible, improve community health and safety
	Biosphere	eliminate or minimize impacts at all levels
		where possible, improve health of the environment
Responsibilities of stakeholders	Employees	protect others from risks
		comply with established procedures
		identify and communicate environmental issues
	Customers	inform others about risks
		protect others from risks
		increase weight of environment in purchase decision
	Suppliers	meet appropriate environmental obligations and
		disclose relevent information
	Business partners	meet appropriate environmental obligations and
		disclose relevent information

Critical aspects of the company's relationships with stakeholders regarding the Environment

- Responsibilities to stakeholders
- Responsibilities of stakeholders
- Conflicts with stakeholders
- Cooperation with stakeholders

—Continued

Continued

The Classification of Content

The text of each code was analysed in order to classify each paragraph by issue, topic or content. The analysis included the primary topics as well as other topics under which the paragraph might also be included. Each paragraph or statement was also classified by "approach", a concept developed by the Ethics Resource Center (1990). The types of approach that they identified were Rule (rr), Seek Advice (sa), Act and Disclose (ad), and Guiding Principle (gp). General administrative elements in the codes are classified as Miscellaneous (ms).

This two dimensional classification system meant that each code statement was located in a matrix, with the horizontal rows designating the topics or issues and the vertical columns describing the approach. An abbreviated form of the matrix for the employee stakeholder group is shown below.

ISSUE		APPROACH				
		rr	sa	ad	gp	ms
2.1	Employees General					
2.2	Conflict of Interests					
2.2.1	Inappropriate Gifts, Favors, Entertainment Bribes					
2.2.2	Hiring of Relatives/ Associates					
2.2.3	Self-Dealing					
2.2.4	Membership on Boards of Directors					
2.3	Nondiscrimination					
2.4	Personal, Professional Conduct; Personal, Sexual Harassment					
2.5	Employee Privacy					
2.5.1	General; Confidentiality of Employee Records					
2.5.2	Health Screening					
2.6	Worker Health and Safety					

The Stakeholder Management Model generates a framework for analysing and revising extant codes and for developing new ones. As a result of addressing the basic question of stakeholder management: "Who is affected?", it is possible to move away from the topical or issue approach towards an analytical approach. The stakeholder framework reveals clearly the relative emphasis which a corporation places on the different stakeholder groups. Analysis of the topics and issues addressed in a particular code also highlights omissions and imbalances.

The Classification of Approach

Each of the four approaches identified by the Ethics Resource Center is different. The four approaches are: the use of rules; seeking advice; acting and then disclosing; and the use of guiding principles. Each approach represents different views about controlling the behavior of employees and each expresses corporate values and ground rules which are qualitatively and managerially distinct. The company which relies upon a simple but deeply held credo demonstrates a very different set of assumptions about its employees and the behavior that can be expected from them than does the company whose code consists primarily of a long list of rules and prohibitions.

In order to clarify this distinction and the difference in the assumptions about behavior which they imply, an additional scale was developed and superimposed on the four approaches. This scale is based on the unifying principle of defining the "source of control" implicit in each approach. One end of the scale is identified as "Imposed Control", because control is imposed on employees by means of rules and prohibitions, with stated penalties in the event of transgression. The other end of the scale is identified as "Self-Control", because guiding principles, values, and ethics have been stated, together with the expectation that the behavior of employees will be governed accordingly.

Source of Control

Imposed		$\longleftrightarrow$		*Self*
rr	sa	ad	gp	ms
Rule	Seek Advice	Act and Disclose	Guiding Principle	Misc. & Admin.

"Seek Advice" is classified as a modified form of "Imposed Control", because clearly this entails going to a superior person in the workplace in order to seek and get an interpretation of a rule or prohibition. "Act and Disclose" is classified as a modified form of self-control, because the employees are authorized to use their own judgment in order to make decisions and take action before advising superiors. The miscellaneous administrative elements in the codes are classified as 'ms', Miscellaneous.

The criteria used for classifying the content of codes by approach are as follows:

—Continued

Continued

Rule (rr)

The focus here is on specific required and prohibited behavior. Examples of rules would be: when the company prohibits an employee from falsifying records and expense statements, giving money to government officials, and taking gifts over $100 from suppliers. The degree of imposed control is very high.

Seek Advice or Approval (sa)

Here the focus is on seeking supervisory approval before one acts. For example, an employee may be required to obtain approval prior to communicating with the public or government on behalf of the company, choosing a supplier or participating in municipal politics. The locus of control is external as the employee must seek prior approval before he or she acts. Generally, the approval is required to come from one's immediate supervisor in writing, but some codes require approval from a specified company officer or committee.

Act and Disclose (ad)

The emphasis here is on the disclosure of an employee's activities and interests after the employee has acted, as opposed to seeking prior approval before the act. It occurs most frequently within the context of conflict of interest guidelines, annual sign-off procedures, and when an employee's outside or personal interests change significantly so as to affect professional decision-making. The locus of control is internal as the employee is expected to exercise his or her judgment when acting. When Act and Disclose and Seek Approval overlap (for example, disclosing the conflict and then seeking approval), Seek Approval is chosen when approval precedes the act whereas, with Act and Disclose, disclosure is subsequent to the employee's actions.

Guiding Principle (gp)

These statements occur in the general context of company values and culture—how things are done and the principles and guidelines by which employees are expected to govern their actions. They do not refer to specific ethical issues and choices, but rather focus on the matter in which the company conducts its business with stakeholders and employee expectations of judgment and behavior.

Miscellaneous (ms)

The rationale for this category is to include residual material not able to be classified in the rr, sa, ad, or gp categories. It includes material of a definitional, explanatory or general organizational nature. Examples include: "this code sets forth minimum standards all employees are expected to follow"; "code has been adopted by the Board of Directors"; and "customers, employees and shareholders have information from the company so as to judge the company and its activities."

THE CORPORATE CODE PROFILE

As a result of applying the Stakeholder Management Model to the analysis of each code, an index was developed which includes all the issues or topics that have been identified in the codes. In this Stakeholder Index for Corporate Codes (see insert box) there is a total of forty-five issues, which are organized and indexed by stakeholder group. Issues and topics were also analysed in each company's code in order to determine their position on the "source of control" scale.

In order to develop a Code Profile for each company, the data were entered into the ETHIDEX Code Database. A volume analysis was then performed for individual corporate codes, using the character count for each issue. This analysis shows the issues that are being covered in each company code, together with those issues that have been omitted. By highlighting issues that have not been covered, a quick check on the completeness of a particular code is provided. The analysis also shows the company's approach to the control of employee behavior. The printout for a particular company constitutes its Code Profile.

At this stage in the research, it is not possible to show that the character count for an issue can necessarily be equated with its importance to the company. Such a proposition, however, remains reasonable until it can be disproved.

Computer Company's Code Profile

Appendix 1 shows the Code Profile for *Computer Company*. The issue with the highest character count is "Proprietary Knowledge", which is clearly a subject of great importance to a technology based company. It comprises 22.7% of the total number of characters in the code. "Fair Dealing" is also an issue of major importance, accounting for 9.8% and 7% of the character count in the Competitor Relations and Customer Relations groups respectively. This again is not surprising in view of the company's settlement with the U.S. Justice Department arising out of the lawsuits against the company some years ago. Competitors are an important stakeholder group for this company, accounting for 18% of the total character count, compared with 20% devoted to Employee Relations.

In terms of *Computer Company's* approach to the control of behavior, rules and seeking advice, or Imposed Control, applied to 51% of issues. Act and advise and guiding principles, or Self-control, applied to 12% of issues. In terms of

—Continued

Continued

Stakeholder Index for Corporate Codes

1. The Company
1.1   Mission, Philosophy

1.2   Adherence to Applicable Laws, Regulations

1.3   Commitment to Ethical Conduct

1.4   Use of Corporate Assets

     1.4.1   Integrity of Books, Records

     1.4.2   Goodwill

     1.4.3   Internal Communications

     1.4.4   Proprietary Knowledge

     1.4.5   Company Time

     1.4.6   Physical Assets

1.5   Communication and Education

1.6   Compliance Procedures, Monitoring and Enforcement

2. Employees
2.1   Employees General

2.2   Conflict of Interests

     2.2.1   Inappropriate Gifts, Favors, Entertainment Bribes

     2.2.2   Hiring of Relatives/Associates

     2.2.3   Self-Dealing

     2.2.4   Membership on Board of Directors

2.3   Nondiscrimination

2.4   Personal, Professional Conduct; Personal, Sexual Harassment

2.5   Employee Privacy

     2.5.1   General; Confidentiality of Employee Records

     2.5.2   Health Screening

2.6   Worker Health and Safety

3. Shareholders
3.1   Shareholders General

3.2   Disclosure Process

3.3   Rights and Remedies

4. Customers
4.1   Customers General

4.2   Conflict of Interest

4.3   Confidentiality of Customer Information

4.4   Product, Service Quality

4.5   Product, Service Safety

4.6   Truth of Advertising Statements

4.7   Third Party Relations (Agents, Representatives, Distributors)

4.8   Fair Dealing

5. Suppliers
5.1   Suppliers General

5.2   Conflict of Interest

6. Public Stakeholders
6.1   Government Relations

6.1.1   Relations With Government Representatives

6.1.2   Political Activities and Contributions

6.2   Foreign Business Practices

     6.2.1   General

     6.2.2   Conflict Between Host & Domestic Country's Laws, etc.

     6.2.3   "Facilitating" Payments

     6.2.4   International Trade Boycott

6.3   Community, Public Relations

     6.3.1   General

     6.3.2   Charitable Contributions

     6.3.3   Profit from Non-Public Information

6.4   Environmental Protection

     6.4.1   General Statement, Policy

     6.4.2   Specific Environmental Issues

7. Competitors
7.1   Competitors General

7.2   Conflict of Interest

7.3   Information Gathering, Sabotage

7.4   Disparagement, Sabotage

7.5   Fair Dealing

—Continued

Continued

business conduct, *Computer Company's* code covers thirty issues or topics, omitting none of importance.

Air Line's Code Profile

Appendix 2 shows *Air Line's* Code Profile, based on an analysis of the Corporate Policy and Guidelines on Business Conduct, published in 1986. It is significantly, shorter than *Computer Company's*. This is primarily the result of covering only twelve issues or topics, compared with thirty for *Computer Company*. *Air Line's* approach to control also shows that rules or seeking advice apply to 49% of issues, while act and disclose or guiding principles apply to 29% of issues. However, *Air Line* devotes 36.6% of its code to Issue 1.6, "Compliance procedures, monitoring, and enforcement", whereas *Computer Company* does not have any coverage of this issue. The defensive approach of *Air Line* to its employees is also highlighted by the proportion of coverage given in the code to 2.2 "Conflict of Interests", 30% compared with 11% for *Computer Company*. Clearly the language in *Air Line's* code has been drafted by lawyers, which would account for this code's emphasis on the protection of company assets and the emphasis on compliance procedures.

Packaged Goods Company's Code Profile

Appendix 3 shows *Packaged Goods Company's* Code Profile, which is based upon analysis of their Credo and the Policy on Business Conduct. 21% of the code's content is devoted to Issue 2.2, Conflicts of Interest, and 16% to Issue 1.6, Compliance Procedures.

34% of the issues are governed by rules or seeking advice, or imposed control, 23% of the issues rely on the approach of self-control: guiding principles or acting and disclosing. Relations with all groups of stakeholders are covered by at least one entry in each section. A total of twenty four issues or topics are covered. A culture which values autonomy, responsibility, and strong performance is reflected in the content and approach to this code.

The data described above for the three companies can be compared as follows:

	Imposed Control	Self Control	Topics Covered	Topic 1.6	Topic 2.2
Computer Company	51%	12%	30	0%	11%
Air Line	49%	29%	12	37%	30%
Packaged Goods Company	34%	23%	24	16%	21%

Additional analysis and study are necessary before valid conclusions can be drawn, but some obvious differences between these three sets of codes can be described on the basis of these data. *Air Line's* code is heavily weighted towards compliance procedures and by concern about potential conflicts of interest. It is, in effect, a legal document, and there appears to be a lower level of trust in employees than is found in the other two codes. The other two codes cover many more issues, which means that there is proportionately less emphasis on compliance and issues related to conflicts of interest. Both *Computer Company's* and *Packaged Goods Company's* codes are managerial rather than legal in language and viewpoint. They are written from the viewpoint of the Board of Directors and the CEO telling employees what they believe the company stands for and what behavior is expected from them in their relationships with each other and with the company's different stakeholders. The Language of *Air Line's* code shows clearly that it comes from the Chief Legal Officer rather than from the CEO.

FUTURE RESEARCH

Expanding the Codes Database

The basic weakness of the present collection of codes is the lack of depth in many industries. A diverse set of industries is represented. In order to be more useful, the database should include a reasonable number of examples from industries such as oil and gas, forestry products, the chemical, mining and steel industries, manufacturing, food processing, financial services (banking, trust companies, insurance, investment banking), transportation, computers and telecommunications.

This extended Code Database could then become a major source of data about codes in many important industries and provide current and relevant information for corporations, researchers, students and governments, as follows:

i.   Generic information about codes of ethics, conduct, and practice, and a description of the analytic system and evaluation process in use.

ii. A current index of general corporate issues common to most codes, together with descriptions and language of 'best practices'.

iii. An index of issues relating specifically to the environment, health, and safety, together with examples of 'best practice' language.

iv. An index of issues relevant and important to specific industries, together with examples of 'best practice' language.

Codes are part of the control and evaluation system of a company which makes possible the management of transactions and relationships with its many stakeholders. In order for these codes to be useful as a tool for effective manage-

—Continued

Continued

ment they must be clear, consistent, and congruent with corporate culture, values, policies, and actions. The analytic framework which has been developed and the current 'best practice' data that would be available from the extended database will provide the means by which the content and approach of codes can be evaluated and made more effective. Effective codes make explicit the values and principles which are the basis of ethical behavior and proactive social performance.

The Stakeholder Performance Profile

Another step in this research program is to establish a measurement of the relationship between a company's Code Profile, the content and approach of a company's code, and its Stakeholder Performance Profile (SPP). The Stakeholder Performance Profile is defined as the evaluation of a company's management of its relationships with its principal stakeholders: employees, customers, shareholders, and suppliers and with its external environment including competitors, communities, and other public stakeholders.

Recent legal decisions make it evident that one way for directors and officers to demonstrate due diligence is by the implementation of effective codes. In order to be effective, codes must be clear, consistent, and congruent with corporate culture, values, policies, and actions. By establishing a method of comparing systematically the elements of a corporate code and of the stakeholder performance profile, this project will provide an objective measure of effectiveness. This measurement will be stated in terms of the distance, if any, between what the company says (its code) and what it does (its social performance).

There is, as any researcher in this area knows, a great deal of skepticism about the value and effectiveness of codes. Are they just window dressing, bearing little relationship with the way that corporations actually behave, reflecting only input from the public relations department? Or do codes actually influence the behavior of corporations and the management of their relationships with their stakeholders?

The next page of this research program will be to develop a Stakeholder Performance Profile for each company in the Social Performance Database by evaluating the data as defined in the 'Guide to Performance Data' (Clarkson, 1991, Appendix 2). The Stakeholder Performance Profile will show the fifty issues contained in the Inventory and Index listed on the left hand side of the form and the RDAP scale across the top (Clarkson, 1991, p. 341). The profile will be developed by showing the applicable evaluations from the Social Performance Database.

This profile would then be compared with the same company's Code Profile contained in the Codes Database. Discrepancies between the two profiles will show that there is a gap between what the company says and what it does.

On the other hand, congruence between the two profiles will provide evidence that the company means what it says, and that its behavior is consistent with its intent as stated in its code. Codes, to be effective, must be implemented. The purpose of this research program is to develop analytical methods that enable corporations to formulate and implement effective codes.

SOURCE: Reprinted with permission from the authors and the Center for Corporate Social Performance & Ethics, University of Toronto

REFERENCES

Brooks, L. J., "Survey on the Effectiveness/Compliance of Corporate Codes of Conduct in Canada", October 1990, The Centre for Corporate Social Performance & Ethics, University of Toronto.

Clarkson, M. B. E., "Defining, Evaluating, and Managing Corporate Social Performance: the Stakeholder Management Model". To be published in *Research in Corporate Social Performance and Policy*, Vol. 13, 1991. JAI Press.

Ethics Resource Center, *Creating a Workable Company Code of Ethics*. Washington, D.C.; Ethics Resource Center, 1990.

APPENDIX 1

Index: *Computer Company Code Profile*

		size	percent	it	sa	ad	gp	ms
1. The Company	1.1 Mission, Philosophy	153	0.3	0	0	0	0	99
	1.2 Adherence to Applicable Laws, Regulations	0	0	0	0	0	0	0
	1.3 Commitment to Ethical Conduct	1020	2.01	0	0	0	25	75
	1.4 Use of Corporate Assets	0	0	0	0	0	0	0
	1.4.1 Integrity of Books, Records	1360	2.68	49	0	0	0	51
	1.4.2 Goodwill (Use of Company Name etc.)	163	0.32	99	0	0	0	0
	1.4.3 Internal Communications	673	1.33	65	34	0	0	0
	1.4.4 Proprietary Knowledge	11523	22.74	30	33	4	0	34
	1.4.5 Company Time	875	1.73	100	0	0	0	0
	1.4.6 Physical Assets	1480	2.92	29	55	0	0	16
	1.5 Communication and Education	1883	3.72	0	22	0	16	62
	1.6 Compliance Procedures, Monitoring and Environment	0	0	0	0	0	0	0
		19130	38	31	27	2	3	36
2. Employee Relations	2.1 Employees General	429	0.85	0	0	0	0	100
	2.2 Conflict of Interests	2923	5.77	12	25	0	26	36
	2.2.1 Inappropriate Gifts, Favors, Entertainment Bribes	1414	2.79	36	46	0	0	18
	2.2.2 Hiring of Relatives/Associates	0	0	0	0	0	0	0
	2.2.3 Self-Dealing	1373	2.71	31	0	0	0	68
	2.2.4 Membership on Boards of Directors	0	0	0	0	0	0	0
	2.3 Nondiscrimination	1619	3.2	0	46	0	54	0
	2.4 Personal, Professional Conduct; Personal, Sexual Harassment	1822	3.6	33	0	0	27	39
	2.5 Employee Privacy	0	0	0	0	0	0	0
	2.5.1 General; Confidentiality of Employee Records	572	1.13	0	0	100	0	0
	2.5.2 Health Screening	0	0	0	0	0	0	0
	2.6 Worker Health and Safety	0	0	0	0	0	0	0
		10152	20	19	21	6	21	33
3. Shdr	3.1 Shareholders General	0	0	0	0	0	0	0
	3.2 Disclosure Process	0	0	0	0	0	0	0
	3.3 Rights and Remedies	0	0	0	0	0	0	0
		0	0	0	0	0	0	0
4. Customers	4.1 Customers General	0	0	0	0	0	0	0
	4.2 Conflict of Interests	0	0	0	0	0	0	0
	4.3 Confidentiality of Customer Information	449	0.89	0	0	0	100	0
	4.4 Product, Service Quality	0	0	0	0	0	0	0
	4.5 Product, Service Safety	0	0	0	0	0	0	0
	4.6 Truth of Advertising Statements	298	0.59	100	0	0	0	0
	4.7 Third Party Relations (Agents, Representatives, Distributors)	1108	2.19	29	0	0	0	70
	4.8 Fair Dealing	3569	7.04	12	18	0	0	69
		5424	11	19	12	0	8	60
5. Sp	5.1 Suppliers General	1276	2.52	100	0	0	0	0
	5.2 Conflict of Interest	1462	2.89	81	19	0	0	0
		2738	5	90	10	0	0	0
6. External Relations	6.1 Government Relations	0	0	0	0	0	0	0
	6.1.1 Relations With Government Representatives	592	1.17	0	0	0	55	45
	6.1.2 Political Activities and Contributions	329	0.65	100	0	0	0	0
	6.2 Foreign Business Practices	0	0	0	0	0	0	0
	6.2.1 General	0	0	0	0	0	0	0
	6.2.2 Conflict Between Host & Domestic Country's Laws, etc.	0	0	0	0	0	0	0
	6.2.3 "Facilitating" Payments	0	0	0	0	0	0	0
	6.2.4 International Trade Boycott	0	0	0	0	0	0	0
	6.3 Community, Public Relations	0	0	0	0	0	0	0
	6.3.1 General	1930	3.81	17	20	0	30	32
	6.3.2 Charitable Contributions	0	0	0	0	0	0	0
	6.3.3 Profit from Non-Public Information	1048	2.07	83	0	0	0	16
	6.4 Environmental Protection	0	0	0	0	0	0	0
	6.4.1 General Statement, Policy	0	0	0	0	0	0	0
	6.4.2 Specific Environmental Issues	0	0	0	0	0	0	0
		3899	8	39	10	0	23	27
7. Compt	7.1 Competitors General	733	1.45	0	0	0	0	100
	7.2 Conflict of Interests	2098	4.14	0	21	0	62	17
	7.3 Information Gathering, Sabotage	1500	2.96	0	0	0	0	100
	7.4 Disparagement, Sabotage	0	0	0	0	0	0	0
	7.5 Fair Dealing	4923	9.85	54	28	0	0	18
		9324	18	29	20	0	14	37
		50667		31%	21%	2%	11%	36%

APPENDIX 2

Index: *Air Line Code Profile*

		size	percent	rr	sa	ad	gp	ma
1. The Company	1.1 Mission, Philosophy	708	7.37	0	0	0	100	0
	1.2 Adherence to Applicable Laws, Regulations	0	0	0	0	0	0	0
	1.3 Commitment to Ethical Conduct	0	0	0	0	0	0	0
	1.4 Use of Corporate Assets	0	0	0	0	0	0	0
	1.4.1 Integrity of Books, Records	0	0	0	0	0	0	0
	1.4.2 Goodwill (Use of Company Name etc.)	253	2.63	0	100	0	0	0
	1.4.3 Internal Communications	0	0	0	0	0	0	0
	1.4.4 Proprietary Knowledge	538	5.6	100	0	0	0	0
	1.4.5 Company Time	135	1.41	99	0	0	0	0
	1.4.6 Physical Assets	0	0	0	0	0	0	0
	1.5 Communication and Education	684	7.12	0	0	0	0	100
	1.6 Compliance Procedures, Monitoring and Enforcement	3519	36.65	66	24	6	0	4
		5837	61	51	19	4	12	14
2. Employee Relations	2.1 Employees General	0	0	0	0	0	0	0
	2.2 Conflict of Interests	1579	16.44	15	0	24	0	61
	2.2.1 Inappropriate Gifts, Favors, Entertainment Bribes	599	6.24	0	0	53	0	47
	2.2.2 Hiring of Relatives/Associates	0	0	0	0	0	0	0
	2.2.3 Self-Dealing	416	4.33	0	0	100	0	0
	2.2.4 Membership on Boards of Directors	326	3.4	0	0	100	0	0
	2.3 Nondiscrimination	0	0	0	0	0	0	0
	2.4 Personal, Professional Conduct; Personal, Sexual Harassment	0	0	0	0	0	0	0
	2.5 Employee Privacy	0	0	0	0	0	0	0
	2.5.1 General; Confidentiality of Employee Records	0	0	0	0	0	0	0
	2.5.2 Health Screening	0	0	0	0	0	0	0
	2.6 Worker Health and Safety	0	0	0	0	0	0	0
		2920	30	8	0	49	0	43
3. Shdr	3.1 Shareholders General	0	0	0	0	0	0	0
	3.2 Disclosure Process	0	0	0	0	0	0	0
	3.3 Rights and Remedies	0	0	0	0	0	0	0
		0	0	0	0	0	0	0
4. Customers	4.1 Customers General	0	0	0	0	0	0	0
	4.2 Conflict of Interests	441	4.59	0	0	100	0	0
	4.3 Confidentiality of Customer Information	0	0	0	0	0	0	0
	4.4 Product, Service Quality	0	0	0	0	0	0	0
	4.5 Product, Service Safety	0	0	0	0	0	0	0
	4.6 Truth of Advertising Statements	0	0	0	0	0	0	0
	4.7 Third Party Relations (Agents, Representatives, Distributors)	0	0	0	0	0	0	0
	4.8 Fair Dealing	0	0	0	0	0	0	0
		441	5	0	0	100	0	0
5. Sp	5.1 Suppliers General	0	0	0	0	0	0	0
	5.2 Conflict of Interests	0	0	0	0	0	0	0
		0	0	0	0	0	0	0
6. External Relations	6.1 Government Relations	0	0	0	0	0	0	0
	6.1.1 Relations With Government Representatives	0	0	0	0	0	0	0
	6.1.2 Political Activities and Contributions	404	4.21	100	0	0	0	0
	6.2 Foreign Business Practices	0	0	0	0	0	0	0
	6.2.1 General	0	0	0	0	0	0	0
	6.2.2 Conflict Between Host & Domestic Country's Laws, etc.	0	0	0	0	0	0	0
	6.2.3 "Facilitating" Payments	0	0	0	0	0	0	0
	6.2.4 International Trade Boycott	0	0	0	0	0	0	0
	6.3 Community, Public Relations	0	0	0	0	0	0	0
	6.3.1 General	0	0	0	0	0	0	0
	6.3.2 Charitable Contributions	0	0	0	0	0	0	0
	6.3.3 Profit from Non-Public Information	0	0	0	0	0	0	0
	6.4 Environmental Protection	0	0	0	0	0	0	0
	6.4.1 General Statement Policy	0	0	0	0	0	0	0
	6.4.2 Specific Environmental Issues	0	0	0	0	0	0	0
		404	4	100	0	0	0	0
7. Compt	7.1 Competitors General	0	0	0	0	0	0	0
	7.2 Conflict of Interests	0	0	0	0	0	0	0
	7.3 Information Gathering, Sabotage	0	0	0	0	0	0	0
	7.4 Disparagement, Sabotage	0	0	0	0	0	0	0
	7.5 Fair Dealing	0	0	0	0	0	0	0
		0	0	0	0	0	0	0
		9602		38%	11%	22%	7%	22%

Index: *Packaged Goods Company Code Profile*

		size	percent	rr	sa	ad	gp	ms
1. The Company	1.1 Mission, Philosophy	0	0	0	0	0	0	0
	1.2 Adherence to Applicable Laws, Regulations	0	0	0	0	0	0	0
	1.3 Commitment to Ethical Conduct	89	0.69	0	0	0	99	0
	1.4 Use of Corporate Assets	0	0	0	0	0	0	0
	1.4.1 Integrity of Books, Records	747	5.79	43	0	0	0	56
	1.4.2 Goodwill (Use of Company Name etc.)	0	0	0	0	0	0	0
	1.4.3 Internal Communications	0	0	0	0	0	0	0
	1.4.4 Proprietary Knowledge	349	2.71	0	0	0	0	100
	1.4.5 Company Time	0	0	0	0	0	0	0
	1.4.6 Physical Assets	265	2.05	76	0	0	0	23
	1.5 Communication and Education	218	1.69	0	0	0	0	100
	1.6 Compliance Procedures, Monitoring and Enforcement	2075	16.08	49	31	21	0	0
		3743	29	41	17	12	2	28
2. Employee Relations	2.1 Employees General	321	2.49	0	0	0	0	99
	2.2 Conflict of Interests	1740	13.49	0	0	100	0	0
	2.2.1 Inappropriate Gifts, Favors, Entertainment Bribes	1674	12.97	14	0	0	0	86
	2.2.2 Hiring of Relatives/Associates	0	0	0	0	0	0	0
	2.2.3 Self-Dealing	347	2.69	0	0	0	0	100
	2.2.4 Membership on Boards of Directors	434	3.36	0	0	0	0	100
	2.3 Nondiscrimination	226	1.75	0	0	0	0	99
	2.4 Personal, Professional Conduct; Personal, Sexual Harassment	0	0	0	0	0	0	0
	2.5 Employee Privacy	0	0	0	0	0	0	0
	2.5.1 General; Confidentiality of Employee Records	0	0	0	0	0	0	0
	2.5.2 Health Screening	0	0	0	0	0	0	0
	2.6 Worker Health and Safety	95	0.74	0	0	0	0	99
		4837	37	5	0	36	0	59
3. Shdr	3.1 Shareholders General	292	2.26	0	0	0	19	80
	3.2 Disclosure Process	0	0	0	0	0	0	0
	3.3 Rights and Remedies	0	0	0	0	0	0	0
		292	2	0	0	0	19	80
4. Customers	4.1 Customers General	156	1.21	0	0	0	99	0
	4.2 Conflict of Interests	0	0	0	0	0	0	0
	4.3 Confidentiality of Customer Information	0	0	0	0	0	0	0
	4.4 Product, Service Quality	361	2.8	0	0	0	20	79
	4.5 Product, Service Safety	0	0	0	0	0	0	0
	4.6 Truth of Advertising Statements	0	0	0	0	0	0	0
	4.7 Third Party Relations (Agents, Representatives, Distributors)	1019	7.9	100	0	0	0	0
	4.8 Fair Dealing	0	0	0	0	0	0	0
		1536	12	66	0	0	15	19
5. Sp	5.1 Suppliers General	86	0.67	0	0	0	0	99
	5.2 Conflict of Interest	0	0	0	0	0	0	0
		86	1	0	0	0	0	99
6. External Relations	6.1 Government Relations	0	0	0	0	0	0	0
	6.1.1 Relations With Government Representatives	0	0	0	0	0	0	0
	6.1.2 Political Activities and Contributions	393	3.05	0	100	0	0	0
	6.2 Foreign Business Practices	0	0	0	0	0	0	0
	6.2.1 General	0	0	0	0	0	0	0
	6.2.2 Conflict Between Host & Domestic Country's Laws, etc.	0	0	0	0	0	0	0
	6.2.3 "Facilitating" Payments	0	0	0	0	0	0	0
	6.2.4 International Trade Boycott	0	0	0	0	0	0	0
	6.3 Community, Public Relations	0	0	0	0	0	0	0
	6.3.1 General	183	1.42	0	0	0	58	42
	6.3.2 Caritable Contributions	101	0.78	0	0	0	99	0
	6.3.3 Profit from Non-Public Information	1145	8.87	53	0	13	0	33
	6.4 Environmental Protection	0	0	0	0	0	0	0
	6.4.1 General Statement, Policy	127	0.98	0	0	0	99	0
	6.4.2 Specific Environmental Issues	0	0	0	0	0	0	0
		1949	15	31	20	8	17	23
7. Compt	7.1 Competitors General	0	0	0	0	0	0	0
	7.2 Conflict of Interests	459	3.56	0	0	0	0	100
	7.3 Information Gathering, Sabotage	0	0	0	0	0	0	0
	7.4 Disparagement, Sabotage	0	0	0	0	0	0	0
	7.5 Fair Dealing	0	0	0	0	0	0	0
		459	4	0	0	0	0	100
		12902		26%	8%	18%	5%	42%

Completely at Sea

Kenneth S. Gunning
CA Magazine, April 1989.

It's hard to feel otherwise when conflicts of interest can hit with the force of a tidal wave, sucking us under and the only vessel that can keep us afloat—the professional conduct code—is quickly taking on water.

If there's one attribute that distinguishes our profession, it's objectivity. The fundamental attest role of the chartered accountant is to render professional services that must be entirely uninfluenced by personal or corporate interests—ours or the client's. As the foreword to the profession's rules of conduct describes it, our outlook must be "essentially objective," and we have "a responsibility to subordinate persona interests to those of the public good."

It's on the basis that the public accepts and relies on our audit and other attest assurances and that the government has turned to us to establish accounting and auditing standards. It is also with this understanding in mind that clients come to us for independent advice on estate and personal financial planning, business and personal investments. We are relied on not only for our specialized technical and professional knowledge but also for our ability to provide an objective and disinterested viewpoint—in short, for our integrity. We must be seen to have no personal axe to grind.

Financial Conflicts

Our provincial conduct rules are full of proscriptions and restrictions regarding financial interests or potential benefits that might in some way affect not only an audit's objectivity but now other types of attest services as well. Our American and United Kingdom counterparts have similarly exhaustive requirements designed to ensure financial disinterestedness.

The fact is, the prohibited investments can be so remote that they sometimes verge on the ridiculous. Nevertheless, it's just that kind of assurance the public probably expects, and it is much better for the profession to err on the side of too much restriction than too little.

About the only real problem related to financial self-interest in the attest area concerns the fact that auditors have a financial interest in collecting fees directly from their clients for such attest services and for any other services they might render the same clients. This problem seems almost entirely beyond solution since no one has come up with a sensible alternative; but except in extreme situations, it doesn't normally pose any real threat to the accepted objectivity requirement in attest services. The provision of other services to the very same clients magnifies this financial self-

interest problem and creates other threats to audit objectivity, which I'll discuss later.

All in all, as far as avoiding financial self-interest is concerned, the profession's rules are generally well established and adhered to.

Personal Involvements

To be truly objective, CAs must not be personally involved in making key management decisions or performing key control functions for enterprises that are also relying on their attest services. Again, the professional conduct codes contain a number of proscriptions designed to ensure objective professionals aren't personally identified with or committed to decisions they may have made previously or at least participated in.

For example, auditors cannot serve as officers, directors or key controlling employees of an entity and then be expected to remain objective in judging its affairs. This area is well documented, and I think the public properly expects and accepts that CAs can be truly objective only if they have no direct management involvement of any sort.

Still, potential dangers do exist: the line between decision making and offering advice leading to key decisions cannot always be drawn definitely—an ever-present danger for firms that provide ancillary services to their audit clients.

Personal Relationships

Now we're getting into murkier waters, areas less well defined and understood by either ourselves or the public as far as our objectivity is concerned. The profession's rules state, and it's generally understood, that CAs must avoid relationships that impair their objectivity or that might appear to do so. The professional should and normally will avoid forming personal or business friendships that become so close that they make it difficult to frame an objective judgment uncolored by them.

In the real world, though, to work effectively with others, one must be sociable. CAs, like most other business executives, find it important to be "close" to their clients. Club memberships are widely regarded as business development opportunities and good ways to become friendly with clients and other business associates. These types of relationships are subject to general guidance provided in the foreword to the conduct rules.

—Continued

Continued

In my view, personal relationships haven't posed much of a problem to date when any significant questions have been raised about the objectivity of attest services. There is still a potential danger here, however, that is probably most acute with respect to close personal friendships that are formed with owner-executives of smaller businesses. Such friendships could cause an unconscious and unintentional bias to creep into difficult or critical audit judgments.

Where attest services are provided to these types of entities, it's a prudent practice followed by most firms to require a second opinion of a partner not personally involved in servicing the client.

A second precaution, observed by some firms but not as easily achieved, is to periodically (every five years or so) rotate client services between partners. The downside is, while this provides the opportunity for a new and objective viewpoint, it also removes the accumulated benefit of years of knowledge about the business and service to it.

The wise firm will be alert to the closeness of relationships between partners and their clients and will take appropriate precautions when such dangers could affect the total objectivity of professional judgments that must be made in different situations.

Other Threats to our Objectivity

Now let's move on to various other types of conflicts of interest CAs and their firms face. While there is a good deal of very general and sound advice available, particularly in the foreword to the rules of conduct, the guidance is long on generalities and short on specifics. Furthermore, certain aspects of conflict of interest that apply to firms rather than individuals have received relatively little attention from the profession, even though public concerns have been raised about them. Let's examine, then, these potential threats to our objectivity.

For years, concerns have been raised here and in the United States about public accountants supplying other services to clients beyond expressing objective opinions on attest services. Enquiries and hearings have been held in both countries addressing this difficult issue—focusing on potential threats to objectivity from two perspectives.

First, it might be necessary to express an objective attest opinion on transactions previously entered into by a client that were based on advisory services supplied by the same firm—management consulting or taxation advice, say: Often extensive in scope these services may amount to full-blown studies and carefully researched recommendations; but they're still only advisory in nature and may not be accepted and followed by management. For that reason, they don't constitute a conflict resulting from any personal involvement in management decision making.

When the recommendations are followed, however, and circumstances later dictate that a possible writeoff arising from a transaction must be assessed, what firm isn't going to hesitate about recommending or requiring that the loss resulting primarily or partly from its own advice be recognized? Two significant and rather typical types of such advice in this situation might be aggressive reorganizations to minimize corporate tax, and business acquisitions the firm investigated for its client.

Second, the revenues from substantial ancillary services to an audit client increase the possibility of fee loss if an unfavorable audit judgment causes that client to retain a different auditor. Almost every public statistic on the topic tells us these nonaudit services are forming a growing proportion of major accounting firms' total fee revenues—in some cases, the majority. It's a reasonable assumption, then, that a large proportion of these services may be purchased by a firm's audit clients.

The profession appears to be less concerned about these two potentially adverse influences on objectivity than the public. Even the Macdonald commission report, generally a first-rate document, seems to conclude that, contrary to the views of 50% of respondents to its own survey, this posses no serious threat of objectivity—not, in my view, one of the high points of this otherwise excellent report.

The professional conduct codes contemplate conflicting interests arising from providing services to several clients at once. A number of rules require disclosing to clients business connections, interests or financial benefits. Interpretations of these rules, concerning commissions and finders' fees, for example, or an auditor later providing services such as acting as trustee, receiver or liquidator, are set out in the provincial codes. These provisions, however, are either quite general (as in the case of making disclosures to other clients) or tied so specifically to unusual circumstances that they provide little in the way of guidance in more common situations.

Conflicting Obligations

Circumstances can arise where, through no fault of their own, CAs are caught in a situation where professional obligations require them to follow two mutually contradictory courses of action.

For example, CAs are required to maintain a client's affairs in complete confidence but, at the same time, might be required to express an objective opinion for another client concerning, say, an appropriate carrying value for a receivable from the first client. If they possess confidential knowledge that the first client's affairs are such that the

—Continued

Continued

receivable should be written down, can they require and justify this to the second client based on their direct knowledge? And if they don't, can they express an objective opinion and turn a blind eye to the fact that they have confidential knowledge from other sources indicating that opinion to be in error?

There are no clear-cut answers. When there is no publicity available source for such information, and the second client cannot be otherwise convinced, the auditor would do well to seek legal advice.

The same sort of conflicting obligation arises in cases where an auditor may have a stated or implied responsibility to alert regulatory authorities to a client's strained financial circumstances. Here, the problem of conflicting obligations becomes extremely difficult and, as the Macdonald commission notes, may require legislative changes.

What Brought Us To This?

Before immersing ourselves any deeper, let's take a look at where we are and how we got here.

Only relatively recently has complete financial objectivity become a requirement with broad and restrictive practical applications. Less than a professional lifetime ago, it was possible for CAs to make a lot of money while in public practice through business involvements and investments with client owners and executives. Gradually, however, the broadening of the scope of our services and the strengthening of the rules that apply to them restricted the practitioner's opportunities to accumulate personal wealth through entrepreneurial activities. By the 1960s, most of these entrepreneurs had opted to leave public practice to seek their fortunes as business executives.

It was also at about this time that a different potential threat to objectivity began rearing its head—created, ironically, by our governments. The Income Tax Act, for political and other reasons, came more and more to be used as an instrument of economic and social policy. If corporations or individuals invested their money in certain ways, accelerated or extended tax benefits were allowed. A number of social or economic purposes were designated by successive Canadian governments as the beneficiaries of this tax largesse (such as resources exploration and development and industrial research).

Not much later, the emerging tax shelter scene stimulated our creativity and encouraged us to advise our clients on the somewhat complex housing subsidy schemes and opportunities available to defer or minimize taxes. Unfortunately, the investments weren't always as sound as the tax savings.

What's more, the complicated plans needed to navigate the choppy waters of the eligibility rules caused us to focus more of our attention on finding creative ways to be eligible than on accomplishing the legislation's intended purpose. The latest tax fiasco in this country, scientific research tax credits, wasn't created by this profession but was undoubtedly assisted by it—not a proud page in our professional history.

Today, the ever-expanding scope of our professional services poses yet another threat to objectivity. Personal financial planning is one of the latest of such services. By opening up new avenues for investment and acquisition advice by accountants. PFP has probably also contributed to the likelihood of conflicts of interest arising should two of a firm's separate clients become parties to the same transaction.

The world keeps turning, and new rocks lie menacingly ahead. We can probably expect our objectivity to be questioned sometime soon concerning our ability to supply attest services to the same client for both future-oriented financial information and historic financial statements.

Similar to the problem of ancillary services, this purported ability has the potential to impair a firm's objectivity, either in fact or appearance, if it is required to attest in the future to the fairness of a set of historic accounts covering periods in which it had previously expressed an opinion on the consistency and inclusiveness of the assumptions underlying the forecasted results.

The dangers lurking in this area are only directly alluded to in the "acceptance of engagement" and the "procedures" sections of the CICA's reexposure draft on future-oriented financial information. Although the draft's proposed report contains a denial of opinion concerning the potential achievement of forecasted results, it cautions against unduly optimistic or pessimistic assumptions that may raise doubts about the plausibility of the information supplied. It will not be easy guidance to follow, in any event—a problem only compounded if the same firm is later called on to attest to what actually happened.

Competitive Business Pressures

Why are these new or broader types of conflicts becoming more prevalent? One general answer is the increasing emphasis and importance the major firms are giving to revenue growth and business development activities.

There's not the slightest doubt that modern management practices put more of an emphasis on a firm's business development prospects. There is also no question, particularly because of the enhanced risk of lawsuits, that our consciousness of risk is much greater. Where the two come into conflict, however, profitability and competitive motives can threaten to carry the day. This is the hidden danger in the

—*Continued*

Continued

widely held concerns about so-called "opinion shopping." It is also a concern related to providing ancillary services.

Why is the profession in North America so defensive about the benefits and appropriateness of providing unlimited ancillary services to attest clients? (In this we differ from our counterparts in the United Kingdom, for example, where rules generally limit to 15% the percentage of fees that may be derived from one client or associated group, or Italy, where consulting services cannot be provided to audit clients.) Is it perhaps because our heavy emphasis on size and growth, or because of the competitive concerns firms understandably have about their clients retaining competitors to provide such services?

That question will probably remain unanswered, and our North American profession in its wisdom may have made the right judgment. But in the long run, it is the public who must be convinced of that. It's undeniable, however, that our business development objectives, coupled with competitive pressures, have exacerbated the potential for conflict-of-interest problems, particularly as a result of the broadened scope of our services. Firms must be alert to the potential dangers arising from such conflicts, and take steps to ensure they don't occur and undermine public confidence in their objectivity—and ultimately the profession's.

The BC Institute's Letters

In response to this changing professional scene, an interesting development took place in British Columbia in the 1980s. In January 1981, the institute's executive director, with Council's approval, wrote to all CAs in the province warning them "of the various pitfalls . . . in giving investment advice." The letter referred specifically to tax shelters such as MURBS, oil and gas funds and films. It warned CAs that, among other things:

- They must possess and apply professional-level skills in giving investment advice, and could be sued for negligence if they don't.

- They should assume that any written information they hand out will be circulated to others, and it should contain a disclaimer regarding investment visibility.

- If they act for both parties to a purchase/sale transaction, they must by law disclose to each party all information their firm has, no matter the source.

This letter was likely written in response to concerns expressed by securities regulators in both British Columbia and Ontario about the increasing assistance CA firms were giving promoters of tax-shelter vehicles. It was officially withdrawn in September 1988 because Council had by then decided that certain parts of it unduly implied that the competence of CAs was limited in giving investment advice to clients. The withdrawal letter endorsed the earlier warnings as being appropriate for their time and restated the professional concerns, but focused on the rules of conduct rather than on the legal proceedings.

Why are these letters of interest? Because they:

- Reflect important concerns outside the profession about its involvement in expanded service areas.

- Warn about dangers inherent in acting for two parties to the same transaction.

- Warn about "passive association" problems.

- Carry an undefined "semiofficial" status. (Why were they not put into the rules or interpretations?)

- Constitute a graphic illustration of a structural problem in the profession. (Why were these warnings issued only to BC members?)

These issues are of concern to all of us.

Can We Serve More Than One Master?

The BC Institute's letters serve as a warning that there are real and unrecognized dangers in advising two parties to the same transaction. It is not enough to look to the rules of conduct for council interpretations. Aside from a reference in Council Interpretation 204.18 to the "rare instances" (which it fails to define) where it is possible to do so, help is not to be found. The best place to look is in the foreword to the rules for general guidance on integrity, objectivity and avoiding conflicts of interest.

Which raises an important point. There's very real danger we may fail to attach enough importance to the foreword to the rules and regard it as more a flowery introduction or short sermon than a set of general principles. But looking to it for guidance on the intent of the rules is often far more helpful than trying to apply specific interpretations to particular relationships or transactions that might seem analogous but aren't specifically covered by them.

What are the unchartered dangers facing an accounting firm that is advising two clients on the same transaction? One of the key problems is that pointed out to BC members in 1981: a firm might be legally obliged to disclose to both parties all the information related to the transaction that it knows about, but this creates an obvious conflict with the confidentiality rules and would be a course of conduct most firms would find inappropriate to follow—a view unlikely to be shared by the courts.

—*Continued*

Continued

Second, a firm must not only be objective but appear to be. When it might be "associated" with the marketing of an investment, it must do its best to ensure the marketing isn't misleading. When it advises a second client on purchasing that investment, it has an obligation to that other client to provide knowledgeable and objective advice concerning its merits.

In these circumstances, the obvious and classic problem arises: What should or would the firm do when the appropriate advice to one client is such that the other would be damaged? Further, if a firm is involved in negotiating price or other essential terms between the parties, how can it be objective (and appear to be) in serving the interests of each?

As Hugh Rowan observed in "Chinese walls prove paper thin" (*CAmagazine,* October 1987, p. 50), so-called "Chinese walls" can come tumbling down on their creators: "Chinese walls and the conflict of interest created by being the confidential adviser to clients who do business with each other remains 'a dilemma—fit material for a senior partner!' Perhaps the problem should receive the attention of the profession's governing bodies so more guidance can be developed before the problem is raised in the courts."

Unfortunately, it didn't—and it has been.

Association: More Hidden Rocks

Some of these difficulties seem so obvious and fundamental that one might wonder how or why a firm would ever find itself in a conflict position. But a conflict isn't always easy to foresee.

Association is a basic if somewhat elusive concept, a cornerstone of conduct rules in general and of certain *CICA Handbook* examination and reporting standards. But it's not defined in Rule 205(1), where it has long been used (a member shall not "associate himself with" false or misleading financial or other information) or elaborated on in any way in the bylaws, rules, interpretations or the foreword.

Defined in the recent *CICA Handbook* Section 5020, "Association," as a term "generally used within the profession to indicate a public accountant's involvement with an enterprise, or with information issued by that enterprise," it can arise in an "active" (by the accountant's own actions) or "passive" (by the actions of others) way.

Unfortunately, after the introductory part of the *Handbook* section, there is virtually no material of any sort on passive association. The standard suggests only that the auditor consider "further steps, including legal advice," if the passive association was inappropriate and the client refuses to take the necessary action to correct it. As for guidance on active association, it pertains almost exclusively to written communications and consent to the use of the firm's name in financial documents.

As a result, guidance concerning the ways a firm might legally be regarded as "associated" with financially oriented material is so narrowly focused as to be dangerous. This is a problem due largely to deficiencies in the conduct rules, since the *Handbook* is obviously not the place to deal with the actions or conduct of members, or the assumptions of other parties.

This whole area is a problem and a danger largely because the profession, knowingly or unknowingly, has failed to provide important guidance and cautions, especially concerning verbal communications and involvements other than formal engagements related to financial statements.

The profession seems to be unaware of the potential difficulties that can be caused by such conflicts of interest. For example, perhaps as a result of the inadequate advice given in the conduct rules, a surprisingly high proportion of CAs (42% or 334 out of 819) recently surveyed in British Columbia expressed the view that it would be proper to advise more than one party to the same transaction, provided both sides were made aware of it.

For the firm that acts for both the buyer and the seller in a single transaction, the potential problems are often unforeseen at the time, particularly where the parties may feel a degree of assurance or credibility added by the active involvement of a large and reputable firm on behalf of both.

But, if the transaction later turns out to have been to the disadvantage of one party and to the advantage of the other, a fundamental problem may immediately arise in the mind of the disadvantaged party (and his or her legal adviser) concerning the appearance, if not the fact, of a lack of objectivity on the firm's part resulting from the conflicting roles.

The Rules for Lawyers

The rules of conduct for the legal profession in Canada are in sharp contrast to those of the accounting profession when it comes to conflict of interest. "Conflict of Interest," Rule 5 of the Law Society of Upper Canada's professional conduct handbook, sets out more than four pages covering the following requirements and guidance:

- Conflicting interests include the duties and loyalties of the lawyers to any other client.

- Before acting for more than one client in a matter or transaction the lawyer must advise both that no information received from one can be treated as confidential from the other, and that he or she cannot continue to act for one or both if contentious or divergent issues should arise or be foreseen between them.

—Continued

Continued

- The same basic considerations apply where the conflicting interest arises by reason of the lawyer's financial interest or that of a family member, law partner or associate.

- The lawyer should not advise an unrepresented person, nor create or permit the impression that he or she will protect that person's interests.

- The lawyer must advise a client of any error or omission in service that may form the basis of a claim by the latter against the former.

- The term "client" includes any client of the firm the lawyer is a partner or associate of, whether or not the lawyer handles the client's work.

Consider the fact that courts and justice are administered by lawyers. Is the Canadian accounting professional adequately guided and protected by our existing rules and conflict-of-interest provisions?

Other Hidden Reefs Ahead?

A 1986 *Globe and Mail* article by Claire Bernstein outlined a series of related lawsuits filed against a number of parties, including a Canadian accounting firm, that "have the Canadian legal and accounting communities reeling."

The firm in question was allegedly involved in a conflict-of-interest position as a result of having served, all at the same time, as auditor of a large public company, as personal adviser to its controlling shareholders and as trustee for a minority family shareholder whose financial interests were alleged to have been prejudiced by the actions of the client corporation.

Bernstein observed that, regardless of the outcome, "accountants and lawyers will now think twice or even three times, before agreeing to represent both the company and its majority shareholders at the same time."

That comment puts into some question the North American profession's long and strongly held conviction that it is in both the client's and the public's best interests for the same firm to audit parent and subsidiary companies, even though there might be minority shareholdings in a publicly held subsidiary.

Substantial transactions between parents and subsidiaries are quite common, for example, in vertical integrations. What, if any, legal obligation might someday be held to exist by the auditor to a minority shareholder of a subsidiary in the event of a corporate reorganization or even substantial normal purchase/sale transactions, particularly if the auditor had also provided advice on these matters? Is there some basis for alleging a conflict of interest should any losses result from prices held to be at other than fair market value that, as a result, prove detrimental to that shareholder?

Those considerations constitute uncharted waters, and though they might appear to have been encountered so often over the years that the danger is negligible, this is another potential conflict situation that could pose future difficulties for the profession.

Take another example. In 1988, a Canadian accounting firm was removed in a Supreme Court of Ontario judgment as trustee in a bankruptcy case because of an apparent conflict of interest. The firm also acted as auditor for a large secured creditor in the bankruptcy. There was no finding of actual misconduct, but the court held that in this particular case, claims against the secured creditor were crucial to the administration of the estate, and there was both the appearance of and the potential for actual conflict of interest. "The trustee is, in effect, suing its own client," the judge ruled.

It's likely that accounting firms, even in Canada, have faced many more difficulties resulting from conflicting duties to different clients involved in common transactions or relationships than have come to the public's or even the profession's attention. These problems may have been resolved through financial or other settlements without alerting the public, or firms may have gone through the legal process without attracting any notice. I am not aware of any processes followed by provincial institutes to require notice of, or to monitor, civil litigation for CAs' professional services and obligations.

The Uncharted Gap

The recent Macdonald commission extensively surveyed the "expectation gap" in Canada, producing a report that has been widely and rightly commended. It will be of immense help to us if its recommendations are acted upon. As a concerned CA for over 30 years, however, and as one who has enjoyed a challenging and rewarding career in public practice during that time, I cannot fully support its general approach in two significant respects.

First, is understood its conclusion that the profession's existing organization—its standard-setting and regulatory mechanisms and the kinds of business it engages in—doesn't need any basic change (see the foreword to its report).

In particular, I believe some basic structure or "turf" problems urgently need to be addressed, because they are delaying and complicating solutions to very serious problems in the areas of professional conduct, standard setting and education, to name just three.

Second, it has failed to focus directly enough on the real and increasing problems caused by the wide range of conflicts of interest, actual or perceived, facing us. I believe there

—Continued

Continued

are a number of areas related to conflicts of interest where the report's recommendations still leave a gap too wide to bridge between what the public expects—or would expect if it knew more—and what the profession requires, permits and actually does. It's a very wide gap, indeed.

The term "conflict of interest" receives little mention in the Macdonald commission report. It is treated, correctly, as a "narrower concept" than independence (paragraph 6.45), and seems to have been accepted as "more imaginary than real" in relation to the performance of nonaudit services for audit clients (6.46). The term is not even used in the report's index, nor am I aware of its consideration elsewhere. This seems odd to me, because the chairman is a distinguished lawyer, and because of the emphasis, particularly in the past decade or so, the legal profession has given that consideration.

Why were these general approaches taken in these two areas? Is it possible, because its mandate was from the CICA and not from the provincial institutes, that the Macdonald commission felt at all constrained in dealing more specifically or critically with matters concerning the profession's basic structure or with particular rules of conduct? If that was so, it's really unfortunate.

Navigating Without Charts

By focusing on broader issues of independence, and not considering certain fundamental aspects of conflict of interest, our profession has left its members in a position where they must set their own standards and policies. I suspect many firms have no defined policies concerning many types of conflict of interest. The result is twofold: not only will practices differ between firms, but the entire area will receive less attention than it deserves, and the vacuum is likely to remain.

I believe one of the public's fundamental expectations is that audit firms will avoid any type of conflict of interest that would in any material way affect their impartiality in rendering an audit opinion or providing other objective advice or services. Further, there is likely to be a close relationship between public expectations and liability exposure, as commission chairman Bill Macdonald observed. The courts are therefore likely to consider conflict of interest, as it affects impartiality and objectivity, in a much broader context than has to date been specifically codified in either the rules of conduct or the *Handbook*.

To minimize our danger of being run up on the rocks or thrown off course by the turbulent currents of conflict of interest, here are some important navigational aids the profession can and should provide as soon as possible:

- By agreement among the provincial institutes, formalize the requirement for uniform professional conduct rules

and grant to the new interprovincial committee standard-setting authority equivalent to that of the CICA's accounting and auditing standards committees.

- By agreement between the CICA and the provincial institutes, clarify and distinguish clearly between the areas where the *CICA Handbook* sets requirements and those where the provincial conduct rules and interpretations do. (Significant uncertainties remain here, especially concerning the general auditing standard and the question of association.)

- Develop in the rules of conduct, specific requirements and guidance concerning conflict of interest as a subset of independence. And, in doing so, consider and make specific pronouncements regarding the impairment or non-impairment of objectivity resulting from at least the following: conflicting types and extent of services to one client or group of clients; and conflicts resulting from services or obligations to parties with divergent interests, including providing separate services to different parties to a common transaction or relationship.

- Establish guidance in the rules of conduct more comprehensively codifying the association of an individual or a firm with financial information or proposals resulting from not only their own acts (conduct or involvement) but also their assent to, knowledge of and response to assertions by third parties concerning the same.

- More specifically define in the rules requirements concerning services to and relationships with clients seeking investment-related assistance.

- As recommended by the Macdonald commission, remove the anomaly of regulation by the profession only of individuals rather than firms, and provide that both are subject to regulation.

- Deal more adequately in the rules of conduct with opinion-shopping dangers by providing that the second firm consulted may not later accept audit engagements from the client for a reasonable period (say two or three years).

- Adopt a rule requiring any member or firm to inform a designated member of the institute's staff (at the same time he or she informs insurers) of potential or actual claims or lawsuits pertaining to professional services provided, excluding fee disputes. Set up a strictly confidential mechanism within the provincial institutes that would monitor these, and require reporting on the resolution of these matters. Consider a requirement, at least in audit relationships, to report at the same time to the client con-

—Continued

Continued

cerned, where the client may not already be aware of the problem.

- Last but not least (and at the risk of being called a complete heretic), agree between the CICA and the provincial institutes to jointly retain a totally objective consulting firm to study the structural, organizational, elective and administrative processes of the CA profession in Canada and to recommend appropriate and practical longer term changes that would better enable it to serve its members, and its members to serve the public.

Steps the firms can take to set their own course should include adopting the following internal policies pending more definitive CICA rules:

- Prohibiting, without senior management permission, services concerning a transaction being provided to two different clients who become or may become parties to it.
- Prohibiting, without senior management permission, the provision of consulting, valuation, tax planning or other services within an associated group of audit clients that relate to and materially affect intercorporate structures, relationships or transactions.
- Requiring approval by senior management and technical partners before providing a second opinion on accounting or auditing matters of other firms' clients.
- Identifying and establishing stricter controls over the nature, extent and quality of services to high-risk clients (those with a great potential for third-party suits) than for other clients.
- Controlling a firm's activities and involvements and those of its personnel with private or public offerings, particularly those concerning tax-driven incentives or savings.
- Establishing internal review and other quality-control procedures over providing financial planning and investment advice.
- Retaining expert consultants (possibly other accounting firms) to provide objective support for critical valuation or other judgments, or seeking legal advice when serious questions or doubts arise concerning conflict of interest such that impartiality or objectivity might be open to question.

How Will We Respond?

By focusing here on conflict of interest as posing a real danger to our profession, I may be regarded by some as being unduly critical or even alarmist. But am I? Perhaps we should pause for a moment and chart our course with a view to gaining a broader perspective on the closely related matters of professional integrity and public trust.

The professional stature attained by CAs in Canada by the early 1980s was quite high. We had earned credibility and respect in the business community and with the public generally; we had done well by comparison with other Canadian professions; and we had much to be proud of in achieving international recognition in the accounting world.

Today, though, the profession faces some very significant changes and challenges: strong economic and competitive pressures; serious personnel shortages; a near-revolution in technology; a near-crisis in risk management; and some large and very contentious Canadian business and alleged audit failures. All of these have been thoroughly and openly assessed by the Macdonald commission, and the profession is now in the early stages of formulating a response. A lot of action is under way by the institutes.

In framing these responses, we must carefully assess and weigh fundamental issues of objectivity, independence and professional integrity. In the words of the commission:

- "Serious concerns about auditor independence and professionalism exist both inside and outside the profession."
- "Unswerving independence and impartiality in the face of a difficult structure of relationships and strong commercial pressures is the pearl beyond price and the indispensable shield for the profession. "This view pervades each of our recommendations."
- "There is a need at this juncture for the leaders of the profession to reflect upon and project a renewed vision of the profession. This vision should above all seek to preserve the continued independence of the profession, a goal that can only be achieved by deserving the public's trust."

In a very real sense, the profession's response will measure its own commitment to a key "distinguishing element" outlined in the foreword to the professional conduct rules that we see for ourselves and other professions: "Acceptance by the practitioners of a responsibility to subordinate personal interests to those of the public good."

Surely that constitutes the broadest possible conflict of all, and the issues we face today will put that commitment to some real tests. We must resolve these issues if we are to meet the challenges facing us—and in a reasonable fashion that merits public trust.

It's encouraging to see the continuing response of the CICA to the Macdonald commission report in the monthly progress report from its president. The responses of the provincial institutes are less certain. The new Committee to Harmonize the Rules of Professional Conduct may be promising. We can only hope, however, that it fares differ-

—Continued

Continued

NAVIGATIONAL NOTES

Growth Gulf and Business Development Sound[1] form the entrance to the inside route much preferred by all accounting firms in their race to reach the Sea of Great Size. There are several reasons for this. First, it's the shorter route and, taken at the favourable tide,[2] much quicker. Second, the waters lie to the leeward side of the Friendly Contact chain of islands, which offer shelter from the severe storms that often blow in through Proposal Sound from the open waters of Competition Ocean to the west. Finally, taking this route, one can also avoid (except when carrying hazardous cargo) the delays and risks of navigating in the open and rough waters of the Oess Sea in the north, and around the Regulatory Rocks dotting the Essie Sea[3] further to the south.

The first part of the journey, past Prospect Point through Personal Contact Entrance and turning south at New Client Straits, is wide, scenic and pleasant. Passing down the Sound, by Handbook Harbour and into Recommendations Reach, one next enters Independence Inlet. This passage, while becoming progressively narrower, is again very deep and generally calm. The Sea I See, Eh?[4] has mapped this early part of the journey well and its recommendations and background material generally dot the route. Anyone who closely follows the navigational charts[5] will have no trouble getting around the Ancillary Services Islets and on past Objectivity Arm.

Past this point, however, the picture starts to change quickly. The sea floor rises steadily, and as the waters become shallower, the Ethics Eddies start to appear on the surface. Except at slack tide, the water flows very swiftly, but still smoothly until one reaches the well-known Expectations Gap.[6] From here on the route is largely uncharted. The Sea I See, Eh? has been so busy surveying the Gap, and the Provincial Institutes[7] have been so preoccupied with keeping a lookout for submarine threats from the OAG[8] that they have tended to ignore the turbulent waters that lie beyond. The currents rush faster and faster past MURB Point,[9] Opshop Bay and Tax Shelter Cove, and can swing a vessel dangerously close to the PFP Bluffs.[10] Whitecaps and tide ripoffs[11] dot the surface, and the Integrity Island Lighthouse, strategically located at Conflict Corner, is the last and only renavigational aid in this area.

Here, it is vital for the vessel to stay well to the right, and to immediately swing hard to starboard into Judgment Bay, the only calm and sheltered water, to consult navigational charts and tide tables before resuming the journey. Those who fail to do so, or are foolhardy enough to sail these waters without reference to them, are swept to the left around Conflict Corner and into the Conflict-of-Interest Rapids.

The Conflict Rapids and Reefs are a relatively wide but shallow succession of fast-running currents that race through a maze of (sometimes less-than-arm's-length) channels between the Association Shoals and the Remuneration Rocks. "These jagged rocks rise suddenly and steeply, and are usually hidden from view except at the lowest tides."

Warning to vessels: It is essential to chart one's course keeping a close eye on the Integrity Light, ensuring it's always visible, and bearing to starboard whenever in doubt. These dangerous rapids cannot be navigated safely in the fog, or when tide or wind conditions are unfavorable. Vessels not taking due care to keep a cautious watch from the bridge (especially the larger ones known to be heavily loaded with insurance, and which may be much less responsive to the wheel) are in danger of hitting the reefs—though, of course, many are lucky enough to pass between or just over them when the tide is high enough.

Author's note: This article was written from Judgment Bay. While to date, there have been no known shipwrecks with serious loss of vessel or professional life, there have doubtless been serious incidents with damages to ships, both large and small, severe enough to warrant the Sea I See, Eh? and the provincial constitutes to immediately reconsider their hydrographic proprieties. The Macdon-

---

1. Not to be confused, of course, with sound business development.
2. ". . . which taken at the flood, leads on to fortune" (Shakespeare)
3. Identified by other explorers (for example, Luscombe) as a central part of the much larger Osaikanu Sea.
4. Obviously a Canajun organization.
5. Chiefly the *Handbook* and rules of conduct, but where detail isn't provided, its essential to consult other maps published abroad or to follow the usual course of experienced navigators.
6. As distinct from (1) the expectorations gap (usually between the front teeth), (2) GAAP and (3) "GOOP."
7. To be distinguished from the provincial Institutes.

8. Other Accounting Groups.
9. Most Usual Result—Bankruptcy.
10. Plenty of Fish in the Pond.
11. Such as SRTC,15 for example.

—Continued

Continued

ald commission did identify and consider briefly a few of the many rocks to the Conflict Reefs[12] but pressed over them once they did not appear serious enough to require other than an amplified situation in the charts. Until adequately detailed charts and maps of these dangerous reefs are available, the author urges all vessels to proceed with due care and an objective stateroom,[13] and offers some suggestions for national aid and guidance.

12. For example, paragraph 6.45 to 6.50, and Recommendation 29.
13. *CICA Handbook* Section 5100.02–04.

ently than its predecessor, the Interprovincial Committee on Uniform Rules of Ethics, and that the new "IPCURE" is better than the disease. Its mandate, "to reach a consensus on the preferred approach to change in these areas," does not convey to me the sense of purposeful urgency that I believe appropriate and necessary.

But even a unified and vigorous response by all the provincial institutes won't be enough to achieve the goal. The Macdonald commission's report is full of references (in the foreword, and in Chapters 6 and particularly 9) to the need for responses by the major accounting firms and their leaders. An even more urgent warning in this regard was issued by its chairman in his extensive postreport interview with *CAmagazine* (see the July 1988 issue).

The profession's relationship with the investing public is largely formed and established by the big national accounting firms. Their policies and practices, in turn, are largely formed and established by their leaders. A lot is at stake and rests on the actions recommended by this small group of people.

I believe the profession is entitled to a progress report from those firms: not in a defensive or self-promotional way, please, but an honest appraisal of the very real and different problems they face, and a report on the internal policies, practices and plans they're proposing and adopting to overcome them.

One key aspect of these plans should be to establish internal procedures and policies (some I've suggested here) designed to avoid and protect against real or perceived threats to objectivity flowing from a wide range of potential conflicts of interest. A summary of what I would hope it might look like is shown in the response of the newly created Canadian CA firm of *Public, Trust & Confidence* (see the letter).

But in the end, the guidance of our personal, corporate and institutional integrity is the best and only real protection against the hidden dangers posed by such conflicts. As long as we can see the light of integrity, and chart our course by it, we will deserve the confidence of the public. Lose sight of it and we're in danger of losing everything.

SOURCE: Reprinted, with permission, from the April 1989 issue of *CA Magazine,* published by the Canadian Institute of Chartered Accountants, Toronto, Canada.

Kenneth N. Gunning, FCA, is national executive partner of Pannell Kerr MacGillivray. Toronto, and practises in the field of litigation support.

Offices across Canada and Throughout the Universe

Public, Trust & Confidence
Chartered Accountants

STATEMENT OF POLICY

RESPONSE TO THE MACDONALD COMMISSION REPORT

Our firm has carefully studied and evaluated the report and recommendations of the CICA's Commission to Study the Public's Expectations of Audits. Its 50 recommendations are very wide-ranging, and call for prompt action by governments, the profession and its practising firms, and individual professionals.

PT&C strongly supports most of the recommendations in the report, and in some cases goes beyond them. In a few instances, we are concerned that they may prove impractical or unduly costly to implement. In these areas, we are actively working within the profession to come up with better solutions.

PT&C maintains continuing quality controls that fully meet current professional requirements, and our quality control document is available on request. In addition, we now have in place or are implementing the following policies and procedures, which exceed existing institute requirements and are designed to ensure that we will always be able to meet and fulfill reasonable public expectations of auditors.

Objectivity and Conflict of Interest
We observe the following internal requirements to ensure our attest and other services and advice are entirely uninfluenced by any conflicting financial or other interests of clients, personnel or our own firm:

—Continued

Continued

- We will not provide attest services to any client or group of clients whose fees constitute 10% or more of the fee revenue of the office concerned. Where such fees constitute 5% or more of our office's revenue, we require a pre-issue review of financial statements and material accounting or auditing judgments made by specialists in our national office.

- We will not accept continuing engagements with audit clients or related entities where unpaid and outstanding fees equal or exceed one year's normal audit fee for the client or group.

- We require special approval before accepting engagements to supply certain tax planning, financing or consulting advice or other services to attest clients where:

1. Material reorganization proposals may be involved that we might be called on later to express an audit opinion on.

2. The interests of minority shareholders might be seen to be affected injuriously.

3. Our aggregate fees for the year from nonattest services to an audit client or group are likely to exceed our audit fees to that client or group.

    We will not accept such engagements where we believe the circumstances could place us in any significant conflict of interest in, for example, later expressing an audit opinion.

- We will not knowingly provide consulting or advisory services to two different clients who are parties to a common transaction or relationship that could affect the impartiality of our advice to either.

- We will not accept an engagement to express an opinion on auditing or accounting issues faced by a nonclient without that company first agreeing to the following:

1. We will consult fully on the matter with its existing auditors before issuing our opinion.

2. We will require technical approval, by specialists in our national office before issuing our opinion.

3. We will not accept any appointment offered to act as an independent auditor until at least two years after the date we issued our opinion.

    When, despite the above policies, we find ourselves in any position where our potential objectivity might for any reason be reasonably questioned, we will advise our client and will retain independent consultants or legal counsel as appropriate.

Auditing Services

- During the first two years of audits obtained after competitive tendering, and in other circumstances we deem appropriate, we require a special national preapproval of audit plans and programs to ensure our audit scope and standards are not in any way compromised as a result of economic pressures.

- (. . . and so on).

Creating Ethical Corporate Structures

Patrick E. Murphy

Sloan Management Review, Winter 1989, pp. 81–87.

ETHICAL BUSINESS PRACTICES stem from ethical corporate cultures, the author writes. How does an organization go about developing that kind of culture? The most systematic approach is to build and nurture structures that emphasize the importance of ethical considerations. This paper outlines several companies' experiences with three types of ethics-enhancing structures: corporate credos, programs such as training workshops and ethics "audits," and codes tailored to the specific needs of a funcational area. Ed.

WHAT IS AN ETHICAL COMPANY? This question is not easy to answer. For the most part, ethical problems occur because corporate managers and their subordinates are *too* devoted to the organization. In their loyalty to the company or zest to gain recognition, people sometimes ignore or overstep ethical boundaries. For example, some sales managers believe that the only way to meet ambitious sales goals is to have the sales reps "buy" business with lavish entertaining and gift giving. This overzealousness is the key source of ethical problems in mot business firms.

Employees are looking for guidance in dealing with ethical problems. The guidance may come from the CEO, upper management, or immediate supervisors.[1] We know that ethical business practices stem from an ethical corporate culture. Key questions are, How can this culture be created and sustained? What structural approaches encourage ethical decision making? If the goal is to make the company ethical, managers must introduce structural components that will enhance ethical sensitivity.

In this paper, I examine three promising and workable approaches to infusing ethical principles into business:

- corporate credos that define and give direction to corporate values;
- ethics programs where companywide efforts focus on ethical issues; and
- ethical codes that provide specific guidance to employees in functional business areas.

Below I review the virtues and limitations of each and provide examples of companies that successfully employ these approaches.

CORPORATE CREDOS

A corporate credo delineates a company's ethical responsibility to its stakeholders; it is probably the most general approach to managing corporate ethics. The credo is a succinct statement of the values permeating the firm. The experiences of Security Pacific Corporation (a Los Angeles-based national bank that devised a credo in 1987) and of Johnson & Johnson illustrate the credo approach.

Security Pacific's central document is not an ethical code per se; rather, it is six missionlike commitments to customers, employees, communities, and stockholders. The credo's objective is "to seek a set of principles and beliefs which might provide guidance and direction to our work" (see Table 1).

More than 70 high-level managers participated in formulating a first draft of the commitments. During this process, senior managers shared the analyzed examples of ethical dilemmas they had faced in balancing corporate and constituent obligations. An outside consultant, hired to manage the process, helped to draft the language. Ultimately more than 250 employees, from all levels of the bank, participated in the credo formulation process via a series of discussion groups.

Once the commitments were in final form, management reached a consensus on how to communicate these guiding principles to the Security Pacific organization. Credo coordinators developed and disseminated a leader's guide to be used at staff meetings introducing the credo; it contained instructions on the meeting's format and on showing a videotape that explained the credo and the process by which it was developed. At the meetings, managers invited reactions by posing these questions: What are your initial feelings about what you have just read? Are there any specific commitments you would like to discuss? How will the credo affect your daily work? Employees were thus encouraged to react to the credo and to consider its long-run implications.

Security Pacific's credo was recently cited as a model effort, and it serves internally both as a standard for judging existing programs and as a justification for new activities.[2] For example, the "commitment to communities" formed the basis for a program specifically designed to serve low-income

1. P. E. Murphy and M. G. Dunn, "Corporate Culture and Marketing Management Ethics" (Notre Dame, IN: University of Notre Dame, working paper, 1988).

2. R. E. Berenbeim, *Corporate Ethics* (New York: The Conference Board, research report no. 900, 1987), p. 15, pp. 20–22.

—Continued

Continued

constituents in the area. However, this credo should not be considered the definitive approach to ethics management. First, the credo could be interpreted simply as an organizational mission statement, not as a document about ethics. Indeed, the examples supporting the credo and the videotape itself do stress what might just be called good business practice, without particular reference to ethical policies. And second, the credo has not been in place long enough for its impact to be fully assessed.

Any discussion of corporate credos would be incomplete without reference to Johnson & Johnson, whose credo is shown in Table 2. This document focuses on responsibilities to consumers, employees, communities, and stockholders. (The current J&J president, David Clare, explains that responsibility to the stockholder is listed last because "if we do the other jobs properly, the stockholder will always be served.") The first version of this credo, instituted in 1945, was revised in 1947. Between 1975 and 1978, chairman James Burke held a series of meetings with J&Js 1,200 top managers; they were encouraged to "challenge" the credo. What emerged from the meetings was that the document in fact functioned as it was intended to function; a slightly reworded but substantially unchanged credo was introduced in 1979.

Over the last two years, the company has begun to survey all employees about how well the company meets its responsibilities to the four principal constituencies. The survey asks employees from all fifty-three countries where J&J operates questions about every line in the credo. An office devoted to the credo survey tabulates the results, which are confidential. (Department and division managers receive only information pertaining to their units and composite numbers for the entire firm.) The interaction at meetings devoted to discussing these findings is reportedly very good.

Does J&J's credo work? Top management feels strongly that it does. The credo is often mentioned as an important contributing factor in the company's exemplary handling of the Tylenol crises several years ago. It would appear that the firm's commitment to the credo makes ethical business practice its highest priority. One might question whether the credo is adequate to deal with the multitude of ethical problems facing a multinational firm; possibly additional ethical guidelines could serve as reinforcement, especially in dealing with international business issues.

When should a company use a corporate credo to guide its ethical policies? They work best in firms with a cohesive corporate culture, where a spirit of frequent and unguarded communication exists. Generally, small, tightly knit companies find that a credo is sufficient. Among large firms, Johnson & Johnson is an exception. J&J managers consciously use the credo as an ethical guidepost; they find that the corporate culture reinforces the credo.

When is a credo insufficient? This approach does not offer enough guidance for most multinational companies facing complex ethical questions in different societies, for firms that have merged recently and are having trouble grafting disparate cultures, and for companies operating in industries with chronic ethical problems. A credo is like the Ten Commandments. Both set forth good general principles, but many people need the Bible, religious teachings, and guidelines provided by organized religion, as well. Similarly, many companies find that they need to offer more concrete guidance on ethical issues.

ETHICS PROGRAM

Ethics programs provide more specific direction for dealing with potential ethical problems than general credos do. Two companies—Chemical Bank and Dow Corning—serve as examples. Although the thrust of the two programs is different, they both illustrate the usefulness of this approach.

Chemical Bank, the nation's fourth largest bank, has an extensive ethics education program. All new employees attend an orientation session at which they read and sign off on Chemical's code of ethics. (This has been in existence for thirty years and was last revised in May 1987.) The training program features a videotaped message from the chairman emphasizing the bank's values and ethical standards. A second and more unusual aspect of the program provides in-depth training in ethical decision making for vice presidents.[3]

The "Decision Making and Corporate Values" course is a two-day seminar that occurs away from the bank. Its purpose, according to a bank official, is "to encourage Chemical's employees to weigh the ethical or value dimensions of the decisions they make and to provide them with the analytic tools to do that." This program began in 1983; more than 250 vice presidents have completed the course thus far. Each meeting is limited to twenty to twenty-five senior vice presidents from a cross-section of departments, this size makes for a seminarlike atmosphere. The bank instituted the program in response to the pressures associated with deregulation, technology, and increasing competition.

The chairman always introduces the seminar by highlighting his personal commitment to the program. Most of

---

3. A more detailed discussion of Chemical's comprehensive program, and of Johnson & Johnson's, appears in *Corporate Ethics: A Prime Business Asset* (New York: Business Roundtable, February 1988).

—Continued

Continued

TABLE 2

JOHNSON & JOHNSON CREDO

We believe our first responsibility is to the doctors, nurses, and patients, to mothers and all others who use our products and services. In meeting their needs everything we do must be of high quality. We must constantly strive to reduce our costs in order to maintain reasonable prices. Customers' orders must be serviced promptly and accurately. Our suppliers and distributors must have an opportunity to make a fair profit.

We are responsible to our employees, the men and women who work with us throughout the world. Everyone must be considered as an individual. We must respect their dignity and recognize their merit. They must have a sense of security in their jobs. Compensation must be fair and adequate and working conditions clean, orderly, and safe. Employees must feel free to make suggestions and complaints. There must be equal opportunity for employment, development, and advancement for those qualified. We must provide competent management, and their actions must be just and ethical.

We are responsible to the communities in which we live and work and to the world community as well. We must be good citizens—support good works and charities and bear our fair share of taxes. We must encourage civic improvements and better health and education. We must maintain in good order the property we are privileged to use, protecting the environment and natural resources.

Our final responsibility is to our stockholders. Business must make a sound profit. We must experiment with new ideas. Research must be carried on, innovative programs developed and mistakes paid for. New equipment must be purchased, new facilities provided, and new products launched. Reserves must be created to provide for adverse times. When we operate according to these principles, the stockholders should realize a fair return.

the two days is spent discussing case studies. The fictitious cases were developed following interviews with various Chemical managers who described ethically charged situations. The cases are really short stories about loan approval, branch closings, foreign loans, insider trading, and other issues.[4] They do not have "solutions" as such; instead, they pose questions for discussion, such as, Do you believe the individual violated the bank's code? Or, What should X do?

Program evaluations have yielded positive results. Participants said they later encountered dilemmas similar to the cases, and that they had developed a thinking process in the seminar that helped them work through other problems. This program, while it is exemplary, only reaches a small percentage of Chemical's 30,000 employees. Ideally, such a pro-

gram would be disseminated more widely and would become more than a one-time event.

Dow Corning has a longstanding—and very different—ethics program. Its general code has been revised four times since its inception in 1976 and includes a seven-point values statement. The company started using face-to-face "ethical audits" at its plants worldwide more than a decade ago. The number of participants in these four-to-six hour audits ranges from five to forty. Auditors meet with the manager in charge the evening before to ascertain the most pressing issues. The actual questions come from relevant sections in the corporate code and are adjusted for the audit location. At sales offices, for example, the auditors concentrate on issues such as kickbacks, unusual requests from customers, and special pricing terms; at manufacturing plants, conser-

4. One of the case studies appears in "Would You Blow Whistle on Wayward Colleague?" *American Banker,* 17 June 1988, p. 16.

—Continued

Continued

vation and environmental issues receive more attention. An ethical audit might include the following questions.

- Are there any examples of business that Dow Corning has lost because of our refusal to provide "gifts" or other incentives to government officials at our customers' facilities?

- Do any of our employees have ownership or financial interest in any of our distributors?

- Have our sales representatives been able to undertake business conduct discussions with distributors in a way that actually strengthens our ties with them?

- Has Dow Corning been forced to terminate any distributors because of their business conduct practices?

- Do you believe that our distributors are in regular contact with their competitors? If so, why?

- Which specific Dow Corning policies conflict with local practices?

John Swanson, manager of Corporate Internal and Management Communications, heads this effort; he believes the audit approach makes it "virtually impossible for employees to consciously make an unethical decision." According to Swanson, twenty to twenty-three meetings occur every year. The Business Conduct Committee members, who act as session leaders, then prepare a report for the Audit Committee of the board. He stresses the fact that there are no shortcuts to implementing this program—it requires time and extensive interaction with the people involved. Recently the audit was expanded; it now examines internal as well as external activities. (One audit found that some salespeople believed manufacturing personnel needed to be more honest when developing production schedules.) One might ask whether the commitment to ethics is constant over time or peaks during the audit sessions; Dow Corning may want to conduct surprise audits, or develop other monitoring mechanisms or a more detailed code.

When should a company consider developing an ethics program? Such programs are often appropriate when firms have far-flung operations that need periodic guidance, as is the case at Dow Corning. This type of program can deal specifically with international ethical issues and with peculiarities at various plant locations. Second, an ethics program is useful when managers confront similar ethical problems on a regular basis, as Chemical Bank executives do. Third, these programs are useful in organizations that use outside consultants or advertising agencies. If an independent contractor does not subscribe to a corporate credo, the firm may want to use an ethical audit or checklist to heighten the outside agency's sensitivity to ethical issues.

When do ethics programs come up lacking? If they are too issue centered, ethics programs may miss other, equally important problems. (Dow's program, for example, depends on the questions raised by the audit.) In addition, the scope of the program may limit its impact to only certain parts of the organization (e.g., Chemical Bank). Managers who want to permanently inculcate ethical considerations may be concerned that such programs are not perceived by some employees as being long term or ongoing. If the credo can be compared with the Ten Commandments, then ethics programs can be likened to weekly church services. Both can be uplifting, but once the session (service) is over, individuals may believe they can go back to business as usual.

TAILORED CORPORATE CODES

Codes of conduct, or ethical codes, are another structural mechanism companies use to signal their commitment to ethical principles. Ninety percent of Fortune 500 firms, and almost half of all other firms, have ethical codes. According to a recent survey, this mechanism is perceived as the most effective way to encourage ethical business behavior.[5] Codes commonly address issues such as conflict of interest, competitors, privacy, gift giving and receiving, and political contributions. However, many observers continue to believe that codes are really public relations documents, or motherhood and apple pie statements; these critics claim that codes belittle employees and fail to address practical managerial issues.[6]

Simply developing a code is not enough. It must be tailored to the firm's functional areas (e.g., marketing, finance, personnel) or to the major line of business in which the firm operates. The rationale for tailored codes is simple. Functional areas or diversions have differing cultures and needs. A consumer products division, for example, has a relatively distant relationship with customers, because it relies heavily on advertising to see its products. A division producing industrial products, on the other hand, has fewer customers and uses a personal, sales-oriented approach. A code needs to reflect these differences. Unfortunately, very few ethics codes do so.

Several companies have exemplary codes tailored to functional or major business areas. I describe two of these below—the St. Paul Companies (specializing in commercial

---

5. Touche Ross, *Ethics in American Business* (New York: Touche Ross & Co., January 1988).
6. Berenbeim (1987), p. 17.

—Continued

Continued

and personal insurance and related products) and International Business Machines (IBM).

The St. Paul Companies revised their extensive corporate code, entitled "In Good Conscience," in 1986. All new employees get introduced to the code when they join the company, and management devotes biannual meetings to discussing the code's impact on day-to-day activities. In each of the five sections, the code offers specific guidance and examples for employees to follow. The statements below illustrate the kinds of issues, and the level of specificity, contained in the code.

- Insider Information. For example, if you know that the company is about to announce a rise in quarterly profits, or anything else that would affect the price of the company's stock, you cannot buy or sell the stock until the announcement has been made and published.

- Gifts and Entertainment. An inexpensive ballpoint pen, or an appointment diary, is a common gift and generally acceptable. But liquor, lavish entertainment, clothing, or travel should not be accepted.

- Contract with Legislators. If you are contacted by legislators on matters relating to the St. Paul, you should refer them to your governmental affairs or law department.

The "Employee Related Issues" section of the code is the most detailed; it directly addresses the company's relationship to the individual, and vice versa. This section spells out what employees can expect in terms of compensation (it should be based on job performance and administered fairly), advancement (promotion is from within, where possible), assistance (this consists of training, job experience, or counseling) and communications (there should be regular feedback; concerns can be expressed without fear of recrimination). It also articulates the St. Paul Companies' expectation of employers regarding speaking up (when you know something that could be a problem), avoiding certain actions (where the public's confidence could be weakened), and charting your career course.

The company also delineates employee privacy issues. The code outlines how work-related information needed for hiring and promotion is collected. (Only information needed to make the particular decision is gathered; it is collected from the applicant/employee where possible. Polygraphs are not used.) The St. Paul informs employees about what types of information are maintained. Finally, information in an individual's file is open to the employee's review.

The code covers other important personnel issues in depth, as well. It touches on equal opportunity by mentioning discrimination laws, but the emphasis is on the company recognition of past discrimination and its commitments to

"make an affirmative effort to address this situation in all of its programs and practices." Data acquired from the St. Paul supports this point. Between 1981 and 1986, hiring and promotion increased 60 percent for minorities in supervisory positions and 49 percent for women in management—even though overall employment rose only about 3 percent during this time. In addition, the code informs employees that the company will reimburse all documented business expenses. And it covers nepotism by stating that officers' and directors' relatives will not be hired; other employees' relatives can be employed, so long as they are placed in different departments.

Being an ethical company requires providing clear guidelines for employees. The St. Paul Companies' extensive discussion of personnel policies does just that. Employees may strongly disapprove of certain policies, but they are fully informed. The termination policy, for example, states that employment is voluntary and that individuals are free to resign at any time; the company, too, can terminate employees "at any time, with or without cause." Some people may consider that policy unfair or punitive, but at least the rules of the game are clear. One limitation of the code is that all sections are not uniformly strong. For example, the marketing section is only one paragraph long and contains few specifics.

The second illustration is of a code tailored to the company's major line of business. IBM's "Business Conduct Guidelines" were instituted in the 1960s and revised more recently in 1983. New employees receive a copy and certify annually that they abide by the code. It has four parts; the most extensive section is entitled "Conducting IBM's Business." Since IBM is, at its core, a marketing and sales organization, this section pertains primarily to these issues.

Six subsections detail the type of activities IBM expects of its sales representatives. First, "Some General Standards" include the following directives, with commentaries: do not make misrepresentations to anyone, do not take advantage of IBM's size, treat everyone fairly (do not extend preferential treatment), and do not practice reciprocal dealing. Second, "Fairness in the Field" pertains to disparagement (sell IBM products on their merits, not by disparaging competitors' products or services). In addition, it prohibits premature disclosure of product information and of selling if a competitor already has a signed order. Third, "Relations with Other Organizations" cautions employees about firms that have multiple relationships with IBM (deal with only one relationship at a time, and do not collaborate with these firms).

—Continued

Continued

The fourth and fifth sections address "Acquiring and Using Information for or about Others." The code spells out the limits to acquiring information (industrial espionage is wrong) and to using information (adverse information should not be retained). Employers must determine the confidentiality of information gathered from others. The final section outlines IBM's policy on "Bribes, Gifts, and Entertainment." The company allows customary business amenities but prohibits giving presents that are intended to "unduly influence" or "obligate" the recipient, as well as receiving gifts worth more than a nominal amount.

One might contend that it is easy for a large, profitable company like IBM to have an exemplary code. On the other hand, one could also argue that a real reason for the company's continued success is that its sales representatives do subscribe to these principles. Is this a perfect code? No. The gifts area could use more specificity and, even though the company spends millions of dollars a year on advertising, that subject is not addressed in any section of the code. Further, IBM's legal department administers the code, which may mean that problems are resolved more by legal than ethical interpretation.

When should a company use a tailored code of ethics? If a company has one dominant functional unit (like IBM), or if there is diversity among functional areas, divisions, or subsidiaries, then a tailored code might be advisable. It allows the firm to promulgate specific and appropriate standards. Tailored codes are especially useful to complex organizations because they represent permanent guidelines for managers and employees to consult.

When should they be avoided? If a firm's leaders believe specific guidelines may be too restrictive for their employees, then a tailored code is an unsatisfactory choice. Codes are not necessary in most small firms or in ones where a culture includes firmly entrenched ethical policies. If a credo is similar to the Ten Commandments, and programs are similar to religious services, then tailored credos can be considered similar to the Bible or to other formal religious teachings. They provide the most guidance, but many people do not take the time to read or reflect on them.

CONCLUSION

My research on ethics in management suggests several conclusions that the corporate manager may wish to keep in mind.

- **There Is No Single Ideal Approach to Corporate Ethics.** I would recommend that a small firm start with a credo, but that a larger firm consider a program or a tailored code. It is also possible to integrate these programs and produce a hybrid: in dealing with insider trading, for example, a firm

could develop a training program, then follow it up with a strongly enforced tailored code.[7]

- **Top Management Must Be Committed.** Senior managers must champion the highest ethical postures for their companies, as James Burke of J&J does. This commitment was evident in all the companies described here; it came through loud and clear in the CEO's letters, reports, and public statements.

- **Developing a Structure Is Not Sufficient by Itself.** The structure will not be useful unless it is supported by institutionalized managerial processes. The credo meetings at Security Pacific and the seminars at Chemical Bank are examples of processes that support structures.

- **Raising the Ethical Consciousness of an Organization Is Not Easy.** All the companies mentioned here have spent countless hours—and substantial amounts of money—developing, discussing, revising, and communicating the ethical principles of the firm. And in fact there are no guarantees that it will work. McDonnell Douglas has an extensive ethics program, but some of its executives were implicated in a recent defense contractor scandal.

In conclusion, let me add that managers in firms with active ethics structures—credos, programs, and tailored codes—are genuinely enthusiastic about them. They believe that ethics pay off. Their conviction should provide others with an encouraging example.

The author would like to thank Bernard Avisbai, Gene Laczniak, Michael Mokwa, Lee Tavis, and Oliver Williams, C.S.C., for their helpful comments on an earlier version of this article.

Patrick E. Murphy is Associate Professor of Marketing at the College of Business Administration, University of Notre Dame. Dr. Murphy holds the M.B.A. degree from the University of Notre Dame, the M.B.A. degree from Bradley University, and the Ph.D. degree from the University of Houston. He is currently editor of the Journal of Public Policy and Marketing.

7. G. L. Tidwell, "Here's a Tip—Know the Rules of Insider Trading." *Sloan Management Review*, Summer 1987, pp. 93–99.

Approaches to Ethical Decision Making

Purpose of the Chapter

When a professional accountant faces an ethical decision, the first recourse for guidance should be professional and corporate codes of conduct. Unfortunately, these codes often do not apply specifically to the problem faced but require interpretation to fit the circumstances. When such interpretation is required, the decision maker should refer to principles that will lead to ethical decisions. This chapter discusses those principles and suggests frameworks that can be used to lead to ethical decisions.

Index of Chapter Headings

Introduction

When the broad principles or specific rules embodied in codes of conduct do not specifically apply to the particular problem a professional accountant is facing, the decision maker can be guided by general ethical principles to arrive at a defensible ethical decision. What are these general ethical principles and how should they be applied? This chapter explores these ethical principles within a framework involving how the proposed action would affect the stakeholders to the decision. This framework is generally known as *stakeholder impact analysis*.

Stakeholder Impact Analysis

OVERVIEW

Since John Stuart Mill coined the concept of *utilitarianism* in 1861, an accepted approach to the assessment of a decision and the resulting action has been to evaluate the end results of the action. To most businesspeople this evaluation has traditionally been based on the decision's impact on the interests of the company's owners or shareholders. Usually these impacts have been measured in terms of the profit or loss involved, because profit has historically been the measure that shareholders want to maximize.

This traditional view of corporate accountability has recently been modified in two ways. First, the assumption that *all* shareholders want to maximize *only* short-term profit appears to represent too narrow a focus. Second, the rights and claims of many non-shareholder groups with a stake or interest in the outcome of the decision, or in the company itself, are being accorded status in corporate decision making. Modern corporations are now accountable to shareholders *and* nonshareholders, both of which form the set of *stakeholders* to which a company responds. Some observers have gone so far as to suggest that a company cannot reach its full potential, and may even perish, if it loses the support of one of a select set of its stakeholders known as *primary stakeholders*.

The assumption of a monolithic shareholder group who is only interested in short-term profit is undergoing modification because modern corporations are finding their shareholders are also made up of persons and institutional investors who are interested in longer-term time horizons and in how ethically business is conducted. The latter, who are referred to as *ethical investors,* apply two screens to investments: (1) Do the investee companies make a profit in excess of appropriate hurdle rates? and (2) Do they earn that profit in an ethical manner? Because of the size of the shareholdings of mutual and pension funds, and other institutional investors involved, corporate directors and executives have found that the wishes of ethical investors can only be ignored at their peril. Ethical investors have developed informal and formal networks through which they inform themselves about corporate activity, decide how to vote proxies, and how to approach boards of directors to get them to pay attention to their concerns in such areas as environmental protection, excessive executive compensation, and human rights activities in countries such as South Africa.

Ethical investors and many other investors tend to be unwilling to squeeze the last ounce of profit out of the current year if it means damaging the environment or the rights of other stakeholders. They believe in managing the corporation on a broader basis than short-term profit only. Usually, the maximization of profit in a longer than one-year time frame requires harmonious relationships with most stakeholder groups and their interests. A negative public relations experience can be a significant and embarrassing price to pay for a decision-making process that fails to take the wishes of stakeholder groups into account. Whether or not special interest groups are also shareholders, their capacity to make corporations accountable through the media is evident and growing. The farsighted executive and director will want these concerns taken into account before offended stakeholders have to remind them.

FUNDAMENTAL INTERESTS OF STAKEHOLDERS

The multiplicity of stakeholders and stakeholder groups makes it desirable to identify a set of commonly held interests to be used to focus analyses and decision making on ethical dimensions. Fortunately, decision makers can consolidate the interests of stakeholder groups into the following three commonly held or fundamental interests, shown below:

1. Their interest(s) *should be better off* as a result of the decision.
2. The decision *should result in a fair distribution of benefits and burdens.*
3. The decision *should not offend any of the rights* of any stakeholder, including the decision maker.

To some extent these fundamental interests have to be tempered by the realities facing decision makers. For example, although a proposed decision should maximize the betterment of all stakeholders, trade-offs often have to be made between stakeholders' interests. Consequently, the incurrence of pollution control costs may be counter to the interests of short-term profits, which are of interest to some current shareholders and managers. Similarly, there are times when all stakeholders will find a decision acceptable even though one or more of them, or the groups they represent, may be worse off as a result. In recognition of the requirement for trade-offs and for the understanding that a decision can advance the aggregate of all even if some individuals are personally worse off, this fundamental interest should be modified to focus on the *well-offness* of stakeholders rather than only on their betterment.

Once the betterment principle is relaxed to become the well-offness principle, the need to analyze the impact of a decision in terms of all three of the fundamental principles listed in Table 4.1 becomes apparent. It is possible, for example, to find that a proposed decision may produce an overall benefit, but the distribution of the burden of producing that decision may be so debilitating to the interests of one or more stakeholder groups that it may be considered grossly unfair. Alternatively, a decision may result in an overall net benefit, and be fair, but may offend the rights of a stakeholder and therefore be considered not right. For example, deciding not to recall a marginally flawed product may be cost effective but would not be considered to be "right" if users could be seriously injured. Consequently, *a proposed decision can be declared unethical if it fails to provide a net profit, or is unfair, or offends the rights of a stakeholder.* Testing a proposed decision against only one principle is definitely shortsighted and usually results in a faulty diagnosis.

TABLE 4.1

FUNDAMENTAL INTERESTS
OF STAKEHOLDERS*

Well-offness	The proposed decision should result in more benefits than costs.
Fairness	The distribution of benefits and burdens should be fair.
Right	The proposed decision should not offend the rights of the stakeholders and the decision maker.

*All three interests must be satisfied for a decision to be considered ethical.

Measurement of Quantifiable Impacts

PROFIT

Profit is fundamental to the interests of stakeholders and is essential to the survival and health of our corporations. In inflationary times, profit is essential simply to replace inventory that is priced at higher levels. Fortunately, the measurement of profit is well developed and needs few comments about its use in ethical decision making. It is true, however, that profit is a short-term measure and that several important impacts are not captured in the determination of profit. Both of these conditions can be rectified as indicated below.

ITEMS NOT INCLUDED IN PROFIT: MEASURABLE DIRECTLY

There are impacts of corporate decisions and activities that are not included in the determination of the profit of the company that caused the impact. For example, when a company pollutes, the cost of cleanup is usually absorbed by individuals, companies, or municipalities that are downstream or downwind. These costs are referred to as *externalities,* and their impact can often be measured directly by the costs of cleanup incurred by others.

In order to see a complete picture of the impacts of a decision, the profit or loss from a transaction should be modified by the externalities it creates. Frequently, corporations that ignore their externalities over time will find that they have underestimated the true cost of the decision when fines and cleanup costs are incurred, or bad publicity emerges.

ITEMS NOT INCLUDED IN PROFIT: NOT MEASURABLE DIRECTLY

Other externalities exist where the cost is included in the determination of the company's profit, but where the benefit is enjoyed by persons outside of the company. Donations and scholarships would be examples of this kind of externality. Obviously it would be attractive to be able to include an estimate of the benefits incurred from such externalities when evaluating a proposed decision. Unfortunately, the benefit cannot be measured directly. Nor can the costs of some negative impacts such as the loss of health suffered by persons absorbing pollution be measured directly, but they should be included in an overall assessment.

Although it is impossible to measure these externalities directly, it is possible to measure them indirectly through the use of *surrogates* or mirror-image alternatives. In the case of the scholarship, a surrogate for the benefit could be the increase in earnings gained by the recipient. The value of the loss of health could be estimated as the income lost plus the cost of medical treatment plus the loss of productivity in the workplace involved as measured by the cost of fill-in workers.

The accuracy of these estimates will depend on the closeness of the mirror-image measure. It is likely, however, that the estimates arrived at will understate the impact involved; in the example above, no estimate was made for the intellectual gain of the education permitted by the scholarship or the pain and suffering involved as a result of the loss of health. Nevertheless it is far better to make use of estimates that are generally accurate rather than make decisions on the basis of direct measures that measure precisely only a fraction of the impact of a proposed decision.

The measurement and use of surrogates to estimate external impacts of corporate decisions is discussed further in the article by Brooks (1979), which appears later in this chapter.

BRINGING THE FUTURE TO THE PRESENT

The technique for bringing future impacts of a decision into an analysis is not difficult. It can be handled in a parallel manner to capital budgeting analysis, where future values are discounted at a rate that reflects the interest rates expected in future years. This approach is demonstrated as part of *cost-benefit analysis* (CBA) in Brooks (1979). Using the net present value approach of capital budgeting analysis, the benefits and costs of a proposed action can be assessed as follows:

$$\begin{array}{c}\text{Net Present Value} \\ \text{of Proposed Action}\end{array} = \begin{array}{c}\text{Present Value} \\ \text{of Benefits}\end{array} - \begin{array}{c}\text{Present Value} \\ \text{of Costs}\end{array}$$

where benefits include revenues plus good externalities, and costs include costs plus bad externalities.

Frequently, executives who have learned the hard way to keep their focus on short-term profits will reject the idea of including externalities in their analyses. However, what is *being advocated here is not abandonment of short-term profit as a yardstick but consideration of impacts that are now externalities that have an excellent chance of affecting the company's bottom line in the future.* It is likely, for example, that pollution costs will manifest themselves as fines and/or cleanup costs. Moreover, the advantages bestowed through donations will strengthen society and allow the corporation to reach its full potential in the future. What cost-benefit analysis allows a decision maker to do is to bring these future benefits and costs into the present for a fuller analysis of a proposed decision. For example, Table 2 in the article by Brooks (1979) could be reformatted as follows (see Table 4.2) to give the decision maker a clearer view of present and possible future impacts on profit.

DEALING WITH UNCERTAIN OUTCOMES

Just as in capital budgeting analysis, there are estimates that are uncertain. However, a full range of techniques has been developed to factor this uncertainty into the analysis of proposed decisions. For example, the analysis can be based upon best estimates, upon three possibilities (most optimistic, pessimistic, and best estimate), or upon expected values developed from a com-

TABLE 4.2

COST-BENEFIT ANALYSIS: SHORT- AND LONG-TERM PROFIT IMPACT

	POLLUTION CONTROL EQUIPMENT *Impact on Profit*			UNIVERSITY ADMISSION SCHOLARSHIPS *Impact on Profit*		
	Short-Term	*Long-Term*	*Total*	*Short-Term*	*Long-Term*	*Total*
Benefits (Present Valued at 10%)						
Reduction in worker health costs		$500,000	$500,000			
Increase in worker productivity	$200,000		200,000			
Improvement in level of earnings of scholarship recipients					$600,000	$600,000
Total benefits	200,000	500,000	700,000		600,000	600,000
Costs (Present Valued at 10%)						
Pollution equipment	350,000		350,000			
Scholarships paid				$400,000		400,000
Total costs	350,000		350,000	400,000		400,000
Net benefit-costs	($150,000)	$500,000	$350,000	($400,000)	$600,000	$200,000

puter simulation. All of these are *expected values,* which are combinations of a value and a probability of its occurrence. This is normally expressed as follows:

$$\text{Expected Value of an Outcome} = \text{Value of the Outcome} \times \text{the Probability of That Outcome Occurring}$$

The advantage of this expected value formulation is that the cost-benefit analysis framework can be modified to include the risk associated with outcomes to be included. This new approach is referred to as *risk-benefit analysis* (RBA) and can be applied in the following framework:

$$\text{Risk Adjusted or Expected Value of Net Benefits} = \text{Expected Present Value of Future Benefits} - \text{Expected Present Value of Future Costs}$$

DIFFERENT CAPACITIES TO WITHSTAND OUTCOMES: RANKING INTERESTS

The measurement of profit augmented by externalities discounted to the present and factored by riskiness of outcome is much more useful in assessing proposed decisions than profit alone. However, there are occasions when the simple adding up of benefits and costs does not reflect the capacity of the stakeholder who suffers the cost necessary to withstand the impact. For example, if stakeholders are poor, they will not be able to buy remedial treatment, or alternatively their reserves may be so low that other family members—perhaps children—will suffer. On the other hand, a scholarship to a poor recipient could create a benefit for that person and others of significantly greater impact than to a person who is well off. In these situations, the values included in the CBA or RBA can be weighted, or the net present values created can be ranked according to the impact created on the stakeholders involved. The ranking of stakeholders and their impacts based on their situational capacity is also used when nonmeasurable impacts are being considered.

Relative financial strength does not provide the only rationale for ranking the interests of stakeholders. In fact, several more compelling reasons exist, including the impact of the proposed action on the life or health of a stakeholder or on some aspect of our flora, fauna, or environment that is near a threshold of endangerment or extinction. Usually, the public takes a very dim view of companies that put profits ahead of life, health, or the preservation of our habitat. In addition, making these issues a high priority will often trigger a rethinking of an offending action so as to improve it by removing its offensiveness.

The illustrative case solution provided later in this chapter extends the concept of ranking stakeholders to correlate legal rights, financial and psychological capacity to withstand the impact, and the resulting probable public impact of the action. It is interesting that an item may not be "material" to a lay investor in an accounting sense but may be quite significant to stakeholders. In the long run, such sensitivity by stakeholders to offending corporate decisions may rebound negatively on the shareholders through the bottom line. In time, the *concept of materiality* as we know it may become inadequate and need to be expanded.

SUMMARY

The approaches to the measurement of impacts of proposed decisions can be summarized as in Table 4.3.

Assessment of Nonquantifiable Impacts

FAIRNESS AMONG STAKEHOLDERS

Although fair treatment is a right that individuals and groups can properly expect to receive, it is treated here on its own because of its importance to eth-

TABLE 4.3

APPROACHES TO THE MEASUREMENT OF QUANITIFIABLE IMPACTS OF PROPOSED DECISIONS*

A. Profit or loss only

B. A. plus externalities
    (i.e., cost-benefit analysis [CBA]

C. B. plus probabilities of outcomes
    (i.e., risk-benefit analysis [RBA])

D. CBA or RBA plus ranking of stakeholders for the seriousness of impacts

*Optimal decisions usually result from the most thorough approach.

ical decision making. The concern for fair treatment has been evident in society's recent preoccupation with such issues as discrimination against women and others in matters of hiring, promotion, and pay. Consequently, a decision will be considered unethical unless it is seen to be fair to all stakeholders.

Fairness is not an absolute concept. It is evidenced by a relatively even distribution of the benefits and burdens springing from a decision. For example, it is possible that a decision to increase taxes may weigh more heavily on high income earners but be seen as relatively fair in terms of their capacity to pay those taxes. Reasonability and perspective are required to judge fairness accurately.

RIGHTS OF STAKEHOLDERS

A decision will only be considered ethical if its impacts do not offend the rights of the stakeholders impacted upon and the rights of the person(s) making the decision. This latter point can be seen in the case of a decision being made by executives who subscribe to values that lead them to be offended by tax child labor laws or by low standards of worker safety in Third World countries. The executives making the decision are stakeholders to it in their own right.

An individual stakeholder or a stakeholder group in North America may generally expect to enjoy the rights listed in Table 4.4.

Some of these rights have been accorded protection under laws and legal regulations, while others are enforced through common law or through public sanction of offenders. For example, employees and consumers are protected under statute for health and safety, whereas dignity and privacy tend to be subject to common law, and the exercise of conscience is subject to public sanction.

In many cases, even where protection is afforded through statute, considerable judgment is required to know when an individual's rights are being violated. Drug testing in the form of urinalysis, for example, appears to be warranted when the health of the worker and fellow workers is at stake, but the degree of jeopardy has to be severe. Airline pilots are considered worthy of urinalysis but, at the moment, truck drivers are not. Among the reasons for this apparent inconsistency are the lack of accuracy and timeliness of the tests, and the stigma attached to a false accusation. However, it appears to be reasonable to test a truck driver's reflexes and hand-eye coordination using computer games just prior to his or her shift, so evidently the stigma of failing a computer game related closely to the task to be performed is acceptable in today's society. This complex interplay of statute, regulation, common law, and judgment

TABLE 4.4

STAKEHOLDER RIGHTS

Life

Health and safety

Fair treatment

Exercise of conscience

Dignity and privacy

Freedom of speech

based on values makes it advisable to give any apparent infringement of a stakeholder's rights very careful scrutiny.

Comprehensive Decision-Making Approaches

5-QUESTION APPROACH

The 5-question approach, or 5-box approach as Graham Tucker has called it in his article (which appears later in this chapter), involves the examination of a proposed decision through the five questions presented in Table 4.5. The proposed decision is challenged by asking each of the questions in turn. If a negative response is forthcoming (or more than one) when all five questions are asked, the decision maker can attempt to revise the expected action to remove the negative and/or offset it. If the revision process is successful, the proposal will be ethical. If not, the proposal should be abandoned as unethical.

Asking these questions in a sequential manner implies a ranking of stakeholder interests as follows:

First	Shareholders' interests, usually short-term
Second	Legally enforceable rights
Third	Fairness of all
Fourth	Other rights of all
Fifth	Specific rights

This ranking may not be appropriate for many reasons and should be changed where desirable. In addition, the first question focuses on profit, which is a substantially less comprehensive measurement tool than cost-benefit analysis or risk-benefit analysis, with or without the ranking of stakeholders on their ability to withstand the impact of the decision. Again, this approach calls for revision as the situation requires. As it stands, however, the 5-question framework is a very useful approach to the orderly consideration of problems without many externalities and where a specific focus is desired by the decision-process designer. For an expanded treatment of this approach, refer to the article by Graham Tucker (1990), which appears later in this chapter.

TABLE 4.5

5-QUESTION APPROACH TO
ETHICAL DECISION MAKING

The following five questions are asked in sequence about a proposed decision:

Is the decision:

1. profitable?
2. legal?
3. fair?
4. right?
5. going to further sustainable development?

Question 5 is an optional question designed to focus the decision-making process on a particular issue of relevance to the organization(s) or decision maker involved.

MORAL STANDARDS APPROACH

The moral standards approach to stakeholder impact analysis builds directly on the three fundamental interests of stakeholders identified in Table 4.1. It is somewhat more general in focus than the 5-question approach, and leads the decision maker to a more broadly based analysis of net benefit rather than just profitability as a first challenge to proposed decisions. As a result, it offers a framework that is more suited to the consideration of decisions with significant impacts outside the corporation than the 5-question framework, which begins with profit considerations.

The three standards making up the moral standards approach are listed in Table 4.6. Questions that spring from each standard and that ought to be applied to each decision are also offered.

As shown in Table 4.6 the satisfaction of the utilitarian principle is examined through a question that focuses on cost-benefit analysis or risk-benefit analysis rather than just profit. Consequently, the full range of options discussed in Table 4.3 can be employed as befits the need.

In addition, as explained in Velasquez (1992), the examination of how the decision respects individual rights looks at the impact of the decision on each stakeholder's right as noted in Table 4.4, as well as the process by which the final impact is arrived at. For example, has deception, manipulation, or some form of coercion been used, or has there been some other limit placed on information made available to the individuals impacted upon, or upon their freedom to choose a response or limit their redress. If so, their rights have not been respected. One of the interesting questions raised in this regard is whether notification of the intent to undertake an action implies the consent of those individuals impacted upon. Usually, notification does not imply consent unless the notification provides full information, allows time for consideration, and implies that reasonable options are at hand to avoid the impact.

The question focusing on distributive justice, or fairness, is handled in the same way as in the 5-question approach.

For a full treatment of the moral standards approach, refer to *Business Ethics: Concepts and Cases* by Manuel G. Velasquez (1992).

TABLE 4.6

MORAL STANDARDS APPROACH TO ETHICAL DECISION MAKING*

MORAL STANDARD	QUESTION OF PROPOSED DECISION
Utilitarian: Maximize net benefit to society as a whole	Does the action maximize social benefits and minimize social injuries?
Individual rights: Respect and protect	Is the action consistent with each person's rights?
Justice: Fair distribution of benefits and burdens	Will the action lead to a just distribution of benefits and burdens?

*All three moral standards must be applied; none is a sufficient test by itself.

PASTIN'S APPROACH

In his book *The Hard Problems of Management: Gaining the Ethics Edge* Mark Pastin (1986) presents his ideas on the appropriate approach to ethical analysis, which involves examining the four key aspects of ethics noted in Table 4.7.

Pastin uses the concept of ground rule ethics to capture the idea that individuals and organizations have grounded rules or fundamental values that govern their behavior, or their desired behavior. If a decision is seen to offend these values, it is likely that disenchantment or retaliation will occur. Unfortunately, this could lead to the dismissal of an employee who acts without a good understanding of the ethical ground rules of the employer organization involved. In order to understand the prevailing ground rules, to correctly gauge the organization's commitment to proposals, and to protect the decision maker, Pastin suggests that an examination of past decisions or actions be made. He calls this approach *reverse engineering* a decision, because the attempt is made to take apart past decisions to see how and why they were made. Pastin suggests that individuals are often guarded (voluntarily or involuntarily) about expressing their values, and that reverse engineering offers a way to see, through past actions, what their values are.

In his concept of end-point ethics, Pastin suggests employing the full extent of the treatments summarized in Table 4.3. The application of these techniques to the Ford Pinto case (which appears in this chapter) should illuminate the concept of utilitarianism and illustrate the pitfalls of focusing an analysis on only short-term profit.

The concept of rule ethics is used to indicate the value of rules that spring from the application of valid ethical principles to an ethical dilemma. In this case, the valid ethical principles involve the respect for and protection of the rights of individuals as discussed in Table 4.4 and derivative principles such as the golden rule of "Do unto others as you would have them do to you." The establishment of rules based on respect for individual rights can prove helpful when an interpretation is particularly difficult, or when senior executives want to remove ambiguity about what they believe should be done in certain situations. For example, Pastin suggests that rules formulated by senior executives to assist their employees can divide possible actions into those that are obligatory, or prohibited or permissible. Similarly, rules can be crafted so as to make them categorical (i.e., no exceptions allowed) or prima facie (exceptions are

TABLE 4.7

PASTIN'S APPROACH TO STAKE-HOLDER IMPACT ANALYSIS

KEY ASPECT	PURPOSE FOR EXAMINATION
Ground Rule Ethics	To illuminate an organization's and/or an individual's rules and values
End-Point Ethics	To determine the greatest net good for all concerned
Rule Ethics	To determine what boundaries a person or organization should take into account according to ethical principles
Social Contract Ethics	To determine how to move the boundaries to remove concerns or conflicts

allowed in certain circumstances), or to trigger consultation with senior executives. As such, rule ethics represent Pastin's examination of the impact of proposed decisions on the rights of the individuals involved.

The concept of fairness is incorporated by Pastin into his idea of social contract ethics. Here he suggests that formulating the proposed decision into an imaginary contract would be helpful because it would allow the decision maker to change places with the stakeholder to be impacted upon. As a result, the decision maker could see if the impact was fair enough to freely enter into the contract. If the decision maker found that he or she was not prepared to enter into the contract with the roles reversed, then the terms (or boundaries) of the contract should be changed in the interest of fairness. This technique of role reversal can prove to be quite helpful, particularly in the case of strong-willed executives who are often surrounded by "yes" men or women. In the case of a real contract, this approach can be useful in projecting how proposed actions will affect the contract, or whether a contract change (such as in a union contract) will be resisted.

EXTENDING AND BLENDING THE APPROACHES

From time to time, an ethical problem will arise that doesn't fit perfectly into one of the approaches described. For instance, a problem may fit the 5-question approach, except that there are significant long-term impacts or externalities that call for cost-benefit analysis rather than profitability as a first-level question. Fortunately, cost-benefit analysis can be substituted or added to the approach to enrich it. Similarly, the concept of ground rule ethics can be grafted onto a non-Pastin approach, if needed in an in-house company decision. Care should be taken when extending and blending the approaches, however, to ensure that each of the areas of well-offness, fairness, and impact on individual rights is examined in a comprehensive analysis; otherwise the final decision may be faulty.

Commons Problems

The term *commons problems* refers to the inadvertent or knowing overuse of jointly owned assets or resources. The concept first arose when villagers in old England overgrazed their livestock on land that was owned in common, or jointly, with everyone else in the village, and the term *commons* was used to identify this type of pasture.

The problem of overgrazing could not be stopped because everyone had a right to use the pasture and thus could not be prevented from doing so. Only when the majority of villagers agreed to regulate the commons did the overgrazing stop. Sometimes, when they could not agree, outside authority was called upon to settle the matter. Outdated though these issues seem, the problem of the commons is still with us in modern times. For example, pollution represents the misuse of the environment, a commons we all share. Similarly, if everyone in a business attempts to draw on capital funds or an expense budget or a service department, the result will be akin to overgrazing.

The lesson to be learned is that frequently the decision maker, who is not sensitized to the problem of the commons, will not attribute a high enough value to the use of an asset or resource, and therefore make the wrong decision. Awareness of the problem should correct this tendency and improve decision making. If an executive is confronted by the overuse of an asset or resource, he or she would do well to employ the solutions applied in olden times.

Developing a More Ethical Action

One of the advantages of using a framework such as the 5-question, moral standards, Pastin's, or commons approach is that the unethical aspects of a decision can be identified and modified in order to make the overall impact of the decision acceptable. For example, if a decision is expected to be unfair to a particular stakeholder group, perhaps the decision can be altered by increasing the compensation to that group, or by eliminating or replacing the offending words, image, or specific action. At the end of every application of stakeholder impact analysis there should be a specific search for a win–win–win outcome.

Conclusion

Stakeholder impact analysis offers a formal way of bringing into a decision the needs of an organization and its individual constituents (society, really). Trade-offs are difficult to determine, and can benefit from such advances in technique. It is important not to lose sight of the fact that the concepts of stakeholder impact analysis reviewed in this chapter need to be applied, not as single techniques, but together as a set. Only then will a comprehensive analysis be achieved and an ethical decision made. Depending on the nature of the decision to be faced, and the range of stakeholders to be affected, a proper analysis could be based on the 5-question, moral standards, or Pastin's approach taking into account the possible existence of commons problems that might arise.

A professional accountant can use stakeholder analysis in making decisions about accounting, auditing, and practice matters, and should be ready to prepare or assist in such analyses for employers or clients just as is the case in other areas. Although many accountants will be wary of becoming involved with the "soft" subjective analysis which typifies stakeholder analysis, they should bear in mind, that the world is changing and placing a much higher value on nonnumerical information. They should beware of relying too much on numerical analysis lest they fall into the trap of the economist, who, as Oscar Wilde put it, "knew the price of everything and the value of nothing."

As described above, the assessment of stakeholder impacts, when combined with the ranking of the stakeholder's ability to withstand the action, represents a helpful expansion of the accounting concept of materiality which has guided financial disclosure. As expanded, the "stakeholder significance/materiality" concept could assist in making decisions by projecting their ultimate impact on the company.

ILLUSTRATIVE CASE APPLICATION OF STAKEHOLDER IMPACT ANALYSIS

In order to illustrate and consolidate the techniques of analysis developed in this chapter, a brief case related to a possible audit adjustment is described and an approach to a solution offered.

The Proposed Audit Adjustment Case and suggested solution are located before the cases for students to solve.

QUESTIONS FOR DISCUSSION

1. Is it wise for a decision maker to take into account more than profit when making decisions that have a significant social impact? Why?

2. If a framework for ethical decision making is to be employed, why is it essential to incorporate all three considerations of well-offness, fairness, and individual rights?

3. Is the 5-question approach to ethical decision making superior to the moral standards or Pastin's approach?

4. Under what circumstances would it be best to use each of the following frameworks: 5-question, moral standards, and Pastin's approach?

5. How would you convince a CEO not to treat the environment as a cost-free commons?

6. How can a decision to downsize be made as ethical as possible by treating everyone equally?

CASES

- The Ford Pinto case is a classic which shows in stark relief the danger of ignoring the social impacts of a decision in favor of maximizing short-term profit. The original cost-benefit analysis was quite faulty, and our appreciation of safety has changed a lot since the Pinto was created, but the same problems continue to recur.

- The Kardell Paper Co. case involves the possible pollution of a river with possibly life-threatening consequences. In addition to dealing with uncertainty, the reader learns to appreciate issues such as whistleblowing, representative corporate governance at the Board level, and due diligence requirements on the part of executives and Board members.

READINGS

The two readings provided for this chapter are intended to offer further elaboration on cost-benefit analysis and the 5-question approach to ethical decision making.

REFERENCES

Brooks, L. J. "Cost-Benefit Analysis." *CAmagazine* (October 1979): 53–57.

Pastin, M. *The Hard Problems of Management: Gaining the Ethics Edge.* San Francisco, CA: Jossey-Bass, 1986.

Tucker, G. "Ethical Analysis for Environmental Problem Solving." *Agenda for Action Conference Proceedings,* The Canadian Centre for Ethics & Corporate Policy, Toronto, Canada, 1990, 53–57.

Velasquez, M. G. *Business Ethics: Concepts and Cases.* Englewood Cliffs, NJ: Prentice Hall, 1992.

Illustrative Application of Stakeholder Impact Analysis
Proposed Audit Adjustment Case

Larry Plant, the Chief Financial Officer of Castle Manufacturing Inc., was involved in a lengthy discussion with Joyce Tang of the company's auditing firm, Bennett & Sange, at the conclusion of the audit fieldwork.

"Look, Joyce, we just can't afford to show that much profit this year. If we do record the $1.5 million after-tax adjustment you proposed, our profit will be 20 percent higher than we had two years ago and 5 percent higher than we reported last year. On the other hand, without the adjustment, we would be close to last year's level. We are just about to enter negotiations with our labor unions, and we have been complaining about our ability to compete. If we show that much profit improvement, they will ask for a

huge raise in wages. Our company will become noncompetitive due to higher labor rates than our offshore competition. Do you really want that to happen?

"But, Larry, you really earned the profit. You can't just ignore it!"

"No, I'm not suggesting that, Joyce. But virtually all the goods making up the profit adjustment were in transit at our year end—so let's just record them as next year's sales and profits."

"But, Larry, they were all sold FOB at your plant, so title passed to the buyer when they were shipped."

"I know that, Joyce, but that was an unusual move by our overzealous sales staff, who were trying to look good and get a high commission on year-end numbers. Anyway, the cus-

tomer hadn't inspected them yet. Just this once, Joyce, let's put it into next year. It's not really a significant amount for our shareholders, but it will trigger a much bigger problem for them if the unions get hold of the higher profit numbers. As you know, about 40 percent of our shares were willed to the United Charities Appeal here in town, and they could sure benefit by higher profits and dividends in the future. I bet the difference in their dividends could be up to $400,000 per year over the life of the next five-year contract."

QUESTION

1. What should Joyce do?

Illustrative Solution

Three approaches to ethical decision making are presented in Chapter 4: the 5-question approach, the moral standards approach, and Pastin's approach. In this illustrative solution, the 5-question framework will be used to start, with expansions, where necessary, drawn from the other approaches.

The 5-question approach calls for the identification of the stakeholders impacted on by the decision and then poses five questions or challenges to assess whether these impacts are ethical or not. If some aspect of the decision is considered not to be ethical, the proposed decision/action may be altered to mitigate or remove the unethical element.

In this case, the auditor has recommended that a $1.5 million adjustment be made to increase the profitability of the client, Castle Manufacturing Inc. The CFO is resisting, proposing instead that the impact on profit be put into the next year so as to gain a bargaining advantage over the company's unions, who will use the profit figures to negotiate a new five-year agreement. Joyce Tang, the auditor, must decide whether the

proposal to shift the adjustment to the next year is ethical: If not, she must either convince the CFO to record the adjustment or qualify her audit report. It is not immediately apparent whether the adjustment is material or not: If it was, the correct action would be to qualify the audit report if the CFO were to hold fast to his proposal.

Identification of Stakeholders and Their Interests

The CFO's proposal would impact on the following stakeholders:

Directly Impacted:

Current shareholders wishing to sell their shares in the short run. They would want the adjustment recorded in the current year to boost profit and share values.

Current shareholders wishing to hold on to their shares. They would want the adjustment deferred to minimize the labor settlement and maximize future profits and dividends.

Continued

Continued

Future shareholders. They would want an accurate assessment of profitability to properly assess whether or not to buy into the company. If profits are depressed, they might not buy in, so the increased future profits may not be relevant.

Employees. They would want profits accurately stated to provide a higher basis for negotiation, assuming this would not jeopardize the long-term viability of the enterprise.

Company management. Depending on their bonus arrangements and their altruism, they would want short- or longer-term recognition of the adjustment.

Directors. They would want the long-run profit improvement, provided they would not be sued for sanctioning something illegal.

Creditors, suppliers, and lenders. If the labor negotiations result in higher profitability and liquidity, these stakeholders would want the adjustment deferred.

Governments and regulators. They would want profits accurately stated because this would result in higher taxes and fewer potential complaints from other stakeholders (e.g., unions, etc.).

Joyce Tang and her audit firm. They would want to minimize the chance of legal and professional challenges arising from the audit that could result in fines and/or loss of reputation, but also would wish to continue auditing a healthy client.

Indirectly Impacted:

Recipients of the funds generated by the United States Charities Appeal. They would want the adjustment deferred.

Altruistic management of the United Charities Appeal. They would want the adjustment properly dealt with, which would probably mean that they would side with the employees.

Host communities. They would want the highest labor rate settlement possible without jeopardizing the long-term health of the enterprise.

The auditing profession. They would want to avoid loss of reputation for the profession.

Ranking of Stakeholders Interests

The stakeholder's interests in the decision identified above can be ranked as to their importance on "possessing legal rights", "ability to withstand both financially and psychologically," (a rank of "1" is worst) and "probable public reaction on behalf of" scales, as follows:

	Possess Legal Rights	Rank of Ability to Withstand	Probable Public Reaction For
Current shareholders–wishing to sell	First (yes)	3	Low
Current shareholders–wishing to hold	Tie (yes)	3	Low
Future shareholders	yes	3	Low
Employees-	None (no)	2	Strong
if contract is GAAP based	yes	2	Strong
if financial statement is used in negotiation	yes (poss.)	2	Strong
Company management–dependent on contract	yes or no	3	Low
Directors	yes	2	Low
Creditors, suppliers	no	4	Low
lenders–dependent on contract	no or yes	4	Low
Governments & regulators	yes	4	Moderate
Joyce & her audit firm	yes	2	Strong
Recipients of charity funds	no	1	Strong
Altruistic management of charity	no	3 or 2	Strong
Host communities	no	4	Moderate
Auditing profession	no	3	Strong

It is evident from these rankings that the strength of legal rights do not correspond to the rankings of the stakeholder's ability to withstand the decision or to the probable public reaction on behalf of each stakeholder if the decision to defer the adjustment becomes public. Moreover, the legal rights of stakeholders with differing interests are equal. The "probable public reaction" scale, which corresponds strongly to the "ability to withstand" scale, offers a good idea of how politicians, governments, and regulators will react. Consequently, decision makers would be unwise to focus only on the legality of stakeholders positions.

Of course, the likelihood of the deferment becoming public has to be estimated. Unfortunately, most decision makers overlook the possibility of an altruistic or disgruntled whistleblower making the disclosure public or, alternatively, revealing it to the union bargaining team.

Continued

Continued

As a result, the valid probability of revelation is usually far higher than the decision maker's assessment.

Application of the 5–Question Approach
Question 1: Profitability
There is no doubt that the deferment of an upward adjustment of $1.5 million to profit will decrease profit this year and increase it the next. In addition, there is some possibility, if the decision doesn't become public or known to the union, that the company's profits over the life of the contract will rise substantially if the dividends will rise by $1 million per year ($400,000/40%). On the other hand, if the decision becomes known, the union may retaliate and bargain harder; lawsuits may be launched against the company, the executives, and the auditors; and governments may levy tax penalties and fines. Consequently, the outcome on the profitability question is uncertain for the company, and therefore for its shareholders and their dependents (and for the auditor, for that matter).

Question 2: Legality
Given that the decision to defer the adjustment is in the gray area of Generally Accepted Accounting Principles (GAAP); (it is not clearly material, nor is it contravening usual company practice, the customers have not inspected the goods as may be their custom, and it is a conservative treatment), it would probably be declared reasonable in a court of law. However, the legal process, which usually covers the company, its management and directors, and the auditor as being joint and severally liable, will involve legal fees, expert witness testimony, commitment of time (which soaks up billable time), and the potential of having to pursue other co-defendants for restitution if they are found to be culpable rather than the auditor. Of course, the auditor could mitigate these legal consequences by qualifying her report, but that would obviate the exercise and could create ill will with the CFO and possibly the rest of the management and directors. Because the legal interests do not coincide, and a lawsuit is likely if the deferment becomes known, the decision maker may not be able to take comfort from the fact that the deferment could be within the boundaries of GAAP and therefore legal.

Question 3: Fairness
Although the decision to defer the $1.5 million adjustment may not be considered material to an investor making the decision to invest or divest, it may be very significant to the employees and their union, and to the charity and its dependents. Consequently, not to disclose the $1.5 million this year may be unfair to these interest groups. If the decision becomes public, this unfair treatment may result in lawsuits, and may bring the company, its auditors, and the auditing profession into disrepute with the public. The claim would be that these parties were not acting in the public interest, that the auditors failed to lend credibility to the financial statements and thereby failed to protect the public.

Question 4: Impact on Rights
To the extent that a proposed decision impacts negatively on the rights of stakeholders, in terms of life, health, privacy, dignity, etc., (i.e., rights other than fairness and legal rights which are canvassed in questions 2 and 3), the decision would be considered unethical. In this case, there are no lives at stake, but conceivably the health and well-being of the employees and particularly the ultimate recipients of the charity are at stake. The extent of this infringement would be revealed by further investigation. Given the information in the case, the degree of infringement on stakeholder rights is unclear.

Question 5: Does it contribute favorably to sustainable development and/or survivability?
From the environmental perspective, the deferment decision appears to have nothing to do with the company's impact on sustainable development. Also, there is probably no impact on the ability of the company to survive because the $1.5 million adjustment appears to be only 5 percent of the after-tax profit before the adjustment. However, it is unlikely that the deferment could be repeated year after year without offending GAAP.

Summary of Findings of the 5-Question Approach
This analysis has shown that the proposed deferment could be legal, but may not be profitable, fair, or respectful of stakeholders' rights. Certainly the examination of just a one-year time frame would have proven to be misleading. Further analysis appears needed to reach a conclusive decision on many issues, and even then reflection will be needed to weigh the trade-offs between interests.

Extensions of the 5-Question Approach
As stated earlier, the stakeholder impact challenges inherent in 5-question approach, the moral standards approach, and Pastin's approach can be grouped into three areas: well-offness, fairness and rights.

On the dimension of well-offness, it is evident that looking only at the profitability of the decision focuses discussion on the interests of shareholders rather than stakeholders. The way to broaden the focus is to prepare an analysis over a longer rather than shorter time frame so some of the externalities are included; use cost-benefit analysis to account for intangibles such as the loss of qual-

Continued

ethics case

Continued

ity of life; and use risk-benefit analysis to include probabilities of occurrences. These enhancements have been included intuitively in the above analysis, but could be sharpened with further investigation and presented formally to the decision maker, perhaps in the following format:

Projected Revenues/ cost savings/benefits Costs/opportunity costs	Short-term Profit	Five-year Profit	Cost-benefit Analysis	Risk-benefit Analysis
Net Profit/Net Benefits	_____	_____	_____	_____

This presentation would allow the decision maker to see what the short-term and longer-term impact on profit was, and what the overall net benefits were likely to be for all stakeholders. Frequently, the benefits and costs accruing to stakeholders ultimately accrue to shareholders, so this presentation will allow a decision maker to project what may result from the decision. In this case, we do not have enough information to develop estimates for the costs and benefits associated with the positions of many stakeholders.

With regard to fairness, the concept of ranking stakeholders on several dimensions has already been employed. If the fairness of an impact is ever in doubt, one way to assess it is to put yourself in the position of the stakeholder being assessed. If you would be willing to change places with the other party, then the decision is probably fair. If not, the decision may be made fair by altering or reengineering its impact in some way.

The consideration of impacts on stakeholder rights can be enhanced beyond the level employed in this analysis by an heightened awareness of commons problems. Sometimes rights shared with others are taken for granted, and should not be. The environment is one example of this, but there may be others on which specific decisions may have an impact.

In this decision, there doesn't appear to be much room for reengineering to make its impact more ethical, so it must be faced as it is.

Conclusion

Although the proposed decision appears to hold some promise of profitability, and could be within GAAP and legal, it does not appear to be fair or right to several stakeholders. *Although its impact may not be material to investors, it is significant to several stakeholers.* Consequently, it is somewhat unethical and may result in significant negative reaction for the directors, auditor, and auditing profession. Because the interests of the public are not being protected, which may lead to repercussions, at the very least the auditor should ensure that the decision and its consequences are fully explained to the Audit Committee of the Board of Directors, who should assess the trade-offs and make the final decision for or against the decision for the client. If the Audit Committee votes for the decision, the full board should be advised and the auditor should consult within her firm to arrive at a consensus position on whether or not to qualify the audit report. In this way, the decision can be shared among those who would be held responsible.

Ford Pinto*

In order to meet strong competition from Volkswagen as well as other foreign domestic subcompacts, Lee Iacocca, then present of Ford Motor Co., decided to introduce a new vehicle by 1970, to be known as the Pinto. The overall objective was to produce a car at or below 2,000 pounds with a price tag of $2,000 or less. Although preproduction design and testing normally requires about three and a half years and the arrangement of actual production somewhat longer, design was started in 1968 and production commenced in 1970.

The Pinto project was overseen by Robert Alexander, Vice President of Car Engineering, and was approved by Ford's Product Planning Committee, consisting of Iacocca, Alexander, and Ford's Group Vice President of Car Engineering, Harold MacDonald. The engineers throughout Ford who worked on the project "signed off" to their immediate supervisors, who did likewise in turn to their superiors, and so on to Alexander and MacDonald and, finally, Iacocca.

Many reports were passed up the chain of command during the design and approval process,

including several outlining the results of crash tests, and a proposal to remedy the tendency for the car to burst into flames when rear-ended at 21 miles per hour. This tendency was caused by the placement of the car's gas tank between the rear axle and the rear bumper such that a rear-end collision was likely to drive the gas tank forward to rupture on a flange and bolts on a rear axle housing for the differential. The ruptured tank would then spew gas into the passenger compartment to be ignited immediately by sparks or a hot exhaust.

The remedies available to Ford included mounting the gas tank above the rear axle, which would cut down on trunk space, or installing a rubber bladder in the gas tank. Ford experimented with the installation of rubber bladders but apparently decided they were not cost-effective. Later, as part of a successful lobby effort against government regulations for mandatory crash tests (crash tests were delayed eight years, until 1977), Ford's cost-benefit analysis came to light in a company study entitled "Fatalities Associated With Crash-Induced Fuel Leakage and Fires." As the details below show, the

costs of installing the rubber bladder vastly exceeded the benefits.

Ford took the $200,000 figure for the cost of a death from a study of the National Highway Traffic Safety Administration, which used the following estimates:

Component	1971 Costs
Future Productivity Losses	
Direct	$132,000
Indirect	41,300
Medical Costs	
Hospital	700
Other	425
Property Damage	1,500
Insurance Administration	4,700
Legal and Court	3,000
Employer Losses	1,000
Victim's Pain and Suffering	10,000
Funeral	900
Assets (Lost Consumption)	5,000
Miscellaneous	200
Total per Fatality:	**$200,725**

QUESTIONS

1. Was the decision not to install the rubber bladder appropriate? Use the 5-question framework to support your analysis.

2. What faults can you identify in Ford's cost-benefit analysis?

3. Should Ford have given its Pinto customers the option to have the rubber bladder installed during production for, say, $20?

---

*More comprehensive cases on the Pinto problem can be found in: Donaldson, T., & Gin., A. R. *Case Studies in Business Ethics.* Englewood Cliffs, NJ: Prentice-Hall, 1990, pp. 174–183 (original Case by W. M. Hoffman); and Valasquez, M. G., *Business Ethics: Concepts and Cases.* Englewood Cliffs, NJ: Prentice-Hall, 1988, pp. 119–123.

Ford's Cost-benefit Analysis

Benefits: Savings	Unit Cost	Total
180 Burn Deaths	$200,000	$36,000,000
180 Serious Burn Injuries	67,000	12,060,000
2,100 Burned Vehicles	700	1,470,000
Total Benefits		**$49,530,000**

Costs: Number of units		
11 million cars	11	$121,000,000
1.5 million light trucks	11	16,500,000
Total Costs		**$137,500,000**

The Kardell Paper Co.

Background

The Kardell paper mill was established at the turn of the century on the Cherokee river in southeastern Ontario by the Kardell family. By 1985, the Kardell Paper Co. had outgrown its original mill, and encompassed several facilities in different locations, generating total revenues of $1.7 billion per year. The original mill continued to function and was the firm's largest profit centre. The Kardell family no longer owned shares in the firm, which had become a publicly traded company whose shares were widely held.

Kardell Paper Co. was a firm with a record of reporting good profits, and had a policy of paying generous bonuses to the chief executive officer and other senior executives.

Kardell's original mill was located near Riverside, a community of 22,000. Riverside was largely dependent on the mill, which employed 500 people. The plant, while somewhat outdated, was still reasonably efficient and profitable. It was not designed with environmental protection in mind, and the waste water that discharged into the Cherokee River was screened only to remove the level of contaminants required by provincial regulation. There were other industrial plants upstream from the Kardell plant.

The residential community of Riverside, five miles downstream from the plant, was home to many of the Kardell plant's management, including Jack Green, a young engineer with two children, ages one and four.

Jack, who was assistant production manager at the Kardell plant, was sensitive to environmental issues and made a point of keeping up on the latest paper mill technology. Jack monitored activity at the plant's laboratory, which in 1985 employed a summer student to conduct tests on water quality in the Cherokee River immediately downstream from the plant.

These tests were taken across the entire width of the river. The tests conducted nearest the plant's discharge pipe showed high readings of an industrial chemical called sonox. Further away from the plant, and on the opposite shore of the river, the water showed only small trace amounts of sonox. Sonox was used in the manufacture of a line of bleached kraft paper that Kardell had begun to make at its plant in recent years.

The Issue

The student researcher discovered that the plant lab was not including the high readings of sonox in its monthly reports to management. So the student showed the complete records to Jack. In the summer of 1985, Jack made a report to the CEO with a recommendation that in-depth studies be conducted into the situation and its implications for public health and long-term effects on the ecology.

In recommending that Kardell carry out an "environmental audit" of its operations, Jack pointed out that local doctors in Riverside had been expressing concern over what appeared to be an unusually high rate of miscarriages and respiratory disorders in the community. Jack told the CEO there was data suggesting a possible link between health problems and sonox, but no definite proof. Medical research into sonox's possible effects on humans was continuing.

In bringing his concerns to the CEO's attention, Jack offered as a possible solution the option of Kardell adopting a new processing technology which used recycling techniques for waste water. This technology, already employed by a handful of plants in Europe, enabled a plant to operate in a "closed cycle" that not only protected the environment, but reclaimed waste material which was then sold to chemical producers. Thus, in the long term the new process was cost-effective. In the short run, however, refitting the existing Kardell plant to incorporate the new technology would cost about $70 million, and during the retrofit, the plant would have to operate at reduced capacity levels for about a year and possibly be closed down altogether for an additional year to make the change-over.

The Response

Kardell's traditional response to environmental concerns was reactive. The company took its cues from the regulatory climate. That is, the provincial environment ministry would apply control orders on the plant as new limits on emissions of various compounds came into effect, and Kardell would then comply with these orders.

In raising his concerns in 1985, Jack pointed out that the Ministry of Environment, responding to the serious nature of concerns raised by the sonox issue, was considering internal proposals from its staff that additional research be done into the sources and implications of sonox. Given the early stage of work in this area, Jack could offer no indication of when, if ever, the Ministry would enact new regulations to do with sonox. He argued, however, that the ground rules might change, as they had with previous compounds; and that Kardell should give some thought to the worst-case scenario of how the sonox issue could turn out down the road.

Kardell's CEO was sympathetic to the concerns raised by Jack, a val-
Continued

Continued

ued employee of the company who had proved himself in the past by identifying many cost-efficiency measures. The CEO felt obliged, however, to match Jack's concerns about sonox against the substantial cost of refitting the plant. The CEO felt there simply was not enough data upon which to base such an important decision, and he was wary of any external force that attempted to influence the company's affairs. The CEO told Jack, "We simply can't let these 'greens' tell us how to run our business."

While the CEO did not feel it would be appropriate for Kardell to adopt the recommendations in Jack's report, the CEO did take the step of presenting the report to the board of directors, for discussion in the fall of 1985.

Kardell's board of directors represented a cross-section of interest groups. Everyone on the board felt a responsibility toward the shareholders, but, in addition, some members of the board also paid special attention to community and labor concerns. The board was composed of the CEO and president of the firm, along with several "outside" directors: two local businesspeople from Riverside, a representative of the paperworkers' union at the plant, a mutual-fund manager whose firm held a large block of Kardell shares on behalf of the fund's investors, an economist, a Riverside city councillor and the corporation's legal counsel.

Each member of the board spoke to Jack's report from his or her perspective. The Riverside representatives—the city councillor and the two businesspeople—wanted assurances that the community was not in any danger. But they also said, in the absence of any firm proof of danger, that they were satisfied Kardell probably was not a source of harmful emissions.

The lawyer pointed out that legally Kardell was in the clear: it was properly observing all existing regulations on emission levels; and, in any case, there was no clear indication that the Kardell mill was the only source of sonox emissions into the Cherokee River. While acknowledging the health concerns that had recently arisen over sonox, the lawyer thought it prudent to wait for the government to establish an acceptable limit for sonox emissions. Besides, the lawyer added, while liability actions had been initiated against two or three other mills producing sonox, these claims had been denied through successful defense actions in court on the grounds of lack of clear evidence of a significant health hazard.

The labor representative expressed concern about any compound that might affect the health of Kardell employees living in the area. But the labor official also had to think about the short-term consideration of job loss at the plant; and the fact that with the plant shut down, there were few other employment opportunities in the area to fill the gap. The board representatives from Riverside pointed out that, obviously the local economy would be severely affected by the shutdown to refit the plant. And the mutual fund manager agreed with the CEO that, at least in the short term, Kardell's profitability and share price would suffer from a decision to undertake a costly overhaul of the facility.

The Decision

After much debate, the board decided to defer consideration of Jack's proposals pending the results of government research into this issue. It also asked Jack to continue monitoring the regulatory climate so that the plant would always be in basic compliance with provincial emission standards.

During the next two years, Jack presented similar warnings to the board regarding sonox, and continued to meet with the same response. As a precautionary measure, he kept copies of his reports in his own files so there could never be any question of the timing or substance of his warnings to the board. During this same period, an above-average incidence of miscarriages, birth defects and respiratory ailments was reported in the Riverside area.

The Kardell case was prepared by David Olive, Graham H. Tucker, Tim J. Leech and David Sparling. Mr. Olive, Senior Writer at *Toronto Life,* is author of *Just Rewards: The Case for Ethical Reform in Business,* and edits *Management Ethics,* the newsletter of the Canadian Centre for Ethics & Corporate Policy. Mr. Leech is Managing Director of NCM Control and Security Services Ltd., Toronto. Previously he was responsible for directing the control and risk management services practice with The Coopers & Lybrand Consulting Group in Toronto. David Sparling is a manager with the Ontario Ministry of Government Services.

SOURCE: Agenda for Action Conference Proceedings, the Canadian Center for Ethics & Corporate Policy, 1990, pp. 20–21.

Reprinted with the permission of the Canadian Center for Ethics & Corporate Policy.

Cost-Benefit Analysis

Leonard J. Brooks, Jr., CA

CAmagazine, October 1979

Corporate management has become increasingly aware that business decisions often have an impact that cannot be easily measured by traditional accounting analysis. Governments and special interest groups have been quick to point out that many costs resulting from business decisions are not reflected in (or are external to) corporate accounts. Pollution damage costs, for instance, must be borne by neighbours, not by the companies causing the problems. Understandably, then, corporate executives are searching for analytical techniques that will take account of such external costs and benefits when they are deliberating company policy, resource allocation (to pollution controls, for example), desirability of potentially harmful projects and other programs that will have an impact on the general public. Inevitably, they are looking to their accountants to develop the required cost-benefit analyses to supplement usual rate of return projections.

There are many reasons why management will continue to voluntarily ask for and use cost-benefit analyses. The best managers usually try to reduce uncertainty in their decision making as much as possible, and knowing in advance the costs and benefits of an action could forestall inciting an unpleasant reaction by an angry populance. Furthermore, data developed using cost-benefit techniques can serve as an excellent predictor of cash costs that will show up later in the traditional accounts. Also, the social choices governing the implementation of government programs and regulations are often based on cost-benefit analyses. It may even be that organizations, both profit and non-profit, will someday be forced to justify their social existence in terms of cost-benefit analyses. Already, about 90% of the *Fortune 500* companies make social responsibility disclosures in their annual reports.[1]

There are already many indications that the use of cost-benefit analysis may become mandatory. For example, governments are about to require summaries of social costs and benefits before allowing new chemical plants to be built. A growing number of public-spirited shareholders are demanding increased disclosure of corporate contributions to society. An increasingly burdened electorate is challenging government largesse and is insisting on documented justification of new or further spending programs. Thus, in view of such pressures, accountants would be well-advised to become more familiar with the techniques and potential problems of cost-benefit analysis.

---

1. *Social Responsibility Disclosure: 1977 Survey of Fortune 500 Annual Reports* (Cleveland: Ernst & Ernst, 1977).

Cost-benefit analysis (CBA) can be used to (a) determine whether projects should be undertaken, and (b) to monitor the performance of a company or project. Table 1 provides a partial list of the areas where CBA is now being used in both the private and public sectors of our economy. The format for presentation of these impacts, their scope and other factors will be discussed later; first, it is useful to see how CBA differs from traditional accounting analyses in terms of scope and focus.

SHORTFALLS OF TRADITIONAL ACCOUNTING DATA

In comparison with cost-benefit analysis, traditional accounting analysis falls short on four counts:

1. It focuses on past actions, which are not as relevant as future actions for decision making.

2. It does not take into account external factors.

3. It considers some resources to be free, or to have no cost.

4. Its focus is far more narrow, relating almost always to shareholders' interests, rather than stakeholders' (or society's) interests.

The first shortfall, decision-time orientation, will not be news to most readers. The classic cartoon portraying the manager as an airline pilot flying a plane while looking backwards epitomizes the situation of decision makers using only historical financial reports in their deliberations. Fortunately, CBA looks ahead at what might happen so that decisions can be tempered by foresight.

Not taking external factors into account, the second shortfall, is more serious. In the case of pollution, the cost of clean-up or health damage is rarely shown in the accounts of the corporation responsible, since it is not borne by the company but by someone else. Yet such costs are undeniably real, and to omit them from the net profit figure significantly weakens it as a measure of the polluter's "contribution to society." To be fair, we should point out that the reverse (i.e., costs borne by a company and benefits reaped by society; company-funded scholarships, for example), also exists and should be taken into a corporation's analysis of costs and benefits.

The third type of shortfall noted in traditional accounting analysis is the consideration of many resources as being free. This usually occurs where no market mechanism exists to exact payment for resource use. Air and water are the most

—Continued

TABLE 1

USES OF COST-BENEFIT
ANALYSIS

PRIVATE SECTOR ORGANIZATIONS

- Support for government subsidy, grant or tariff.
- Estimate of impact of pollution on society.
- Valuation of employee time spent on public activities.
- Evaluation and allocation of resources to public projects or causes.
- Monitor mechanism for net corporate social contribution to society for the year and to date.
- Individuals
- Support for damage claims arising from loss of life, eyes, limbs, etc.
- Valuation of leisure time.

PUBLIC SECTOR

Evaluation of social program alternatives leading to allocation of resources for:

- Health programs.
- Education programs.
- Recreation facilities.
- Conservation projects (flood control dams, reservoirs).
- Transportation improvement projects (airports, subways, tunnels, etc.).
- Formulation of regulations for pollution control.

ready examples of "free" resources, but governments are already moving to regulate their use to protect the interests of other members of society, both present and future. Consequently, capital investment decisions should from now on reflect the potential costs of air and water regulation.

The fourth shortfall, the narrow focus of accounting analysis, is a result of the traditional desire to reflect the impact of corporate actions on the interest of shareholders. But corporations affect, and are responsible to, many other groups in society as well, and these are becoming more vocal in corporate affairs. These groups (employees, neighbours, customers, suppliers, bankers, etc.) are usually referred to as stakeholders, and stakeholder interest has been the focus of a number of recently developed accounting systems.[2]

Currently, however, there is considerable debate over the scope of these new hybrid accounting systems. In 1972, Linowes proposed that a "net social corporate contribution to society" be calculated; curiously, however, he limited the calculations to voluntary expenditures, and did not include, for example, costs involuntarily incurred to comply with government regulations.[3] Abt. in 1977, proposed that the cost-benefit analysis leading to the determination of corporate net social equity include both voluntary and involuntary expenditures and be integrated into traditional financial statements.[4] The AICPA agreed that an integrated system would be ideal but, because of costs and the fact that CBA is

2. R. Estes, *Corporate Social Accounting* (New York, N.Y.: John Wiley & Sons, 1976).

3. D. Linowes, "An approach to Socio-Economic Accounting, *The Conference Board Record,* Vol. IX. No. 11 (November 1972).
4. C. C. Abt, *The Social Audit for Management* (New York: AMACOM, 1977).

—Continued

Continued

still in an early stage of development, it has opted for a less sophisticated approach focusing on the organization's impact on, in turn: the environment, human resources, suppliers, etc.[5]

Indeed, although others have suggested even more complex approaches to organizational worth,[6] the long-term answer probably lies in a modification of the Abt Associates, Inc. traditional accounting model plus cost-benefit analysis.[7] But, as the AICPA found, the cost for a moderately large company to set up a system of accounts to duplicate the Abt model, before costing the data assembly each year, could be as much as $300,000—a price too high for most industries to contemplate at this time.[8] In addition, reports generated by this system will be of questionable value until industry standards of comparison are available and the knowledgeability of traditional financial report readers has been improved. Finally, time is required to thoroughly determine the interrelationships of the various comprehensive models.

Obviously, then, costs and other practical considerations will probably mean that the incorporation into financial reports of the disclosure of significant corporate impacts on society will happen gradually, taking into account one area at a time. Yet there should be no illusion that this type of one-dimensional analysis is all that is needed. As a part measure, however, it will make information available to relevant stakeholder groups and allow governments to provide, for instance, pollution standards by which corporate performance can be measured. And, regardless of whether CBAs are used to facilitate decisions or to monitor corporate performance, the basic techniques should be understood.

TECHNIQUES OF COST-BENEFIT ANALYSIS

Instead of the normal captions "revenue," "expense" and "net profit," CBA terminology would be "benefits," "costs" and "excess of benefits over costs." The CBA concepts of benefits and costs are broader than revenues and expenses, because they take into account future and hitherto external values. Projects should be undertaken if benefits exceed costs or the benefits/cost ratio is greater than one. Usually, the larger the benefit/cost ratio, the more attractive the pro-

ject; but occasionally, if a company has only limited funds to invest, small projects that are attractive from a benefit point of view must be bypassed in favour of larger projects that produce higher absolute levels of benefit. In other words, if only part of the resources available to be invested will be absorbed by the project(s) with the highest benefit/cost ratio, it is preferable to choose a project with a slightly lower benefit/cost ratio which uses more of the resource base and contributes overall benefits.

To illustrate, an unsophisticated yet typical CBA is set out in Table 2. The values used are hypothetical but readily attainable by means we'll discuss later.

The general framework for CBA is identical to the discounted cash flow approach used in capital budgeting analysis. For example, the present value of net costs or net benefits may be derived from the sum of the future values discounted at an appropriate discount rate, or

present value of net costs or net benefit

$$= \frac{B_1 - C_1}{(1+r)^1} + \frac{B_2 - C_2}{(1+r)^2} + \frac{B_3 - C_3}{(1+r)^3} + \cdots\cdots^{\infty}$$

$$= \sum_{n=1}^{\infty} \frac{B_n - C_n}{(1+r)^n}$$

where:

B is the benefit for the year, accruing at the end of the year.
C is the cost for the year.
r is the discount rate per annum reflecting the opportunity cost for capital invested in projects of comparable risk.
1, 2, 3, ... n specifies the period/year with n the final period.

THE DISCOUNT RATE

Monies used to finance projects are necessarily withheld from other uses such as private investment or personal consumption. Therefore, the cost of such financing is properly measured by computing the cost of the opportunity foregone, whether that is the lost after-tax marginal rate of return on other investments or the price consumers would be willing to pay not to forego deferring their consumption. Since such alternative costs are not practically available, the results of CBA studies are usually discounted at a weighted average marginal rate based on the projected sources of financing to be employed. The weighted average marginal cost of capital approach has prevailed in practice even though economists have noted that, in some instances, the

—Continued

5. Committee on Social Measurement, *The Measurement of Corporate Social Performance* (New York: The American Institute of Certified Public Accountants, 1977).
6. In L. J. Brooks, *Canadian Corporate Social Performance* (Hamilton, Canada: The Society of Management Accountants of Canada), 1986. Chapter 3.
7. Abt. *Op. cit.*
8. *Ibid.* pp. 112–113.

Continued

TABLE 2

JM CO. LTD. COST-BENEFIT
ANALYSIS OF SOCIAL IMPACT
PROPOSALS: MARCH 1979

	POLLUTION CONTROL EQUIPMENT PROTECTING WORKERS IN PLANT	UNIVERSITY ADMISSION SCHOLARSHIPS
Benefits (Present valued at 10%)		
Reduction in worker health costs borne by society	$500,000	
Increase in worker productivity	200,000	
Improvement in level of earnings of scholarship recipients		$600,000
	700,000	600,000
Costs (Present valued at 10%)		
Pollution equipment	350,000	
Scholarships paid		400,000
	$350,000	$200,000
Benefit/cost ratio	2/1	3/2
Decision		
(1) if only one project can be funded	X	
(2) if all projects with a positive benefit/cost/ratio can be funded	X	X

Time horizon: 10 years from March 1979

While there may be some difference of opinion over the validity of considering increased earnings of scholarship recipients as the "benefit" of these payments, such a measure is, on balance, conservative and facilitates a numeric comparison with the project costs and thus results in a more informed decision.

use of a single discount rate may not produce valid integrations of present and future consumption foregone.[9]

In the case of a corporation, the discount rate is usually its average weighted after-tax cost of capital, plus a risk factor depending on the nature of the project's cash flows, less whatever the amount with which the company wishes to subsidize projects with heavy social orientation. A similar approach should be followed for non-profit organizations. For government agencies, however, it has been argued that their size and taxing mandate produces a relatively risk-free cost of capital which, if they used it, would be lower than the cost to firms in the private sector. Over time, the use of the lower governmental rate would result in an increasingly larger rate of investment by the public sector in comparison with that of the private, and the balance of activity would shift further towards the former. To counteract this tendency, the governments of Canada and Britain use a 10% discount rate on most projects.[10]

MEASUREMENT OF COSTS AND BENEFITS

Although there are problems in choosing the appropriate discount rate, they are minor in comparison with the diffi-

9. M. S. Feldstein, "The Inadequacy of Weighted Discount Rates," in *Cost-Benefit Analysis*, ed. R. Layard (Harmondsworth, Middlesex, Eng.: Penguin Books, Ltd., 1973), pp. 311–332.

10. D. B. Brooks, *Conservation of Minerals and of the Environment* (Ottawa: Canada Department of Energy Mines and Resources, 1974).

—Continued

Continued

culties of identifying and measuring the annual future costs and benefits themselves.

Whenever possible, direct measurement is preferable. For example, when assessing the costs resulting from air pollution caused by a generating station, we can measure the saving (benefit) from the use of coal or natural gas instead of oil. The costs could also be partially measured by a direct survey estimate of the increase in local health costs attributable to respiratory problems and to the increased house maintenance costs due to smoke damage.[11]

Unfortunately, many costs and benefits cannot be determined directly, and surrogate or indirect means must be used to estimate the values involved, although, admittedly, it is virtually impossible to capture all of the relevant characteristics in the surrogate value. For instance, and continuing our pollution example, it is impossible to measure directly the aesthetic values that will be lost in the cloud of smoke and smell that will enfold the community if coal is used as a fuel. An indirect or surrogate value could be estimated for this aesthetic loss, however, by surveying the local residents to see how much they would be willing to pay to have the problem improved or removed. From this survey a type of demand curve for smoke and smell abatement could be fashioned and aesthetic values estimated.[12] The cost of a pollution control project could then be compared with the curve to see if the overall demand is large enough to justify going ahead.

Another approach to determining the cost of pollution is to calculate the full cost of health damage incurred based on the value of the time lost by patients while ill. For patients who would not have been working for wages if well, the appropriate approach would be to identify the most lucrative opportunity lost by being ill; and, once this is done, the value loss, or opportunity cost, can be estimated by (for instance) estimating the cost of task delay or of paying someone else to complete the task. If a patient loses wages while ill, then this would be one measure of the opportunity cost of time lost.

A further example of surrogate measurement is the evaluation of the net benefit derived from a company-sponsored training program (total cost $60,000) for 50 personnel. Unable to measure the benefit directly, we make the assumption that the benefit will be reflected by increased earnings (say $5,000 per annum) over the expected 20-year average working life of each employee. Hence the net benefit of the

courses would be $2,068,500 (calculated as 50 x $5,000 $a_{\overline{20}|}$ 10% [i.e., a 20-year annuity at 10% rate of discount] less $60,000) before tax.

Additional CBA approaches are outlined in Table 3.[13]

SHORTCOMINGS OF COST-BENEFIT ANALYSIS

Some accountants will argue that CBA is too subjective and too removed from their traditional pursuits to be worth studying. But this argument overlooks:

- The longevity of CBA, which has been used since before 1844.
- The prominence of CBA in governmental decision making.
- The apparent likelihood that CBA techniques will be employed in the private sector to provide a focus for decisions on corporate programs that will have an impact on society.

Accountants have traditionally assumed a central role in providing data for decisions in the private sector and, if this position is to be maintained, it is in the accountant's best interest to be familiar with CBA techniques and their shortcomings. Furthermore, since accountants are often directly involved with (or indirectly subject to) CBA decisions in the public sector, they will be unable to make decisions properly, to advise less-skilled decision makers, or to challenge specific CBA proposals effectively, unless they are aware of the relevant CBA techniques and their shortcomings. The reasoning behind our stressing the importance of informed advice will become more apparent when the variety and seriousness of CBA shortcomings are understood. The shortcomings can be grouped into three categories:

- Choices available to the preparer.
- Constraints to be considered by the preparer and user.
- Issues not resolvable by CBA.

THE CHOICES AVAILABLE

The choices are many and, if too inaccurate, would bias a CBA to the point where unwise decisions would result. There are methods by which bias and unreasonableness can be mitigated, but first the decision maker must understand the potential problems.

11. M. O. Alexander and J. L. Livingstone, "What are the Real Costs and Benefits of Producing 'Clean Electric Power'?" *Public Utilities Fortnightly* (August 30, 1973).

12. Estes, *Op. cit.,* pp. 111–114.

13. J. L. Knetsch and R. K. Davis, "Comparisons of Method for Recreation Evaluation," in *Water Research,* ed. A. V. Kneese and S. C. Smith (Baltimore: the Johns Hopkins Press for Resources for the Future, Inc., 1966).

—*Continued*

Continued

TABLE 3

DIFFERENT METHODS OF
EVALUATING THE BENFITS
OF A RECREATION FACILITY

Calculation of:

1. Gross expenditure by users on travel, equipment, etc.
2. Market value of fish caught (production or output value).
3. Production cost of project (input value).
4. Market value of recreation services produced x number of users.

Survey of:

1. Users' willingness to pay for use.
2. Users' (and other interested parties') willingness to pay to prevent deprival of use or enjoyment.

When beginning a CBA, the preparer must make certain assumptions such as the rate of discount (r%) and the time horizon over which costs and benefits will be taken into account. Obviously, the choice of a long time horizon might favour some projects, even though the uncertainties of estimation are too great to warrant the inclusion of costs and benefits to be incurred 20–25 years from now. If too high a discount rate is chosen, distant costs and benefits will have less impact on the CBA than they should and, even if no longer-term costs and benefits exist, decision makers might reject proposals when their existing opportunities for investment are far less than r%.

Since it is essential that an accurate opportunity cost be estimated for the monies to be used to finance each CBA project, is the 10% test rate used by Canadian and British governments appropriate? For instance, if 10% is too low, there will be a tendency for the public sector to accept more projects than the private sector would. On the other hand, since private sector capital budgeting decisions do not incorporate all the costs or external factors that public sector CBAs do (thereby inflating projected rates of return), maybe the 10% test rate is acceptable. Surely accountants should have a thorough understanding of this fundamental issue.

Which costs and benefits to include or exclude is another basic choice to be made, one that reflects the special interests of the group making the CBA decision. If the decision makers are an upstream town council, they may be unwilling to include in their analysis the cost incurred by a downstream town to clean up pollution put into the river by the upstream municipality. If, in the same situation, all filtration costs were borne by the province (a larger political jurisdiction to which both towns belong), then the costs of clean-up would be recognized. In other words, decision makers can be led astray if the boundaries of the CBA analysis are not broad enough.

Bias can enter CBA through unfortunate choices of surrogates and of the methods used to assess people's values. Surrogates are rarely mirror images of what one is attempting to measure. Table 3 indicates a wide range of alternatives available to evaluate a park or other recreation facility. Some alternatives listed are more conservative than others, so decision makers should examine surrogates closely to avoid being misled. It should also be kept in mind that the surrogates chosen will most often focus on output or production values, rather than on consumption values. For instance, when evaluating the time of an unemployed person, the conventional CBA approach focusses on his or her production opportunity loss (nil since he/she is unemployed) and he is not asked how much his inactivity or leisure is worth.

Having listed some of the pitfalls, it is comforting to note that a wary review, looking for each item mentioned, can be aided greatly by sensitivity analysis. The discount rate, the time horizon and the choice of surrogate can be varied to see if the CBA outcome changes and in what way. Since CBA is a technique used most frequently to rank several possible projects, it is not essential that a project be valued exactly, but rather that it may be ranked better or worse than other alternatives.

CONSTRAINTS

With respect to the constraints that must be considered by CBA preparers and users, it is imperative that projects be mutually exclusive; or, if a joint project is under consideration, that the CBA analysis include all aspects of the project. Furthermore, accepted projects must meet legal requirements and be amenable to administration. Occasionally, budgetary constraints are removed and decision makers are told

—*Continued*

ing social choices for all of us based on cost-benefit analysis.
Accountants, therefore, would be well advised to increase
their understanding of cost-benefit analysis and its pitfalls, or
else lose their place at the right hand of decision makers.

14. J. Dupuit, "On the Measurement of Utility of Public Works"
(translated from the French published in 1844). *International Economic Papers,* Vol. 2 (London: Macmillan & Co. Ltd.), 1952.

Leonard J. Brooks, Jr., MBA, CA, is an associate professor in the
department of political economy at the University of Toronto and
the discipline representative for commerce at the university's
Erindale College in Mississauga. He is also a former audit manager
with Touche Ross & Co. in Toronto.

Reprinted with the permission, from the October 1979 issue of
CAmagazine, published by the Canadian Institute of Chartered
Accountants, Toronto, Canada.

Continued

to spend their predetermined budget without regard to the
opportunity cost (r%) of the money spent. In this case, however, only analyses using an appropriate discount rate will
ultimately be defensible.

UNRESOLVABLE ISSUES

The CBA decision maker must realize that many issues can
never be fully resolved by CBA techniques. CBA doesn't take
into account issues of equity, such as the advisability of penal-
izing one group to the advantage of another. Moral issues are
likewise excluded or abstractly incorporated. For instance,
the $600,000 spent earlier on scholarships might feed 50,000
children in southeast Asia. Similarly, the loss of an eye, limb
or human life is valued by the discounted earnings stream
foregone, whereas, fortunately, society is willing to pay large
amounts to maintain the lives of leukemia victims and provide dialysis equipment for kidney patients whose future
incomes may be nil. Even value judgments on issues of less
importance than human life may not be handled to everyone's satisfaction. Beauty is in the eye of each beholder and
to impute an aesthetic judgment for a whole group based on
the average of several individual opinions may not provide
an accurate picture. On the other hand, decision makers'
judgments often depend on external factors and are therefore enhanced by quantitative CBA analysis, however rough
and imperfect.

CBA IS HERE TO STAY

Society in general, public organizations, private corporations
and individuals are increasingly looking beyond traditional
accounting analysis for broader impact measurements. Traditional accounting will remain valuable; but, in advanced
societies, organizations must be aware and take account of
their external impacts as well. Governments are already mak-

Ethical Analysis for Environmental Problem Solving

Graham Tucker
Canadian Centre for Ethics & Corporate Policy, 1990

INTRODUCTION

Today, no company can claim to be "ethical" unless it is demonstrating a concern for the environment. The focus of this conference is on the tools of ethical analysis and problem solving that can provide a practical framework for action.

Before finalizing a business decision, an executive should ask a series of questions designed to ensure the best possible choice is made both for the shareholders as well as other stakeholders. These questions ought to be asked in the following order to canvass the values shown:

1. Is it profitable? (market values)

2. Is it legal? (legal values)

3. Is it fair? (social values)

4. Is it right? (personal values)

5. Is it sustainable development? (environmental values)

These questions have been built into the "five-box" framework for ethical analysis which is shown in Figure 1.

FIGURE 1

A FRAMEWORK FOR ETHICAL ANALYSIS—CHANGING GROUND RULES AND A SUSBSTAINABLE FUTURE

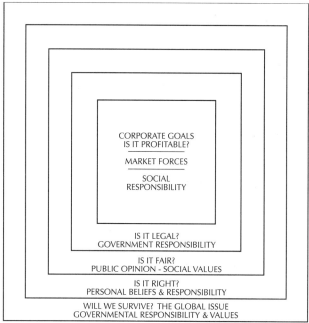

CORPORATE GOALS
IS IT PROFITABLE?

MARKET FORCES

SOCIAL
RESPONSIBILITY

IS IT LEGAL?
GOVERNMENT RESPONSIBILITY

IS IT FAIR?
PUBLIC OPINION - SOCIAL VALUES

IS IT RIGHT?
PERSONAL BELIEFS & RESPONSIBILITY

WILL WE SURVIVE? THE GLOBAL ISSUE
GOVERNMENTAL RESPONSIBILITY & VALUES

FIGURE 1 QUESTIONS

The focus on values is critical to the proper analysis of business decisions because morality, which is becoming more and more critical to the health of corporations and society, cannot be legislated. It depends on the value system of corporate leaders and employees. Moreover, the tough choices required among alternatives often defy quantification and must be based on the values of the decision-maker.

Nowadays, it is not safe to judge a prospective action just on its contribution to profits, because the action may not be legal. Even if it is profitable and legal, society will penalize the company if the action is not also perceived to be fair and right. Recently, as the fragility of our global environment has become clear, society has begun to demand that corporate actions fit into the sustainable development of our economy.

The application of the "five-box" framework for analysis will be developed in the analysis of the Kardell Paper Co. case, after a discussion of some terms used in ethical analysis and the outlining of a framework for ethical problem solving.

SOME IMPORTANT DISTINCTIONS

It's important that we make important distinctions (a) between management and leadership and (b) between being legal and being ethical. Lack of clear distinction in these areas causes a lot of confused thinking in business ethics.

When managers are successful, usually it is because they are high-energy, hard-driving individuals who know how to play by the rules of the game. They efficiently and single-mindedly strive to achieve the goals of the organization. But they may or may not be leaders.

Robert Greenleaf, author of the book *Servant Leadership,* defines leaders as "those who better see the path ahead and are prepared to take the risks and show the way." The characteristic which sets leaders apart from managers is their intuitive insight and the foresight which enables them to go out ahead and show the way. Why would anyone accept the leadership of another, except that the other sees more clearly where it's best to go? The manager, by contrast, tends to be part of the bureaucracy that wants to preserve the status quo. The managerial role determines the values. Managers do what's expected of them. That role often overrides the managers' personal values.

Role responsibility can be very powerful. The management of Johns-Manville knew for years that its product asbestos was linked by scientists to lung cancer in its employ-

—Continued

Continued

ees. Similar situations existed with the Ford Pinto and the Dalkon Shield.

Managers often feel powerless to act outside of their prescribed role; they feel that they don't have the authority to buck the system. The corporate authority may be sanctioning the unethical behavior. It takes the moral authority of a leader to change the system, and this is often notably lacking in both politics and business.

Robert Greenleaf points out that the failure of businesspeople to use foresight and take creative action before a crisis arises is tantamount to *ethical failure,* because managers in these cases lack courage to act when there is still some freedom to change course. Many managers opt for short-term profit at the expense of long-term viability. On that basis there are probably a lot of people walking around with an air of innocence which they would not have if society were able to pin the label "unethical" on them for their failure to foresee crises and to act constructively when there was freedom to act.

Similarly, it is important that we distinguish between being legal and being ethical. The law is frequently quite distinct from morality. It is mainly concerned with the minimum regulation required for public order, whereas ethics attempts to achieve what is "best" for both the individual and society. Thus it's possible to be operating within the law and yet be unethical. The legal limits for a certain pollutant may have been established before it was discovered to be unsafe at that level. The company may be operating legally. Yet by knowingly endangering the health of workers or the community, the company is acting in an unethical manner.

Many corporate codes of ethics express a commitment to keeping the letter of the law, but that may not protect them from censure when the new data becomes public knowledge. Obviously we have to have laws and regulations to avoid the chaos of a lawless society. However, the ethical crunch that is being experienced by the business world today is that the communications revolution is putting more information in the hands of the public. It used to be possible to exercise power and control by withholding or concealing information. If you don't know that asbestos dust is giving you lung cancer you can't do anything about it. The public now finds out very quickly what is going on, and it is demanding ethical conduct because this affects its well-being.

We have recently witnessed dramatic changes in Eastern Europe, as shared information has empowered previously powerless people to rise up and take control of their own destiny in seeking a better life. Precisely the same power is at work in our society, changing the rules of the game for business. Five years ago, the concern for the environment ranked sixth in the value system of the Canadian public. Today it

ranks number one. This in turn is empowering government to enact much tougher regulations. Those companies that are either too entrenched in the old rules or lack the foresight to see the long-term consequences of what is now perceived by the public to be unethical behavior will fail. Whereas those companies which use a combination of ethical foresight and good business and have the courage to make the changes required will survive and prosper.

Legislation may provide a level playing field, but legislation alone cannot solve the problem. Similarly, strong corporate statements about environmental values also are useless if business does not have the ethical will to comply with them. The health of our environment depends more than anything else upon corporate moral leadership, which reflects the personal values of executives and employees. And this is where we move from theory to the realm of applied ethics, which is concerned with the practical outcome of business decisions.

VALUE JUDGMENTS

The name of the game is making value judgments in the light of our personal values. I want to say a few words about values so that we can have a common language in this conference.

Values are the criteria by which we make our judgments or choices, and establish our goals and priorities. For most of us, there is a bit of a gap between our ideal personal values and our actual or operative values, and we need to be honest about what our values really are.

The situation is complicated for us today as social values are changing, and this is redefining ethical standards. The ground rules are changing.

Studies have shown the following characteristics resulting from people having clear or unclear values:

Unclear values	Clear values
Apathetic	Know who they are
Flighty	Know what they want
Inconsistent	Positive
Drifter	Purposeful
Role player	Enthusiastic
Indecisive	Decisive

Both individually and corporately, it is to our advantage to develop a clear set of values, because confused values will result in confused ethical decisions.

Ethical analysis usually uncovers value conflicts which occur below the surface of our thinking. They can't be settled by rational argument. Only as we listen respectfully to

—Continued

Continued

A FRAMEWORK FOR ETHICAL PROBLEM SOLVING

Consider the following issues while employing the eight steps listed below:

1. **Establish objectivity.**
   Who is doing the analysis and what interests do they represent? What are the ground rules of the company and of the decision-making group?
2. **Scan the situation; identify the problem.**
   Separate out the "core problem" from the subproblems. Whose problem is it? Why is it a problem?
3. **Analyze the problem.**
   Use the "five-box," or "five-question" framework (the chart on the following page) to analyze the situation. What are the operative ground rules or values from the perspective of corporation's existing rules, as well as the legal, public, personal and environmental implications? Who makes the decision? Who are the stakeholders? What are their ground rules? Is it fair to all concerned?

4. **Determine the cause of the problem.**
   Why and how are the rules being broken? Are the rules being broken Prima facie or Categorical? Is there any justification? Specify the cause.
5. **Establish the objective.**
   Describe the desirable outcome, or end-point. Is it achievable? How would you measure it? What is the time frame?
6. **Explore the options.**
   Brainstorm possible solutions. Create alternative courses of action.
7. **Decide on the best solution.**
   Who will be affected by each option? Evaluate the impacts from each option on each group of stakeholders. Which option maximizes the benefits and minimizes the burden? Will it pass the five-box ethics test?
8. **Plan and implement the solution.**

---

each other's value perspective it is possible to find a reasonable accommodation of the difference. This is why stakeholder analysis is so important.

RULE ETHICS

This brings us to the two-basic ethical concepts we will apply in our case study today. The first is rule ethics.

Rule ethics states that you make your decisions about right or wrong on the basis of valid ethical principles, norms or ground rules. In other words, we ask, "Will this proposed action be violating civil law, or company policy in the code of ethics?" This is a good place to start, but as mentioned before, it may not produce ethical decisions. The decisions that result may be legal—but if the ground rules have changed, they may not be ethical.

The next level of Rule Ethics consists of the rules or principles that come out of our moral traditions, which in our society are mainly the Judeo-Christian moral norms such as "Thou shalt not kill, steal, lie, cheat or oppress."

The underlying question in Rule Ethics is, Whose rules are you following? It used to be that the corporation had its own rules, which related only to market forces, and it was not felt to be necessary to consider the values of society. That is, "What's good for General Motors is good for the rest of us." Cynically, the Golden Rule has become, "He who has the gold makes the rules."

UTILITARIANISM, OR END-POINT ETHICS

John Stuart Mill said that, "To determine whether an action is right or wrong, one must concentrate on its likely conse-

quences—the end point or end result. What is the greatest benefit for the greatest number?"

This led to cost-benefit analysis: does the benefit justify the cost? And to risk-benefit analysis: does not benefit justify the business risk?

In other words, you begin with Rule Ethics, in which the stakeholders test a decision by asking:

Is it legal?

Is it fair?

Is it right?

Is it environmentally sound?

Then you move to the end-point ethics, which seeks the greatest benefit for the greatest number—and this, finally, forces us to make some trade-offs to achieve the greatest good.

So far, we have been considering the process of ethical analysis. However, there is a tendency to think that having analyzed the problem we have solved it. Unless we take it to the next step of rational problem solving, nothing much is going to happen.

The process I am going to introduce is ethically neutral. The thing that makes it ethical is the particular values and ground rules you apply in the process. If the ethical analysis has been done thoroughly, you will have already sorted out the values that you will apply at the various decision points in the problem-solving process.

Creative problem solving involves lateral thinking, or second-order thinking.

—Continued

Continued

First-order thinking is the obvious course of action that first occurs to the mind of the manager or executive.

Second-order thinking involves "reframing" the problem and considering it from a different perspective.

For example, if you look at a business problem from the perspective of each of the five boxes on the chart, you might generate some creative alternatives which might not come to mind if only the corporate box is considered. It will take courage for every business enterprise to make the ethical shift for a sustainable future, but some can and *are* leading the way.

Graham H. Tucker is founder and Director of the King-Bay Chaplaincy in Toronto, and acting executive director of the Canadian Centre for Ethics & Corporate Policy. Rev. Tucker is author of *The Faith-Work Connection.*

SOURCE: Tucker, G. "Ethical Analysis for Environmental Problem Solving" *Agenda for Action Conference Proceedings,* The Canadian Centre for Ethics & Corporate Policy, 1990, 53–57.

Reprinted with the permission of the Canadian Center for Ethics & Corporate Policy.

PART III

Important Ethical Issues and Opportunities

Introduction

Part 3 explores the important ethical issues and opportunities facing the professional accountant now, as well as those on the horizon. Building upon the awareness of ethical issues, public expectations and developments in business and professional ethics covered in Part 1, and on the codes of conduct and decision-making techniques of Part 2, readers will be well positioned to appreciate Part 3.

Conflicts of interest are unavoidable for professional accountants, so Chapter 5 begins with a review of why this is the case, and an ethical analysis of the types of conflict which professionals must face. Practical advice is offered on dealing with important conflicts concerning services offered, improper use of influence, and aspects of confidentiality including misuse of information for insider trading and abuse of client trust.

Special problems are then examined including the "slippery slope" dilemma. In this chapter, in addition to discussion questions, cases and readings, commentary is offered on the Arthur Andersen & Co. videos. One of these, concerning the handling of a "Late Order", is particularly useful in understanding the end result of a slippery slope.

The final section of Chapter 5 covers problems that the professional accountant should be involved with if he or she wishes to contribute to the full potential that a professional education in accounting allows, and the organizations dealt with could benefit from. Topics dealt with include: common problems, developing and managing codes of conduct, measuring impacts on the environment and other stakeholders, reporting on and auditing corporate social performance, and how to manage a crisis ethically. If accountants are not prepared to step forward to help solve some of these problems, then other professionals will take over some of the dominant role of professional accountants in the designing of corporate scorecards and systems, and in the provision of sound advice to management so they might avoid slippery slopes. At the same time, the proper handling of these imperfectly understood challenges to the profession and to business, will provide significant opportunities for the betterment of the professional accountant, the accounting profession, clients and employers, and society in general.

CHAPTER **5** Important Ethical Issues and Opportunities

5

Important Ethical Issues and Opportunities

Purpose of the Chapter

Earlier chapters have provided an understanding of the changing ethical environment in which business functions and how business is reacting to such change. The role of a professional accountant in this new environment is explored, with reference to the usual range of sources for ethical guidance. Three approaches to ethical problem solving are offered to assist when codes of conduct are not specific or applicable. All of this information is designed to provide a platform that can be used by the professional accountant for the ethical analysis and understanding of today's important ethical issues and opportunities.

Index of Chapter Headings

Introduction

Investigating the proper application of techniques of ethical analysis and of principles found in codes of conduct to problems facing professional accountants is the one of the objectives of this chapter. The other is to put forward a number of contributions a professional accountant can and should make to several emerging issues of governance; of the management, audit, and reporting of corporate ethical performance; and of the sound steering of organizations faced with crises. These latter contributions represent interesting opportunities for personal and practice development, and are a reasonable extension of the values, judgment, and expertise developed by professional accountants.

Conflicts of Interest Are Unavoidable

Accountants are often faced with decisions whose outcomes are not covered by a code of conduct or by generally accepted accounting principles (GAAP). The prime considerations in making these decisions remain ethical, of course, but frequently involve sorting out a variety of conflicting interests.

An audit itself, for example, involves several conflicts of interest. Auditors are asked to report on the fairness of information prepared by the people in management who usually have had a major influence on their appointment. Also, the effectiveness of the audit will depend significantly upon the information that management are willing and prepared for the auditor to have. For instance, although auditors are entitled to any information they request, management may not be sufficiently forthright to trigger more penetrating questions that would lead to a proposed audit adjustment. Moreover, because the fairest form of financial disclosure is not always clear either, considerable pressure on the auditor's ability to form impartial opinions.

Accountants in management are no less immune from competing pressures from GAAP, their management, their owners, or from their own self-interests. Consequently, conflicts of interests are unavoidable. It is critical, therefore, that both accountants in management and auditors be continually conscious of the ways in which their judgment can be diverted from their ethical objective and obligation.

Ethical Analysis of Conflicts of Interest

OVERVIEW

A conflict of interest is a situation that could undermine the judgment of a professional accountant. As a result, stakeholders impacted by the biased judgment could be adversely affected. At a minimum, they would be unable to count on the judgment rendered fulfilling their expectations of independence, integrity, and objectivity, which ought to be forthcoming as part of the trust inherent in a fiduciary relationship. For example, professional accountants who invest in a company and then provide an audit opinion on the same company could be reluctant to qualify their opinion in order that the value of their investment not be decreased. In this case there would be a conflict between the personal interest of the auditor and the interests of future, and perhaps current, shareholders.

There are two general types of conflict of interest: *real* and *latent or potential*. A real conflict of interest is one that has affected a judgment about a problem: a latent or potential conflict of interest is one that may affect judgment in the future. An example of the latter would be where an auditor's practice revenue is dominated by one large client. Although this condition may cause no difficulty for years, a time may come where a negative adjustment of profit is required at the large client, whose management threatens to move the audit to another professional if the adjustment is pressed upon the company. Obviously it is best to avoid potential conflicts of interest so they don't become a problem. Firms have sometimes merged to avoid the dominance of one client.

A professional's reputation, which depends upon independence, integrity, and objectivity, takes a long time to acquire, but can be lost very quickly. In fact, because of the importance of unbiased judgment to the fiduciary relationship, reputation can be lost just as quickly as a result of a *perceived* conflict of interest as of one that is real. Unfortunately, and most importantly, a perceived conflict of interest can be real, potential, or *even imaginary*. It is parallel to the situation of Caesar's wife, whom it was said had not only to be above suspicion but also to be *seen* to be above suspicion. Again, it is vital for professionals to avoid situations that may appear to present conflicts of interest. If the role of an audit is to add credibility, the perception of the auditor's independence is critical. This is why large auditing firms forbid their personnel, even those located in offices far from a particular client, from trading in the shares of that client, and ban trading by the close families of those personnel.

When a professional accountant suspects that he or she could be confronted by a conflict of interest situation, a stakeholder impact analysis should be performed that looks particularly at *fairness* to each stakeholder and impingment on the *rights* of each. In order to establish whether the situation is unfair, the professional accountant would be wise to mentally switch places with the other stakeholders as described in the discussion of *Social Contract Ethics* in chapter 4. When assessing impacts on the rights of stakeholders, the professional accountant should keep in mind the responsibilities inherent in a *judiciary and/or professional relationship* that place the rights of the professional accountant last in priority. Employing these techniques of ethical analysis will assist in keeping decision makers on sound ethical ground.

CATEGORIZATION OF CONFLICTS OF INTEREST

Common manifestations of conflicts of interest can be grouped into four categories of stakeholder impact, where:

1. the self-interest of the professional conflicts with the interests of the other stakeholders;
2. the self-interest of the professional and some other stakeholders conflicts with the interests of some other stakeholders;
3. the interests of one client are favored over the interests of another client, or for a management accountant, one employer over another;
4. the interests of one or more stakeholders are favored over the interests of one or more other stakeholders.

SPHERES OF ACTIVITY AFFECTED

The first category pits the professional accountant against the other stakeholders in several spheres of activity. The undermined independent judgment of the professional can be evident in the services offered, the improper use of influence, and the misuse of information. The second category, where the professional sides with some stakeholders to the disadvantage of others, also offers opportunities for poor judgment in terms of the services offered, as does the third category, which refers specifically to clients. The fourth category, which involves stakeholder groups focuses primarily on the proper use of information and particularly on issues of confidentiality. These relationships are summarized in Table 5.1, and it is to a discussion of how judgment can be undermined in each of these spheres of activity that we now turn.

CONFLICTS OF INTEREST INVOLVING SERVICES OFFERED

Self-interest is a very powerful motivator which can disadvantage clients, the public, and other stakeholders through a degradation of the services offered by a professional accountant, whether the professional is serving as auditor or management accountant. Many of the temptations auditors succumb to arise because the auditor's "business" side dominates his or her "professional" side, and the drive for profit or personal gain dominates the values needed to maintain the trust expected in a fiduciary relationship. When this needed trust breaks down, it does so because one or more of the essential aspects of professional service expected are not delivered in a manner that protects or furthers the stakeholder's interests.

For instance, the desire for profit can lead to services being performed at *substandard levels of quality*. Due to the pressures of rising costs, or in an effort

TABLE 5.1

CONFLICTS OF INTEREST FOR PROFESSIONAL ACCOUNTANTS: CATEGORIES, SPHERES OF ACTIVITY AFFECTED AND EXAMPLES

STAKEHOLDER CATEGORY	SPHERE OF ACTIVITY AFFECTED	EXAMPLES
Self versus others	Services offered	Conflicting services, shaving quality
	Improper use of influence	Improper purchases of client goods
	Misuse of information	Improper investments by relatives
Self and others versus others	Services offered	Over involvement with management or Directors, resulting in an erosion of objectivity
Client versus client Employer versus employer	Services offered	Serving competing clients at the same time
Stakeholder versus stakeholder	Misuse of information (confidentiality)	Whistleblowing, reporting to government or regulators

to increase profit, services may be performed at substandard levels of quality. This may happen through the use of junior or unskilled staff, or if staff are not adequately supervised by senior, and more costly, personnel. It may lead to pressures on staff to increase their working hours beyond reasonable levels, or to encourage staff to work long hours but not to charge the clients for the total time spent. In either of these cases, the fatigue factor that results is not only unfair to staff but also can result in diminished capacity to detect errors on the audit. While diminished services clearly affect clients and the public, these working conditions also present the staff involved with the very real ethical problem of how to react: should they complain and, if so, how much and to whom? These issues will be addressed later in this chapter.

The quality of services provided can suffer for other reasons as well. A professional may be tempted to *lowball fee quotations* to clients in an effort to gain new business or retain old clients. Later, the reality of the low fee may present the dilemma of having to meet audit budgets that are too tight, which can again lead to substandard service quality and/or pressures on staff to bury or forget about time spent beyond budget allowances. Lowballing is occasionally justified on the basis of anticipated future price increases for audit services or the garnering of additional high-margin work in tax or consulting services. However, subsequent audit planning frequently focuses just on the audit, and the pressure for profit results in time budgets that are too tight. Moreover, the anticipated high-margin revenue sources may not subsequently materialize in any event. These exigencies have been understood for a long time, and were the major reason why many professional societies prohibited the quotation of *fixed fees*. When something unexpected occurs, in a fixed or lowballed fee situation the additional time spent comes right out of the auditor's pocket, thereby raising the pressure for cutting corners or service quality. Fees set on the basis of hourly rates per level of staff employed allow for quality service to be incorporated in the total fee even when unexpected problems arise during an audit.

Self-interest can also lead to the offer of services in situations leading to conflicts of interest with other stakeholders. For example, an auditor is in an excellent position to offer *management advisory services* because he or she has developed, through the audit, a thorough knowledge of the client's affairs and personnel. On the other hand, if an auditor accepts an engagement to install an internal control system, there may be a reluctance to acknowledge its flaws when these become clear during a subsequent audit. Such reluctance can arise even when nonaudit personnel from the same firm are used. Unfortunately, living with a faulty system of internal control is like living with a time bomb, with the enhanced risk being borne by the client and the public. Another example, which presents itself frequently, involves a partner who is negotiating with a client's chief financial officer (CFO) on the adequacy of a provision for bad debts, knowing that next week the CFO will decide whether to award his or her firm, or a competitor, a very large consulting assignment. The threat of objectivity is obvious and overwhelming, yet the partner is expected to be objective nonetheless.

What are the remedies for such situations involving so-called *conflicting services* that involve self-criticism? Refusal to provide such services is one option but could lead to the client incurring unnecessary costs and the professional losing revenue. At present, the established position of the accounting profession is to rely on the personal integrity of the professionals involved to be able to criticize themselves in the event they or their associates perform conflicting services. Whether this reliance is misplaced remains to be seen, but it is interesting to note that the future of such activities depends upon the values, strength of character, and ethical awareness of the professionals involved.

The self-interest of professional accountants can cause the professional to want to side with certain stakeholder groups, to the detriment of others. Professional accountants can easily and inadvertently become overinvolved with clients or suppliers or other stakeholders. Sometimes this *overinvolvement* can make the professional judgment susceptible to bias in favor of their newfound friends or compatriots. Gifts can create pressures for continuance. Involvement in management friendships and decisions can create the desire not to be critical, as can the continued, close involvement of the auditor with the board of directors. To borrow from the hierarchy of human needs developed by Maslow (1954), professionals can be subject to influence attempts directed at their ego, their social needs, or even their basic financial needs that can threaten the professional's independence. Frequently, overinvolvement begins very innocuously, then builds imperceptibly to a condition that gets out of hand. Constant vigilance is required to avoid overinvolvement.

The examples of self-interest cited in Table 5.1 put the professional's reputation at risk because the interest of the client, employer, or public may not be considered before the professional's self-interest as is expected in a fiduciary relationship. For example, the lure of personal profit (big stock price gains for the investor-professional accountant) from investment positions in clients may lead to the manipulation of accounting disclosure or the choice of accounting principles that do not communicate the real state of affairs to shareholders. Fortunately, most professional codes have barred such investment for years. Similarly, skimping on quality of service, particularly of audit service, has proven difficult to resist in the past. As competition on the basis of price of services becomes more intense, professionals would be well advised to consider the longer term possibilities of loss of reputation, fines, and higher insurance premiums.

It is possible but very risky, for both a professional accountant and the professional's clients, for the professional to *represent more than one client in a transaction*. Even if a professional is very knowledgeable about the matter, such as would be the case if an audit client were being sold, and the buyer and seller are good friends, it is frequently impossible to do your best for one client except at the expense of the other. Later, if the buyer or seller becomes disenchanted, he or she may suspect that his or her interest has been shortchanged and launch a lawsuit. Therefore, even if more than one client who is party to a transaction wants a professional accountant to act on his or her behalf, the clients should at least be advised that each should have independent representation. Sometimes it will be advisable to select and serve only one of the clients even if they insist otherwise.

For the accountant in management, it is similarly risky to consider *serving two or more employers*. Serving two or more masters has, over the years, proved very difficult because of the real, latent, and imaginary conflicts of interest that inevitably arise even where the employers are not competitors. Where the employers are competitors, it is sheer folly. A variant of this ethical problem surfaces when an accountant in management *invests in a competitor*. Care must be taken to ensure that conflicting interests do not influence judgment or work performance adversely for the employer.

Blind self-interest can prove to be the undoing of professional accountants, just as blind ambition has proven to be the bane of many managers. Frequently, however, professional accountants do not suffer from blind or rabid self-interest, but will lose sight of *whether they are in a profession or in business*. They would do well to remember that few businesses are accorded the privilege of engaging in fiduciary relationships. A balance is called for which involves placing the interest of the public, the client, the profession, the firm, or the employer before the professional's own self-interest.

CONFLICTS OF INTEREST INVOLVING IMPROPER USE OF INFLUENCE

The desire to improve the professional's own lot can lead to the improper use of influence such that the independent judgment of the professional is undermined. For example, a professional accountant employed by a corporation might be successful in arranging for a friend to be hired by the company. In so doing, however, the professional may put himself or herself in a position to be approached by management who wants a *favor in return*—a favor that may take the form of nondisclosure of a financial matter, or the delay of such disclosure, or the minimization of the disclosure. The public, shareholders, other management, and the auditors can be misled in the process.

An auditor may also be unsuspectingly trapped by use of his or her influence. From time to time, auditors will want, and be encouraged by clients, to *purchase goods or services from the client* at substantial discounts beyond those available to the public. Such preferential treatment could create a desire on the part of the auditor to subjugate public interests in favor of the interests of the management. Similarly, a professional employed by a corporation may wish to *buy goods or services from a supplier* at a discount. Is this a reasonable thing to do? The answer depends on the circumstances.

Alternatively, a professional in audit practice or employed by a corporation can be offered a *gift, or a meal, or entertainment, or a trip, or preferential treatment* by a client or a supplier. Is it ethical to accept such a gift? Again, the answer depends on the circumstances.

Fortunately, there are guidelines that can be used to avoid the real or potential conflicts of interest that could develop when the giver expects a favor in return. These are outlined in Table 5.2. They are intended to assess whether the offering is likely to sway the independent judgment of the professional. Obviously something worth a very modest amount, perhaps under $100, which is offered to a group of people as a publicity venture, is much less of a problem

TABLE 5.2

GUIDELINES FOR THE ACCEPTANCE OF A GIFT OR PREFERENTIAL TREATMENT

1. Is it nominal or substantial?
2. What is the intended purpose?
3. What are the circumstances?
4. What is the position of sensitivity of the recipient?
5. What is the accepted practice?
6. What is the firm/company policy?
7. Is it legal?

that an expensive item offered to one person who has considerable influence over the fortunes of the giver.

CONFLICTS OF INTEREST INVOLVING THE USE OR MISUSE OF INFORMATION (CONFIDENTIALITY)

The misuse of information by a professional accountant can be detrimental to other stakeholders of the client or company involved. For example, the use of information by the professional before others have the right to use such information is unfair and considered unethical. Thus anyone who is privy to *inside information* about a company by virtue of being the auditor or an employee (i.e., an "insider") must take care not to use that information personally or indirectly for *inside trading*. In order to ensure the basic fairness of stock markets so that the public and other noninsiders will wish to enter the market, regulatory bodies like the Securities and Exchange Commission or the Ontario Securities Commission require management insiders to wait until company information is released to the public before allowing the trading of stock; even then insiders must disclose these trades to the public. The prospect of a "rigged game" would not be in the public interest or, in the long run, in the interest of the corporations using the market for fund raising. Insider trading rules also apply to the families of the insider, extending to those who are not part of the immediate family but to whom the insider has an obvious ability to influence. In fact, insider trading rules apply, in some jurisdictions, to persons beyond family members and adherents who are "tipped off" by an insider. Some individuals with high-profile jobs in the public service go to extremes to avoid such conflicts of interest. In order to be seen to be entirely ethical, some politicians have gone so far as to place their holdings, and those of their dependents, in so-called "blind trusts" which are managed by someone else with instructions not to discuss trades or holdings with the politician.

The situation for auditors is somewhat different in that the ownership of shares or financial instruments of a client is forbidden to prevent the real or potential conflict of interest that would be created as discussed earlier in this book. Most auditing firms extend this ban in two ways. First, the ban is applied to the auditor's family and persons who would be considered significant dependents or subject to influence. Second, the ban often applies to any client of the firm even if that client is serviced through a wholly separate office (for international firms, even in another country) with which the individual does not have contact on a normally occurring basis. The extent of attention to the prevention of insider trading and the perception of it is indicative of the alarm with which most firms view its prospect.

Confidentiality is the term used to describe the keeping confidential of information that is proprietary to a client or employer. The release of such information to the public, or to competitors, would have a detrimental effect on the interests of the client, and it would be contrary to the expectations of trust of a fiduciary relationship. In the case of an auditor, this expectation of trust and privacy is vital to the client's willingness to discuss difficult issues, which are quite germane to the audit, in order to get the opinion of the auditor on how they might be dealt with in the financial statements and notes. How frank would the discussion of a contentious contingent liability be if there were a possibility the auditor would reveal the confidence? How could a contentious tax treatment be discussed thoroughly if there was the possibility of voluntary disclosure to the tax collection authorities? It is therefore argued that the maintenance of client confidences is essential to the proper exercise of the audit function, and to the provision of the best advice based on full discussion of the possibilities.

There are, however, limits to privacy which some professions have enshrined in their codes of conduct or which have been spelled out in regulating frameworks. Engineers, for example, must disclose to appropriate public officials when they believe a structure or mechanism is likely to be harmful to the users, as in the potential collapse of a building due to violations of the building code. In Canada, the recent bankruptcy of two chartered banks has resulted in the requirement that auditors report client conditions directly to the Federal Office of the Superintendent of Financial Institutions. In the U.S. and United Kingdom, standards for the reporting of client irregularities have been promulgated. There appears to be an increasing focus on the public responsibility of auditors and an increasing expectation of action rather than silence.

The trade-off between the interests of client, management, public, regulators, the profession, and management promises to be a growing conundrum for accountants in the future. One issue that is not well understood is the consequences of a professional accountant observing strict confidentiality about the malfeasance of an employer and being directed by his or her professional code to resign if the employer cannot be convinced to change his or her behavior. Such action would follow from the codes of conduct that require no disclosure of client/employer confidences except in a court of law or subject to a disciplinary hearing, and at the same time require resignation in order to avoid association with a misrepresentation. In the event of a resignation in silence, the ethical misdeed goes unrecognized by all stakeholders except the perpetrators and the silent professional. How does this protect the interests of the public, the shareholders, or the profession? A discussion of this issue earlier in this book gave rise to an argument for the modification of the strict confidentiality of codes and the introduction of assisted confidentiality involving consultations with officials of the relevant professional institute. Perhaps through such consultations a means can be found to better judge what information needs to be kept confidential, when and how disclosure ought to be made, and how the professional's and public's interests can be protected. For an auditor, the situation is different. When an auditor is discharged or replaced, the incoming auditor has the right to ask the outgoing auditor (and the client) what the circumstances were that led to his or her dismissal or resignation (or removal). In some jurisdictions, the removed auditor even has the right to address the shareholders at their annual meeting, or by mail, at the expense of the corporation involved.

One aspect of confidentiality that ought to be examined is what action should be taken when a professional accountant realizes that a client or employer is engaged in *tax evasion*. Tax evasion involves the misrepresentation of facts to the taxation authorities resulting in the commission of a fraud and the cheating of the public treasury. At present, the established practice is not to be involved in the misrepresentation, to counsel against it, but not to report the problem to the authorities. As a result, the perpetrators need not fear their misdeed will be reported by a *whistleblower* to the tax authorities or the public. Consequently, the interests of the public, and, when the deed is found out, the shareholders and the profession, will suffer. Hopefully, the corporation will recognize the large cost of not encouraging whistleblowers to come forward through protected internal channels so that unknown problems can be corrected and pubic disgrace, and fines, can be avoided.

Looking the other way when confronted with tax evasion doesn't appear to make ethical sense. In some cases the professional involved may believe that the interpretation involved is debatable so that the problem is one of *avoision* and its borderline nature is worthy of support until the authorities find and rule on the problem. *Avoidance* of taxes is, of course quite legal; avoision reflects borderline practices, and evasion is both illegal and unethical (Lynch, 1987). The boundaries are blurred, so access to confidential consultation on these matters is essential to proper ethical action by clients.

Special Problems Facing Professional Accountants in Management

The foregoing discussion dealt with many topics that are relevant to professional accountants employed in management, including:

- overinvolvement, which biases objectivity and independence;
- working for, or investing in, two or more masters;
- blind self-interest;
- favors, gifts, bribes, or preferential treatment;
- insider trading and other misuse of information;
- respecting employer confidences; and
- misrepresentations in tax and other matters.

There are, however, several special problems facing accountants in management that remain to be addressed. First, there may be a point in his or her career when an accountant in management ceases to be a member of a profession and becomes a member of management. At that point, presumably, the person would cease to adhere to the profession's code of ethics because a situation would demand that he or she act in the interests of the employer. What kind of a situation would this be? Would it require dishonesty, misrepresentation, or duplicity, or could it be that to aspire to the post of CEO would require that the accountant have no divided loyalties? It would seem, if these possibilities were real, that the corporation would be on ethically shaky ground—properly ethical corporate action would not require a professional to renounce fundamental professional principles.

So, in a strictly ethical company, an individual could happily be a professional and an executive. An interesting question arises where bargaining and bluffing are required to arrive at a reasonable valuation or deal for the accountant's shareholders. Is bluffing ethical? The answers appears to be, it depends. If, for example, the transaction is in a marketplace where bluffing is traditional or expected, the other party to the transaction will not be harmed by it. If, however, the other party lacks the capacity to anticipate or deal with the bluff, then it could be unethical. For example, selling a faulty used car to an inexperienced, trusting senior citizen would likely be unethical: bargaining hard with a leasing manager would not. Again, given the situation, professional accountants should be able to bluff and bargain so as not to allow their clients or employing company to be taken advantage of.

Second, because accountants in management cannot afford to resign and walk away from their employment as readily as auditors (who have many clients) can from a client, other ways of making known their views on unethical actions ought to be explored. Hopefully the company involved will have an ombudsperson or an ethics officer, an ethics committee of the board, access to board members, or an anonymous/protected whistleblowing system to enable reporting of potential misdeeds. According to Singer (1992, reproduced as a reading in Chapter 1) those whistleblowers who become ethical heroes without a safety net usually suffer substantially. Intelligent people, no matter how upset, will not come forward to report malfeasance unless some protection is afforded and a fair hearing process is developed for those accused. The development of such a system should be the priority of all professional accountants for their own sakes as well as their employers. It should also be noted that documentation of misdeeds to superiors and/or to one of the portals mentioned may prove vital in the later assessment of the ethics of the professional accountant.

Third, from time to time, professional accountants in management will enter into an action or decision without knowing it is unethical, but as later events unfold and subsequent decisions are made, the ethics involved become questionable and questioned. How should a management accountant get off such a *slippery slope* and extract him or herself from these situations? If the safe-reporting mechanisms mentioned above are in place, they would be one option to reverse the entire scheme. Alternatively, the frameworks for ethical decision making could be employed with the view of revising the offending action to make it ethical. If neither approach worked then the professional accountant should consult a lawyer or an ethics counselor provided by the professional's society, or an outside ethics consultant as to the appropriate course of action.

APPLICATION OF STAKEHOLDER IMPACT ANALYSIS TO A SLIPPERY SLOPE PROBLEM

Suppose a professional accountant were faced with the decision of whether the bad debt provision of a corporation should be increased such that it could trigger the bankruptcy of the corporation. In this case, the accountant had been party to the setting of the bad debt provision in earlier periods and had hoped that the fortunes of several delinquents would turn around so that their debt could become current. Although conditions had been worsening in each period, to the point that the situation had been borderline for some time, you were worried about the consequences of a higher bad debt provision.

A stakeholder impact analysis of the situation would begin with an identification of the stakeholders involved, including: shareholders, auditors, management, lenders, employees, suppliers, creditors, and the accountant of the corporation. Secondary stakeholders would include the dependents of the above set, who would be influenced directly. As a group, shareholders should be broken into current and future subsets in order not to lose sight of the potential impact on people from the public who are not yet involved. Once identified, the impact on each stakeholder should be gauged, as well as the ability of each stakeholder group to withstand that impact. This would lead to and facilitate a ranking of the stakeholders' positions.

A trade-off would probably arise between (a) the interests of the employees whose jobs would be extended somewhat and the current shareholders who might sell their shareholdings in the period of extended life, and (b) the interests of the future shareholders who would buy in, the lenders and suppliers whose positions would weaken, the potential loss of reputation to the accountant and his or her profession, as well as to the auditor and the employees and current shareholders who might have benefited by a more accurate assessment of the financial picture and acted to remedy the situation.

Of course, no one knows when the brink of bankruptcy will be passed, so judgment comes into play. But the identification of each stakeholder group and their interest, and the attempt to judge the proposed action on the basis of overall well-offness, of fairness, and of the impact on the rights of individuals can be helpful. At some stage the allowances made by the accountant will no longer be worth the risk to the offended stakeholders and a decision to increase the provision will be made. Sometimes the early identification of stakeholder interests can lead to better arrangements in terms of timing, soliciting buyouts, and determining other lending accommodations that can ease the dilemma.

Potential Contributions by Professional Accountants to Ethical Issues

The professional accountant can be viewed as part, if not the chief engineer, of the process of measurement of economic events, communication of a message about those events, and decision making related to those events. This viewpoint covers and incorporates the system of internal control, which governs the entire process; the resolution of difficulties that arise to impede its operations; and the enhancement of decisions required of management. As the world evolves, accountants will have to expand their expertise at the same pace, or lose out to competing professionals. For example, as the need emerges for decisions to be made using nonfinancial indicators, the professional accountant should be able to help with the measurement, communication, and decision making by building upon the financial-event skills already developed and by developing new techniques.

Several ethical issues impact on the measurement, communication, and decision-making process, and therefore ought to fall within the professional accountant's purview. Commons problems, discussed in Chapter 4, threaten the resource allocation process. Codes of conduct are intended to guide behavior as ethical dilemmas become more pervasive and, as such, are a constructive part of the internal control system which has been very much within the ambit of the professional accountant. Similarly, as our society evolves, the measurement of corporate impacts on the environment and other stakeholders will become much more important to the assessment of corporate activities, as will the measurement, audit, and reporting of this broad-based corporate social performance. When all of the proactive planning responses fail and disaster befalls the corporation, ethics are often forgotten in the turmoil. If ethics are important in normal day-to-day activities, then they should be front and center when the crisis management is being practiced. Often poor ethics created the crisis in the first place, so professional accountants should be prepared to make sure the remediation is done properly.

Each of these modern-day aspects of the evolving measurement, communication, and decision-making process is dealt with below, or in the accompanying readings, to alert and prepare accountants for their proper role in dealing with new ethical frontiers related to their core function.

TABLE 5.3

Descriptive analysis
Numerical indicators:

      Space and issues counts

      Attitude surveys

      Media analysis: frequency, tone

Expenditure analysis
Cost-benefit analysis
Categorization:

      How far along is a process for improvement?

      Decision style/character

      Governance process

RESOLVING COMMONS PROBLEMS FACING MANAGEMENT

Commons problems, as discussed in Chapter 4, involve individuals competing for relatively unprotected resources—unprotected because it is assumed they are for common use, or because they are jointly owned and no stakeholder is strong enough to enforce rules of use. In the case of budget allocations, or the use of engineering or marketing support or other centrally funded expert resources, the resources involved may well be oversubscribed as a result. The most pervasive commons problem outside of the corporation is the use of our environment. Whether resources inside or outside the company are involved, the problem of overuse deserves attention.

There are several remedies to commons problems. Most involve creating more structure in the relationship between users and the resource. For example, a professional accountant has typically introduced user fees or internal charges to regulate the use of central services. Where all stakeholders are equal, it may be attractive to arrange a coalition of the equals to influence the rest to obey some rules established for the good of all. Perhaps a pecking order may be established to regulate use or access, where the order can be determined by the stakeholder analysis techniques described above.

CREATING, IMPLEMENTING, MONITORING, AND USING CODES OF CONDUCT

The need for an effective code of conduct as part of the internal control system is explained in Chapter 3, as is the role of the professional accountant in the creation, implementation, and monitoring of a proper code. Particularly in the compliance/use of codes can the expertise of professional accountants be well employed. The kinds of monitoring and compliance mechanisms referred to in the *Survey of the Effectiveness/Compliance of Corporate Codes of Conduct in Canada* (Brooks, 1990, reproduced as a reading in Chapter 3) are well within the capacity of professional accountants to advise on and be involved with. Indeed there is so much scope for improvement in the effectiveness and compliance of codes that this presents a very desirable area in which professional accountants can provide excellent, helpful service to management.

FIGURE 5.1

THE CORPORATE SOCIAL
PERFORMANCE MODEL

SOURCE: S. L. Wartick and P. L. Cochran
(1985), with "implementation" added by M. B.
E. Clarkson the author as the fourth stage of
Social Issues Management.

PRINCIPLES	PROCESSES	POLICIES
Corporate Social Responsiblities	Corporate Social Responsiveness	Social Issues Management
(1) Economic	(1) Reactive	(1) Issues Identification
(2) Legal	(2) Defensive	(2) Issues Analysis
(3) Ethical	(3) Accommodative	(3) Response Development
(4) Discretionary	(4) Proactive	(4) Implementation
Directed at:	Directed at:	Directed at:
(1) The Social Contract of Business	(1) The Capacity to Respond to Changing Societal Conditions	(1) Minimizing "Surprises"
(2) Business as a Moral Agent	(2) Managerial Approaches to Developing Responses	(2) Determining Effective Corporate Social Policies

MEASUREMENT, ANALYSIS, AND DISCLOSURE OF IMPACTS ON THE ENVIRONMENT AND OTHER STAKEHOLDER INTERESTS

There is a growing trend for companies to measure, analyze, and disclose their impacts on the environment. This interest, as has been noted in Chapter 3, has been galvanized by the realization that fines for environmental malfeasance can be very high, and in some jurisdictions executives or directors can face personal fines and even jail. In the face of these traumatic possibilities, the need to monitor and report activities internally to company officials and externally to the public can go a long way toward raising the awareness of employees and preventing problems. The need for reporting of company impacts (such as those related to gender, health and safety) on employees, consumers, and other stakeholder groups is only slightly less acute.

The old saying, "If you can't measure it, you can't manage it," is quite applicable to such impacts. Much has already been done to identify the nature of what should be measured, and significant stakeholder groups such as government, customers, and banks even require *compliance disclosures* before completing contracts, considering bids, or advancing loans. Studies are underway on what is expected to be the ameliorated impact of "bad news" on corporations that have previously created favorable images due to their disclosure of their efforts at environmental management and performance. Such disclosures might take the generic forms identified in Table 5.3.

Although some of these techniques are self-evident, others require elaboration. For example, Figure 5.1 presents a framework developed by Wartick and Cochran (1985) for the categorization of the principles, processes, and policies used to govern a company. This framework, as amended by Professor Max Clarkson (1989), has been used by students at the University of Toronto as the basis for the audit and ranking of the social performance of almost seventy companies. Their findings are available to researchers and participating firms on a computerized data base. Governing principles are assessed based on their dominant motivation, processes on the basis of their proactivity, and com-

FIGURE 5.2

ASSESSMENT OF
ENVIRONMENTAL PRACTICE AT
INFORMATION TECHNOLOGY
COMPANIES IN 1993

SOURCE: "Ethical Performance Comparison of
Selected Information Technology Companies".
Corporate Ethics Monitor. Published by EthicScan
Canada, Toronto. March–April 1993, p. 21.

MANAGEMENT PRACTICE	EXTENT OF COMMON PRACTICE		
	Rare	Some Companies	Many Companies
Issue public sustainable development report	•		
Report internally on environmental performance		•	
Formal environmental code		•	
Ethical procurement standards	•		
Routine environmental audit of all operations	•		
Environmental committee of Board	•		
Regular quarterly reports to Board	•		
Employees with full time environmental responsibilities	•		
Annual report printed on recycled paper			•
Internal staff environmental committee	•		

pany policies based on the stage of their development. (Articles by Wartick and Cochran, and Clarkson appear in Chapter 1, and by Clarkson in Chapter 5.)

Figures 5.2 and 5.3 (see page 262) illustrate how many issues might be assessed for a wide variety of stakeholders. These figures are taken from the *Corporate Ethics Monitor,* which presents reviews of selected companies in two different industries every two months. Figure 5.2 shows a list of items to be considered when assessing environmental management practices, and Figure 5.3 offers a more complete information set of interest to many stakeholder groups.

There will be measurement problems to be faced, including those discussed in earlier chapters and identified in Table 5.4.

TABLE 5.4

CORPORATE SOCIAL
PERFORMANCE REPORTING:
MEASUREMENT PROBLEMS

Which impacts should be measured:
    Direct and/or indirect?
    Inside and/or outside the company?
    Voluntarily created or not?
Objectivity:
    Is the information objective enough to be helpful?
Surrogate measures:
    Are they accurate enough representations to be helpful?
Comprehensiveness:
    One-sided reports can result in loss of credibility.
    Comprehensive reports are best in the long run.

In spite of concerns over measurement problems and conceptual frameworks, disclosure of environmental impacts has begun. Such disclosure is being driven in the U.S. and Canada by SEC, FASB, and CICA regulations and exposure drafts. In 1993, KPMG published its *International Survey of Environmental Reporting* in ten countries. The highlights are summarized in Table 5.5.

TABLE 5.5

ENVIRONMENTAL REPORTING:
KPMG INTERNATIONAL SURVEY
HIGHLIGHTS

SOURCE: *International Survey of Environmental Reporting*, KPMG Peat Marwick Thorne, Toronto, Canada, 1993, p. 26.

Number of separate environmental reports				105
Number of mentions in annual report				400
Number commenting in Director's report or MD&A				183
Number giving details of an environmental policy statement				287

Nature of disclosure:

	U.S.	Canada	UK	Germany
Environmental costs:	25%	0%	0%	57%
Capital expenditures	21%	8%	13%	7%
Remediation costs	28%	23%	27%	0%
Contingent liabilities	21%	9%	7%	7%
Future commitments	3%	46%	13%	0%
Accounting policies	2%	14%	40%	29%

Policy Statements:	World-wide coverage
Emissions to air, land and water	20%
Resource conservation	20%
Legislative compliance	19%
Employee involvement	15%
Local community issues	12%
Health and safety	14%

Targets/quantitative data reported:	Targets	Data
Air emissions	13%	17%
Effluent discharges	10%	13%
Waste management	13%	15%
Energy conservation	11%	12%
Legislative compliance	11%	
Supplier performance	5%	
Product design	13%	
Employee involvement	9%	
Developing Environmental Mgt. System	7%	
Environmental auditing	4%	
Sustainable development	4%	
Accidents and incidents		9%
Environmental costs		18%
Environmental benefit		16%

CORPORATE SOCIAL PERFORMANCE: AUDIT AND REPORTING

The foregoing section presented the concepts and problems involved in the measurement of corporate social performance. Not surprisingly, there has been a desire to report this performance to the corporation's external stakeholders, and to lend credibility to those reports through an audit. Internal and external audits have also been commissioned as a way of finding out what significant impacts and potential problems a corporation has to deal with. Such an audit helps greatly in planning a strategy for responsible operation, facilitating cleanup, installing a corporate social performance measurement system, and providing benchmarks for future monitoring.

CRISIS MANAGEMENT

Crises are pervasive in the current business environment. Surveys of executives have revealed that in excess of 50 percent face a potential crisis within a twelve-month period, and almost 40 percent of those escalate into an acute crisis (Fink, 1986). More than 70 percent of the crises reported were subject to media scrutiny and to a lesser extent attracted the scrutiny of regulators, interfered with normal operations, and damaged the bottom line as well as the reputation of the corporation and the CEO involved. As a result, executives have learned that crises are to be avoided, but if avoidance is not possible, that the crisis is to be managed so as to minimize the harm done.

Unfortunately, the nature of a crisis is such that the emphasis is on survival, not ethical niceties which, consequently, are largely forgotten. A crisis can be defined as an unstable time or state of affairs in which a decisive change is impending. Proper crisis management should involve the art of removing much of the risk and uncertainty in order to achieve more control over your own destiny (Fink, 1986). In reality, crisis-driven reactions rarely approach this objective unless advance planning is extensive and is based upon a good understanding of crisis management techniques, including the importance of ethical behavior.

TABLE 5.6

FOUR PHASES OF A CRISES

PHASE	DESCRIPTION, REMEDY
Warning	Precrisis, detection
Acute	Some damage has been done
	How much additional damage depends on you
	Try to control crisis
	If you can't, try to influence where, when, and how the crisis will erupt
Chronic	Cleanup, recovery
	Postmortem, self-analysis
	Further crisis-management planning
	Can linger
Resolution	When patient is well and whole again

If ethical behavior is considered to be of great importance by a corporation in its normal activities, then, because crisis resolution decisions frequently cast the die or chart the company's course for the future, ethical considerations should be even more important in crisis situations. Not only are crisis decisions among the most significant defensive actions by a corporation, opportunities may be lost if ethical behavior is not a definite part of the crisis management process. For example, avoidance of crisis may be easier if employees are ethically sensitized to stakeholder needs; phases of the crisis may be shortened if ethical behavior is expected of employees; and/or damage to reputations may be minimized if the public expects ethical performance based on past corporate actions. Moreover, the degree of trust that ethical concern instills in a corporate culture will ensure that no information or option will be withheld from the decision maker. Finally, constant concern for ethical principles should ensure that important issues are identified and the best alternatives canvassed to produce the optimal decision for the company.

TABLE 5.7

CRISIS MANAGEMENT: ADVANCE PLANNING CONSIDERATIONS

Crisis forecasting and ranking:

Score each potential crisis from 0–10 on these dimensions:

Will it: escalate in intensity?

fall under close scrutiny from government or media?

interfere with normal operations?

jeopardize positive public image?

damage bottom line?

Add the score for each dimension and calculate average crisis impact value

Estimate probability of occurrence

Plot average score and probability on a grid to identify crises with high-impact scores and high probability of occurrence

Develop early warning devices to show: what, where, who is involved

Consider a crisis management team, with:

Designated replacements

Outside experts

Public Spokesperson

Current list of phone numbers for: employees, media (day and night), regulators

Consider: Who are responsible for notifying: employees, media, provincial or federal agencies?

Who are the backup notifiers?

What will the switchboard operators say?

Who will brief them?

Will the message be bilingual?

To whom will they refer rumor/special calls?

Should a rumor-control hotline be set up?

TABLE 5.8

CONSIDERATIONS FOR
MANAGING A CRISIS

Identify the crisis quickly:

    Can you influence the outcome?

    Consider:

        crisis impact value

        probability of occurrence

        cost of intervention

Focus only on the crisis:

    Nothing should take precedence over a crisis

Avoid:

    Decision paralysis

    Bunker mentality (waiting too long for all the facts before taking action)

    Taking the counsel of your fears (Being too afraid of various concerns to take any action.)

Make plan fluid, contingent

Integrate ethics into the decision making:

    Assign watchdog responsibility

    Use a checklist

Fundamental to the proper management of a crisis is the understanding of the four phrases of a crisis—warning, acute, chronic, and resolution—which are outlined in Table 5.6. Obviously, the main goal of crisis management should be to avoid crises. If this is not possible, then the impacts should be minimized. This can be done by endeavoring to minimize the time between warning and resolution phases, and/or by reducing the acute phase. These goals can best be achieved by proper advance planning and by effective decision making during the crisis.

Advance planning for a crisis may seem to be an unlikely activity. However, it can be done effectively by looking for potential problem areas, ranking those found and concentrating on the most damaging. Second, red flags or warning lights can signal those activities/events so that effective action can be taken. A crisis management team can be structured that can devote its attention to the crisis and not be diverted by day-to-day activities. Other considerations related to notification of the public, employees, and the media ought to be planned in advance so as not to be lost sight of when an emergency arises. These aspects of advance planning are expanded upon in Table 5.7.

Managing the crisis once it has happened can also be vital to the achievement of crisis management goals. Quick identification and assessment of a crisis can be instrumental in influencing the outcome efficiently and effectively. Undivided attention to the crisis and avoidance of the problems that can befuddle decision makers will result in better decisions, just as will the making of plans on a contingency basis and the integration of ethics into the decision-making process. These issues are developed in Table 5.8.

Ethics can be integrated into the decision-making process for crisis management in many ways. Specific instances involving prevention and warning,

TABLE 5.9

HOW TO INCORPORATE ETHICS
INTO CRISIS MANAGEMENT

Prevention and warning:
  Code of conduct: adopt, emphasize and make effective
  Training: emphasize how to identify "red flags" and what to do
    about them
  Examples in practice: cite, and award "paper medals"
Analytical approach:
  Apply a stakeholder-analysis framework:
    5-question approach
    Moral Standards approach
    Pastin's approach
  Ethics expert on the crisis management team
  External ethics consultant
  Checklist or specific time to consider:
    ethics issues
    alternatives
    opportunities
Decision itself:
  Apply a template including ethics
Communications on ethical intent to:
  Outsiders: customers, media, etc.

inclusion in an analytical approach, focusing a decision, and framing communications are outlined in Table 5.9.

Conclusion

One of the most difficult but enduring lessons to be learned by professional accountants is that technical brilliance without sound ethical values is hazardous to themselves, their organization, their fellow professionals, and society as a whole. This lesson is too important to be left to trial and error. Although ethical learning might begin at a parent's knee, the perspectives, frameworks, and analyses discussed herein will become more and more worthy of specific study in the future.

QUESTIONS FOR DISCUSSION

1. Which type of conflict of interest should be of greater concern to a professional accountant: real or imaginary?

2. An auditor naturally wishes his or her activity to be as profitable as possible, but when, if ever, should the drive for profit be tempered?

3. If the provision of management advisory services can create conflicts of interest, why are audit firms still offering them?

4. If you were an auditor, would you buy an new car at a dealership you audited for 17 percent off the list price?

5. If you were a management accountant, would you buy a product from a supplier for personal use at 25 percent off the list price?

6. If you were a professional accountant, and you discovered your superior was inflating his or her expense reports, what would you do?

7. How could you monitor compliance with a code of conduct in a corporation?

8. Descriptive commentary about corporate social performance is sometimes included in annual reports. Is this indicative of good performance, or is it just window dressing? How can the credibility of such commentary be enhanced?

9. Should professional accountants push for the development of a comprehensive framework for the reporting of corporate social performance? Why?

10. Do professional accountants have the expertise to audit corporate social performance reports?

11. Why should professional accountants be concerned that ethical decision making is incorporated into crisis management?

CASES

The cases provided to illuminate the issues developed in this chapter are surprisingly realistic and engage the reader quickly. The specific scenarios, many of which involve conflicting interests and conflicts of interest, are as follows:

- The "Tax Return Complications Case" introduces the prospect of "bending the rules" to keep a client happy, as well as having to decide to admit an error or attempt to hide it. This case provides a very good illustration of the slippery slope problem.

- "Locker Room Talk," which is located in Chapter 3, provides an excellent illustration of confidentiality and conflict of interest.

- "Minimal Disclosure" investigates how an audit partner would deal with a client who wanted to avoid disclosing the amount of income made from derivative securities, details of a lawsuit, and the financial situation in a consolidated subsidiary.

- "Opinion Shopping" looks at some reasons for seeking a new auditor, and at the responsibility of an auditor likely to lose an audit to a firm willing to be more lenient in deciding on the acceptability of some accounting practices.

- "Lowballing a Fee Quotation" is a common temptation. Are there reasons why it is appropriate?

- The "Interesting Times" case, which deals with crisis management, can provide some spectacular role-playing opportunities.

VIDEOS

Several excellent videos are available from a variety of suppliers. Those listed below are available from Arthur Andersen & Co. in Chicago, a firm that recognized the importance of professional ethics to the accounting profession and created a "Business Ethics Program" which sponsors seminars for academics, and develops and distributes print material, cases, and videotape vignettes to assist in the understanding of business and professional ethics.

- *Gambling and the Tax Return* presents a partner in a small CPA firm with the prospect of losing an important client if a newly appointed professional accountant is unwilling to bend her principles.

- *The Error* shows a management accountant who realizes he has made too optimistic a forecast on which management has acted. Should he tell management? Offsetting factors may hide his problem for a while.

- *Eating Time* portrays a common scenario where a manager is facing an overrun situation and is asking an inexperienced auditor to understate the audit time charged to an audit client.

- *The Recommendation* focuses on a professional accountant in a public accounting firm's management consulting group who has to recommend a new general ledger package to a client. Her choice is between two packages: the firm's and an outside supplier's. Pressure is being applied.

- *The Order* illustrates the *slippery slope* concept by presenting three progressively more complex scenes. An order is accepted late in the year to meet a sales budget. But as the situation degenerates from an innocent beginning, less than ethical actions are called for. Developing the capacity to project where the slippery slope will lead is an essential aspect of becoming a fully qualified professional accountant who can stay out of trouble.

READINGS

The readings that follow are intended to provide background on areas where accountants can make a contribution or avoid unethical behavior in the future, both in the practice of public accounting and in the activities of corporations they serve. The drive to manage corporate social performance better will not subside, so articles by Clarkson and Mitroff et al. should be essential reading. Challenging practice problems in general, in auditing, and in tax practice are the subjects of the articles by Finn et al. Gunz and McCutcheon, and Lynch respectively.

REFERENCES

Brooks, L. J. "A Survey of the Effectiveness/Compliance of Corporate Codes of Conduct in Canada." Centre for Corporate Social Responsibility & Ethics, University of Toronto, 1990.

Clarkson, M. B. E. "Towards CSR_4: Defining Economic and Moral Responsibilities." Centre for Corporate Social Responsibility & Ethics, University of Toronto, 1989.

Corporate Ethics Monitor, a bimonthly publication published by Ethic-Scan Canada, Toronto, Canada.

Fink, S. *Crisis Management: Planning for the Inevitable.* New York, N.Y. AMACOM, 1986, pp. 220–223.

Finn, D., Chonko, L. B., & Hunt S. D. "Ethical Problems in Public Accounting: The View from the Top." *Journal of Business Ethics* (July 1988): 605–615.

Gellerman, S. W. "Why Good Managers Make Bad Choices." *Harvard Business Review* (HBR 86402).

Gunz, S., & McCutheon, J. "Some Unresolved Ethical Issues in Auditing." *Journal of Business Ethics* (October 1991): 777–785.

Lynch, T. "Ethics in Taxation Practice." *The Accountant's Magazine* (November 1987): 27, 28.

Maslow, A. H., *Motivation and Personality.* New York: Harper and Row, 1954.

Mitroff, I. I., Shrivastava, P., & Udwadia, F. E. "Effective Crisis Management." *Academy of Management Executive* 1(3) (1987): 283–292.

Singer, A. W., "The Whistle–Blower: Patriot or Bounty Hunter", *Across the Board,* November 1992 p. 16–22. (Refer to reading in Chapter 1).

Wartick, S. L., Cochran, P. L. "The Evolution of the Corporate Social Performance Model." *Academy of Management Review,* 10 (1985): 758–769. (Refer to reading in Chapter 1).

FIGURE 5.3

TELEPHONE UTILITY COMPANIES: ETHICAL PERFORMANCE COMPARISON

	BCE MOBILE COMMUNI-CATIONS INC.	BRITISH COLUMBIA TELEPHONE COMPANY	BRUNCOR INC.	MARITIME TELEPHONE AND TELEGRAPH COMPANY	QUEBEC TELEPHONE	ROGERS CANTEL INC.	TELEGLOBE INC.	TELUS CORPORATION
Code of Ethics								
Existence	Yes	Yes	Yes	No	Yes	No	Yes	Yes
Date (original/most recent update)	1988/1992	1967/1988	No info/1991	Not applic	1988/None	Not applic	1992	No info/1988
Reinforcement/ethics training	Yes	No	No	Not applic	Yes	Not applic	Yes	No
Annual Sign-Off	Yes	Yes	No	Not applic	No	Not applic	Yes	No
Direct Job Creation								
Current employment Canada	1,858(1)	14,411	2,424(3)	3,734	1,750	2,450	1,448	10,066
One-year change (1992/91) Canada	(137)	(604)	(73)	(383)	(49)	250	(892)	(171)
Five-year change (1992/88) Canada	411	(746)	(190)	(618)	(221)	No info	(627)	(408)
Employment of Women								
Directors (#)	1 of 10	2 of 11	0 of 9	1 of 14	0 of 11	1 of 12	0 of 13	2 of 15
Senior management (%)	33.0	28.0	0	0	0	17	0	14.7
Management (%)	25.0	29.0	20.0	No info	18.7	29	22	42.9
Workforce (%)	57.0	45.0	40.0	No info	42.5	No info	31	43.1
Hiring and Promotion Programs								
Employment equity	Yes	Yes	Yes	Yes	Yes	Yes	Yes	Yes
Affirmative action	No	Yes	Yes	Yes	No	No info	No info	Yes
Minority hiring	No	Yes	Yes	Yes	No	No info	Yes	Yes
Disabled hiring	No	Yes	Yes	Yes	Yes	No info	Yes	Yes
Aboriginal peoples hiring	No	Yes	Yes	Yes	No	No info	Yes	Yes
Charitable Donations								
Company amount 1991 ($)	80,000	1.2 million	315,104	627,000	180,000	No info	295,000	705,380
Employee among 1991 ($)	No info	1.1 million	142,386	No info	12,200	No info	52,000	421,330
Total amount 1991 ($)	80,000	2.3 million	457,490	No info	192,000	No info	347,000	1,126,710
% of profit before/after taxes	No info	At least 1.0	0.85 after	0.56/1.06	0.47/0.70	No info	No info	No info
'Caring Company' commitment (Imagine Campaign)	No	Yes	No	No	No	No	No	Yes

—CONTINUED

FIGURE 5.3

TELEPHONE UTILITY COMPANIES: ETHICAL PERFORMANCE COMPARISON—*Continued*

	BCE MOBILE COMMUNI-CATIONS INC.	BRITISH COLUMBIA TELEPHONE COMPANY	BRUNCOR INC.	MARITIME TELEPHONE AND TELEGRAPH COMPANY	QUEBEC TELEPHONE	ROGERS CANTEL INC.	TELEGLOBE INC.	TELUS CORPORATION
Community Relations								
Scholarship fund for employees	No	No	Yes	No	No	No	No	No
Scholarship fund for employees' children	No	Yes	Yes	No	Yes	No	Yes	No
Matching gift program	No	Yes	No	Yes	No	No	No	Yes
Athletic/sports team support	No	Yes	Yes	Yes	Yes	No info	Yes	Yes
Health/medical support	No	Yes	Yes	Yes	Yes	No info	Yes	Yes
Cultural/arts support	No	Yes	Yes	Yes	Yes	No info	Yes	Yes
Social/welfare support	Yes	No info	Yes	Yes	Yes	No info	Yes	Yes
Progressive Staff Policies								
Corporate sponsored daycare	Referral	No	No	On site	No	No	No	No
Extended maternity leave	Yes	Yes	Yes	Yes	Yes	No	Yes	No
Formal employee assistance program (EAP)	No	Yes	Informal	Yes	Yes	Yes	Yes	Yes
Health promotion plans (HPP) (#)	2	3	2	1	3	0	4	3
Company training programs (1991 $ per employee)	320	1,112	1,010	No info	1,529	No info	1,003	1,489
Training programs (intuition/book compensation)	Up to $1,000/0	100%/100%	100%/100%	Yes	100%/0	No info	100%/0	100%/100%
Communications programs (#)	5	4	4	3	3	3	3	4
Retirement counselling	No	Yes	Yes	Yes	Yes	Yes	Yes	Yes
Employee Gainsharing Opportunities								
ESOP—yes/no/employer contribution	No	Yes/20%	Yes/20%	Yes/25%	Yes/20%	No	Yes/25%	Yes/matching shares
Stock option plan—yes/no	Yes	Yes	Yes	No	Yes	No	Yes	Yes
—who eligible	Key employees and officers	Sr. mngmt.	Key execs	Not applic	Officers and key employees	Not applic	Sr. mngmt.	Officers and key employees

—*CONTINUED*

FIGURE 5.3

TELEPHONE UTILITY COMPANIES: ETHICAL PERFORMANCE COMPARISON—*Continued*

	BCE MOBILE COMMUNICATIONS INC.	BRITISH COLUMBIA TELEPHONE COMPANY	BRUNCOR INC.	MARITIME TELEPHONE AND TELEGRAPH COMPANY	QUEBEC TELEPHONE	ROGERS CANTEL INC.	TELEGLOBE INC.	TELUS CORPORATION
Profit sharing—yes/no	No	No	Yes	No	No	No	Yes	No info
—who eligible	Not applic	Not applic	Non-unionized employees	Not applic	Not applic	Not applic	Key mngmt	No info
Labour Relations/Health and Safety								
Unionized (% of workforce)	18.0	70.0	37.0	67.0	94.8	No	57.0	67.5
Formal job security policy	No	Yes	No	No	Yes	No	No	No
Strikes/lockouts in last 10 years	0	2(2)	0	0	3	Not applic	0	0
Data on workplace inquiries supplied (1989/1990/1991)	No	Yes	Yes	No	Yes	No	Yes	Yes
Workplace fatalities (1989/1990/1991)	0/0/0	0/0/0	0/0/0	No info	0/0/0	No info	0/0/0	No info
Unjust dismissal cases (#)	0 on record	0 on record	0 on record	1	0 on record	0 on record	2	0 on record
Environmental Management								
Formal environmental code	No	Yes	Pamphlet	Policy statement	No	Yes	No	No
Date (original/recent update)	Not applic	1988/No info	Not applic	Not applic	Not applic	Not applic	Not applic	1992/1992
Undertaken environmental audits	No	Yes	Yes	No	No	No	No	Yes
Frequency of environmental audits	Not applic	As required	Yearly	Not applic	Not applic	Not applic	Not applic	To be determined
Employees with full-time environmental responsibility	0	2	0	0	0	0	0	1
Senior position with full-time environmental responsibility	Not applic	Director	Not applic	Not applic	Not applic	Not applic	Not applic	Manager
Internal staff environmental committee	No	Yes	No	Yes	No	No	Yes	Yes
Environmental committee of the board of directors	No	No	No	No	No	No	No	No

—CONTINUED

FIGURE 5.3

TELEPHONE UTILITY COMPANIES: ETHICAL PERFORMANCE COMPARISON—*Continued*

	BCE MOBILE COMMUNI-CATIONS INC.	BRITISH COLUMBIA TELEPHONE COMPANY	BRUNCOR INC.	MARITIME TELEPHONE AND TELEGRAPH COMPANY	QUEBEC TELEPHONE	ROGERS CANTEL INC.	TELEGLOBE INC.	TELUS CORPORATION
Environmental reports to the board of directors (#/year)	0	As required	As required	No info	0	No info	0	1
Internal recycling programs (#)	7	6	7	3	4	6	4	6
Charitable giving to environmental organizations	No	Yes	No	No	No	No info	Yes	Yes
Environmental Performance								
Prosecutions in last 10 years	0	0	0	0	0	No info	0	0
Control orders in effect	0	0	1	No info	0	No info	No info	0
Environmental expenditures ($/1991)	0	No info	100,000	No info	No info	No info	No info	830,000
International Relations (South Africa)								
Canadian Company/Subsidiary Operations	No	No	No	No	No	No	No info	No
Parent Company Operations	Yes	No	Yes	Yes	No	No info	No	Not applic
Military involvement								
Telephone equipment and service	No	Yes	Yes	Yes	Yes	No info	Yes	Yes
Military operations contracts	No	Yes	No info	No info	Yes	No info	Yes	Yes
Candor Quotient								
% of questions answered	97	97	98	84	98	57	90	93

Notes

1 1991 figure

2 A partial walkout in 1988 due to province-wide labour action

3 Includes major operating subsidiary

Information for this comparison is drawn from the files of EthicScan Canada. Where the performance of a company is described as "No info," the company may have a salutary record, but the facts are not known to EthicScan researchers. The regular fact checking process involves corporate database reviews, interviews, and two requests that the company review, update and validate the major findings on file.

SOURCE: Ethical Performance Comparison: Selected Utility Companies, *Corporate Ethics Monitor,* Published by EthicScan Canada Ltd, January–February 1993, pp. 3–4.

Tax Return Complications

As Bill Adams packed his briefcase on Friday, March 15, he could never remember being so glad to see a weekend. As a senior tax manager with a major accounting firm, Hay & Hay, Bill was on the fast track for partnership. Today, however, he was worried that the events of the week could prove to be detrimental to his career.

Six months ago the senior partners had rewarded Bill for his hard work by asking him to be the tax manager for Zentor Inc., a very important client of the firm in terms of both prestige and fees. Bill had worked hard since then ensuring that his client received impeccable service, and he had managed to build a good working relationship with Dan Rim, the Chief Executive Officer of Zentor Inc. In fact, Dan was so impressed with Bill that he recommended him to his brother, Dr. Larry Rim, a general medical practitioner. As a favor to Dan, Bill agreed that Hay & Hay would prepare Dr. Rim's tax return.

This week a junior tax person prepared Dr. Rim's tax return. When it came across Bill's desk for review today he was surprised to find that although Dr. Rim's gross billings were $480,000, his net income for tax purposes from his medical practice was only $27,000. He discussed this with the tax junior, who said he had noted this also but was not concerned as every tax return prepared by the firm is stamped

with the disclaimer "We have prepared the return from information provided to us by the client. We have not audited, or otherwise attempted to verify its accuracy."

On closer review Bill discovered that the following items, among others, had been deducted by Dr. Rim in arriving at net income:

- $15,000 for meals and entertainment. Bill felt that this was excessive and probably had not been incurred to earn income given the nature of Dr. Rim's practice.
- Dry-cleaning bills for shirts, suits, dresses, sweaters, etc. Bill believed these to be family dry-cleaning bills that were being paid by the practice.
- Wages of $100 per week paid to Dr. Rim's twelve-year-old son.

Bill telephoned Dr. Rim, who confirmed Bill's suspicions. When Bill asked Dr. Rim to review the expenses and remove all that were personal, Dr. Rim became very defensive. He told Bill that he had been deducting these items for years and his previous accountant had not objected. In fact, it was his previous accountant who had suggested he pay his son a salary as an income-splitting measure. The telephone conversation ended abruptly when Dr. Rim was paged for an emergency, but not before he threatened to inform his brother that the accounting firm he thought so high-

ly of was behind the times on the latest tax-planning techniques.

Bill was annoyed with himself for having agreed to prepare Dr. Rim's tax return in the first place. He was afraid of pushing Dr. Rim too far and losing Zentor Inc. as a client as the result. He could not anticipate what Dan's reaction to the situation would be. Bill was glad to have the weekend to think things through.

Just as Bill was leaving the office, the tax senior on the Zentor Inc. account informed him that they had missed the deadline for objecting to a reassessment, requiring Zentor Inc. to pay an additional $1,200,000 in taxes. (The deadline had been that Wednesday!) The senior added that he was able to contact a friend of his at the Tax Department who agreed to process the Notice of Objection if it was dated March 13, properly signed, and appeared on his desk Monday, March 18.

Bill left his office with some major decisions to make over the weekend.

QUESTIONS

1. Identify the ethical issues Bill Adams should address.

2. What would you do about these issues if you were Bill?

Prepared by Joan Kitunen, University of Toronto, 1994.

Minimal Disclosure

Ted Lopez was the manager and Carl Nance the partner on the audit of Smart Investments Limited, an investment company whose shares were traded on the NASDAQ exchange. Ted was detailing to Carl the issues to be debated at the upcoming Audit Committee meeting to finalize the financial statements and audit for the current year.

"As I see it, Carl, we have three problems that are going to be difficult to resolve because it's not in the interests of the CEO, CFO, and some Directors to go along with our recommendations. Remember all those stock options that may be exercised next month at $7.50 per share. Well the stock is trading at $9.50 now, so they aren't about to upset the price with negative news."

"Anyway, the rules call for segmented disclosure of significant lines of business, and this year the company has made 55 percent of its profit through the trading of derivative securities. It's awfully high risk, and I'm not sure they can keep it up, so I think they ought to add a derivative securities disclosure column to their segmented disclosure information. They are going to argue that they are uncertain how much profit relates to derivative securities trading by itself and how much was realized because the derivative securities were part of hedging transactions to protect foreign currency positions."

"The second issue concerns their reluctance to reveal the potential lawsuit by their client Bonvest Mutual Funds for messing up the timing and placement of orders for several mining securities. I believe it should be mentioned in the Contingent Liabilities note, but they may be dragging their feet on calculating the size of the problem. They don't want to disclose an amount anyway, because they argue that Bonvest will set that figure as the lower bound for their claim."

"Finally, as you know, the statements we are auditing are consolidated and include the accounts of the parent and four subsidiaries. One of these subs, Caribbean Securities Limited, is in tough shape, and I think they may let it go broke. That's the sub that is audited by the Bahamian firm of Dodds & Co., not our own affiliate there. There is no qualification on the Dodds & Co. audit opinion, but I know how these guys at Smart think."

"I realize that a lot of this is speculative, but each of these issues is potentially material. How do you want to play each of them?

QUESTION

1. What should Carl Nance plan to do?

Opinion Shopping

"We have had Paige & Gentry as our auditors for many years, haven't we, John? They have been here since I became President two years ago."

"Yes, Bob, I have been the Chief Financial Officer for seven years, and they were here before I came. Why do you ask?"

"Well, they were really tough on us during the recent discussions when we were finalizing our year-end audited statement—not at all like I was used to at my last company. When we asked for a little latitude, our auditors were usually pretty obligating. Frankly, I'm a little worried."

"Why, Bob, we had nothing to hide?"

"That's true, John but let's look ahead. We're going to have difficulty making our forecast this year, and our bonuses are on the line. Remember, we renegotiated our salary/bonus package to give us a chance at higher incentives, and we have to be careful."

"Looking ahead, we've got a problem with obsolete inventory that's sure to require discussion for a second year in a row. We've got the warranty problem with the electrical harness on mid-range machines, which is going to cost us a bundle, but we want to spread the impact over the next three years when the customers discover the problem and we have to fix it up. And don't forget the contaminated waste spill we just had—how much is that going to cost to clean up, if we ever get caught?"

"These are potentially big-ticket items. Bill Paige, the guy who is in charge of our audit, is not going to let these go by. He said the inventory problem was almost material this year, and we had to argue really hard. You are a qualified accountant. Tell me how we can handle this."

"Well, Bob, we could have some informal discussions with other auditors—maybe even the ones at your old company—to see how they would handle issues like these. The word will get back to Bill: he may be more accommodating in the future and will probably shave his proposed audit fee for next year when he meets with our Audit Committee next month. If you really wanted to play hardball, we could talk the Audit Committee into calling for tenders from new auditors. After all this time, it's logical to check out the market anyway. We would have advance discussions during which we would sound out the prospective auditors on how they would assess materiality in our company's case. Our audit fee in getting pretty large—almost $50,000 this year—so some big firms will be really interested."

"John, let's play hardball. Get a list of audit firms together for the tender process, and I will approach the Audit Committee. Be sure to list some small firms, including Webster & Co., the firm auditing my old company."

QUESTIONS

1. Who are the major stakeholders involved in this situation?

2. What are the ethical issues involved?

3. Is this situation unethical? Why, and why not?

4. What should John do if Webster & Co. looks like the choice the Audit Committee will make and recommend to the Board of Directors?

Lowballing a Fee Quotation

"Look, Nancy, I've been told that the competition for the audit of Diamond Health Services is really competitive, and you know what it would mean to both of us to bring this one in. You would be a sure bet for the Executive Committee, and I would take over some new audit responsibility as your backup partner. Let's quote the job really competitively and get it."

"I'm not sure, Andy. After all, we have to make a reasonable profit or we're not pulling our weight. Anyway, you don't know what problems we may meet, so you should build in a cushion on the front end of the job."

"But, Nancy, if we quote this job the usual way—on an hourly rate and estimated total time basis—we are going to miss it! The CFO as much as told me we would have to be lower than the current auditor, and we would have to guarantee the fee for two years. Now are we in, or not? I plan to put our best staff on the job. Don't worry, they won't blow it. What's the matter, don't you think I can get the job done?"

"Well, Andy, I suppose there would be some overall savings to our firm because this audit is the only one of six companies in the Diamond Group that we don't audit.

We certainly don't want any other auditors getting a foothold in the Diamond Group, do we? What are you proposing anyway, a fee that's at a lower margin than normal, or one that's below the projected cost for this job? Either way, it's unethical, isn't it?

QUESTION

1. Should Nancy agree to lowball the fee quotation?

Interesting Times*

You are the executive vice president—the number-two person in charge—of Wei-Ji Pharmaceutical Labs, a privately held (but soon to go public) Los Angeles-based manufacturer of prescription drugs. The Food and Drug Administration is only days away from approving your firm's request to manufacture and market Sneezex, a time capsule that will cure the common cold. In fact, your contact at the FDA told you a month ago on the telephone—off the record, of course—that the formal approval was pro forma and would be issued in a month.

When you reported this good news to your boss, the president, he decided to begin manufacturing and distribution to pharmacies and physicians early, in order to be ready immediately when the FDA approval was issued. You pointed out that this was illegal, but he ordered you to do it anyway and told you to put carefully worded warning labels on the packages, stating that the medication was not to be dispensed until the official approval came from the FDA and the go-ahead was given by Wei-Ji Labs. Feeling only somewhat mollified by the warning labels, you followed your boss's orders.

As soon as the FDA approval is given, Wei-Ji Labs plans to go public. Because of the almost-certain success of Sneezex, as well as your own position in the company, you stand to make about $5 million and retire at an early age.

The prospect of this personal success—which you can almost taste—is about the only thing keeping you going. You dislike your job and hate your boss; you have long thought that he has a serious drinking problem that, on more than one occasion, you believe has clouded his

otherwise sound business judgment. However, the ten years you have devoted to Wei-Ji Labs are about to pay off—big.

But outside pressures are wearing you down, too. You have been having difficulty making ends meet financially. You suspect your spouse is having an affair. There has been a lot of nagging about buying an expensive ski chalet in Aspen, and you think that if you buy the chalet your spouse will end the affair. You need to put your oldest daughter through college and get braces for your youngest daughter. And last night at dinner, your 16-year-old son announced that he is gay.

This morning your spouse has been calling you incessantly: first to report that the college-bound daughter is pregnant and to blame you for causing your son to be gay; second, to tell you that the real estate broker just called to report that she had located a beautiful "fixer-upper" in Aspen that was a steal at $1.5 million, but you had to act fast; and last, to warn you that you had better not be late getting home again tonight.

A little while ago, your doctor also called to report that the results of your last physical examination could have been better and that you have to slow down. Your blood pressure, she reminded you, is too high and, she said, if you aren't careful, you could become a candidate for a coronary. The thought of slowing down made you laugh. Later you would recall that it was the only laugh you had that day.

You had lunch with your stockbroker, who tried to explain why your portfolio was in bad shape. On the way back to the office, you were involved in a minor fender-bender with an uninsured motorist.

Although the events that followed have become somewhat of a blur because they happened so fast, you recall that the sequence was as follows:

- 2:00—You returned from lunch to find a message to report to the president's office immediately.

- 2:01—Your spouse called to tell you that your in-laws had flown into town and would be taking you both out to dinner tonight.

- 2:15—You take a call from the Canadian Testing Lab, which has been running tests on mice relative to Sneezex. The call should have gone to your boss, but they couldn't reach him. They just wanted to let you know that "another mouse died" and to ask "what should we do?" You had never heard of *any* mice dying, but they tell you that the president has known for two weeks. You'll get back to them.

- 2:30—Another "urgent" message from the boss's secretary. "Please report to the president's office at once."

- 2:45—A prominent doctor, whose name you know from all the publicity he seems to generate about himself, reaches you on the telephone to tell you that two of his patients (one with asthma and one with bronchitis) have died and four more are in hospitals on the critical list after having taken Sneezex. You ask him why he didn't obey the warning label, but he sidesteps this issue, demands an explanation, and threatens to go to the press, even though he admits that his suspicions about Sneezex are just conjecture.

—Continued

Continued

- 3:00—A security guard shows up at your office to "escort" you to the president's suite. On your way out, you tell your secretary to have the public relations director, the chief of testing, the head of production, the biochemist who headed the Sneezex research and development team, and your in-house legal counsel meet you in the president's suite.

- 3:15–You find the president passed out on the couch in his office, and his secretary is obviously quite distraught. He is in a drunken stupor, but is clutching a bunch of fancy brochures for yachts, cruises, expensive cars, and vacation homes. At his feet is a two-week-old report from the Canadian Testing Lab reporting the death of three mice involved in the tests. The deaths are "inconclusive, but suspicious." Periodically the president can be heard to be singing "We're in the Money."

- 3:30—The head of production and distribution arrives and demands to know what the president has decided to do about the "glue problem." You don't know what he's talking about. He explains that the warning labels came in from the outside supplier with a "substandard" glue that "doesn't stick too well" on the Sneezex packages. He's also afraid some of the packages were delivered without the labels.

- 3:45—The president's secretary relays a message to you from your spouse, who has given the real estate broker a $15,000 check to open escrow on the ski chalet. Be sure to cover the check before 5 P.M. Oh, and is the blue suit O.K. for dinner?

- 3:47—The public relations director shows up and reports that she just got off the phone with the Associated Press. AP has "reason to believe that there is a problem with Sneezex" and demands to speak directly to the president for comment. They are on a 6 P.M. deadline for making the morning papers and must speak to the CEO immediately or they will go with the story they have: "Prominent Doctor Reports Death of Patients Due to Sneezex Pill."

- 4:00—The president's secretary sticks her head in to say, "I don't know if this is important, but the FDA called at 2 P.M. to say that they are holding a news conference tomorrow at 9 A.M. in Washington, D.C., regarding Sneezex." She does not know the nature of the press conference. You tell her to get the FDA on the phone, but she comes back to report that it is now 7 P.M. on the East Coast and no one is answering the phone there.

- 4:05—Everyone you requested to be in the president's office has arrived—the public relations director, the chief of testing, the head of production, the R&D biochemist, the in-house legal counsel, as well as the security officer, who is still hanging around, not to mention the incapacitated CEO.

- 4:06—You sit in the president's chair to take a call from a Midwest pharmacist, who wants to know when her next shipment of Sneezex will arrive. She's almost out of the initial shipment.

- 4:10—The chief financial officer shows up to report there is not enough cash in the bank to make the payroll tomorrow morning.

- 4:15—The security officer's walkie-talkie crackles out an urgent message that there is a bomb scare in the building, but it could be "another hoax." The question is whether or not to evacuate, and what to do about the second shift, which is due in an hour.

- 4:20—The personnel director strolls in to report that the switchboard is getting a lot of "weird rumor calls" about the safety of Sneezex. The switchboard operators are upset. What should he have them say to the callers?

- 4:25—Your spouse barges in unannounced to tell you that your son has threatened to leave home, "or worse," if his gay lover cannot move in with him.

- 4:30—Your head is pounding, you are perspiring profusely, and breathing is difficult. Every light on the telephone is lit up. The president is now singing loudly and rolls off the couch with a thud. Everyone ignores him. Two and a half hours ago things looked pretty good. Now your life and your company may be coming down around your ears unless something is done soon. You realize for the first time that you are sitting in the president's chair, and all eyes are on you.

  The time has come to act.

QUESTIONS

1. In what order of priority should you act on the problems facing you? Why?

2. What should your actions be?

3. How should ethics be integrated into your decision-making process?

SOURCE: *This is a revised version of a case that appears in *Crisis Management* by Steven Fink (New York: AMACOM, a division of American Management Association, 1986). Reprinted with permission.

Towards CSR₄: Defining Economic and Moral Responsibilities

Max B. E. Clarkson, Director
Centre for Corporate Social Performance & Ethics
Faculty of Management University of Toronto

ABSTRACT

Corporate Social Responsibility should be defined in normative terms that include both the profit-making or economic imperative and the public policy or moral imperative. Corporate Social Responsibility is comprised of both economic responsibilities and moral responsibilities: CSR = ER + MR. The fundamental strategic question for the corporation is the reconciliation of these two different kinds of responsibility, and the resolution of the inherent conflict between cost/benefit analysis, or end point ethics, and the ethics of moral rules, distributive justice and social contracts.

A business organization fulfils its social responsibilities by being profitable over an extended period of time and by responding to the changing values, needs, and expectations in the society of which it is a part. There have been significant changes in the relative importance of some key values. The needs of different groups and segments of society to exert influence on corporate decision-making have resulted in significant changes in the management of corporate stakeholders, which have led to turn to changes in the role of the manager.

Our subject of inquiry is business in society, not business and society. Effective, satisfactory social performance is both ethical and profitable.

Frederick (1986) has written about three phases in the conceptualization of the relationship between business and society, CSR₁ being the initial phase of discussion and definition of Corporate Social Responsibility and CSR₂ being the phase of Corporate Social Responsiveness. He defined the third phase, CSR₃, as that of Corporate Social Rectitude. Preston (1986) also identified three phases in the development of the social issues/public policy field. Evidence indicates that we are now entering a fourth phase in this continuing search for conceptualization and definition of Corporate Social Responsibility. This fourth phase has evolved from those which have preceded.

This evidence can be found in three areas of significant changes in society's view about *Values*, about the relative importance of different classes of *Stakeholders* in the corporation, and about the *Role of the Manager*. These changes have now made it possible to define Corporate Social Responsibility in terms of its two principal components, economic responsibility and moral responsibility: CSR₄ = ER + MR.

The development of this formulation has its origins in Carroll's (1979) model of Corporate Social Performance, which, for the first time, recognized and incorporated economic performance as the first principle of social responsibility, but without excluding the other and necessary legal, ethical and discretionary responsibilities. Wartick and Cochran (1985) developed a model, based on Carroll's construct, and Clarkson (1988) tested the validity of this model and its conceptual foundations, as part of a major research project to evaluate corporate social performance. A key conclusion of this study was as follows:

> The Wartick and Cochran model, based on the Carroll construct, provides a usable and relevant framework analyzing, and evaluating CSP. As a result of this approach, economic responsibility and public policy responsibility are integrated into the definition of social responsibility. No longer is it possible to view economic responsibility as being inconsistent with, or in opposition to, social responsibility. Economic responsibility is. . . . .the first and most important social responsibility, but it is not the only one. Business does not carry on its affairs in a compartment labelled "economic", separate from the society of which it is a part. Average or above-average economic performance in an industry group over several years is related to the integration of social, ethical and discretionary responsibilities and goals with the strategic planning of the company, which is, in turn, linked with management performance and decision-making at the operating level. To be socially responsible is to be ethically responsible and profitable. (Clarkson, p. 263)

The single most important feature of the Wartick and Cochran model is that it recognizes and incorporates economic performance as the first among the principles of social responsibility without excluding other responsibilities, which are defined in the model as legal, ethical and discretionary. It is these three components which should be subsumed under the single rubric of Moral Responsibility.

Democracy has been defined as "a moral process for the resolution of conflict in a pluralistic society." (Benne, 1981) Business conducts its affairs in a democratic society and is not separate therefrom. To talk and write about "Business and Society" has led to the belief that they are in separate compartments. It is this compartmentalisation which has led in turn to the false antitheses between business and society.

—Continued

This in turn has led to the fruitless and sterile debates which have been the result of the separation of economic from social responsibilities. As soon as this distinction can be seen for what it is, theoretically convenient but realistically false, we can revise a well-known dictum by stating that the "business of business is business in society" and move on.

If a business organization cannot fulfil its economic responsibilities, clearly it cannot fulfil any social responsibilities, no matter how they are defined. "The basic proposition is that managerial organizations cannot operate successfully over the long run in conflict with their environments". (1986 Preston). A business organization fulfils its social responsibilities by being profitable over an extended period of time and by responding to changing values, needs and expectations in the society of which it is a part. Our subject of inquiry is business *in* society, not business *and* society.

The line of inquiry leads to the conclusion that Corporate Social Responsibility can be defined only in normative terms that include both the profit-making or economic imperative and the public policy or moral imperative.

These three areas or domains in society of values, needs and expectations are interrelated. There have been significant changes in the relative importance of some key values. The needs of different groups and segments of society to exert influence on the processes of corporate decision-making have resulted in significant changes in the management of corporate stakeholders. The expectations of society and of corporate stakeholders have resulted in a significant change in perceptions of the role of the manager.

VALUES

The values of technology and of profit have taken priority over human values throughout most of the 20th century. The technological imperative has had us in its grip: if it could be built, it should be built, whether it was a ten lane superhighway on land or its equivalent in space. The imperative of profit maximization has led us into environmental and social dilemmas that can be ignored no longer.

The imperatives of technology and of profit require that managers ignore any ethics but utilitarianism or end-point ethics. Utilitarianism, achieving the greatest good for the greatest number, is basically indifferent to the welfare of the individual. When the 'greatest number' is the shareholders and managers of a corporation, the harm or benefit to individual members of society is irrelevant to the corporate manager and his decision making processes. Utilitarianism has been constrained and has become the ethic of cost-benefit analysis, where the ends of greater technological efficiency or greater profits justify whatever are the necessary means. And those means, as we now know full well, can result in pol-lution, unsafe products, unhealthy working conditions, 'ends' or results which, judged by other moral standards, are unethical.

These results, or ends, are judged unethical when we weigh them using human values on our scales, values such as justice, equity, security, self-respect and respect for individual human rights. Utilitarianism does not confront these human values or try to deal with them very effectively. Thus what we are experiencing today in this context is the struggle to give human value some kind of parity with the values of technology and profit in corporate and governmental decision-making processes. And, of course, as soon as we allow the consideration of human values, of rights, justice, equity and self-respect into the calculus of decision-making we have entered the domain of ethics and of moral responsibility.

The increased level of concern with ethics in business and in government shows that we are beginning to understand that, unless we can bring human values back into our decision-making processes, we shall be condemning ourselves to a contaminated world, an environmentally wounded world, a world unfit for human life, unable to maintain the five billion who are here now or the ten billion who will be inhabiting the earth in less than fifty years. Human values, the values of survival and security, of justice, equity and self-respect, are also changing our views about stakeholders in the decision-making processes of corporations.

STAKEHOLDERS

It has become clear in recent years that the stakeholder is no longer the sole or even the primary stakeholder in a corporation. The concept of the shareholder and profit maximization is being replaced by the concept of stakeholders, of whom the shareholder or investor is only one class. This represents a profound change in the ideology of business in North America. The shareholder is no longer the preeminent stakeholder.

There still may be some unreconstructed Friedmanites, some economic isolationists, who maintain that the nature, purpose and responsibility of a corporation is solely economic; that capitalist society is constructed in such a way that everything to do with free enterprise and profit-seeking takes place in a separate compartment, insulated in some mysterious way from the rest of society and labelled 'economic', a compartment in which corporate managers can pursue their own and their shareholders' self-interest by maximizing profits, regardless of the results, as long as their actions are within the letter of the law. But they are a minority, as society, government and corporations themselves recognise the claims

—Continued

Continued

of other stakeholders for just and equitable treatment. Today the customer comes first in many corporate statements of mission or purpose. These same statements promise the shareholders a "fair return", in effect admitting that maximizing shareholder returns is incompatible with the effective management of the claims of competing stakeholders. Employees, suppliers, the communities in which corporations have their operations and even competitors are all recognised now as stakeholders. And of course environmental groups and special interest groups have a place at the corporate table, whether or not they have been invited.

The moment that we recognise the existence and legitimacy of several or multiple stakeholder groups, we have entered the domain of moral principles and ethical performance. So long as managers could maintain that shareholders and their profits were supreme, the claims of other stakeholders could be subordinated or ignored. There was no need for the manager to be concerned with fairness, with justice, or even with truth. The single minded pursuit of profit justified any necessary means, so long as they were not illegal.

We have seen the results and there is no need to dwell on them now, except to point out that the whole subject of inquiry called "Corporate Social Responsibility" is a direct outcome of what was perceived, by an increasing number of people, as Corporate Social Irresponsibility.

As soon, therefore, as we talk and act in terms of stakeholder management we have entered the territory of moral principles and ethics. We have been slow to recognise this, since we have been brought up to deny the moral responsibility of corporations and their managers for the results of their activities. We forget that Adam Smith was Professor of Moral Philosophy. In order to manage the interests of different stakeholders, ethical analysis of business decisions, a concern for the results of decisions on different stakeholders and on human beings, must become as integral a part of our decision-making processes as cost benefit analysis, risk assessment, internal rate of return, and all the other analytical tools available to the modern manager.

The time has come therefore to redefine "Corporate Social Responsibility" in terms of its two principal components: ethics and profits. Corporate Social Responsibility is both economic and moral: CSR = ER + MR. This definition leads us to confront the fundamental strategic question, which is how to reconcile these two different kinds of responsibility and how to keep them in balance. How do we resolve the inherent conflict between the cost benefit analysis or end points ethics and the ethics of moral rules, of distributive justice and of social contracts?

Just as corporations have learned to be explicit about their marketing and financial objectives and responsibilities,

so they must now learn to be explicit about their stakeholder objectives and their responsibilities towards stakeholder groups. The time has come when corporations must define their objectives, and consequently their responsibilities, towards their customers, employees, suppliers and competitors, towards government and the communities in which they operate, just as they have defined their economic objectives and responsibilities toward their shareholders.

What about our customers? Do we consider them as 'means' or as 'ends'? Do we believe in 'caveat emptor', so that customers are regarded primarily as the means by which we increase our profits, at the expense of safety, health, quality or truthfulness? Or do we value the customer as an end, to be satisfied and maintained, to be served honestly and fairly as well as profitably?

What about our employees? Do we intend to treat them as 'means' or 'ends'? Do we regard them as means, as instruments to be used in order to maximize profits, to be terminated or laid-off when no longer immediately useful? Or do we manage people as ends in themselves, individuals entitled to respect and fair treatment? Are we prepared to state what we mean by 'respect' and 'fair treatment'?

Similar questions must be asked and answered about the corporation's relationship with suppliers and competitors, with the community, the environment and government. Are these relationships governed primarily by a utilitarian, cost-benefit calculus, in which the 'other' is simply a means towards the end of greater profit? Or do we also determine and define our relationships with these other stakeholders on the basis of our moral responsibilities towards them? This then requires that we define the ground-rules of justice, equity and rights that will govern our behavior in these relationships. These are questions of fundamental strategic importance. The answers will determine our behaviour and have a profound influence on the processes of decision-making.

In many statements of corporate purpose or mission today we find such words and phrases as 'ethical, integrity, fairness, quality, respect for the individual, service to the customer'. These words and phrases of moral responsibility and ethics are common currency today even though we are still learning to speak the new language of business ethics. 'Fairness, rights, discrimination, affirmative action; duties, obligations, loyalties; environmental pollution'. We need to understand more clearly the implications and meaning of these words in terms of our behaviour and our decision-making.

For example, if Exxon and Aleyaska had been obliged to define clearly their objectives and responsibilities towards their stakeholders, including the communities of Valdez and

—Continued

Continued

Prince William Sound, the local people and their governments would have known that these two companies were prepared to spend no more than $x on standby equipment and $y on emergency crews, because additional costs could not be justified by cost/benefit and risk assessment analysis. The communities would have known that the companies' objectives were to move a maximum number of barrels of oil through the pipeline, into the tankers, and down the coast at a defined cost per barrel. Such a cost would allow for certain clearly stated precautions, which, based on risk assessment assumptions, were deemed sufficient to prevent or contain disastrous situations.

But the companies were not obliged to be explicit about anything, not even to justify how little they were doing except to have claimed, in 1981, that they were doing too much at too high a cost. From the viewpoint of human values and stakeholder management the fundamental flaws and inadequacies in the processes of cost/benefit analysis and risk assessment are revealed clearly and tragically in this disaster, as has happened so many times before: Bhopal, Challenger, the Dalkon Shield and asbestos are merely at the head of the list, for the time being.

It does not seem unreasonable, therefore, to require that corporations define not only their economic or market responsibilities to society, but also define their responsibilities to the different stakeholder groups who are actively or passively involved in the corporation's activities, those groups, in effect, without whom the corporation could not operate or make a profit, and those groups who may be affected by the corporation's actions.

THE ROLE OF THE MANAGER

What is the role of the manager? To whom is the manager responsible? Is the role of the manager solely that of the loyal and faithful agent of the corporation and its shareholders, as Milton Friedman and other conservative economists would have us believe, or does it involve responsibilities to stakeholders other than the shareholders? These are important and fundamental questions, the answers to which have profound impact on the decisions and behaviour of managers.

In a free-enterprise, private property system, a corporate executive is an employee of the owners of the business. He has direct responsibility to his employers. That responsibility is to conduct the business in accordance with their desires, which generally will be to make as much money as possible while conforming to the basic rules of the society, both those embodied on law and those embodied in ethical custom. . . . . .the key point is that in his capacity as a

corporate executive, the manager is the agent of the individuals who own the corporation. . . ., and his primary responsibility is to them. (Friedman, 1970)

The "resource converter" model presents a difficult definition of the role of the manager:

The basic function of managers in society is to convert resources. . . into outputs. The managers are the middlemen who keep the conversion process going . . . . As a resource converter the manager is cast in a role that is clearly vital to society. He is not a protagonist for any one resource group. Instead, the social values that the manager seeks to satisfy when he makes decisions for his company are the values of all the various resource contributors.

Of course, two crucial and complicating factors qualify this simplified source of values. First, all wishes of contributors cannot possibly be met . . . . Second, the desires of resource contributors changes . . . . Thus, the manager is an active participant in shifting values.

In this framework the manager is no reluctant Scrooge. Rather, his success depends to a large extent on how well he perceives value issues and how ingenious he is in meeting highest priorities. He is moral because he is responsive to human wants.

Picturing the manager as a resource converter at least emphasizes one point—future managers will be inextricably concerned with change in social values. (Newman, 1978)

In business, which comes first when the manager must resolve conflicting needs and values: the profits of the corporation, the well-being of the employees, customer satisfaction, paying suppliers on time, respecting the environment? Which has priority? What happens when it is not possible to satisfy all these different stakeholders? Which comes first?

The responsibility of the manager: is it only to the corporation and its owners or shareholders? Or is the manager responsible also to the corporation's employees, its customers and suppliers, and to society as a whole for the results or effects of his or her decisions, the implementation of policies and strategies?

There has been a significant change in the way these questions are being answered today from the answers of not so many years ago. This change was documented by Feldman, Kelsay and Brown. (1986) They analysed articles in the *Harvard Business Review* from 1940–1980 and showed that there has been a shift in the concept of managerial responsibility from a narrowly focussed 'role' to a more widely oriented 'moral' responsibility.

—Continued

Continued

Under the concept of Role Responsibility, the manager:

a) is answerable only to the claims of the owners/ stockholders for the corporation's profits, survival and growth,

b) promotes the corporation's profitability and thereby its bottom-line, using cost-benefit calculations in order to maximize the productive and efficient use of its resources,

c) is not directly answerable to the claims of society, of employees, or of consumers,

d) and can justify breaches of ordinary moral norms, such as truthfulness, with reference to the claims of other interest groups of stakeholders, such as employees, consumers, society. Thus misleading advertising, bluffing, deception and even bribery can all be justified.

e) finally the manager is answerable only to the stockholders and the corporation, and justifies all actions, regardless of their ethical significance, with reference to the claims of these overarching constituencies.

Under the concept of Moral Responsibility, however, the manager:

a) is answerable to the claims of members of society, consumers and labor

b) is obliged to answer the claims of persons affected by company policies and decisions, whether inside or outside the company,

c) and is obliged to observe ordinary moral norms, and can justify breaches of one norm only when it is overridden by another.

In the *Harvard Business Review* of the 1940s–1960s, the concept of 'role' responsibility was preeminent. This meant that the manager's responsibility was to the market system, to the system of free enterprise, and not to the people who were assumed to be the beneficiaries of the working of the invisible hand. Actions and decisions were justified primarily on the basis of their beneficial consequences for the corporation and the market system. The implicit norm was the utilitarian cost benefit calculus, whatever provided the greatest good for the shareholder and the corporation. "What's good for General Motors is good for the country" represented this viewpoint perfectly.

The manager's primary commitment was to "the rules of the game" (Carr 1968), and thus he could justify deception and other practices that are normally viewed as violations of the ordinary obligations due persons. Under 'role responsibility' the manager experiences a totally different purpose and meaning of his business life than in his personal life. The values of the free enterprise system and of the corporation justify any actions that will contribute to success and profit

(ends justify means). Consequently the principle of respect for persons, for individuals, does not apply to the manager. Any lingering sense of moral responsibility on the part of the manager must be subordinated to the responsibility of the role as an agent of the employer. Managers have been trained to hang up their personal values and ethics with their coats as they enter the office.

In recent years Feldman et al. identified that there has been a shift, as reflected in the pages of the *Harvard Business Review,* and stress is now being placed on a wider sense of responsibility, which may be called 'moral'. It is now being argued that, since corporate strategies and decisions are made by managers, who as individuals possess the capacity for moral reasoning, the corporation itself is responsible for taking 'the moral point of view'. This argument rests on the premise that managers can and do inject their own values into the culture and decision-making processes, a view strongly expressed by Andrews (1971). This view has also received significant support from "The Pursuit of Excellence" (Peters and Waterman, 1982) and the tidal wave of books which have followed. Values, culture and ground rules come from the top, and so do ethics. Role responsibility and moral responsibility cannot be compartmentalized. Both are essential for the successful management of stakeholders with conflicting or competing claims on the corporation.

THE PROBLEM OF BALANCE

Defining Corporate Social Responsibility in terms of its two principal components, economic responsibility and moral responsibility, makes it essential to confront the difficulty of reconciling these responsibilities when they are in conflict and of keeping them in balance.

When the value system of a corporation gives unquestioning priority to the values of profit and technology, then economic responsibilities will be emphasised at the expense of moral responsibilities, the purpose of the corporation will be to maximize profits for the shareholders and the role responsibility of its managers will be solely to the corporation and its shareholders. Its economic orientation, its emphasis on the bottom line, will be at the expense of its social, or moral, orientation. Profits take priority over ethics.

By contrast, when the value system of a corporation explicitly acknowledges the importance of human values by granting them parity with the values of profit and technology, then economic responsibilities will be balanced with moral responsibilities, the corporation will seek to balance the interests of the stakeholders without sacrificing its economic responsibilities, and the responsibilities of its man-

—*Continued*

Continued

agers will be not only to the corporation and its shareholders but also to other stakeholders. Its economic orientation will not be at the expense of its social, or moral orientation. Profits and ethics coexist.

A recent research study, evaluating the social performance of forty-two large corporations (Clarkson, 1988), concluded that "emphasis on the bottom-line (economic orientation) at the expense of social orientation is shown to be related to economic performance which is below average within an industry groups". Corporations, however, whose proactive economic orientation was balanced by a proactive social orientation, were profitable at average or above-average levels in their industries. In the corporations included in this research project, unbalanced concentration on the maximization of profits was counter-productive and resulted in lower ratios of profitability than their competitors during the preceding three to five years. There was, in these less-profitable companies, no evidence of a conscious attempt "to weave social concerns into their long-term, strategic planning. . . (or) to ensure that social performance is built into the whole organization, its policies and day-to-day practices. There is a lower level of awareness and analysis of social and public policy issues, and consequently of policy development and implementation."

'Balance', clearly, is not an easy concept to define in the context of social responsibility. The measurement of economic performance is governed by a multitude of generally accepted accounting principles. The balance sheet of corporation 'balances' assets and liabilities, but no mechanisms exist whereby moral responsibilities and ethical performance can be quantified or measured in such a way as to satisfy accountants or academics, let alone the general public. The imperative of quantification must be resisted. Instead of attempting to quantify the unquantifiable, the principle elements of moral responsibility and ethical performance must be defined and analysed, together with the corporate data necessary in order to evaluate levels of performance.

DEFINING ECONOMIC AND MORAL RESPONSIBILITIES

Managers enter the domain of moral principles and ethics, whether they know it or not, as soon as they recognise the existence and legitimacy of several or multiple stakeholder groups. The sophisticated cost/benefit analytical tools of end-point ethics cannot by themselves alone provide satisfactory answers to dilemmas and problems involving moral rules, distributive justice or social contracts. Corporations which are morally aware understand this difficulty. They confront it by explicit statements about their mission, about codes of ethics or conduct, and in the basic principles by which the company is managed.

For example, in 1986, a large industrial company, as an integral part of a major strategic restructuring, made explicit statements about its corporate purpose, principles and policies, and initiated an ongoing program of communication and education for all employees. The CEO stated that the purpose was

"to remind ourselves of what we, as a corporation, are trying to become, to clarify our corporate purpose and identify those basic, enduring values or principles that bind all units of the company together. These essential elements taken together form the very heart and corporate character of (the company) and are critical to our success." (Clarkson 1987)

The four "basic, enduring values or principles" of the company can be summarised as follows:

1) The company "is in business to serve the needs of its customers" by producing high quality products and services and by providing value to customers through continuing effort to increase productivity.

2) "Profit is essential and the ultimate measure of corporate performance." Shareholders are entitled to an "appropriate" return on investment, and profits are intended to contribute to the well-being of all stakeholders in the company.

3) "Employees make the crucial difference." This principle provides the basis for the company's policies covering human resources, health and safety.

4) "In all its dealings (the company) must act reasonably and with a sense of public accountability".

Thus this company defines both its economic and its moral responsibilities, and aims to achieve a balance between them: customers are mentioned first, ahead of profits and the shareholders, who are entitled to a fair but not a maximum return, so that all stakeholders can benefit from their association with the company.

From these four principles established by this company major policies were derived, covering the management of human resources, care of, and responsibility for, products, and the environment, and the safety, security and maintenance of physical assets. Finally, the Code of Business Conduct serves as a special statement of policy, which provides guidance to individuals in their business dealings and is based on the fundamental ethical principles of honesty and integrity.

This company shows how economic, moral and social issues can be integrated in the formulation and implementa-

—Continued

Continued

tion of strategic goals. The statements of principles are qualitative in nature, excluding numbers and quantification. They are not, however, motherhood statements or variations on the Golden Rule. As statements of purpose, of values and of principles they can be made operational only by means of policies and objectives derived from them, which in turn must be linked with management style and performance at the operating level.

Role responsibility and moral responsibility are both essential for the successful management of stakeholders with conflicting or competing claims on the resources and capabilities of the corporation. In order to exercise moral responsibility, managers must have, from top management, the guidance and support of clear corporate statements, which explicitly affirm the importance in policy and decision making of human values, moral rules, distributive justice and social contracts. The behaviour and performance of senior managers must demonstrate their belief in, and understanding of, these principles and values. Otherwise cynicism and corporate social irresponsibility will prevail.

The business of business is not just business. The business of business is business *in* society. Effective and satisfactory social performance is both profitable *and* ethical. Corporate social responsibility is both economic *and* moral.

REFERENCES

Andrews, K. E., *The Concepts of Corporate Strategy,* Richard Irwin, 1971.

Bennis, W., Chin, R., and Benne, K., *Moral Dilemmas* 1981.

Carroll. A. B., "A Three-Dimensional Conceptual Model of Corporate Performance," *Academy of Management Review,* 1979, Vol. 4, No. 4, 497–505.

Clarkson, M. B. E., "Corporate Social Performance in Canada 1976–1986". *Research in Corporate Social Performance and Policy,* Vol. 10, 1988, JAI Press, 241–265.

Clarkson, M. B. E., "The Strategic Management of Corporate Social Performance," Administrative Sciences Association of Canada, 1987 Conference Proceedings.

Feldmann, J. D., Kelsay, H., Brown, H. E., "Responsibility and Moral Reasoning: A Study in Business Ethics", *Journal of Business Ethics,* 1986, No. 5, 93–117.

Frederick, W. C., "Towards CSR_3: Why Ethical Analysis is Indispensable and Unavoidable in Corporate Affairs," *California Management Review,* Vol. XXVIII, No. 2, Winter 1986, 126–155.

Newman, W. H., "Managers for the Year 2000", Prentice Hall, 1978.

Peters, T. J., Waterman, R. H., *In Search of Excellence,* Harper and Row, 1982.

Preston, L. E., "Social Issues and Public in Business and Management: Retrospect and Prospect". Centre for Business and Public Policy, University of Maryland, 1986.

Wartick, S. L., Cochran, P. L., "The Evolution of the Corporate Social Performance Model", *Academy of Management Review,* 1985, Vol. 10, No. 4, 758–769.

SOURCE: Reprinted by permission of the author. This paper was subsequently published as: "The Moral Dimensions of Corporate Social Responsibility in *Morality Rationality and Efficiency: New Perspectives on Socio-Economics,* Richard M. Coughlin, ed., M. E. Sharpe, Inc. Armonte, N. Y., 1991, pp. 185–196.

Ethical Problems in Public Accounting: The View from the Top

Don W. Finn
Lawrence B. Chonko
Shelby D. Hunt

Journal of Business Ethics, July 1988

ABSTRACT. *The authors empirically examine the nature and extent of ethical problems confronting senior level AICPA members (CPAs) and examine the effectiveness of partner actions and codes of ethics in reducing ethical problems. The results indicate that the most difficult ethical problems (frequency reported) were: client requests to alter tax returns and commit tax fraud, conflict of interest and independence, client requests to alter financial statements, personal-professional problems, and fee problems. Analysis of attitudes toward ethics in the accounting profession indicated that (1) CPAs perceive that opportunities exist in the accounting profession to engage in unethical behavior, (2) CPAs, in general, do not believe that unethical behavior leads to success, and (3) when top management (partners) reprimand unethical behavior, the ethical problems perceived by CPAs seem to be reduced.*

The accounting profession recently has been under increased scrutiny by the House Subcommittee on Oversight and Investigations (Congressman John D. Dingell, Chairman) concerning activities which undermine the integrity of financial statements. These activities may include detection of overstated company earnings and financial condition, falsification of corporate records, lying, covering up practices, improperly applying accounting principles, and false disclosures.

In a report by the American Institute of Certified Public Accountants (AICPA) "Restructuring Professional Standards to Achieve Professional Excellence in a Changing Environment", the profession is looking to the future by reforming standards and requiring new compliance and education requirements. Extensive revisions by the AICPA Tax Division Executive Committee [1986] concerning "Statements on Responsibilities in Tax Practice" are being developed. Committee efforts are being focused on updating the statements, clarifying them, and increasing tax preparer awareness of penalty situations. Furthermore, the AICPA, on an Institute-wide basis, is in the process of issuing a report on overall professional standards [Anderson 1985; Anderson and Ellyson, 1986].

In addition to the efforts to update ethical standards, Davis [1984] found that CPAs were not knowledgeable about specific applications of their ethical code. He concluded that adherence to the ethics code could only result from self-regulated educational programs designed to increase code of ethics understanding. His suggestions for

improving educational requirements for the profession are well within the new guidelines recommended by the AICPA special committee on standards of professional conduct for CPAs.

Clearly, efforts by the AICPA and others are directed at reducing, if not eliminating, government and public criticism of the accounting profession and restoring the public confidence that was once more prevalent. The present study reports the results of ethical problems that accounting professionals experience in practice, which may give some insight into the problems that accountants can expect to face during a career in public accounting. Specifically, this paper empirically examines the nature and extent of ethical problems confronting senior level AICPA members (CPAs) and examines the effectiveness of partner actions and codes of ethics in reducing ethical problems. The research addresses four questions.

1. What are the most difficult ethical problems confronting senior level AICPA members?

2. How do these problems compare to the issues addressed by the AICPA code of ethics?

3. How extensive are the ethical problems of AICPA members?

4. How effective are the actions of partners in reducing the ethical problems of AICPA members?

THE NATURE OF ETHICAL PROBLEMS IN ACCOUNTING

Ethical Conflict

Ethical problems occur only when an individual interacts with other people. They are relationship kinds of problems. Bartels [1967] succinctly states the nature of ethical conflict.

In a pluralistic society not one but many expectations must be met. Therefore, resolution of what is right to do produces a balance of obligations and satisfactions. Ideally, full satisfaction of the expectations of all parties would continue the most ethical behavior. This is impossible, for expectations are often contradictory and sometimes exceed social sanction. Therefore, skill and judgment must be used to guide one in determining the point at which his own integrity can be best maintained.

—Continued

Continued

Ethical conflict occurs when people perceive that their duties toward one group are inconsistent with their duties and responsibilities toward some other group (including one's self). They then must attempt to resolve these opposing obligations. For example, suppose a subordinate in an accounting firm learned that a partner had accepted a contingent fee arrangement (a violation of the AICPA Code of Ethics). The interest of self, partner, firm, client, and society would probably conflict. Some of the actions the subordinate might take in this situation would include: (1) resigning his/her position, (2) informing the client's management, (3) informing legal authorities, (4) informing other partners of the firm, (5) directly confronting the partner, or (6) doing nothing. The subordinate choice of action determines which interests are satisfied and which are not. None of the alternatives can completely satisfy all the interests for all parties.

How well does the accounting profession govern itself? Research efforts do not agree. O'Riordan and Hirschfield [1982] point out the high level of prestige that exists for the profession as a result of self regulation. Graber [1979] and Fusco [1982] indicate the need for improvement through self regulation. However, no empirical research has documented the kinds of, and extent to which, ethical problems actually exist in the accounting profession from the CPA's perspective. In general, research has taken a situation specific approach, focusing on perceptions of ethics and concluding with philosophical exhortations cast as general guidelines for improving moral behavior. The preceding discussion suggests that two of the research questions addressed in this paper warrant investigations: "What are the major ethical problems confronting AICPA members?" and "How extensive are the ethical problems of AICPA members?" The next section examines management actions and codes of ethics for the last two research questions of the study.

Management Actions and Codes of Ethics

Previous researchers have proposed that top management actions can help reduce ethical conflicts experienced by others in their organizations through various mechanisms. They usually draw three conclusions. First, senior managers (partners) can serve as role models by not sending ambiguous or conflicting messages (i.e. verbally endorsing one set of standards while practicing another). Second, top managers (partners) can discourage unethical behavior by promptly reprimanding instances of unethical conduct. Third, corporate and industry codes of conduct can be developed, promoted, and enforced. Many writers propose that top management sets the ethical tone for an organization. This has been implicitly referred to as "the organization ethic" by Alderson [1964], Westing [1967], and Pruden [1971].

Codes of ethics have been specifically suggested as a means to encourage higher ethical standards in business [Berkman, 1977; Boling, 1978; Ferrell *et al.*, 1983; throughout Kramer, 1977; Woelfel, 1986]. CPAs have adopted Rules of Conduct of the Code of Professional Ethics. These general Rules of Conduct are designed to guide and establish high professional standards for members of the AICPA.

Many major corporations also have developed codes of ethics. Brenner and Molander [1977] reported that respondents believed that codes are "limited in their ability to "change human conduct." Nevertheless, "the mere existence of a code, specific or general, can raise the ethical level of business behavior because it clarifies what is meant by ethical conduct."

Based upon the preceding discussion of top management actions and codes of ethics, two additional research questions may be examined: "How effective are the actions of partners in reducing the ethical problems of AICPA members?" and "To what extent does the AICPA code of ethics address the major ethical problems of AICPA members?"

RESEARCH METHOD

The data used in this research was obtained from a self-administered questionnaire sent to 1250 AICPA members. Accounting practitioners were randomly selected (using a random number table) from a complete membership listing of the AICPA. Educators were excluded from the sample frame since the focus of the study was on practitioners.

The questionnaire was pretested using a convenience sample of 100 accountants, also AICPA members. The final set of mailings consisted of the questionnaire itself, a cover letter, and a stamped, pre-addressed reply envelope. An identical follow-up mailing packet was also sent to the entire sample mailing list approximately two weeks after the original questionnaire was mailed. A total of 332 usable questionnaires were returned, for a response rate of 26.6 percent. Table 1 presents the profile of the respondents for the sample.

As indicated by Table I, participants generally have accounting and business education backgrounds, and, as expected, almost all have college degrees. The respondents span a wide range of ages and income. Ninety-five percent of the respondents were either partners or sole proprietors of firms with less than 100 employees.

Trend analysis provided a basis for investigating the direction of nonresponse bias [Armstrong and Overton, 1977]. Constructs of job satisfaction, age, and income were compared to determine if responses between early and late ques-

—Continued

readings

Continued

TABLE I

CHARACTERISTICS
OF THE SAMPLE GROUP

CHARACTERISTIC	PERCENT	CHARACTERISTIC	PERCENT
Job Title		**Sex**	
Partner	77	Male	97
Sole proprietor	18	Female	3
Manager/Vice President	5	**Number of Employees in Firm**	
Years in Current Position		1	7
One or less	5	2	8
2 to 3	11	3	7
4 to 5	13	4	9
6 to 10	32	5	8
11 to 15	16	6 to 10	28
16 or more	23	11 to 15	12
Years with Current Firm		16 to 99	18
2 to 5	12	100 or more	3
6 to 10	20	**Educational Level**	
11 to 15	19	Bachelor's degree	76
16 or more	49	Master's degree	24
Total Business Experience		**Major Field of Study**	
Two years or less	1	Accounting	86
3 to 5	1	Other business	10
6 to 10	5	Non-business	4
11 to 15	17	**Income**	
16 to 20	17	Less than $10000	2
21 to 25	17	$10000 to $19999	1
26 or more	42	$20000 to $29999	6
Number of Firms Worked For		$30000 to $39999	13
1	22	$40000 to $49999	14
2	39	$50000 to $59999	12
3	24	$60000 to $69999	12
4	9	$70000 to $79999	9
5 or more	6	$80000 to $89999	5
		$90000 to $99999	7
		$100000 or more	19

CONTINUED

—Continued

Continued

TABLE I

CHARACTERISTICS
OF THE SAMPLE GROUP
—*Continued*

CHARACTERISTIC	PERCENT	CHARACTERISTIC	PERCENT
Age			
20 to 29	2	60 or more	16
30 to 39	24	*Marital Status*	
40 to 49	31	Married	91
50 to 59	27	Single	9

tionnaires differed. No significant response differences were found.

RESULTS

The first research question asks "What are the major ethical problems confronting AICPA members?" The lack of previous research on this question necessitated an exploratory research procedure. Accountants were asked to respond to the following open-ended question.

> In all professions (e.g., law, medicine, education, accounting, etc.), managers are exposed to at least some situations that pose a moral or ethical problem. Would you please briefly describe the job situation that poses the most difficult ethical or moral problem for you personally?

The question was phrased in this way because of the sensitivity of the subject of ethics. Pre-test information from a similar study by Chonko and Hunt [1985] indicated that many professionals believed that the purpose of these kinds of studies was to isolate their profession and criticize it as unethical. Indeed, this was not our purpose. The first phrase attempts to "desensitize" the issue and subjects were much more willing to respond to the ethics question.

Fifty-four percent of the subjects responding provided answers to this question. The response rate may have been lower, at least in part, to some subjects still perceiving the question as sensitive or threatening.

The ethical problems described by respondents were coded according to the issues involved. Table II presents the results concerning ethical issues. The ethical issue (i.e. problems) most often cited by AICPA members was "client proposals of tax alteration and/or tax fraud." Other issues frequently cited were those concerning conflicts of interest, alteration of financial statements, and fee problems.

The client proposals of tax alteration and/or tax fraud category accounted for 47 percent of all responses and includes client efforts to alter tax reporting or efforts to commit tax fraud. Respondents indicating this type of problem used descriptions such as "questionable deduction", "fudged amounts", "under-reporting", "requests to deduct personal expenses", "requests to cut tax liabilities", "deductions which were not 100 percent supportable", "cheat to reduce taxes", "lie", and "utilize the underground economy". The response in this category was qualified as being a request to "avoid" tax (a legal act) or to "evade" tax (an illegal act). The determination that this category included both tax "avoidance" issues and tax "evasion" issues was made on the basis that in most cases respondents did not state whether their ethical description was a legal or illegal request.

An individual practitioner described the following situation.

> Preparing income tax returns whereby the basis of taking a deduction on the tax return is not 100 percent supportable (in other words a "grey area"). In this situation, the preparer is compensated by the client yet the [Internal][1] Revenue Service can subject the preparer to penalties unless the preparer can show he relied on "SUBSTANTIAL" authority. It seems the regulations are enacted to pressure the preparer into making tax decisions which favor the IRS. This can, at times, be a moral dilemma.

The following responses indicated CPAs whose clients specifically requested some form of tax evasion. Tax evasion is not only highly unethical, but illegal as well. One partner described his most difficult ethical problem as "confronting a client that is attempting to fraudulently misstate his tax information" while another partner stated:

---

1. Respondents occasionally used slang expressions or incomplete sentences. Every effort was made to leave each response intact; however, for those cases where understanding would be enhanced a [ ] phrase was inserted.

—Continued

Continued

TABLE II

ETHICAL ISSUES IN THE ACCOUNTING PROFESSION[a]

RANK	ISSUE[b]	FREQUENCY	(%)
1	Client proposals of tax alteration and tax fraud	98	(47%)
2	Conflict of interest and independence	35	(16%)
3	Client proposals of alteration of financial statements	26	(12%)
4	Fee problems (billing, collection, contingent fee problems, or competitor bids)	22	(10%)
5	Other issues	32	(15%)
		213[c]	(100%)

[a]Response to open-ended question: "In all professions (e.g., law, medicine, education, accounting, etc.), managers are exposed to at least some situations that pose a moral or ethical problem. Would you please briefly describe the job situation that poses the most difficult ethical or moral problem for you personally?"

[b]Note that all of the issues listed (except for 5 "Other Issues") are distinctly accounting related.

[c]Although respondents were asked to describe only one ethical problem, 51 respondents described two coequal problems. Therefore, *n* is the number of problems described by all valid responses, i.e., 178 (54%) respondents described 228 situations. Of the 178 responses fifteen respondents reported that they did not have any ethical problems in their job situation, therefore *n* = 213. Of the total of 332 AICPA members who responded to the questionnaire, 154 (46%) chose not to respond to the question identified in footnote a.

The most difficult ethical or moral problem I personally face is unreported income or unallowable deductions. In the tax environment clients may inadvertently pass information which may disclose unreported income or unallowable deductions. I invariably say: (1) it is your return, (2) you are responsible, and (3) give me the figures you want to report and I will report them if you are not in a fraud situation or if your deductions are in the grey area. I will not be a party to fraud nor will I be a party to gross over deduction.

The second ethical issue labeled "conflict of interest and independence" comprised 16 percent of the responses. This category includes activities such as conflict of interest for "not for profit" boards, client-accountant privilege when testifying, audit of close friends and associates' businesses and solicitation issues. One managing partner stated:

Being in a small town, there are often conflicts of interest. One client may be interested in purchasing another client and you as the CPA may have additional information, for either party, that is really confidential [and might have a significant impact on the potential purchase].

Another partner was concerned about firms "wining and dining" to obtain and maintain client relationships. A senior was concerned about independence and solicitation and stated:

A situation that creates an ethical problem is that of independence and solicitation. A situation where you really get involved with a client and independence is questionable. Same situation where you really get involved with client (independence is already questionable) and you seek other clients through existing clients. I believe independence and solicitation [are interrelated].

The client proposals of financial statement alteration category accounted for 12 percent of all responses and includes client efforts to alter financial statement presentation. This category included client proposals to alter outcomes from CPA prepared financial statements. These requests ranged from disagreements about line items to requests to "modify" the financial statements for creditor or investor purposes.

One respondent was concerned about clients using "proper accounting practices such as the proper valuation of

—Continued

Continued

inventory, etc." and "hidden income (for) businesses dealing with cash". A second CPA stated that he had an occasional problem of "having to refuse client requests to ignore rules and regulations in the preparation of income". Another CPA stated that his problem was:

> Ethical—Occasionally new clients want you to classify certain accounts to make it look better for financing. [I] have to explain why I can't do that even though I would like to have them as clients. Ninety percent understand and go along. Ten percent understand but won't agree.

A sole practitioner had difficulty "convincing clients (management) to use proper accounting practices" in determining the company's gain. Another sole practitioner was concerned about the proper use of GAAP and stated:

> The situation where a company wants to handle a situation contrary to GAAP and the item is not a substantially material, significant item. However, treatment pursuant to GAAP could affect the client's ability to obtain credit or the amount of taxes he will have to pay.

Fee problems were the fourth most frequently mentioned ethical problem (10 percent). This category included CPA concerns about accepting finder's fees and collecting unpaid fees from clients whose businesses are in jeopardy. One partner expressed concern over contingency fees and stated that he had difficulty in

> . . . promoting a certain product or service to a client because you are offered a fee or commission by the sales representative. We are not allowed to receive contingent fees of any kind; however, the number of offers of this type increases each year.

A partner expressed concern over retaining or releasing clients who cannot afford CPA services. Conversely, another CPA reported a reverse fee problem:

> When I have done work for a client that is of much greater value than the normal hourly billing rate, occasionally I have billed it based on "(fair) value". However, I tend to feel guilty when doing so.

The final set of issues comprising nine percent of the responses included, in order: concerns over technical competence, integrity in admitting mistakes made by the firm, unethical practices of other CPAs, employee problems within the firm that do not come under the direct authority of a code of ethics, difficulty in reporting unethical activities of other CPAs (without becoming involved in a lawsuit), and questions concerning the ethical considerations of advertising for clients even though it is no longer a professional taboo.

A major problem reported by some CPAs was a concern that they could not "keep up" with the technical changes that were taking place in the accounting profession and the temptation they had to "cover up" mistakes by their firm.

One fifty-seven year old CPA expressed a personal dilemma concerning professional integrity.

> On occasion, because of time pressures and/or changes in tax laws, we fail to file a return by the required date. The moral problem then arises whether to admit the mistake or shift the blame to someone else (associates and/or clients). Over the years, honesty has proven the best policy. By admitting the mistake and reimbursing the client for any interest or penalty incurred, you keep your personal honor and retain the client. Any cover up attempt leads to worse problems. We're all human and make mistakes (as little as possible); but; lying about [a mistake] just compounds the problem.

Another problem that was noted was how to report unethical activities of other CPAs without becoming involved in a lawsuit. Some CPAs questioned the ethical standing of CPAs who would advertise for clients. Finally, one CPA expressed overall frustration with the entire accounting profession thus:

> Attempting to keep up with rapid changes in professional ethics, income taxation, auditing, accounting matters, payroll taxation, etc., so that I am not inadvertently compromised by not knowing some development through not being able to sift through the mountains of mail and information coming to my sole practitioner firm (including your questionnaire).

The AICPA Code of Ethics

Our second research question asks, "To what extent does the AICPA code of ethics address the major ethical problems of AICPA members?"

The AICPA code has fourteen rules which are to be followed. Comparing the results in Table II with the code reveals that seventy-four percent of the ethical problems (issues 1 through 3) reported by the CPAs relate to Rule 101 (Independence) or Rule 102 (Integrity and Objectivity). Additional issues noted in previous sections are also addressed in the ethics document. However, while the code addresses contingent fee and commission problems (issue 4), it does not address the issue of collection of fee problems which is essentially a management credit policy question. Issues reported by our respondents and not specified in the AICPA code are personal-professional decisions (issue 5)

—Continued

Continued

which are again management policy questions. Personal-professional issues mentioned in this study (issues of confidentiality) are mentioned in other studies [Chonko and Hunt, 1985], Overall, our finding suggest that the AICPA code is sufficiently inclusive to provide a working guideline for practicing CPAs for those activities which are accounting related. The AICPA Code of Ethics, in substance, addresses the ethical issues about which CPAs are most concerned.

Extent of Ethical Problems

In the preceding discussion, the most difficult ethical problems faced by the CPAs were reported and compared with the existing AICPA Code of Ethics. The third research question asks "How extensive are the ethical problems of AICPA members?" Table III summarizes responses to items specifically directed at assessing the extent of ethical problems in accounting environments. The items are grouped according to the following categories:

1. Opportunities for unethical behavior (items A1 and A2);

2. Frequency of unethical behavior (items B1 and B2); and

3. The relationship between success and generally unethical behavior (items C1 and C2).

Table III also reports three items on top management actions and unethical behavior (D1, D2, and D3).

The results in Table III indicate that a substantial number of AICPA members (35 percent) perceive opportunities for CPAs employed in their firm to engage in unethical activities. However, very few AICPA members (3 percent) agreed that "CPAs in their firms often engage" in unethical behaviors. Similarly, although many AICPA members (76 percent) agree that there are numerous opportunities for them to engage in unethical activities outside of their firm, a much smaller percentage (42 percent) considered other CPAs to "often engage" in unethical activities. These finding are consistent with those of Chonko and Hunt [1985] and Ferrell and Weaver [1978] who reported that managers seem to believe that their firms have higher ethical standards than other organizations.

Trade publications report that managers feel pressured to engage in unethical behaviors to achieve corporate goals [Business Week, Jan. 31, 1977]. If managers agree that there is relationship between unethical behavior and success, these perceptions would serve as a strong motivator for unethical behavior. However, only nine percent of the AICPA members who participated in this study believe that generally unethical behaviors lead to success in CPA practice (item C1). Similarly, few AICPA members (10 percent) agree that it is necessary to compromise one's ethics in order to be successful.

Actions of Partners

Our fourth research question asks "How effective are the actions of partners in reducing the ethical problems of AICPA members?" Two measures were used to address this question: (1) the extent of ethical problems perceived by CPAs and (2) the extent of partner actions. Since no previous scale for measuring the extent of partner actions (top management) existed, a scale was developed. Items D1, D2, and D3 in Table III describe top management behaviors that other writers have suggested should be undertaken to deter unethical behavior. A factor analysis of these items (shown in Table IV) yielded a one factor solution (alpha coefficient—0.76) suggesting that the three items may be treated as a single scale measuring the latent construct "partner actions". The factor analysis procedure was used to reduce the number of variables in the analysis and thus simplify the results (in Table V) and conclusions [Kim and Mueller, 1978].

A similar approach was attempted for the development of a scale to measure the extent of ethical problems in the accounting profession. Four items (A1, B1, C1, and C2) in Table III relate to ethical problems in the respondents' firms. However, a factor analysis of these items yielded an alpha coefficient of only 0.41 and an explained variance of 0.35 for these four items suggesting that the four items cannot be treated as a single latent construct "ethical problems of CPAs". Therefore, recursive regressions for each variable were used to test for significance with respect to partner actions. The use of recursive regressions was used in order to test for significance of each variable and variable combination.

Exploratory analysis was used to examine a number of demographic variables to determine if they were correlated with ethical problems. Several of the demographic variables were correlated with ethical problems (see Table V); however, only income was significantly correlated with more than two of the ethical questions. In general, respondents with higher incomes perceived fewer ethical problems within their firms which was consistent with results found in a study by Hunt and Chonko [1985].

On the basis of other researchers' findings, it was expected that specific actions by top management to encourage ethical behavior and discourage unethical behavior would decrease the extent of ethical problems perceived by CPAs. The results indicated in Table V show that, of the two variables included in the regressions, the actions of partners are the best predictor of perceived ethical problems of CPAs explaining 7 percent to 11 percent of the variance in each dependent variable. Although income, as a control variable, was significant in all but one of the regressions, it explains very little of the variance.

—Continued

Continued

TABLE III

QUESTIONNAIRE ITEMS FOR
ETHICS[a]

QUESTIONNAIRE ITEMS	AVERAGE RESPONSE[b]	STANDARD DEVIATION	PERCENT AGREE[c]
A. Opportunities for unethical behavior			
1. There are many opportunities for CPAs in my firm to engage in unethical activities	4.6	2.1	35
2. There are many opportunities for CPAs outside my firm to engage in unethical activities	2.7	1.6	76
B. Frequency of unethical behavior			
1. CPAs in my firm often engage in behaviors that I consider to be unethical	6.2	1.2	3
2. CPAs outside my firm often engage in behaviors that I consider to be unethical	3.9	1.7	42
C. Success and unethical behavior			
1. Successful CPAs in my firm are generally more ethical than the unsuccessful	5.5	1.6	9
2. In order to succeed in my firm it is often necessary to compromise one's ethics	6.2	1.4	10

CONTINUED

CONCLUSIONS

The findings indicate that CPAs are confronted with a wide variety of ethical problems. The problems concerning tax alteration and tax fraud were most frequently cited. However, conflicts of interest and independence, alteration of financial statements, and fee problems also were frequently cited. Together, these issues account for 84 percent of the ethical problems identified by CPAs. Because of the relatively equal number of responses to issues 2 through 5 represented in Table II, care should be taken in not over-interpreting the rank ordering of these items. Readers are reminded that CPAs were asked to describe the job situation that poses the most "difficult" ethical or moral problem for them. Therefore, these results should not be interpreted as the issues that occur most "frequently". However the nature of the respondents' comments suggest that CPAs perceive significant ethical problems in the areas identified.

Findings in Table III suggest that CPAs perceive both fewer opportunities for, and less frequent participation in, unethical behavior for their own firms than for their competitors. This finding is consistent with those of Ferrell and Weaver [1978] who reported that "respondents believe they made decisions in an organizational environment where peers and top management have lower ethical standards than in their own." In both studies, respondents consider themselves as more ethical than others.

The findings suggest that the individual respondent's income was significant in explaining perceptions of ethical problems. CPAs with high income levels reported fewer ethical problems that did their colleagues at lower levels. No theoretical rationale for this finding is known. However, it is consistent with other empirical research [Chonko and Hunt, 1985].

—Continued

Continued

TABLE III

QUESTIONNAIRE ITEMS FOR
ETHICS[a]—*Continued*

QUESTIONNAIRE ITEMS	AVERAGE RESPONSE[b]	STANDARD DEVIATION	PERCENT AGREE[c]
D. Top management actions and unethical behavior			
1. Partners in my firm have let it be known in no uncertain terms that unethical behaviors will not be tolerated	2.0	1.4	87
2. If a CPA in my firm is discovered to have engaged in unethical behavior that results primarily in personal gain (rather than the firm's gain) he/she will be promptly reprimanded	1.9	1.5	84
3. If a CPA in my firm is discovered to have engaged in unethical behavior that results primarily in the firm's gain (rather than personal gain) he/she will be promptly reprimanded	2.0	1.2	84

[a]$n = 301$.
[b]Each respondent was asked to indicate a response on a seven point Likert scale from strongly agree (1) to strongly disagree (7).
[c]Percent responding "slightly agree", "agree", or "strongly agree".

The results in Table V indicate that partners believe that unethical behavior is inversely related to top management actions (e.g. the standardized beta coefficient for each variable is negative). Partners who let it be known that unethical behavior will not be tolerated believe that the incidence of unethical behavior will decline as indicated by over 80 percent of respondents.

SUMMARY

Five conclusions are suggested by the findings in this research.

1. The most often mentioned ethical problem faced by participating senior level AICPA members is client pressure to alter tax reporting. Four other issues (financial statement alteration, conflict of interest and independence, fee problems, and personal and professional problems) were also frequently cited as difficult ethical issues.

2. Respondents perceive opportunities in their firms and industries to engage in unethical behaviors. However, they report that few CPAs frequently engage in such behaviors.

3. Respondents do not believe that unethical behaviors in general lead to success. And, most believe that successful CPAs do not engage in certain specific unethical behaviors investigated here.

4. When top management discourages unethical behavior, the ethical problems perceived by participating CPAs seem to be reduced.

5. The AICPA Code of Ethics, in substance, addresses the ethical issues about which participating CPAs are most concerned.

—Continued

Continued

TABLE IV

FACTOR ANALYSIS OF
PARTNER ACTIONS SCALE

QUESTIONS	FACTOR[a]
D1	0.39
D2	0.88
D3	0.99
Eigen value	1.93
Variance Explained	64%
Coefficient Alpha	0.76

[a]Orthogonal solution, minimum eigen value -1.

TABLE V

REGRESSION:
PARTNER ACTIONS RELATED
TO ETHICAL PROBLEMS

DEPENDENT VARIABLE—ETHICAL PROBLEMS		STANDARDIZED BETA COEFFICIENTS FOR INDEPENDENT VARIABLES		ADJUSTED R^2	*"F"*
Dependent variable		*Income[1]*	*Partner actions*		
A1[d]	I	0.01	—	0.00	0.03
	II	—	-0.21[a]	0.05	12.87[a]
	III	-0.04	-0.22[a]	0.05	6.62[a]
B1[d]	I	0.07[c]	—	0.00	1.25[c]
	II	—	-0.29[a]	0.08	24.52[a]
	III	0.00	-0.29[a]	0.08	12.22[a]
C1[d]	I	0.18[a]	—	0.03	9.16[a]
	II	—	-0.32[a]	0.10	31.07[a]
	III	0.12[a]	-0.29[a]	0.11	17.62[a]
C2[d]	I	0.11[b]	—	0.07	3.13[b]
	II	—	-0.27[a]	0.07	21.93[a]
	III	0.05	-0.26[a]	0.07	11.28[a]

[1]Regressions were calculated as follows:
   I: Independent Variable—Income.
   II: Independent Variable—Partner Actions.
   III: Independent Variable—Income and Partner Actions.
[a]Significant at 0.01 level.
[b]Significant at 0.05 level.
[c]Significant at 0.10 level.
[d]See Table III for questions.

—*Continued*

Continued

Finally, our findings indicate several fertile areas for additional research on ethical problems for CPAs. How do CPAs "solve" ethical problems? What ethical trade-offs do CPAs make between behaviors and outcomes? How do CPAs adjust these trade-offs as relevant role partners change? Are the actions of top managers effective in reducing all types of unethical behavior, or are they only useful in deterring selected unethical behaviors? All these issues warrant further research.

The finding in this study were concerned with ethical problems of upper echelon CPAs. Additional research to explore the perceptions of lower level CPAs may provide supportive evidence toward the notion that top management (partners) determine and provide guidance for ethical behavior of lower level CPAs.

In conclusion, it was encouraging to find that so many of our respondents were concerned about ethical issues in accounting. The future challenge lies in improving our knowledge with respect to accounting ethics and behaviors. Both academics and practitioners have roles to play. Academicians can help improve knowledge through research aimed at understanding the ethical decision-making process. Practitioners can help to improve behavior by establishing organizational climates that deter unethical behavior and reward ethical behavior.

Don W. Finn is Associate Professor of Accounting at Texas Tech University in Lubbock, Texas. Professor Finn has published over twenty articles on business, accounting, and budgeting topics which have appeared in professional publications such as The Accounting Review, Omega, Oil & Gas Tax Quarterly, Cost and Management, *and* Managerial Planning. *Dr. Finn also has co-authored two monographs on accounting topics. He is also active in the American Accounting Association and the National Association of Accountants.*

Professor Shelby Hunt is currently Distinguished Professor and Horn Professor of Research in the Marketing Department at Texas Tech University. He has published extensively in Journal of Marketing Research, Journal of Marketing, *and many other prestigious journals. Recently, he was editor-in-chief for the* Journal of Marketing.

Professor Lawrence B. Chonko has published in Journal of Marketing Research *and other prestigious marketing journals. He is currently director of consumer research at Baylor University.*

SOURCE: Reprinted by permission of *Kluwer Academic Publishers.* © 1988 *Journal of Business Ethics* 7 (1988) 605–615.

REFERENCES

Alderson, Wroe: 1964, 'Ethics, Ideologies, and Sanctions', in *Report of the Committee on Ethical Standards and Professional Practices*, Chicago, Il.: American Marketing Association.

Anderson, George D.: 1985, 'A Fresh Look at Standards of Professional Conduct', *Journal of Accountancy* (September 1985), pp. 91–106.

Anderson, George D. and Robert C. Ellyson: 1986, 'Restructuring Professional Standards: The Anderson Report', *Journal of Accountancy* (September 1986), pp. 92–104.

American Institute of Certified Public Accountants: 1986, *Restructuring Professional Standards to Achieve Professional Excellence in a Changing Environment*, New York.

American Institute of Certified Public Accountants: 1973, *Rules of Professional Conduct*, New York (1976), pp. 1481–1482.

American Institute of Certified Public Accountants: 1975, *Statements on Responsibilities in Tax Practice*, New York, pp. 1–30.

Armstrong, Scott J. and Kenneth L. Bernhardt: 1977, 'Estimating Non-Response Bias in Mail Surveys', *Journal of Marketing Research* (August 1977), pp. 396–402.

Bartels, Robert: 1967, 'A Model for Ethics in Marketing', *Journal of Marketing* 31, pp. 20–26.

Baumhart, Raymond C.: 1961, 'How Ethical Are Businessmen?', *Harvard Business Review* 39, pp. 6–19 and 156–167.

Berkman, H. W.: 1977, 'Corporate Ethics: Who Cares?', *Journal of the Academy of Marketing Science* 5, pp. 154–167.

Boling, T. Edwin: 1977, 'The Managerial Ethics "Crisis": An Organizational Perspective', *Academy of Management Review* 2, pp. 360–365.

Brenner, Steven N. and Molander, Earl A.: 1977, 'Is the Ethics of Business Changing?' *Harvard Business Review* 55, pp. 57–71.

Chonko, Lawrence B. and Hunt, Shelby D.: 1985, 'Ethics and Marketing Management: An Empirical Examination', *Journal of Business Research* 13, pp. 339–359.

Davis, Robert R.: 1984, 'Ethical Behavior Reexamined', *The CPA Journal* (December 1984), pp. 32–36.

Ferrell, O. C. and Weaver, Mark K.: 1978, 'Ethical Beliefs of Marketing Managers', *Journal of Marketing* 42 (July 1978), pp. 69–73.

Fusco, C. R.: 1982, 'Ethics and Public Accounting', *Review of Business* 3(4), pp. 12–15.

Graber, Dean E.: 1979, 'Ethics and Public Accounting', *Review of Business* 3(4), pp. 12–15.

Kim, Jae-On and Charles W. Mueller: 1978, *Factor Analysis: Statistical Methods and Practical Issues*, Sage Publication.

—*Continued*

Continued

Kramer, Otto P.: 1977, 'Ethics Programs Can Help Companies Set Standards of Control', *Administrative Manager* 38, pp. 46–49.

O'Riordan, Maureen and Hirschfield, Arthur S.: 1982, 'Aspects of the Profession's Code of Ethics', *The CPA Journal* (August 1982), pp. 30–33.

Pruden, Henry O.: 1971, 'Which Ethics for Marketers?', in *Marketing and Social Issues,* John R. Wish and Stephen H. Gamble (eds.), New York: John Wiley and Sons, Inc., pp. 98–104.

Tax Division of the AICPA: 1986, 'Executive Committee Minutes', New York (September 29, 30, 1986), pp. 1–13.

U.S. Congress, House: 1986, *Financial Fraud Detection and Disclosure Act of 1986* (H. R. 5439), 99th Cong., 2nd Sess. (August 15, 1986).

U.S. Congress, Senate: 1977, *Subcommittee on Reports, Accounting and Management of the Committee on Governmental Affairs.*

Westing, J. Howard: 1967, 'Some Thoughts on the Nature of Ethics in Marketing', in *Changing Marketing Systems,* Reed Moyer (ed.), Chicago, Il: American Marketing Association, pp. 161–163.

Woelfel, Charles J.: 1986, "Standards of Ethical Conduct for Management Accountants', *Journal of Business Ethics* 5(5), pp. 365–372.

Some Unresolved Ethical Issues in Auditing

Sally Gunz
John McCutcheon
Journal of Business Ethics, 1991

ABSTRACT. *Independence is a fundamental concept to the audit. There is a clear relationship between independence and conflict of interest in all professions. This paper examines this relationship in the auditing profession and in the context of three specific practices. The paper analyses these practices by using the Davis model of conflict of interest. The results of this analysis give rise to some interesting questions for the ethical practices of the auditing profession.*

INTRODUCTION

This paper looks at the auditing profession and its understanding of the relationship between independence and conflict of interest. Independence has been called the unique quality of the audit that distinguishes it from other professions and professional activities.[1] While other professions might query this distinction—independence, after all, is said to be intrinsic to all professions and a quality that distinguishes them from other forms of endeavor[2]—there can be no dispute that independence is a fundamental requirement of the audit. It is essential that the auditor maintain a state of mind independent of biasing influences.

When we talk of conflict of interest we mean, very generally, that situation where an auditor "has a private or personal interest sufficient to influence or to appear to influence the objective exercise of his or her duties.[3] We include within this definition both conflicts of obligations and conflicts of interest.[4] That is, we include conflicts which arise because of obligations assumed by the auditor to different interests and conflicts between obligations and self-interest. Our curiosity about the conflict of interest/independence relationship in auditing comes from our observation of certain practices

within the profession which look strange to us as outsiders, particularly when measured by the ethics of other professions such as the law.

This is no trivial issue. The auditing profession is under considerable pressure today because of its failure to deliver what the public expects of it. In its defense the profession says that the public does not understand the nature of the audit. We will make the case that it is the "strangeness" of some of the profession's current practices which feeds public dissatisfaction.

In this paper we first unravel the meaning of independence and conflict of interest to the auditor. We then consider three specific practices which could be said to place the auditor in a conflict of interest. We use a formal model of conflict of interest by which to analyze the practices. We then consider the implications of our analysis for the relationship between conflict of interest and auditor independence. Finally, we return to the question posed above and discuss what this means for the present practice of auditing.

AUDITOR INDEPENDENCE AND CONFLICT OF INTEREST: THE PROBLEM

It would be misleading for us to imply that auditors see no relation between independence and conflict of interest. Their codes of professional practice state that auditors should not perform an audit, say, where the subject corporation is one in which they or a family member have some pecuniary interest.[5] This prohibition is justified in terms of the need for the auditor to have and to be seen to have an objective mind untainted by self interest. At the same time, however, certain practices are allowed to persist that might appear to contradict these prescripts.

To understand how this might be the case it is necessary to understand the concept of independence in auditing. An audit is "the process by which a competent independent person accumulates and evaluates evidence about quantifiable information related to a specific economic entity for the purpose of determining and reporting on the degree of correspondence between the quantifiable information and estab-

1. See, for example the statement by Pearson, M. A.: 1987, 'Auditor Independence Deficiencies & Alleged Audit Failures', *Journal of Business Ethics* 6, p. 285.
2. Larson, M. S.: 1977, *The Rise of Professionalism; A Sociological Analysis* (University of California Press, Berkeley, California); Saks, M.: 1988, "Removing the Blinkers? A Critique of Recent Contributions to the Sociology of the Professions', *Sociological Review* 31(1), pp. 1–21.
3. Kernagham, K. and Langford, W.: 1990, *The Responsible Public Servant* (The Institute for Research on Public Policy and the Institute of Public Administration of Canada), p. 134.
4. Kipnis, K.: 1986, *Legal Ethics* (Prentice-Hall Series in Occupational Ethics, United States), pp. 40–62.

5. See rule 101 and interpretations 101–1 of the American Institute of Certified Public Accountants Code of Professional Conduct or Rule 204 and its interpretations of the Rules of Professional Conduct of the Institute of Chartered Accountants of Ontario.

—Continued

Continued

lished criteria.[6] For present purposes we restrict the discussion to the audit or attest of corporate financial statements. Independence means "taking an unbiased viewpoint in the performance of audit tests, the evaluation of the results, and the issuance of the audit report."[7] Auditors have an ethical obligation to the clients on behalf on whom they are employed. Legally the client is defined as variously the shareholder[8] or as the Board of Directors.[9] It is for these classes of persons that the audit is primarily performed. The auditor also has a wider duty of care to the public in general which might rely upon the audit report. The auditor has an ethical duty to ensure the publication of a fair and appropriate set of financial statements and in doing so becomes the servant not only to the client but the economics and financial structure of the licensing jurisdiction.[10] The duty of the client and to the public at large might conflict. Further, there will be circumstances in which the duty to either the client or the public or both might conflict with the perceived self-interest of the auditor.

In a specified sense, that of the audit not accounting in general, we are describing that "deepseated and unavoidable source of conflict and paradox" that Westra identified.[11] The auditor is a servant to different user groups with distinct and sometimes competing interests. We, however, argue that the paradox is not necessarily unresolvable. It is here that we would distinguish our analysis from that of Beach.[12] In his analysis Beach addresses the dilemma of the Code of Ethics that prescribes forms of behavior which are inherently contradictory in certain circumstances. The circumstances we discuss allow for a resolution.

In order to set the stage for our analysis we describe three ethical problems which are of concern to auditors. They are:

1. An audit firm is hired by two separate corporations to conduct two different audits. There is a pre-existing relationship between the two audit clients. In the course of one audit, information relevant to the other arises.

The ethics of the profession require the auditor to maintain confidentiality. Information obtained in one audit is not to be released to another client. In practice an exception is, however, often made where the information obtained might reflect upon the financial statements of the second client. For example, the confidential information might lead the auditor to restate the accounts receivable of the second audit client. The rationale is first, that the information is not being given to the client but rather to the auditor of the client. More generally, it is said that in providing the information the auditor is fulfilling its service to society through ensuring audit accuracy.[13] In this way it might even be said that large audit firms are better than small because the potential for information sharing increases.[14]

2. The second example concerns the relationship between the audit and other services offered by the firm. The question of how independence can be maintained in such circumstances has been the topic of a great amount of research and government attention. For example, it could be argued that there is an inherent conflict in allowing the same firm to provide management consulting or tax advice to the client it also audits.

The audit firms are satisfied that the various tentacles of the firm are not threats to independence. Indeed, when new clients are solicited, selling features that are emphasized are the amount, quality, and variety of the additional services offered by the firm. This has to be the case because, at least between comparable size audit firms, the audit is a comparable commodity. We posed the question to an auditor of what would happen if there was

6. Lemon, W. M., Arens, A. A., and Loebbecke, J. K.: 1987, *Auditing: An Integrated Approach* (Canadian Fourth Edition, Prentice-Hall Canada Inc.), p. 2.
7. Lemon *et al., op. cit.,* p. 81.
8. The Canadian position.
9. The U.S. position.
10. This role is a consequence of the audit most often being a statutory mandated function. If the audit was not a mandatory act it would be difficult to argue that the auditor's obligations extended beyond the interest of the particular client.
11. Westra, L. S.: 1986, 'Whose "Loyal Agent"? Towards an Ethic of Accounting', *Journal of Business Ethics* 5, pp. 127–128.
12. Breach, J. E.: 1984, 'Code of Ethics: The Professional Catch 22', *Journal of Accounting and Public Policy* 3, pp. 311–323.

13. Some of the literature describes the concept of a Chinese Wall constructed between audits. This will be breached by a neutral partner if and when it becomes apparent that relevant information will not be discovered unaided by the other audit team. (Rowan, H.: 1987, 'Chinese Walls Prove Paper Thin', *CA Magazine* (October), pp. 50–51. Other auditors that we discussed this way say that information is passed freely between audit teams and they had no difficulty with this practice. We note that our "puzzlement" about these practices is not unique. For example, Gunning S.: 1989, 'Completely at Sea', *CA Magazine,* (April), p. 24, at p. 32, had similar concerns.
14. For a more detailed discussion of the conflict between the confidentiality rule and the rule of disclosure in the code of professional ethics, see the Beach, *op. cit.* This is not a trivial issue and has led, at least in the United State, to conflicting jurisprudential interpretations which are discussed in the Beach article.

—Continued

Continued

a falling out between a client and, say, a tax partner such that the client threatens to switch all services to another firm. We were told that there would be a meeting of all those concerned at the firm and the client and that a change of tax partner would likely result. Similarly, a dispute between the client and the audit partner over non-audit matters would result in a change of that partner. This is undoubtedly a reflection of the negative consequences to the individual partner of being seen to be responsible for losing a client.[15] No one suggested that it would be proper for this to occur in the case of a auditor/client dispute over audit issues.

3. Assume that Company *P* purchases 70 percent of the voting shares of Company *S*. The auditors of *P* are engaged to audit *S* in lieu of *S*'s former auditors. This is a relatively common situation and one that makes sense given the potential for lower audit fees.

What if Company *P* charges a management fee to *S* and also buys or sells goods or services to or from *S*? Accounting standards require the disclosure of the magnitude of such transactions. If the transactions with related parties are made on the same terms as with unrelated parties, the fact that they are is considered proper disclosure.[16] What if the transfer prices and management fees are inequitable to Company *S*? Ignoring the problem of how you determine whether these fees or pricing system are unfair, it is evident that the interests of the minority and majority stakeholders are in conflict. The auditors are engaged by those responsible to the shareholders, but to which set? The majority interest or the minority interest? While this is not a reporting problem it certainly concerns public expectations from an audit. The auditors' response to such situations is, in essence, "trust our professionalism."

Each example appears to place the auditor in a conflict of interest. In its defense, the profession would argue first, there is not necessarily a conflict of interest and second, if there is, that conflict does not impact upon independence. It has studied the second example extensively and is comfortable with its retention while examples of one and three have not often been studied. This implies that research has been focused from the point of view of professional codes of conduct which deal in depth with the problem of non-audit services but do not focus on the other two examples. We find

this intriguing, particularly as the audit profession includes in its code of ethics the requirement that independence must exist in perception as in fact. Clearly the examples warrant further examinations.

In our analysis we use the useful and thorough model of conflict of interest proposed by Davis in 1982.[17] We select this model because it helps us to structure our examination rigorously. Our analysis has two stages: first we see whether there is a conflict of interest; second we consider the impact of any conflict, if it exists, upon independence.

Finally, in the examples some conflicts or potential conflicts relate to the individual auditor while others relate to different auditors within the same firm. It is apparent from the practitioner literature that auditors can live with some conflicts because they occur within very large accounting firms. We have no doubt that, in the normal course of events, different branches of the firm maintain independence or quasi-independence from each other. Ethical dilemmas, however, almost by definition, arise not in the normal course of events. We see no reason why a distinction should be made between the conflict concerning the activities of an individual auditor and that of an audit firm.

ANALYSIS OF EXAMPLES

Davis proposed the following model or statement of conflict of interest:[18]

A person AUD has a conflict of interest in role *R* if, and only if:

a. AUD occupies *R*;

b. *R* requires exercise of (component) judgment with regard to certain questions *Q*;

c. A person's occupying *R* justifies another person relying on the occupant's judgment being exercised in the other's service with regard to *Q*;

d. Person U_1 is justified in relying on AUD's judgment in *R* with regard to Q (in part at least) because AUD occupies *R*; and

e. AUD is (actually, latently, or potentially) subject to influences, loyalties, temptations, or other interests to make AUD's (competent) judgment in *R* with regard to *Q* less

---

15. Kaplan, R. L.: 1983, 'Accountants' Liability and Audit Failures: When the Umpire Strikes Out', *Journal of Accountancy and Public Policy*, p. 5.

16. Skinner, R. M.: 1987, *Accounting Standards in Evolution* (Toronto: Holt, Rinehart and Winston of Canada, Limited), p. 72.

17. Davis, M.: 1982, 'Conflict of Interest', *Business and Professional Ethics Journal* 1, No. 4, pp. 17–27.

18. The structure of Davis' model will be retained. For ease of reading, some of the term descriptions will be adjusted for the present model.

—Continued

Continued

likely to benefit U_1 than AUD's occupying R justifies U_1 in expecting.[19]

This model was developed from the legal profession's handling of conflicts of interest. It is particularly apt for the audit profession because of the emphasis on influence or impact on judgment. Further, it is clear that the determination of whether or not a conflict exists is a function of what U_1 is justified in expecting (not what is actually expected) and that this is a function of R and something over which AUD has no control. Once the auditor assumes R there can be no variation of the objective standards of Q.

In this paper AUD is the auditor. R is the role as auditor of a particular corporation. Q is the information the auditor must attest to in order to fulfill the audit. U_1 is the client and any legitimate user of the audited statements. Because this is an audit, the model should be adjusted to allow for more than one user; so there would be potentially $U_2, U_3, \ldots U_n$. These respective users might be justified in relying on AUD's judgment for differing reasons. A conflict of interest exists whenever AUD's (component) judgment in R with regard to Q is less likely to benefit any of the given or identified users than the users are justified in expecting from AUD.

This model is now applied to the three ethical problems identified earlier in the paper. We shall retain the same ordering of these problems.

Example 1: The Two Audit Problem

In this example the apparent conflict the auditor faces is between the duty to "society" and the duty to the clients. The act of breaching confidentiality is justified in terms of providing a "better audit". The ethical dilemma arises from the audit firm's acceptance of two audit clients with a pre-existing relationship of some sort.

The following analysis is of the two separate relationships the auditor has: the relationships brought about by the acceptance of the audit of Corporation 1 and the acceptance of the audit of Corporation 2. Corporation 1 is the corporation that provides the information relevant to the audit of Corporation 2. In this case AUD is constant to the two audits. We assume the same auditor or the same audit firm performs both audits. R_1 and R_2 are the audits of Corporation 1 and Corporation 2 respectively and Q is the set of appropriate audit techniques or principles applied to the respective corporations. While the general rules of auditing will be common to Q in both cases, Q itself cannot be said to be common. Issues such as assessment of risk will be unique to the particular corporation. In each case there will be at least three categories of users with legitimate expectations arising from the auditor assuming R. We call them.

$U_1 Corp_1$ (shareholders of Corporation 1, or, in Canada, the client)

$U_2 Corp_1$ (all other users of the audited financial information of Corporation 1 such as readers of annual reports, potential investors)

$U_1 Corp_2$ (shareholders of Corporation 2)

$U_2 Corp_2$ (all other users of the financial information of Corporation 2 such as readers of annual reports, potential investors).

U_3 (the financial market place of the jurisdiction in which the audit is conducted). This is common to both audits.

What are the respective users justified in expecting of AUD because of AUD's occupying R_1 and R_2? $U_1 Corp_1$ is justified in expecting that AUD will keep confidential information obtained in the course of the audit that is not essential to the audit. The audit process is viable because managers believe that information obtained in the course of the audit but not relevant to the audit will be kept confidential. If that belief is shattered access to relevant audit information will be threatened. $U_1 Corp_1$ and $U_2 Corp_1$ will have the same justified expectation of AUD. U_3 expects that AUD will retain confidence in the audit process.

In Corporation 2 the justified expectation of all relevant users is that AUD will use all the information available to AUD in the course of asking Q.

Does continuing an audit when the AUD becomes aware of information in the course of auditing Corporation 1 that is relevant to the audit of Corporation 2 constitute a conflict of interest? $U_1 Corp_1$ will argue that AUD is subject to a loyalty to the users of Corporation 2 that results in $U_1 Corp_1$ receiving less of a benefit than it is entitled to receive. Conversely, $U_{1-2} Corp_2$ will argue that if AUD fails to use any information that comes before it as auditor that is relevant to the audit of Corporation 2, the users of the audit of Corporation 2 will be receiving less of a benefit than is their entitlement.

Using the Davis model, AUD in this example is placed in a conflict of interest position. If we revert to Davis' terminology: because of the existence of conditions (a) through (d), condition (e), a conflict of interest, results. The question becomes, does this matter? All professions and society in general are prepared to allow the existence of certain conflicts on the basis that the cost of avoiding them seriously outweigh the benefits that would accrue from proceeding with them in place. Is this such a case?

—Continued

---

19. Davis, *op. cit.*, p. 24.

Continued

AUD will defend the actions by arguing, first, that a better audit of Corporation 2 results through the use of all available information. Our response is that this occurs only because of and at the expense of the breach of confidentiality to Corporation 1. Assume a criminal lawyer elects to represent two co-conspirators. The lawyer further allows the free transfer of evidence between the two clients. In the course of the defence of Client 2 the lawyer uses evidence from Client 1 which results in a finding of innocence for Client 2 and a conviction of Client 1. Professional ethics do not allow the lawyer to defend this action on the basis of a better result "for justice." We see little distinction between this example and the practice of the auditor here.

Second, AUD will argue that all subject information here will become public in any event. The cost of the auditor of losing one or both clients far exceeds any slight public benefit of maintaining at least the perception of confidentiality.[20] There is undoubtedly validity to the first leg of this argument. If, for example, AUD discovers in the course of the audit of Corporation 1 that that corporation will be unable to make good on debts owed to Corporation 2, there is no doubt that at some time in the future Corporation 2 will discover this without being told by the auditor or, more correctly, without the auditor making an adjustment to the financial statements. This issue is, however, a matter of timing. If AUD was not the auditor of Corporation 2 the management of that corporation would be unaware of the true nature of the debt until it became public in the normal course of business affairs. In the meantime, the management of Corporation 1 might be able to make changes which would allow it to become a viable entity. If, however, that information is "prematurely" disclosed by virtue of the relationship AUD has with both corporations, Corporation 1 might suffer more harsh consequences. Potentially, there is a direct cost to $U_1 Corp_1$ of the breach of confidentiality. Again, we come back to the same question, does this matter? More specifically, can and should the conflict be avoided? Is AUD entitled to defend its actions because of the benefits to U_3 and the users of Corporation 2?

As Davis did, we find it useful here to look for a parallel in the ethics parallel in the ethics of another profession, namely the law. Assume one law firm has two clients served by difficult partners of the firm and who, at times, have a business relationship with each other. Let us further assume that, in the course of reviewing the affairs of Client 1, a partner of

the firm discovers that Client 2 has the entitlement to bring a cause of action against Client 1 and that the outcome of that action would likely be favorable to Client 2. What is the ethical obligation of that partner? The partner must notify the other partner of the potential conflict of interest and the firm must notify the respective clients that it is unable to act for either some or all of their work for a particular period of time. There is no doubt that by notifying the clients even of this there is some breach of client confidentiality. Any prudent client would go to another lawyer and ask for a review of the circumstances. However, if nothing was done the consequences would be still more serious. Client 1 is entitled to expect that its lawyer will warn of any potentially negative circumstances arising from its affairs. If the lawyer was to warn and then to send Client 1 elsewhere, Client 1 would remain dissatisfied because of the perception that Client 2 could be receiving an advantage because its lawyer (or law firm) has knowledge of both sides of the case. Is there, however, a countervailing argument such as that in the audit example which says that the duty of U_3. in this case "justice," should outweigh the interests of the individual clients in this case? Could the lawyer say that in some way a better decision would result if the firm retains both clients? It is hard to see how such an outcome could override the need for individual clients to maintain confidence in lawyer/client confidentiality.

Turning back to Example 1, two things should be noted. First, the auditing profession tolerates a conflict of interest here which is not acceptable in, say, the legal profession. Second, the conflict can be resolved by resigning from both audits albeit at some cost to the clients and, in the short term, the audit firm. The audit firm would potentially lose two clients.[21] The extent of this cost is largely a function, however, of the present norms in the industry. Once the practice of releasing clients where conflicts of interest is understood, other client services would be retained by the audit firm as is the case with law firms. Further, any one firm will both gain and lose from such a practice which would not be, in any event, a frequent occurrence.

Finally, we do not and will not argue here that the conflict of interest *per se* must be avoided. That is a function of the impact on auditor independence and will be considered in our concluding section. We do note, however, that simply by allowing a practice that is at the very least questionable in

20. Here we have talked as if the information obtained from the audit of Corporation 1 will be used for the audit of Corporation 2. We would argue that even should it not be used the perception of confidentiality will be breached.

21. The same argument would pertain as with the law that maintenance of either one of the clients would allow the other to perceive an advantage to that client. The auditor of the retained client would potentially have information available to it that the auditor of the released client now lacked.

—Continued

Continued

another profession, the auditing profession fosters that perception of "strangeness" to which we referred in our introduction.

Example 2: Relationship Between the Audit and Other Firm Services

Here all users, U_1 to U_3, have a common question: is AUD subject to influences or loyalties which would make AUD's competent judgment in R with respect to Q less likely to benefit U_{1-3} than they are justified in expecting? In particular, will loyalty to the audit firm be seen actually or potentially to affect the appropriate judgment of AUD?

We are talking here of circumstances where the one accounting firm conducts a range of services to the client corporation. Consider the auditor faced with a judgment decision which, if exercised one way, will anger the client possibly resulting in the client seeking out an alternate firm for the full range of accounting services. The empirical evidence suggests that auditing is less remunerative in comparison to say, management consulting. Further, when a new client comes to the firm the auditor tends to provide audit services at a discount.[22] U_{1-3} are justified in expecting that AUD's judgment in R with respect to Q will not be influenced by any outside factors. There are no circumstances where the interests of the audit firm override these expectations. AUD must satisfy all user groups that it, in perception and in fact, was able to exercise appropriate judgment unhindered by considerations of the financial implications for the firm.

In its defence the profession will argue that, to various degrees, all professionals face equivalent pressures. Whenever AUD proposes an unpopular amendment to financial statements to a client the continued audit relationship is threatened.[23] It is one thing, however, to run the risk of losing an audit client that is your own client and quite another to threaten existing relationships your colleges might have with their clients. Further, there can be no way of avoiding the former conflict. It is inherent to any professional/client relationship. The same cannot be said of the latter example.

Using the cost/benefit argument, audit firms will argue that at least the short-term costs of maintaining independence between the audit and other accounting services will be enormous. These will, for the most part, only be transitional costs, however. If all firms are obliged to adopt the same policy, what any one gains the other will lose and vice versa. The client will face increased costs. If there is independence of auditing and, say management consulting services, there would be an elimination of cross-subsidization by management consulting of the audit. Conversely, there may be pressures of reduce premium pricing of other services where that exists. Arguably, however, these pressures will be felt by accounting firms in any event because of increased competition from non-accounting suppliers. We can see one potentially damaging consequence to the audit firm of a separation of functions. The firm has maintained a competitive advantage in non-accounting functions because of the prestige of the audit. If the functions can no longer be linked in the eye of the market, that advantage may be lost. Our response is that dissatisfaction with current audit practices will also damage this advantage in the long-term. If a loss is to result, it is better that it be a consequence of the rigorous application of ethical standards than not.

Are there any possible benefits that accrue from maintaining the status quo? It could be argued that potential for the free-flow of information goes both ways and that there might be distinct advantages for the users from this potential conflict. For example, in the course of a management consulting assignment the accounting firm partner may discover the existence of a manager in the client firm with a personal problem. Perhaps that person is a heavy drinker and is known to have major personal debts. If that manager is also in a position of trust then that information now becomes relevant, if available to the auditor, to the audit process. The auditor has no duty to seek out fraud, but if put on notice of certain risk factors, that same auditor should consider closer tests. If there is the free-flow of information a better audit could result.

Example 3: The Audit of Related Parties Problem

In the third example U_1 and U_2 are redefined. U_1 represents the shareholders of the parent corporation and the majority shareholders of the subsidiary corporation. U_2 represents the majority shareholders of the subsidiary corporation. U_2 represents shareholders of the subsidiary corporation. Other users will continue to exist but are not relevant for the present discussion.

Again it is useful to think in terms of a concrete example. Corporation P has a majority shareholding in Corporation S.

—Continued

22. Simon D. T. and Francis, J. R.: 1988, 'The Effects of Auditor Change on Audit Fees: Tests of Price Cutting and Price Recovery', *Accountancy Review,* (April) p. 259.

23. It is interesting to note that auditors describe the meeting they have with the client in which they discuss the changes they are recommending to the financial statements as "negotiations." To nonauditors such terminology could challenge their basic understanding of the process.

Continued

This might arise because of a recent acquisition or it might be a longstanding arrangement. Corporation S is not, however, wholly owned: there is a set of minority shareholders, U_2. The rules of accounting require that Corporation P's financial statements be consolidated with those of Corporation S. A separate set of financial statements for Corporation S are prepared primarily for the benefit of P_2. We assume a business relationship between Corporation P and Corporation S which results in transfer payments being made between the two. For example, Corporation P might buy component parts from Corporation S or vice-versa. It is possible for the price paid for those parts to be something other than the market price. Corporation S then suffers a financial disadvantage in comparison to what it would obtain if selling or buying on the open market.

It is standard practice for the same auditor to do the two audits; the audit of the consolidated financial statements and the audit of Corporation S. This is justified, typically, on the basis of cost savings. What happens, however, when the auditor discovers inequitable transfer prices or management fees? The obligation to report the nature and magnitude of the related party transactions may not fully disclose the substance of the parent subsidiary relationship. Could the reporting requirements be strengthened? It is not possible to devise all inclusive reporting standards that would disclose all material information about parent subsidiary transactions. As a result, is the auditor in a conflict of interest situation?

What is U_1 justified in expecting of AUD? U_1 expects that AUD will conduct the audit of the consolidated financial statements in accordance with R. This will include ensuring compliance with the minimal reporting requirements for related parties transactions. Does it matter to U_1 that Corporation S might be receiving less of a benefit because of an unfair pricing practice than it would otherwise receive? Clearly it does not very much. It is to the benefit of U_1 that profits be maximized at Corporation P so they do not have to be shared with U_2. What is U_2 justified in expecting? Again U_2 can expect that AUD will conduct the audit of the financial statements of Corporation S in accordance with R. AUD will argue that this is being done. It complies with the formal requirements Q impose on R. The fact that these requirements are not particularly satisfactory to U_2 is not AUD's responsibility. Is this an adequate response? What could U_2 expect of AUD if AUD was not the auditor of Corporation P? The prudent auditor discovering that the firm is receiving an unfair price for goods sold, albeit to the parent corporation, would typically inform both majority and minority shareholders. However, because AUD elects to perform both audits it is by no means clear to which group of shareholders the auditor's loyalties lie in case of conflict.

We believe, first, this is a clear case of conflict of interest. Second, there can be little doubt that in this case the conflict disadvantages one group of shareholders. Is the conflict avoidable? It is at some cost, namely the cost of obtaining a separate audit. The fact that these practices persist seems largely a function of rather weak auditing standards. If the auditing was required to note unfavorable related party transactions the conflict would become more obvious. The auditor would be forced to confront the conflicting nature of the loyalties to the respective clients. We should repeat that audits of related corporations by the same auditor is a common practice in auditing. Likewise it is not unusual to see inequitable transfer pricing practices. There is one final observation worth making here. The problem may be less acute in the case of transactions between corporations residing in different countries. The taxation authorities in the respective countries will try to ensure that transfer pricing is at fair market value so that appropriate revenues are collected.

CONCLUSION

We analysed the three examples to determine whether they give rise to conflicts of interest. Clearly, in each case conflict exists. The next question is does this have any bearing upon the issue of auditor independence? We may debate that a particular conflict of interest is or is not serious enough to be avoided. If that same conflict actually or potentially threatens the independent state of the auditor's mind, or if it could be perceived as threatening that independent state, there can be no debate that the practice should not persist. The ethics of the auditing profession and, indeed, all professions make that quite clear.

In Example 1 the auditor defends its position in terms of independence. We have already examined the argument that says the breach of confidentiality results in a better audit. In other words it is because the auditor is seeking a state of independence of the individual client demands or interests that the practice is acceptable. There is one basic flaw to this argument that we have not as yet considered. Why do auditors pass relevant information between audit partners? Typically, it is to ensure the other audit team does not miss anything. There is an element of self-interest that creeps into the discussion. "Just missing something" can also typically be a cause of audit failure resulting in litigation against the auditor.

What are we then left with in Example 1? There is a conflict of interest which may or may not be serious and worth preventing. There is also a convenient coincidence of what is good for the audit being good for the audit partnership. Does this affect the independent state of the auditor's mind?

—Continued

Continued

Could we argue that by breaching client confidentiality the ability of the auditor to form an independent judgment in accordance with the rules of the profession is threatened? The answer is no. The auditor might be breaching the responsibility to maintain confidentiality but there is no threat to the auditor's independent state of mind.

The same cannot be said for Examples 2 and 3. In both cases there is again a conflict of interest. How does this impact upon the requisite independent state of mind? In Example 2 the actual or threatened conflict of interest is between the best interest of the audit firm. By admitting there is a conflict of interest here we are also saying there is the potential for the auditor to be unable to exercise judgment in a manner untainted by self-interest. Further, we argue that this conflict and potential lack of independence can be avoided. In Example 3, the dilemma the auditor faces is that there are two masters which must be served. These masters have potentially conflicting interests. In accepting both audits the auditor must provide a lesser quality of service to one client than to the other. Can the conflict be avoided? It can be, although again at some increased cost. The auditor must recognize that there will be no push for enhanced independence from Corporation *S.* The beneficiaries are, after all, the minority shareholders who will likely have little say in the selection of the auditor.

It is interesting to speculate upon why these practices persist in the auditing profession—and we note these are by no means the only examples we could have used. It is easy to assume that their continuance is a reflection of the general contentment amongst financial statement users with the quality and integrity of the audit process. We have already noted, however, the criticisms the profession now faces. There is a well-documented cynicism amongst at least more sophisticated users.[24] We argue that sweeping these ethical issues under the carpet serves no one well. It is no longer good enough for any profession to argue "trust us" and "strange" practices are seen as damaging pracices. A rigorous practice of professional independence is, in the long-term, the best defence against the erosion of professional standards.

Sally Gunz teaches business law at the School of Accountancy, University of Waterloo, Waterloo, Ontario. She is a former legal practitioner whose research interests include ethical and legal issues of concern to auditors and studies of the corporate counsel profession.

John McCutcheon teaches accounting at the School of Business and Economics, Wilfrid Laurier University, Waterloo, Ontario. His research interests include analyses of alternate approaches to the liability auditors for negligence and various issues in management accounting.

---

24. See, Causey, D. Y.: 1979, *Duties and Liabilities of Public Accountants* (Homewood, Illinois: Dow Jones-Irwin), p. 30. In a survey, 26 percent of business executives compared with 50 percent or more of professors, institutional investors, analysts, etc., believed accounting firms bent rules in their client's favor.

Ethics in Taxation Practice

Tom Lynch

The Accountant's Magazine, November 1987

Tom Lynch draws attention to some problem areas where ethical standards come under pressure in particular tax situations.

Taxation practice is no different from any other professional practice in that it should be conducted in accordance with the highest ethical standards backed by the application of a high degree of skill, know-how and competence, to the affairs of clients whose interests will be foremost in the mind of the practitioner.

Taxation services fall broadly into two categories: compliance and advisory. There are, of course, other services such as advocacy before Tribunals, addressing the members of a trade association client and so on., but these are usually ancillary activities which can be ignored for present purposes.

When the word "ethics" is mentioned in taxation circles the first reaction is that it relates to evasion and avoidance. Evasion is illegal and therefore unethical, while avoidance is entirely in order and therefore ethical. It follows from this that if one does not positively evade taxes all is well, and since no self-respecting accountant would do so or assist others to do so, that is the end of the matter. Beyond this ethics may be ignored. There is, of course, a great difference between evasion and avoidance. One can lead to prison while the other leads only to disappointment.

But life is not quite as simple as that. On the one hand there are degrees of culpability in evasion, while in avoidance there is a distinction to be made between straightforward mitigation and complex artificial schemes of tax avoidance. Some writers on the subject have even referred to "avoision" as a hybrid word implying that evasion and avoidance may in some circumstances be indistinguishable. The ultimate effect may be the same in that revenue is lost to the Exchequer, but they are different and they are distinguishable. It is in compliance work that tax evasion is normally encountered while generally speaking advisory work is more likely to involve tax avoidance.

EVASION

Evasion can take many forms but the objective is the same: to evade in whole or in part the tax liabilities which arise on the actual expenditure income, gains and wealth of the taxpayer. Given that the accountant in practice would not consciously assist a client to evade taxes it may be argued that evasion does not concern him. But this is not so and, further, it is a dangerous assumption to make. He, or she, can still become involved in evasion—for example, by failing to notice dis-

crepancies in books or accounts or perhaps by finding out after the event that the client has evaded some or all of his tax liabilities.

The practising accountant must strive to ensure—as far as it is humanly possible to do so—that, as agent, no contribution is made to evasion of tax by a client. Compliance work is not a merely passive exercise when it is done by a professional accountant and it is by accepting unsatisfactory information and explanations that the accountant is most at risk. It must be borne in mind too that an accountant's contribution to evasion could be more reprehensible than the evasion itself.

If the accountant comes to the conclusion that his client is evading his tax liabilities, he must point out the risks and penalties; if the client fails to change his ways, the accountant should cease to act for him. Similarly, if an omission in a return or set of accounts comes to light after they have been submitted (and possibly agreed), the client should be advised to report the error—the client is responsible for what is in the return—and if he does not do so the accountant should withdraw his services. It should be made clear to the client, before doing so, that the Inland Revenue's attitude is very different in cases of voluntary disclosure from those where evasion is discovered only after investigation.

COMPLIANCE

Not all taxpayers are both highly literate and highly numerate. Their accounts and financial records can be a mess. But this is no reason to refuse to act for them even if it is necessary to use estimates in order to complete their accounts and returns. The Inland Revenue acknowledges this as a fact of life and is prepared to settle for estimated assessments in many cases. Provided the extent of the estimation is clearly stated, the accountant cannot be faulted even if evasion on the part of the taxpayer is subsequently discovered. But it is necessary to apply professional skills and common sense to the information and explanations on which the estimates are based and to refuse to accept doubtful information.

When the proprietor of a small local business in a rural area in Scotland tells his accountants that his regular trips to Newmarket are solely for business purposes, it would not be prudent to accept this statement without further enquiry. It may well be that what he says is true—perhaps because it is the one place he can be sure to get hold of a certain important supplier or customer; apart from that he may loathe

—Continued

Continued

crowds in general and racegoing crowds in particular. But on the face of it further enquiry would be expected.

One of the most common problems is the danger of accepting unsatisfactory explanations (or none) in the preparation of accounts because of the pressure of work and time limits—"the General Commissioners' meeting is tomorrow!". The accountant must ensure that work is properly staffed and where there is client-caused delay the accountant must not be stampeded or tempted to "keep things tidy" by throwing fingers into accounts without weighing up their reasonableness and requiring further explanations where this is necessary. Indeed, the more incomplete the records and the greater the delay in getting information to supplement what is there the more watchful the accountant should be and the more inclined to seek to square the accounts and returns with the client's standard of living and wealth. This will often turn out to be a valuable service to the sort of client who is simply careless and who would otherwise get into deep financial trouble or worse over his tax liabilities.

AVOIDANCE

"Avoidance" is rather an unfortunate word with a rather naughty connotation; in fact it covers everything from a simple and real rearrangement of affairs, which is eminently sensible and pure, to complex schemes where affairs are rearranged with no real effect—*ie,* with no substance other than to reduce tax liabilities. These artificial schemes are not illegal but are thought by many to be reprehensible and, more importantly, potentially ineffective.

FORM AND SUBSTANCE

The *obiter dicta* in the Duke of Westminster's case about form being preferred to substance and Lord Tomlin's famous words about it being legitimate to arrange one's affairs so as to avoid the Inland Revenue putting its largest shovel into one's store still hold good despite *Furmiss v Dawson* et al. Form is still important. For example, a grandparent may give a grandchild a simple cash gift each year or may choose instead to pay the same cash under a valid deed of covenant. The gift is the same under either method, but the latter will have a tax saving effect solely because of the form in which the gift is made. The essential point is that the transaction between the grandparent and the grandchild has substance apart from tax saving. It is a real transaction in which real money passes from one person to another. The grandparent's finances would change for the worse after each payment while the grandchild's financial position would correspondingly improve. The form of the transaction is therefore vital.

Where the form of the transaction is not accepted by the courts it is not because the substance is preferred to the form but because the substance is *is* no substance, no real transaction. Whatever form one may choose to give to a nothing, a nonentity, a fiction, it can never be a real transaction and it may therefore be ignored. Such transactions may conveniently be described as artificial avoidance schemes.

ADVISORY SERVICES

Whatever may be said about artificial avoidance schemes, tax mitigation is not reprehensible. Taking advantage of loopholes (with real transactions) may not be quite so commendable, but they are available to all taxpayers and it is up to Parliament to avoid creating them and, where they occur, to close them up as soon as possible.

Clients expect to be given advice on tax planning and mitigation and there is nothing wrong in the accountant giving this sort of advice. A Royal Commission report put it very well:

> "there is no reason to assume that the situation of any one taxpayer at that moment is the fairest possible as between himself and others differently situated: and if there is not, it seems wrong to pronounce any principle that would have the effect of fixing each taxpayer in his situation without allowing him any chance of so altering his arrangements as to reduce his liability to assessment."

A wife who helps her husband in his business may decide not to take a salary. Nevertheless, the true situation is that any profits are jointly earned and if the wife becomes a paid employee or a partner it is possible that the tax liability on the jointly earned income may be less. That the profits are jointly earned is the real substance of a case such as this, but once again it is the form in which the profits are earned that will settle the tax position. The accountant should see that the most tax efficient form is in fact adopted.

The transfer of cash from a building society deposit account (taxed income) to National Savings Certificates (income not taxed) is an example of a transaction which is both tax efficient and entirely acceptable. HM Government itself publicises the tax efficiency of National Savings Certificates using phrases such as "send the taxman away empty handed", phrases which accountants would think twice about using in the exercise of their profession.

On other slightly more complicated matters—such as the timing of an incoming or outgoing partner, or accepting shares rather than cash in a take-over bid—Lord Tomlin's

—Continued

CHAPTER 5 *Important Ethical Issues and Opportunities*

Continued

dictum should be followed with enthusiasm, without risk of blame or stigma.

The situation is not so clear when it comes to artificial avoidance schemes. Certainly accountants should advise on them and indeed it is their duty to point out the risks associated with such schemes, the uncertainties and possible changes in the law which might negate them. It would not, however, be part of his duty to devise and promote such schemes if for no other reason than that the scheme so promoted not only has the blessing of the accountant but, because of his expertise, some sort of guarantee of success which if it fails to materialise may sour the relationship with the client. There is no question of morality here, at least so far as the adviser is concerned. Artificial schemes are best left alone simply because they bring trouble and expense in their wake, and often they do not work.

As regards morality, this is a question solely for the taxpayer. It is not the duty of the accountant as tax adviser to advise on what is or is not moral. Not everyone agrees that what is legal must necessarily also be moral or that any act within the law is not only permissible but even praiseworthy. Moral values are often rather higher than minimum legal requirements and it will be a matter for the individual's own conscience to determine which he or she prefers. The accountant/adviser may want, however, to avoid unduly influencing a client's moral judgment by vigorously promoting artificial schemes of tax avoidance.

CONCLUSION

In compliance work it is important not to be "used" either deliberately or willy nilly to assist evasion. It is all too easy to get caught up in this way and accountants must not allow pressures of any kind to distract them from working to a uniformly high standard. It is also necessary to be entirely firm about disclosing omissions in previous accounts and returns.

In advisory work, mitigation advice may and should be given. Advice should also be given on artificial avoidance schemes, but I suggest that accountants should not promote such schemes.

Tom Lynch, CA, FRSA, is visiting Professor of Taxation at the University of Glasgow and a former senior tax partner in Ernst & Whinney.

SOURCE: *The Accountant's Magazine,* November 1987: 27, 28. Reprinted with the permission of the Editor of *CA Magazine* published by the Institute of Chartered Accounts of Scotland.

Effective Crisis Management

Ian I. Mitroff
University of Southern California

Paul Shrivastava
New York University, Industrial Crisis Center

Firdaus E. Udwadia
University of Southern California
Academy of Management Executive, 1987.

Managers, consultants, and researchers have traditionally focused on problems of financial performance and growth, but have paid little heed to the effective management of corporate crisis. The negative effects of organizational and industrial activities have been treated as minor "externalities" of production. It can be argued that until recently, it was unnecessary to focus on such crises. Today, however, such crises as pollution, industrial accidents, and product defects have assumed greater magnitude. The consequences for many corporations—like Johns-Manville and A. H. Robins—have been near or actual bankruptcy.

Corporate crises are disasters precipitated by people, organizational structures, economics, and/or technology that cause extensive damage to human life and natural and social environments. They inevitably debilitate both the financial structure and the reputation of a large organization. Consider the following examples:

- In 1979, the Three Mile Island Nuclear Power Plant had an accident leading to the near meltdown of the plant's reactor core. The accident not only cost Metropolitan Edison—the company that owned the plant—billions of dollars; it altered the fate of the nuclear power industry in the United States.[1] The plant owners and operators paid $26 million in evacuation costs, financial losses, and medical surveillance; the estimated cost of repairs and the production of electricity via other means was $4 billion.

- In 1982 an unknown person or persons contaminated dozens of Tylenol capsules with cyanide, causing the deaths of eight people and a loss of $100 million in recalled packages for Johnson & Johnson. In 1986 a second poisoning incident forced J&J to withdraw all Tylenol capsules from the market at a loss of $150 million. The company abandoned the capsule form of medication and consequently had to redesign its production facility. The full cost of switching from the production of capsules to the production of other forms of medication was in the range of $500 million.

- In December 1984 the worst industrial accident in history occurred: Poisonous methyl isocyanate gas leaked from a storage tank at a Union Carbide plant in Bhopal, India, killing 3,000 people and injuring another 300,000. The accident caused unknown damage to flora and fauna in the area. Union Carbide was sued by victims for billions of dollars; compensation settlement is likely to be between $500 million and $1 billion. In addition, the company was forced to sell 20% of its most profitable assets to prevent a takeover attack mounted by GAF Corporation, which had acquired Carbide's undervalued stock after the accident.[2]

- In May and June 1985 deadly bacteria in Jalisco cheese caused the deaths of 84 people. The company that produced the product was forced into bankruptcy.

The list of recent corporate disasters is virtually unending. It includes executive kidnappings; hijackings, both in the air and at sea; hostile takeovers; and such acts of terrorism as the bombing of factories and warehouses. Most recently, slivers of glass have been found in Gerber's baby food. Contac—an over-the-counter cold remedy—has also been the object of product tampering.

Such incidents now happen on an ever-increasing basis. Further, the interval between major accidents is shrinking alarmingly.[3] The number of product-injury lawsuits terminating in million-dollar awards has increased dramatically in the past decade: In 1974 fewer than 2,000 product injury lawsuits were filed in U.S. courts; by 1984, the number had jumped to 10,000. In 1975, juries had awarded fewer than 50 compensation awards of greater than $1 million each; in

---

1. C. Perrow, *Normal Accidents*. New York: Basic Books, 1984.

2. P. Shrivastava, *Bhopal: Anatomy of a Disaster*. New York: Harper & Row, 1987.

3. B. A. Turner, *Man-made Disasters*. London: Wykeham Publications, 1978; Shrivastava, op. cit.

—*Continued*

1985, there were more than 400 such awards. The costs of product-and production-related injury is one factor in the current liability insurance crisis. Many forms of liability insurance have simply vanished, and all forms of liability insurance have become so expensive, they are available only for small coverages.

The purpose of this article is to argue that while the situation is grave, it is far from hopeless for managers, researchers, and consultants who are prepared to confront the problem directly. While no one can prevent all disasters—let alone predict how, when, and where they will occur—organizations can adopt a systematic and comprehensive perspective for managing them more effectively. Anything less than such a perspective virtually guarantees that an organization will be less prepared to cope and recover effectively from a crisis.

THE ESSENTIAL PHASES OF CRISIS MANAGEMENT

Exhibit 1 presents a basic model of crisis management. It identifies as many of the phases necessary for effective crisis management as we have been able to discern through our research and consulting. The model, reflecting the variety of organizational patterns possible, can be entered at and exited from any point, and the action can proceed in any direction. We shall discuss this model by starting at the entry point labeled "detection" and proceeding clockwise.

The circle labeled "detection" stands for the organization's early warning systems. Those systems—including computerized process control systems, plant/equipment monitoring systems, management information systems, and environmental scanning systems—scan both the external and the internal environments for signals of impending crises.

We have placed "detection" before the sloping line labeled "prevention/preparation" to indicate that it is difficult, both systematically and comprehensively, to prevent or prepare for crises that one has not detected. For most people and most organizations, detection logically occurs before prevention. Although one may unintentionally prevent what one has not detected, prevention in such instances is based on luck and happenstance, not on deliberate organization intervention.

Point II of the model indicates that no organization can prevent every crisis from occurring. Indeed, prevention of all crises is not the basic purpose of planning and crisis management. But constant testing and revision of plans should allow an organization to cope more effectively with crises that occur, because such efforts help it learn how to "roll with the punches." Prevention and preparation take the form of safety policies, maintenance, procedures, environmental-

impact audits, crisis audits, emergency planning, and worker training.

Point III represents the major structures and mechanisms an organization has in place for guiding recovery. These include emergency plans, public relations plans, crisis management teams, etc. At Point IV, the organization asks itself what it has learned from its past crises and how it can use that knowledge in the future. It also assesses the effectiveness of its crisis handling strategies and identifies areas in which better crisis management capabilities need to be developed.

The more an organization denies its vulnerability, the more it will be focused on the right-hand side of Exhibit 1—the more it will respond *reactively* to crises it anticipates and the more potential crises it prepares for, the more it engages in *proactive* behavior.

The model allows us to draw some vital lessons for effective crisis management. First, and perhaps most important, is that most crises are preceded by a string of early warning signals. To prevent some major crisis, organizations need only learn to read these early warning signals and respond to them more effectively. For example, we have seen that for a year and a half before the Bhopal tragedy, messages repeatedly passed back and forth between Union Carbide's parent company in Danbury, Connecticut, Union Carbide Eastern in Hong Kong, a similar Union Carbide plant in West Virginia, and the Indian plant. The messages warned Bhopal plant management to fix potential problems that could cause a catastrophic explosion.[4] The signals were sent, but the system chose either to ignore them or not to act on them. This assessment holds even if, as Union Carbide contends, the catastrophe was caused by a deliberate act of on-site sabotage by a disgruntled employee.

The jury is still out, but Union Carbide may be legally accountable for the disaster unless it can show that it did everything humanly possible to read the early warning signs of internal sabotage and everything reasonable to lessen the chances of sabotage—even if complete prevention was impossible (Editor's note: Courts in India have subsequently decided that Union Carbide was guilty.). Indeed, because complete prevention may have been impossible, it will be all the more important for legal experts to assess what organizational mechanisms Union Carbide could have actually implemented (not just left on a shelf in paper form) to try to prevent a major disaster, cope with one, and help the company and its surrounding community recover in the event of a disaster.

---

4. Shrivastava, op. cit.

—*Continued*

Continued

EXHIBIT 1

A MODEL OF CRISIS
MANAGEMENT

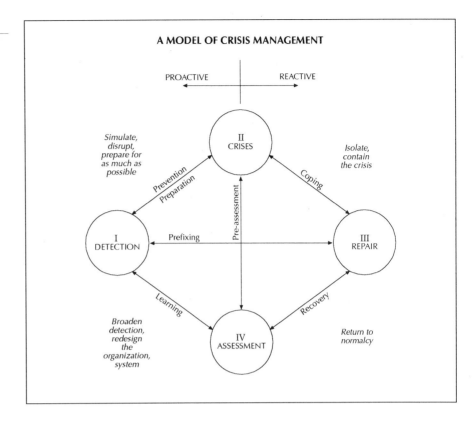

A MODEL OF CRISIS MANAGEMENT

PROACTIVE — REACTIVE

II CRISES

Simulate, disrupt, prepare for as much as possible

Prevention
Preparation

Pre-assessment

Coping

Isolate, contain the crisis

I DETECTION — Prefixing — III REPAIR

Learning

Recovery

Broaden detection, redesign the organization, system

IV ASSESSMENT

Return to normalcy

Given today's extremely litigious environment and a news media that is more vigilant and aware of worldwide events than ever before, organizations can regard it as a virtual certainty that their plans for and performance on every phase of the model in Exhibit 1 will become available to the press.

The field of crisis management is still in its infancy, yet available data seem to indicate that the more potential crises an organization can anticipate and prepare for (regardless of whether it can completely prevent them or not), the more quickly and successfully it will recover from any crises that strike.[5] While planning cannot prevent every crisis, the process of planning teaches an organization how to cope more effectively with whatever does occur. In fact, a cardinal rule of crisis management is that no crisis ever unfolds exactly as it was envisioned or planned for. For this reason, effective crisis management is a never-ending process, not an event with a beginning and an end.

There is, in fact, a fundamental paradox connected with crisis management: The less vulnerable an organization thinks it is, the fewer crises it prepares for; as a result, the *more* vulnerable it becomes. Conversely, the more vulnerable an organization thinks it is, the more crises it prepares for; as a result, the *less* vulnerable it is likely to be. The tragic explosion of Space Shuttle Challenger should be enough to dispel any doubts about the validity of this paradox. The Presidential Commission's report painstakingly examined the contending, probable causes of the disaster and, one by one, ruled them out. Slowly but surely the true cause was revealed: the explosion was caused by the failure of two large, critical O-rings that were supposed to keep highly flammable rocket fuel from spilling over its incasement and igniting with the shuttle's main engines.

The real causes, however, had little to do with technology per se. Having located the technical cause of the disaster, the report then identifies the accompanying human and organizational causes. This part of the report graphically exposes how one of the nation's premier examples of a highly suc-

5. S. Fink, *Crisis Management.* New York: AMACOM, 1986; and I. Mitroff and P. Shrivastava, "Strategic Management of Corporate Crises," *Columbia Journal of World Business,* Vol. 22, No. 1, Spring 1987, pp. 5–12.

—Continued

Continued

cessful and respected organization—NASA—became accident prone through multiple organizational failures.

One of the most powerful aspects of the report is its well-stocked supply of pictures. The report not only recounts, frame by frame, the hundredths and thousandths of seconds leading up to the accident; it also contains detailed photographs of recovered parts from the ocean floor. Although there can be no doubt that the failure of O-rings led to the disaster, the most striking evidence pertains to faulty organization—the underlying cause of the accident. This evidence consists of a seemingly endless series of reproduced memos revealing the anguished cries from deep within NASA's flawed bureaucracy and the bureaucracy of one of its prime subcontractors, Morton Thiokol. If NASA had listened and attended to these early warning signals, in all likelihood it could have prevented the disaster. One of the most striking memos starts with the cry. "Help!" The memo goes on to say that if the shuttle continues to fly with the O-rings as they are designed, then NASA is almost guaranteed a disaster. The evidence shows an organization impervious to bad news. Instead of deliberately designing monitoring systems to pick up danger signals NASA designed, in effect, a management system that would intentionally tune out danger signals or downgrade their seriousness.

The early warning signals associated with crises are not only different for different types of organizations, but are seldom perfectly clear. Rarely, if ever, will a signal say, "The presence of such and such a defect automatically guarantees or invariably leads to disaster Y." Rather, signals will read, "It *appears* that there is a *good chance* that X will cause Y or is associated with its occurrence," or, "The numbers of Xs have been growing noticeably in recent months."

In addition, a big difference exists between warning signals external to an organization and its industry and those internal to them. Those internal to the organization and its industry are more likely to be taken seriously because they "fit in" with the business.

For these reasons, it should not be surprising to find that, based on what preliminary data we have, only 50% of *Fortune* 1000 organizations surveyed have any kind of contingency plan in place to cope with any kind of crisis.[6] Further, those organizations that are prepared have a narrow focus. They are preparing to "fight the last war" because they know how to read the signals and prepare for, cope with, and recover from those crises.

Yet this narrow focus stands in sharp contrast to what we have begun to learn about modern crises and disasters. Unlike previous crises and disasters, modern ones link up

with one another and defy accepted truths. For instance, consider the recent finding of glass in Gerber's baby food. The food industry has long experienced such events, so they are historically well known to the industry. But what happened during the week that slivers of glass were found in Gerber's baby food was not part of the typical historic pattern. That week the Challenger exploded and Tylenol was poisoned for the second time. These events shattered the twin myths that "The worst can and won't happen twice to any organization" and "Lightening won't and can't strike twice in the same place."

As a consequence of these events, the media focused on Gerber's CEO as perhaps never before. Although he may have been right in not withdrawing his products—because withdrawing them may have encouraged "copycat killers"— he was wrong in another, more important sense. By being unwilling to withdraw the products, Gerber's CEO appeared callous toward the most fragile and most precious of all consumers—babies! Contrast this with the behavior of Johnson & Johnson's CEO, who unequivocally withdrew Tylenol from the shelves to demonstrate the company's long-standing commitment to the safety and well-being of its consumers.

AN EXPANDED TYPOLOGY OF CRISES

Clearly, every organization must attend not only to crises that are well known to it and its industry, but to the many disasters that can now happen to any organization and all industries. Such an expanded list of crises is presented in Exhibit 2.

Exhibit 2 differentiates between crises that arise within the organization and those that arise outside it. This distinction is critical because the warning signals will be different for each type of crisis. Exhibit 2 also differentiates between crises caused by technical/economic breakdowns and those caused by people/organizational/social breakdowns. This is because nearly every technical/economic breakdown is associated with a people/organizational/social breakdown, and vice versa. Thus, if we look at only one part of the chain, we miss valuable potential lessons for preparing and correcting the whole system.

Exhibit 3 shows various causes of each type of crisis listed in Exhibit 2. Finally, Exhibit 4 shows the wide variety of actions organizations can take to prepare for, cope with, reduce the effects of, and recover from the various kinds of crises we've identified.

Exhibit 4 shows that when it comes to taking action, we are faced with the problem of choosing between too many options, none of which can guarantee us prevention or complete containment. But then again, perfection is not an

6. Fink, op. cit.

—*Continued*

Continued

EXHIBIT 2

TYPES OF CORPORATE CRISES

	TECHNICAL/ECONOMIC	
Cell 1		**Cell 2**
• Product/service defects		• Widespread environmental destruction/industrial accidents
• Plant defects/industrial accidents		• Large-scale systems failure
• Computer breakdowns		• Natural disasters
• Defective, undisclosed information		• Hostile takeovers
• Defective, undisclosed information		• Governmental crises
• Bankruptcy		• International crises
Internal		**External**
Cell 3		**Cell 4**
• Failure to adapt/change		• Symbolic projection
• Organizational breakdown		• Sabotage
• Miscommunication		• Terrorism
• Sabotage		• Executive kidnapping
• On-site product tampering		• Off-site product tampering
• Counterfeiting		• Counterfeiting
• Rumors, sick jokes, malicious slander		• False rumors, sick jokes malicious slander
• Illegal activities		• Labor strikes
• Sexual harassment		• Boycotts
• Occupational health diseases		
	PEOPLE/SOCIAL/ORGANIZATIONAL	

appropriate criterion for judging the success of crisis management.

Indeed, if an appropriate goal for crisis management is to learn to prepare for as many crises as possible, then a reasonable way of approaching this goal is to form a crisis portfolio based on Exhibits 2, 3, and 4. One way to do this is to select a minimum of one crisis from each of the cells in Exhibits 2 and 3. This way, organizations can avoid the tendency to prepare mainly for the crises listed in Cell 1 of these exhibits and can thus begin to broaden their perspective about potential crises. In the same way, organizations can form a portfolio of coping and recovery mechanisms based on a selection of at least one element from each of the cells in Exhibit 4.

CONCLUDING REMARKS

To manage crises effectively, organizations must first be aware of all the phases and steps involved in the entire process of crisis management. Next, they must be aware of the differences between the phases. For instance, the purpose of the "preparation and prevention phase" in Exhibit 1 is for organizations to ask themselves, "What can/cannot be prevented and/or prepared for?" The goal of this phase is to prepare for as many of the crises and causes of them listed in Exhibits 2 and 3 as possible.

Furthermore, because crises are becoming increasingly complex, a secondary step must be to prepare for the simul-

—Continued

Continued

EXHIBIT 3

CAUSES AND SOURCES OF
CORPORATE CRISES

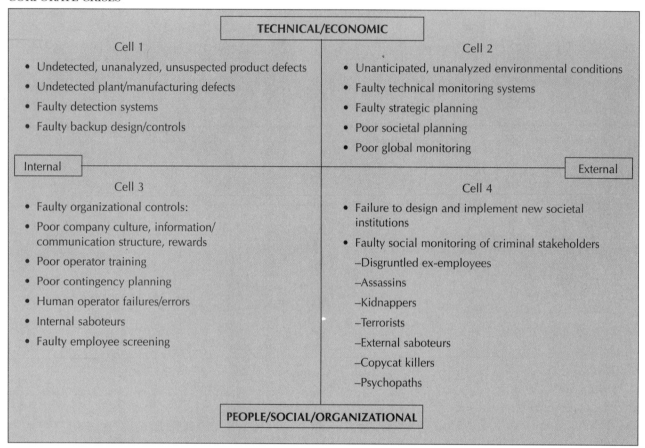

TECHNICAL/ECONOMIC

Cell 1

- Undetected, unanalyzed, unsuspected product defects
- Undetected plant/manufacturing defects
- Faulty detection systems
- Faulty backup design/controls

Cell 2

- Unanticipated, unanalyzed environmental conditions
- Faulty technical monitoring systems
- Faulty strategic planning
- Poor societal planning
- Poor global monitoring

Internal

External

Cell 3

- Faulty organizational controls:
- Poor company culture, information/communication structure, rewards
- Poor operator training
- Poor contingency planning
- Human operator failures/errors
- Internal saboteurs
- Faulty employee screening

Cell 4

- Failure to design and implement new societal institutions
- Faulty social monitoring of criminal stakeholders
  - Disgruntled ex-employees
  - Assassins
  - Kidnappers
  - Terrorists
  - External saboteurs
  - Copycat killers
  - Psychopaths

PEOPLE/SOCIAL/ORGANIZATIONAL

taneous occurrence of crises. Again, the purpose is to broaden the organization's outlook. Preparing for and attempting to prevent crises means constantly testing and simulating as many breakdowns as possible.

The breadth demanded in the prevention and preparation phase stands in sharp contrast to the narrow scope required in the "coping" phase. The goal of the "coping" phase is to draw a tight, narrow net around a crisis that has occurred. This will contain the crisis and prevent it from spreading either inside or outside the organization. To accomplish this, growing numbers of organizations have seen fit to establish special organizational units known as crisis management units or crisis teams. Their full-time responsibility is to prepare for and handle special, emerging situa-

tions. They are free to do this because they are buffered from the normal daily demands of the organization.

Finally, one of the many lessons emerging from the still new field of crisis management is worth stressing. For this lesson, consider an analogy with patients who have been informed that they have terminal cancer. It is believed that people go through four distinct phases upon being informed that their condition is terminal. The first is denial. When denial is no longer effective, one becomes angry at the universe, at God, for "letting this happen to me." At some point deep depression sets in. Most patients who live long enough to make it to the fourth and last stage: acceptance. This stage

—Continued

312

Continued

EXHIBIT 4

PREVENTIVE ACTIONS FOR
ORGANIZATIONS

TECHNICAL/ECONOMIC

One-Shot (Short Term)
- Preventive packaging
- Better detection
- Tighter system security
- Tighter internal operations
- Better operator/management controls
- Tighten design of plants/equipment
- Install chain of command
- Install crisis management units

Repeated (Long Term)
- Design expert monitoring systems, networks
- Hold "continental" planning workshops
- Bring in outside experts; form permanent networks
- Design stores of the future
- Install systems-wide monitoring
- Establish crises command centers
- Perform periodic, mandated reviews

TIME and SPACE

Immediate Environment
(Limited Individual Parts)
- Ensure emotional preparation
- Provide psychological counseling for employees
- Provide security training for all employees
- Provide detection training
- Install social support groups
- Provide media training

Extended Environment
(Systematic)
- Develop profiles of psychopaths, terrorists, copycats, etc.
- Establish preventive hot lines
- Sponsor community watch groups
- Provide consumer education
- Establish political action groups
- Sponsor mental-health programs
- Establish counseling groups
- Re-examine organizational culture
- Establish permanent crisis management units
- Perform organization redesign
- Appoint ombudsmen, whistleblowers
- Establish outside auditing teams to inspect vulnerabilities
- Provide media programs/training for all executives
- Work with industry associations
- Work with research centers
- Establish programs on business ethics

PEOPLE/SOCIAL/ORGANIZATIONAL

—Continued

Continued

EXHIBIT 5

STEPS FOR CRISIS
MANAGEMENT

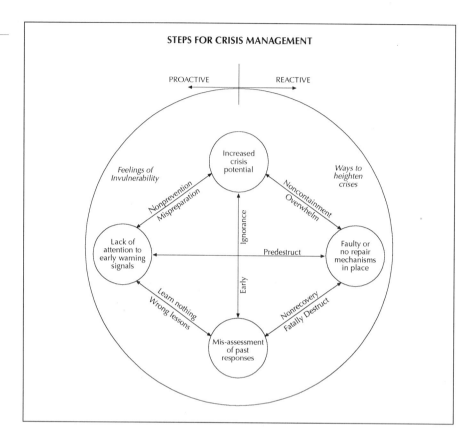

STEPS FOR CRISIS MANAGEMENT

is accompanied by the feeling. "This may be it for me, but at least I can make a last, positive statement with my life and pass something of value on to others."

These steps also apply to organizations managing crises. Keep in mind that denial, anger, and depression are powerful human emotions that are difficult to manage, particularly during a crisis. For this reason, organizations are well advised to raise their anxiety levels when they prepare for the worst, so that they will be able to cope when a real crisis occurs.

No one should ever underestimate the emotional costs of a disaster. While the two Tylenol poisonings cost the company approximately half a billion dollars in total, there were the formidable emotional costs as well. Many executives associated with Tylenol still awake with nightmares on the anniversaries of the poisonings. Also, consider the fact that NASA had to set up special medical hotlines to help its personnel handle the emotional trauma associated with the Challenger disaster. In addition to the explosion itself and the tragic loss of the seven astronauts' lives, more than one member of NASA couldn't handle the question posed by their own chil-

dren: "Daddy (Mommy) were you responsible for killing the astronauts?"[7]

Is your organization prepared to handle the financial and emotional costs of a major disaster? For those who work in the field of crisis management it is no longer a question of whether a major disaster will strike any organization, but only a matter of *when, how, what form will it take,* and *who and how many will be affected?*

Because we started with a simple model (Exhibit 1) that stressed the positive steps organizations can take to blunt crises, we will close with a simple model (Exhibit 5) that shows the steps that almost guarantee an organization will experience a major crisis from which it will not recover. Every organization therefore has a fundamental choice: Practice insurance against disaster or follow almost a guaranteed design for disaster.

---

7. As reported to the first author in direct interviews with NASA officials.

—Continued

Continued

Ian I. Mitroff *is the Harold Quinton Distinguished Professor of Business Policy and co-director of the Center for Crisis Management at the Graduate School of Business, University of Southern California. He received a B.S. in engineering physics, an M.S. in structural mechanics, and a Ph.D. in engineering science and the philosophy of social science, all from the University of California, Berkeley.*

Professor Mitroff is a member of the American Association for the Advancement of Science, Academy of Management, American Psychological Association, American Sociological Association, Philosophy of Science Association, and the Institute for Management Science. He has published over 200 papers and eight books in the areas of business policy, corporate culture, managerial psychology and psychiatry, strategic planning, and the philosophy and sociology of science, and has appeared on numerous radio and television programs. His most recent book is Business Not As Usual: Rethinking Our Individual Corporate, and Industrial Strategies for Global Competition, *published by Jossey-Bass in 1987.*

Paul Shrivastava *is associate professor in the Graduate School of Business Administration, New York University. He has a bachelor's degree in mechanical engineering and masters' and Ph.D. degrees in management. His management research interests include the strategic management of organizations, crisis management, policy-making processes, design of information and learning systems for strategic decision making, and management and administrative problems of developing countries. He has spoken on these topics at national and international meetings and has published over three dozen articles on these topics in professional and scholarly journals.*

Dr. Shrivastava has special expertise in managing decision-making processes in crises, and has chaired and conducted decision meetings

and conference meetings in both corporate and professional environments. He was engaged in several major conflict resolution efforts that involved mediating conflicts between corporate, public, and government agencies. He now serves as executive director of the Industrial Crisis Institute, Inc., a nonprofit research organization devoted to resolving industrial crisis problems.

Dr. Shrivastava is the editor of Industrial Crisis Quarterly, *a coeditor (with Robert Lamb) of* Advances in Strategic Management, *and a contributing editor to the* Journal of Business Strategy. *He has received numerous awards and grants for his research from agencies such as the National Science Foundation, and is currently writing a book entitled* Bhopal: Anatomy of a Crisis, *to be published by Ballinger Publishing Company in 1987.*

Firdaus E. Udwadia *received his M.S. and Ph.D. from the California Institute of Technology and his M.B.A. from the University of Southern California, where he is presently professor of business administration, civil engineering, and mechanical engineering. He is director of the Structural Identification Facility and co-director of the Center for Crisis Management at USC.*

Professor Udwadia has received numerous awards, including the NASA Award for Outstanding Contributions to Technological Innovations, and has been a consultant to government and private industry in the areas of economic and engineering systems modeling, technology transfer, and project management and command, control and communications. His current research interest is in the area of crisis management.

SOURCE: Reprinted with the permission of the Academy of Management.